Epic Season

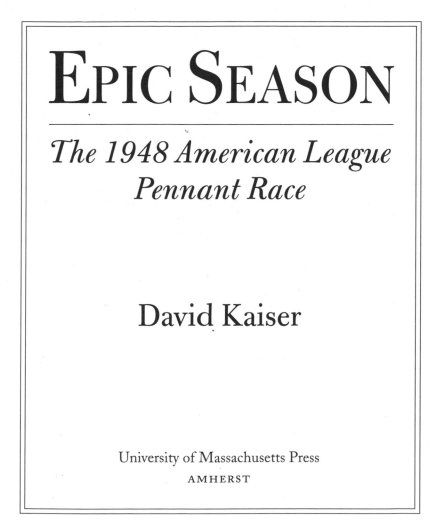

EPIC SEASON

The 1948 American League Pennant Race

David Kaiser

University of Massachusetts Press

AMHERST

Copyright © 1998 by David Kaiser
All rights reserved
Printed in the United States of America
LC 97-43951
ISBN 1-55849-146-5 (cloth); 147-3 (pbk.)
Designed by Jack Harrison
Set in Adobe Caslon and Monotype Bulmer by Keystone Typesetting, Inc.
Printed and bound by Thomson-Shore, Inc.

Library of Congress Cataloging-in-Publication Data
Kaiser, David E., 1947–
Epic season : the 1948 American League pennant race /
David Kaiser.
p. cm.
Includes bibliographical references and index.
ISBN 1-55849-146-5 (cloth : alk. paper). —
ISBN 1-55849-147-3 (paper : alk. paper)
1. American League of Professional Baseball Clubs—History.
2. Cleveland Indians (Baseball team)—History.   3. Boston Red Sox
(Baseball team)—History.   4. New York Yankees (Baseball team)—
History   I. Title.
GV875.A15K35   1998
796.357′64′097309048—dc21   97-43951
CIP

British Library Cataloguing in Publication data are available.

To my favorite baseball fans,
CATHY, DANIEL, AND THOMAS

I turn to the sports pages first because there I find a record of man's achievements, while on the front pages I find only a record of his failures.

—EARL WARREN

1948 was too full a season to put in a capsule. Williams missed 15 games with a rib cracked by Sam Mele—and the team won 13 of the 15 games. Boudreau stole home, and did McCarthy kick catcher Matt Batts at the plate or didn't he? Pitcher Stubby Overmire of Detroit beat the Sox in September, in the 12th inning, with his first hit of the season. Joe DiMaggio got that final day ovation. 1948 was a year to remember.

—HAROLD KAESE, *Boston Globe*, August 14, 1973

CONTENTS

Illustrations follow page 82 and page 186

ACKNOWLEDGMENTS

I have re-created the story of the 1948 American League pennant race mainly with the help of daily newspapers: the *New York Times*, the *New York Herald Tribune*, the *Cleveland Plain Dealer*, the *Boston Herald*, the *Boston Daily Record*, and the *Boston Evening American*. My account also benefited enormously, however, from the reminiscences of nineteen men who participated directly in this great drama. These include Allie Clark, Larry Doby, Bob Feller, the late Ken Keltner, Bob Kennedy, Gene Bearden, and executives Marsh Samuel and Spud Goldstein of the Indians; Matt Batts, Dom DiMaggio, Denny Galehouse, Mel Parnell, and Johnny Pesky of the Red Sox; Billy Johnson, Tommy Henrich, Frank Shea, and Stanley Harris Jr. (the manager's son) of the Yankees; Pete Suder of the Athletics, and umpire Joe Paparella. Other participants or observers who helped me include writers Cliff Keane, Shirley Povich, and Ed Fitzgerald (the season's first chronicler); and Mary Frances Veeck. I also received important assistance from Michael Shulman of Archive Photos, the staff of the Cleveland State University Library, the Boston Public Library, and the Hall of Fame Library. Clark Dougan, my editor at the University Press, played his role well and effectively, never hesitating either to state his own opinion or to remember where final responsibility lay. Andrew Barnes, Mark Caloyer, Jim Davidson, Eliot Quill, and Don Zminda were among those who read versions of the manuscript and made both encouraging and helpful comments, for which I thank them. And Jim Davidson deserves special thanks for that moment back in the summer of 1970 when he looked up from a baseball encyclopedia and remarked, "You know, '48 was such a fabulous year," and the idea of this book was born.

Jim—you had no idea.

EPIC SEASON

1

Baseball after the
Second World War

The late 1940s were a turning point in the history both of baseball and of the United States as a whole. On the one hand, prewar ballplayers took advantage of a revived new market; on the other, various changes in American life were about to threaten baseball's status as the preeminent American pastime, and eventually to transform the structure of baseball in ways that made an epic pennant race impossible.

After four years of war, major league players had returned in 1946 eager to make up for lost time, and encountered the largest, most enthusiastic crowds in the history of the game. The American people emerged from the war with thousands of dollars in savings and tremendous pent-up energy to release, and shifted their gaze from the cataclysmic drama of the Second World War to the more familiar struggle on the ballfield. The effect on baseball was immediate and unprecedented. Virtually every team in baseball broke attendance records in 1946 and 1947, with the 1946 Yankees establishing a new all-time high of 2,265,512. Both leagues shared in the boom, but the American League remained by far the stronger aggregation. Although the senior circuit in 1947 broke the color line and added the sensational Jackie Robinson, they did not have a single player whose stature compared to Joe DiMaggio, Ted Williams, Bob Feller, or Lou Boudreau, and although they had managed to win four of the last eight World Series, they trailed 9–5 in fourteen All-Star games.

As a group, the players of 1948 were old, but eager. The vast majority of them had started their careers before the war, and they were busily trying to make up for lost opportunities with the help of the amazing postwar boom.

1

In addition, the war had largely dried up the supply of young players by making it impossible to begin a baseball career. There were only two twenty-three-year-old everyday regulars in the whole AL in 1948—catcher Les Moss of the Browns and outfielder Vic Wertz of the Tigers—and two twenty-four-year-olds, Larry Doby and George Vico of the Tigers. A trickle of younger players who had missed the war almost entirely, like twenty-two-year-old Red Sox Billy Goodman, was only beginning. The cohort born from 1924 through about 1926 had gone into the armed forces when they would normally have gone into baseball, and few, when they returned, had risked a baseball career. The consequences of this demographic hole—and other consequences of the war and changes in living patterns— would be felt later. For now, prewar stars still dominated the league.

Despite the shortage of young players, however, it was still considerably harder to reach the big leagues in 1948 than it is today. In every era, the major leagues occupy top of a pyramid made up of all those engaged in the game of baseball. And in 1948, baseball employed far, far more Americans than it does even today—not only relatively, but absolutely. To call baseball "the national pastime" in 1948 was simply to state a fact of American life. Americans had two main leisure interests, the movies and baseball, and baseball may well have come first. Baseball was the first organized activity in which boys—and many girls—ever participated. The reminiscences of players and umpires from the 1920–1950 period—collected mainly by Donald Honig and Larry Gerlach—tell a simple story: when children or adults had a free hour, a free afternoon, or a free day, they got together and played, and when they got too old to play, they watched. They played on neighborhood teams, town teams, factory teams, tavern teams, minor league teams, Negro league teams, and, if they were among the true, tiny elite that had the necessary skill and good fortune, the sixteen major league teams.

Anyone who studies interviews with players like Tommy Henrich, Pete Reiser, Ted Williams, Johnny Vander Meer, or Cool Papa Bell, and compares them to the experience of present-day Little Leaguers will understand how much has been lost by the overorganization of children's activities. Kids before 1950 played on their own, playing as much as they wanted and developing at their own pace. Tommy Henrich remembers that he sometimes had as many as fifty hits in a day, but few Little Leaguers today get to swing the bat enough to learn how to hit. As kids grew older, semipro leagues and high school programs gave them plenty of opportunities to keep playing, and almost no one lived beyond the reach of a minor league team that would give them a tryout.

Another source of talent, meanwhile, was becoming available to fill the gap left by the war—at least for those with the courage to take advantage of it. Baseball throughout the first half of the century had been the national pastime for black as well as white Americans, but during the spring and summer it had been rigidly segregated. Knowledgeable fans and players knew that the Negro leagues, as they were called, included numerous players of big-league caliber, but no one had moved seriously to include them in the majors before the war. In the winter, teams of black all-stars did compete against major leaguers in barnstorming tours that brought big league baseball to the hinterlands, and in this way, men like Satchel Paige, Josh Gibson, and Cool Papa Bell had become well known to knowledge-able white fans. Now the war, which had drawn American society together to an unprecedented degree in a struggle for freedom and equality, had played a key role in opening the door of the major leagues to black ball-players like Robinson and Doby, both of whom had served in the army. This development, too, played a crucial role in the story of the 1948 season.

In retrospect, it seems extraordinary how many changes in American life coincided in the late 1940s and early 1950s to change the place of baseball within it. Television, of course, provided a new—though far inferior—form of entertainment; televised major league games quickly cut into the market available to the minors; and the population movement from cities and small towns into the suburbs broke down much of the community life of which baseball had been a part. In the 1950s, jet air travel suddenly made trans-continental leagues a real possibility. Perhaps the biggest change, however, was the increase in higher education that began with the G.I. Bill of Rights, which ensured that the veterans of the Second World War would want to send their children—the baby boomers—to college as well. At the same time that baseball ceased to be the main pastime of children, it also ceased to be a reasonable career option for tens of thousands of young Americans. It was not serious enough, and it would delay college and a career. Baseball in the 1930s and 1940s attracted young men from all walks of life, includ-ing those like Lou Gehrig, Lou Boudreau, Jackie Robinson, Joe Gordon, Larry Doby, Spud Chandler, Buddy Hassett, and Bobby Brown, who were college-educated. It was only in the 1950s that college players became such a rarity, and professional baseball became primarily a pursuit of poorer Americans until the 1970s, when colleges became a source of talent once more.[1]

The major league of that era, it is true, drew on a smaller total popula-tion, and organized baseball was only just opening its doors to black Amer-

---

1. See on this point Jim Bouton and Leonard Schechter, *Ball Four* (New York, 1970), which chronicles the travails of the rare college-educated players of the 1960s.

icans and Latins, who make up so much of the major leagues today. But the major leaguers of the late 1940s represented the cream of a much, much larger crop of professional baseball players than those of the 1990s. There were about 480 fully professional major and minor league teams in the late 1940s, more than twice as many as there are today. According to the Hall of Fame Library, twelve to fifteen thousand men played professional baseball in 1948, only four hundred of whom—about one in thirty—played full-time in the majors. Today, with 28 major league teams and many fewer in the minors, about one in ten professional baseball players plays in the majors. Baseball still dwarfed every other sport in the United States in the late 1940s, with boxing a very poor second and football third. Even today, we forget far too easily that every major leaguer has to outperform ten other fine athletes who, like him, were stars in Little League, high school, college, or American Legion ball. In those days, the majors were *three times* more selective.

The game itself in the late 1940s was played on green grass, in highly individual and distinctive ballparks—most of them twenty to thirty years old—and mostly, though not exclusively, in the daytime. More day games, statistics show, mean more hitting, and the summer of 1948 was destined to be a hot one, increasing hitting further still. The biggest single difference in the baseball of the late 1940s was the greater frequency with which the ball was put in play. Because of night baseball and changes in hitting styles, batters now strike out much more often than in the late 1940s, substantially increasing the time taken up merely by the pitcher and the catcher and decreasing the role of the defense. Defense was both more important and more difficult, since fielding gloves were smaller and the one-hand catch was still a desperation play. Stolen bases had become a very rare part of the game, reserved for certain critical situations, although managers often used the hit-and-run to try to avoid a double play. With the ball in play more often, baseball was a much *faster* game in the late forties than in the nineties. The average game lasted only a little more than two hours, and a close, low-scoring game would frequently be over in an hour and fifty minutes or so. The teams took much less time between innings because they were playing for the fans at the ballpark—not, as they do today, for the advertisers who pay for television broadcasts.

Some evidence suggests that the style of hitting was rather different from that of the 1990s. For various reasons, hitters, and especially good hitters, concentrated on pulling the ball. This had become part of the macho ethic—Joe DiMaggio, in particular, was actually embarrassed to hit an opposite-field home run—but it also reflected the shape of the ballparks hitters had to play in. While today most parks have a maximum distance of only about four hundred feet to center field, in the late 1940s Shibe Park in Philadelphia, Griffith Stadium in Washington, Yankee Stadium, Cleveland's Municipal Stadium, and Comiskey Park in Chicago all had center-field fences well over four hundred feet away, making it virtually essential to pull the ball to hit a home run. Batters tailored their strokes accordingly. In addition, since pitchers threw inside more frequently in the 1940s, batters had more opportunity to pull the ball.

Last, because of the economic structure of the game, the league was less balanced, but more competitive. No network TV or radio contracts provided each team with a large chunk of guaranteed revenue, and the league was not yet dedicated to the idea of "competitive balance," or, to give it another name, organized mediocrity. Rich clubs never lost players to free agency, and could always try to become stronger by buying more good players and winning the pennant; poor clubs could stay in business by selling talent to their richer brethren. As we shall see, a frantic movement of talent from the White Sox, Senators, and above all the Browns to the Red Sox, Indians, and Yankees occurred during the winter of 1947–48. It reflected the economic reality that Boston, New York, and Cleveland had the resources to buy a stronger team, while player sales or sweetened trades could balance the books of a poorer club. These transfers of resources were certain to increase the disparity between the top of the league and the bottom, but they had another, more important, effect as well. They led in 1948 to the emergence of not one, but three truly excellent teams, any one of them capable of winning a pennant in a normal year. Corporate baseball—like most other corporate activity—is not an environment in which excellence is encouraged to flourish. In 1948, baseball organizations were still free to make their teams as good as they could be.

"I don't think baseball has ever been played any better than from 1946 to 1950," Ted Williams wrote in the late 1960s.[2] And while contrary opinions persist, much evidence can be cited to support him. Some players of that era, such as Johnny Pesky—who has remained in the game—also feel that players could maintain their concentration more easily over the long season, because the schedule usually called for a Sunday doubleheader and a day off on Monday, and because train travel provided more time to relax than air travel. And with the end of the war and the Depression, players and fans alike could focus more sharply than ever on the events on the field, where the excitement of the struggle was not diluted by the tragedy of loss of life.

Among the many things that made baseball so consuming in the late

2. Ted Williams with John Underwood, *My Turn at Bat: The Story of My Life* (New York, 1969), 166.

1940s, certainly, was the intimacy of the eight-team league: an organization small enough for any fairly serious fan to know all the major players on all the teams, and to ensure that a three-game confrontation with a team's most hated rival was never more than a few weeks away. Competition was inevitably more intense than it is today. Each pair of teams faced each other twenty-two times during the season—almost twice as often as teams face each other today—and the players were far more familiar with one another's talents, styles, and habits. The eight-team major leagues had formed early in the twentieth century, when population was concentrated in the Northeast and Midwest. All this was changing by the middle of the century, and something had to give, but in 1948, American League fans saw the climax of baseball in the first half of the twentieth century.

2

Setting the Scene

During the first week of October 1947, a wild and profitable year of baseball reached its climax as the Yankees and the Dodgers faced each other in
the World Series. The contest itself was a feast for fans and writers alike, as
the two teams battled for seven games that included Bill Bevens's loss of a
no hitter and a ball game with two out in the ninth, Al Gionfriddo's great
catch off Joe DiMaggio that saved the sixth game for the Dodgers, the fine
relief pitching of Joe Page, Dodger base-running that embarrassed Yankee
rookie catcher Yogi Berra, and several highly controversial managerial
moves by Yankee skipper Bucky Harris. But while these dramas played
themselves out on the field, a series of off-the-field changes and crises
within three American League teams—the Boston Red Sox, the Cleveland
Indians, and the Yankees themselves—set in motion a much different kind
of campaign in 1948. The events of the first week of October 1947 set the
stage for the most remarkable pennant race in the history of the American
League, and perhaps of all time.

The defending league champion Boston Red Sox were finishing up a
disappointing season on September 30, 1947, when the front office announced a managerial change. Joe Cronin, the team's manager since 1934,
became the new general manager, replacing Hall of Famer Eddie Collins,
and Joe McCarthy—the most successful manager in baseball history, and
the winner of nine pennants in twenty years for the Cubs and the Yankees
from 1926 through 1945—replaced him. The next day, the tabloid *Boston
Daily Record* boasted that its famous sports columnist, Dave Egan, had
predicted all these changes nearly a year before, after the pennant-winning

Red Sox had lost the World Series to the Cardinals in seven games. Egan himself declared that another year-old prediction was now certain to come true: that Ted Williams, the team's leading star, who combined a lifetime batting average of more than .350 with a temperamental reputation, would be traded so as to pose no threat to McCarthy's authority.

History lent some support to this position. Twice before Joe McCarthy had taken over a franchise with a rich tradition that had slipped from the top, and each time he had become involved in a dispute with a legendary figure. In Chicago in 1926 the man in question was the legendary but alcoholic pitcher Grover Cleveland Alexander, whom McCarthy dispatched to St. Louis because he could never be sure when "Alex" would actually be able to pitch. In New York, where he took the helm in 1931, McCarthy encountered the greatest star of all, Babe Ruth. Four years (and one pennant) later, Ruth told longtime owner Col. Jake Ruppert that he deserved McCarthy's job, only to find himself palmed off on the Boston Braves. "Joe McCarthy," wrote Egan on October 2, "once told Jake Ruppert of the Yankees to choose between him and Babe Ruth, and now has been given authority to make all the deals for the Red Sox, so that nobody will have to choose between him and Williams."

> Once again, he is in a position where a player will receive more money than he does. Once again, he is in a position where he is managing a player who is above all discipline. And once again, he will do what he did many years ago. He will get rid of a star, and create harmony, and mold a team out of individuals, and win the pennant that the Red Sox should have won this year.[1]

Other Boston columnists and writers quickly followed Egan's lead. "The Red Sox players," wrote Egan's colleague Joe Cashman, "will produce for 'Mac' or be given the gate in a hurry. That goes for everybody, from the highest salaried and most illustrious performer right down to the greenest rookie. That's how McCarthy operates." A few days later, Jack Conway of the *Sunday Advertiser* listed Williams as one of the likely candidates for a trade. "With Joe McCarthy as the Sox manager," Hy Hurwitz of the *Globe* wrote ominously, "business will be conducted along different lines in Fenway Park. And Williams, who has been handled with kid gloves in the past, will be treated just like any other member of the team." Williams himself, nearly always quotable, spoke warmly of McCarthy during the World Series. "He isn't a rookie," he quipped to a reporter. "I played for him in a couple of All-Star games and he really impressed me." But privately, as he admitted twenty years later in his autobiography, *My Turn at Bat,* he worried that his career in Boston was over. Williams, like his tormentors in

1. *Boston Daily Record,* October 2, 1947.

the press box, anxiously awaited the aftermath of the World Series to find out exactly what moves McCarthy had in mind.

A few days later, another major story broke in another American League city. Halfway through the series, the Cleveland papers, in page one headlines, announced that owner Bill Veeck was planning to trade the team's All-Star shortstop and manager, Lou Boudreau, to St. Louis. The explosion that followed set the tone for an astonishing season in Cleveland.

Bill Veeck had literally grown up in a ballpark—Wrigley Field, where his father was president of the Chicago Cubs during their glory days in the late 1920s and 1930s. When Veeck's father died in 1933 he had left Kenyon College to go back into the Cubs operation, and in 1941, with virtually no capital, he managed to scrape together enough financing to purchase the bankrupt Milwaukee Brewers of the International League. He immediately went to work promoting the team, giving away novelties like a two hundred-pound cake of ice and live lobsters to unsuspecting fans, playing morning games (and serving breakfast) for the benefit of night-shift workers in war plants, and, more than incidentally, putting together a winning team. For the whole of his career as an owner, Veeck combined promotional gimmicks with a fierce desire to win.

Veeck had run the Brewers as an independent minor league operator. Farm systems did not as yet control every minor league club, and independent outfits signed players themselves and made much of their income by selling them to the majors. Veeck, like the late commissioner Kenesaw Mountain Landis, understood that the health of baseball around the country depended upon such a system—which gave fans in medium-size cities and smaller towns independent teams of their own to root for—and Veeck fought a lonely, losing battle to keep it alive during the early 1950s. As soon as he experienced any success in Milwaukee, however, Veeck had set his sights on the majors. An attempt to buy the Philadelphia Phillies failed, however, and Veeck joined the Marines in late 1943.

Returning home from the war in 1945, Veeck had sold the Brewers and bought a dude ranch in Arizona, where he and his wife hoped to save their troubled marriage. By the spring of 1946 the experiment was clearly failing, and Veeck was itching to get back into baseball. His old friend Lou Jacobs—the head of the concession business that serviced much of the major leagues—tipped him off that the Cleveland club might be available. Without much capital of his own, he put together a syndicate and purchased the Indians in the middle of 1946.

Veeck had arrived in the majors in the midst of the greatest baseball boom in history. No one was better positioned or better able to take advantage of it. Taking over the team in June 1946, Veeck immediately persuaded

Bob Feller to make a run at the strikeout record. In 1947, he managed to improve the team from 68–86 to 80–74. In June of that year, he broke the American League color line by signing twenty-three-year-old, left-handed-hitting Larry Doby from the Newark Eagles of the Negro National League. While Doby was a fine prospect, the signing was not well handled. Unlike the older and more mature Jackie Robinson, Doby was thrust right into the majors, even though as a second baseman he had no chance of playing his natural position for the Indians. As it turned out he appeared in 29 games, 23 of them as a pinch hitter, and hit just .180 in the waning weeks of 1947. Writers generally dismissed the signing as a publicity stunt, and few expected Doby to be with the Indians on Opening Day 1948.

The World Series of 1947 presented another opportunity to strengthen the team and generate some more publicity, and Veeck had already decided to make the most of it. Sitting with Cleveland reporters, he broached—off the record—the biggest deal of his career. He intended to trade his second-most distinguished player—and manager—shortstop Lou Boudreau.

Boudreau had already had a remarkable career. A graduate of the University of Illinois—where he had been a star basketball player—he had joined the Indians after a few months of minor league experience in 1939. He immediately established himself as a great shortstop and a good right-handed line-drive hitter. In 1942, when Roger Peckinpaugh stepped down as Cleveland's manager, Boudreau seized upon a chance comment by a reporter, marched into the front office, asked for the job, and got it. At twenty-four, the "Boy Manager" was the youngest in modern history. He won a 1944 batting title as well, missing the war because of chronically bad ankles that threatened to shorten his career.[2] Boyishly handsome, he was a crowd favorite all over the American League.

Boudreau showed as much courage and imagination as a manager as Veeck did as a promoter. In June 1946, after losing the first game of a doubleheader to the Red Sox to three homers and eight runs batted in by Ted Williams, Boudreau had tried to stop the "Splendid Splinter" in the second game by moving six fielders—everyone but the left fielder—to the right of second base. The "Boudreau shift" had been widely imitated, and temporarily credited with stopping Williams when he reached June of 1947 hitting just .277 (he righted himself later and won the triple crown). Boudreau liked to play hunches, and during 1947 he tried calling pitches from shortstop. He would sometimes insert pinch hitters and relief pitchers in the middle of an at-bat when the count turned against the Cleveland player.

2. Lou Boudreau with Ed Fitzgerald, *Player-Manager* (Boston, 1949), 16–72.

Like another shortstop-manager, Leo Durocher, he was a gambler, both on and off the field. But Veeck disliked Boudreau's managing. Ironically, Veeck—frequently labeled by his critics as nothing but a prankster and a showman—seems to have regarded the original choice of Boudreau as manager as a publicity stunt. He did not think that Boudreau had a real managerial philosophy, and he wanted to replace him with fifty-six-year-old Casey Stengel, who had managed for him in Milwaukee. According to Veeck, he had already suggested to Boudreau that he might do better to step down as manager, but Boudreau politely declined. The shortstop knew that his ankles were deteriorating rapidly, and was already planning a long-term career as a bench manager. Veeck did not dare risk the wrath of the Cleveland fans by trading him, and the issue was closed—but only, as both men knew, for the moment. As 1947 drew to a close with the Indians in fourth place, Boudreau's contract also expired.

At the World Series, Veeck opened negotiations with Bill DeWitt of the lowly, poverty-stricken St. Louis Browns. He planned to send Boudreau to the Browns in exchange for shortstop Vern Stephens—who hit with more power, and who had led the league in assists in 1947—and several other players, perhaps including pitchers Jack Kramer and Ellis Kinder, infielder Walt Judnich, and center fielder Don Lehner. Veeck, who had smashed Cleveland attendance records with 1,521,978 customers, was also prepared to contribute more than $100,000 to alleviate the Browns' cash flow problems. After making his pitch, Veeck alerted the Cleveland writers off the record. According to Veeck, the deal collapsed because the Browns asked him to pay a large share of Boudreau's salary for the next three years as well. Perhaps this problem would eventually have been worked out, but an item reporting the talks leaked into a Chicago paper. The Cleveland writers caucused and decided to break it themselves—as a story of negotiations in progress. The story knocked the World Series right off the Cleveland front pages, and fans literally took to the streets, foreshadowing the massive protests twelve years later when Frank Lane traded Rocky Colavito, a Cleveland hero of comparable stature, to Detroit.

Reached in New York by a Cleveland executive, Veeck was encouraged to return at once and calm the furor rather than face a lynch mob should he return with Boudreau gone from his roster. The Cleveland papers, which monitored the Indians every bit as closely as the Boston sheets did the Red Sox, printed ballots upon which fans could express their opinion of the trade, and huge majorities rejected it. Met at the airport by an angry mob, Veeck promised not to trade Boudreau if the citizenry insisted. He spent the rest of the night walking the streets and barhopping, assuring one and all that Boudreau's job was safe.

Boudreau—like Bob Feller, Joe DiMaggio, and Ted Williams—was a shrewd businessman as well as a great player, and in new talks he insisted on a two-year contract. In return, Veeck won the right to hire new coaches, and he used it to the full. Bill McKechnie, sixty-one years old, had twenty-five years of National League managerial experience behind him, including four pennants. Veeck hired him, and he became Boudreau's right-hand man. Muddy Ruel, fresh from a year as the Browns' manager, joined the team as well, and Mel Harder, the team's ace pitcher for much of the thirties, became pitching coach. Veeck also hired Cleveland immortal Tris Speaker—manager and star of the city's only pennant winner, the 1920 world champions—as a part-time coach.

The final act of Cleveland's off-season drama was played out at a baseball banquet, at which two writers played Veeck and Boudreau in an improvised skit. "You didn't like the way I ran the ball club, is that it?" asked Boudreau. "Now, I never said that, Lou," replied Veeck, "I never said you were the worst manager in baseball." "I know," said Boudreau. "Well, Joe McCarthy thinks I'm pretty good—that I know what I'm doing." "I think you know what you're doing, too, Lou," replied Veeck. "Only sometimes I'm not sure why." But at the conclusion of the dinner came a real surprise. Boudreau—reversing himself—acknowledged that he did, indeed, have something to prove. For the first time, he offered to step down as manager and remain in Cleveland as a player should Veeck ever decide he should.[3] Boudreau, in effect, was challenging himself to lead the Indians to a much better finish—if not a pennant—in 1948. It would not be just another season.

While Veeck was flying home to pacify Cleveland fandom and the Boston papers were busily forecasting a controversy between Ted Williams and Joe McCarthy, the Yankees were winning their first world championship in four years. And within minutes of their seventh-game triumph on October 6, they too had experienced an extraordinary front-office controversy that changed the face of the team for years to come.

The years 1945–47 in Yankee history resembled the much longer, equally turbulent George Steinbrenner era. The key man in the postwar organization was another electric but unstable personality, Yankee president and part owner Larry MacPhail. After running the Cincinnati Reds in the 1930s, when he introduced night baseball to the majors and built most of a pennant-winning team, and the Brooklyn Dodgers in the 1940s, where he turned a chronic second-division club into a winner, MacPhail had arranged in 1945 to purchase the richest of all franchises from the estate of

---

3. Both the principals described the controversy at length. See Boudreau with Fitzgerald, *Player-Manager*, 87–97, and Bill Veeck with Ed Linn, *Veeck—As in Wreck* (New York, 1962), 93–98, 152–58.

Col. Jake Ruppert. His two partners, Dan Topping and Del Webb, had no baseball experience. For the first time in MacPhail's career he had taken over a winning organization, but he was not content simply to administer a going concern.

While it seems unlikely that Steinbrenner will ever follow MacPhail into Cooperstown, the parallels between them are unmistakable. Forceful and dynamic, MacPhail was highly emotional and prone to sudden outbursts of rage. He chronically second-guessed managers and ballplayers. According to Leo Durocher, his skipper during his glory years in Brooklyn, MacPhail frequently fired him in the evening only to forget the next morning that anything had happened.[4] In the summer of 1942 he informed his defending champion Dodger club, then enjoying a ten-game lead over the Cardinals, that he expected them to lose the pennant because of complacency— a prophecy which they proceeded to fulfill. He publicly feuded with other clubs, accusing the Cardinals in 1940 of purposely throwing at the Dodgers, and accusing Durocher in 1947 of associating with undesirable elements. The Yankee team MacPhail took over in 1945, shaped largely by the late Ed Barrow, was a staid, relatively conservative group, and clashes between the new owner and older members of the organization inevitably occurred.

Joe McCarthy, who completed his fifteenth year as Yankee manager in 1945, was an intense but extremely thoughtful teacher and strategist who valued stability in a club and prided himself on his patience. He had never before had to face a boss like MacPhail, and he refused to put up with his interference. After trying to resign in 1945, only to have MacPhail persuade him to stay, the man who had won seven pennants and six world championships in the last ten years quit MacPhail and the Yankees in the spring of 1946 with a 22–13 record and went home to Buffalo, New York. MacPhail installed veteran catcher Bill Dickey in his place, but couldn't get along with him either. The season reached a climax when MacPhail called Dickey into his office together with Joe Gordon, the star second baseman and MVP in 1942, who was having injury troubles and a poor season in his first year back from the war. MacPhail ordered Dickey to take Gordon out of the lineup, and Gordon had to be restrained from slugging him. Mac-Phail fired Dickey in September, also bringing his career as a player to an end, and replaced him temporarily with coach Johnny Neun, and Gordon went to the Indians after the season. Until Steinbrenner, the record of three Yankee managers in one season looked quite safe. Shortly after the season

---

4. Leo Durocher, *The Dodgers and Me* (Chicago, 1948), 71–140, gives a more thorough account than the later work, Leo Durocher with Ed Linn, *Nice Guys Finish Last* (New York, 1975), 116–57.

ended, MacPhail signed veteran manager Bucky Harris, who had joined the Yankee front office late in 1946, to a two-year contract.

Harris and the Yankees proceeded to win the pennant while MacPhail became involved in further controversies. His feud with the Dodgers resulted early in 1947 in the suspension of Leo Durocher for an entire year by Commissioner Happy Chandler. In the middle of the season MacPhail astonished the baseball world by declaring that Durocher had not deserved the suspension—an out-and-out violation of the commissioner's order silencing all participants in the controversy. Under the steadying hand of Harris, however, the team took control of the pennant race and coasted to a comfortable victory. MacPhail pulled one more rabbit out of his hat late in the season, acquiring colorful, irrepressible forty-year-old pitcher Buck "Bobo" Newsom, who had won 198 games and changed teams eleven times since 1929; he proceeded to go 7–5 with a 2.75 ERA down the stretch.

On the afternoon of October 6, 1947, as the Yankees were wrapping up a 5–2 seventh-game win over the Dodgers behind a strong relief job from Joe Page, MacPhail strolled into the press box and announced loudly that he was quitting. He stole the show for the last time in the locker room a few minutes later by making it official, and promptly got into two fistfights with other club executives during the victory party that followed. Dan Topping and Del Webb bought him out a few days later. The actual direction of the club now passed into the hands of George Weiss, the longtime director of the Yankee farm system. Larry MacPhail—one of the most innovative executives in baseball history—never ran a ball club again.

The events of September and October 1947 ensured that action on the American League trading market would commence almost immediately after the World Series. Both the Boston and Cleveland organizations were determined to strengthen themselves for a run at the Yankees, who in turn needed to make some moves of their own. In Boston, Joe McCarthy wasted no time in making his mark on his new club—although not, as it turned out, in exactly the way that the Boston writers had anticipated.

The team that McCarthy had signed to manage had been built up by Eddie Collins and Joe Cronin for owner Tom Yawkey, who had owned the club for fourteen years and retained it until his death almost thirty years later. The scion of a millionaire timber family, Yawkey had taken over a moribund Red Sox franchise in 1933. During the next four years he spent more than half a million Depression dollars to acquire established stars, including Lefty Grove, George Pipgras, Max Bishop, Wes Ferrell, player-manager Cronin, Bing Miller, Jimmy Foxx, and Doc Cramer. Less successful even than in the 1970s, this strategy got the Red Sox only up to the high eighties in wins and second place in 1938–39. By that time, Yawkey and general manager Eddie Collins had shifted their strategy to the more productive acquisition of West Coast youngsters like second baseman Bobby Doerr, center fielder Dom DiMiggio, shortstop Johnny Pesky, and the magnificent Ted Williams. Helped by these players, the team finished second again in 1941 and 1942, finally cracking 90 wins in 1942, and stormed to the pennant in a romp in the first postwar year of 1946. After barely losing a seven-game World Series to the Cardinals, they crashed to third, fourteen games behind the Yankees, in 1947. The conventional wisdom blamed the decline on the Red Sox pitching staff. As usual in dealing with the Red Sox, the conventional wisdom was dead wrong.

Even in the 1940s, the illusions created by Fenway Park were sufficiently massive to mask the real strengths and weaknesses of the team that played in it. The huge left-field wall was only three hundred feet away from home plate at the foul line, visibility was excellent, and prevailing winds frequently helped balls fly out of the park.[5] Over a five-year period (1946–50), the Red Sox and their opponents scored more than 20 percent more runs in Fenway than out of it. Because of the ballpark, a mediocre hitter who joined the Red Sox suddenly acquired the statistics of a good one, while a mediocre pitcher's new numbers could quickly cost him his job. In 1946, when the Red Sox romped to the pennant, they scored 469 of their league-leading 792 runs at home. Their runs scored on the road, 323, ranked third in the league, behind the Washington Senators (!) and the Tigers. They allowed the second lowest total of runs on the road, however, exceeding the Tigers by just 12 runs. The Red Sox of 1946, in short, had good, but not outstanding, hitting, and excellent pitching. The statistical juggernaut they presented was an illusion created by the visibility and short left-field wall of Fenway Park.

The Red Sox of 1947 showed an even more interesting pattern. True it was that ace pitchers Boo Ferriss, Tex Hughson, and Mickey Harris, who between them had started 113 games and won 62 in 1946, suffered injuries, started only 77 games in 1947, and won just 29. But Joe Dobson, lefty Earl Johnson, and late-season acquisition Denny Galehouse picked up a great deal of the slack, and the team ERA only rose from 3.38 to 3.81. On the road the Red Sox gave up just 314 runs, only 24 more than the league-leading Athletics, *and twelve fewer than the pennant-winning Yankees!* What killed the 1947 Red Sox was their offense, which fell from 323 runs

---

5. The prevailing winds became much less of a factor after the team built roof boxes in the early 1980s, costing Jim Rice an excellent chance of at least 500 home runs.

scored on the road in 1946 to just 299—sixth in an eight-team league—in 1947. Their pitching and defense had fallen from great to good; their hitting, from good to bad. On the eve of the 1948 season, the Red Sox had some major holes to fill.

At first base, Rudy York, acquired rather cheaply from Detroit, had been the second-most valuable offensive player on the 1946 champions, hitting .276 with 86 walks and driving in 119 runs. York was only thirty-two in 1946, but he had a drinking problem. In June of 1947, when they had definitely fallen out of the race, the Sox unloaded York, then hitting just .212, to the White Sox in exchange for a big twenty-six-year-old right-handed first baseman, Jake Jones, who had yet to play regularly for a full season. Jones hit a promising 16 home runs in 404 at bats for the Sox, but batted just .236. According to his teammate Johnny Pesky, American League pitchers had discovered by late 1947 that Jones could not hit a curveball.

Bobby Doerr, on paper, was the outstanding offensive second baseman in the league in 1946, driving in 116 runs with 18 homers. He slipped to 17 homers and 95 RBIs in 1947. Doerr was an excellent hitter in Fenway and a fine fielder, but he had one of the biggest home-road differentials of any player in history. A lifetime .315 hitter at home, on the road he was barely average. In 1947 Doerr hit .237 with 5 homers and 35 RBIs on the road. With his figures, Doerr was a fixture at second, but he would not help the Red Sox win a pennant hitting as he did in 1947. His RBI totals were a function of batting behind Dom DiMaggio, Johnny Pesky, and Ted Williams, as well as his talent for hitting the left-field screen.

Johnny Pesky, a left-handed-hitting shortstop, had emerged in three seasons as one of the finest table-setters in the league. Only five feet nine inches tall and weighing less than 170 pounds, the Oregonian was a fine all-around athlete who had adapted his game to his capabilities. Reaching the majors in 1942 after just two years in the minors, Pesky had gotten more than 200 hits in each of his first three seasons.[6] He had an astonishing lifetime batting average of .330, third in the league behind Ted Williams and Joe DiMaggio. At this stage of his career, moreover, Pesky was not a Fenway Park hitter—his averages were virtually identical at home and away. He had gained weight before the 1947 season, however, and his play at shortstop had fallen off. He had even played 22 games at third, where the Sox had lacked an adequate regular even in 1946, and where Pesky shared the time with Sam Dente (.232) and Eddie Pellagrini (.203) in 1947. The corners of the Red Sox infield obviously presented major problems.

---

6. Pesky had spent 1943–45 in the navy.

The outfield looked much better. Dom DiMaggio was an outstanding center fielder. Five inches shorter and about twenty-five pounds lighter than his more famous brother at five-nine, 168 pounds, Dom D had come to the Red Sox in 1940. He was a good line-drive hitter who hit between .283 and .316 and walked about seventy times a year. He covered the relatively small Fenway Park outfield to perfection. In three full seasons in center he had led the league in putouts once and finished second twice, easily outdistancing his more famous brother every time. Indeed, defensive statistics indicate that in the field Dominic DiMaggio was truly "better than his brother Joe," as the Fenway faithful liked to sing to the tune of "Maryland, My Maryland." Right field had been shared by thirty-six-year-old left-handed-hitting veteran Wally Moses, who hit an inadequate .275, and twenty-four-year-old right-hander Sam Mele, the one promising offensive acquisition of 1947, who weighed in at .302 with 12 homers. In left field, of course, was Ted Williams, the greatest hitter in baseball.

At twenty-nine, Williams had compiled a lifetime batting average of .352, fourth on the all-time list behind Ty Cobb, Tris Speaker, and Joe Jackson. He had developed his swing during thousands of hours on San Diego playgrounds, playing mythical nine-inning, twenty-seven-out games against a single friend when no one else was around to make up a team. Reaching the majors at the age of twenty in 1939, he had now won three batting titles, three home run crowns, and three RBI titles. He had hit .406 in 1941, the last man ever to top .400. Renowned for his amazing discipline and strike-zone judgment, he had walked 145 times or more for four straight seasons. He had won the triple crown in 1942 and 1947. He lived to hit, practicing whenever and wherever he could, ceaselessly studying pitchers, and endlessly rehashing his at bats. So intense was his concentration that he could remember the details of every single major league home run he had ever hit—the situation, the pitcher, the count, and where he had hit the ball.

Ever since his second year in 1940, however, Williams had found himself at the center of one controversy or another. Exuberant and extroverted, Williams had immediately caught the attention of fans around the league in his rookie season, and his .406 average in 1941 established him as an all-time great. Yet from his second year onward, the intense, easily offended, often outspoken kid from San Diego frequently found himself in hot water with the press. After Fenway Park fans booed him for some shaky fielding, he refused, beginning in 1940, to acknowledge their cheers by tipping his cap. In the same year, Williams, whose uncle enjoyed a relaxed and easygoing life as a fireman near New York City, announced in a moment of frustration that he would rather be a fireman than a ballplayer. The press nailed him for ingratitude, and several teams greeted his next appearance with bells, red hats, and on one occasion, a company of firemen in the stands.[7] He became a frequent target of much-read Boston columnists like Austen Lake of the *American*, Bill Cunningham of the *Herald*, Dave Egan of the *Record*, and (less often) Harold Kaese of the *Globe*. The sensitive Williams could not forget bad columns the same way that he forgot a rare 0–4 day.

Williams encountered further controversy in early 1942, when he received a III-A draft deferment on the perfectly true grounds that he supported his divorced mother. Even though most of the league's leading stars played during 1942, he was singled out for criticism, and failed to win the MVP award despite winning the triple crown. Returning in 1946 after three years in the navy, he won the MVP and led Boston to the pennant but became a target once again when he had a poor World Series and the Red Sox lost to the Cardinals. Williams tied a record in 1947 by winning his *second* triple crown, but set yet another one by failing to win the MVP award on either occasion. Analyzing the 1947 voting, Harold Kaese, probably the most brilliant, analytical baseball writer in the country, noted that one writer had apparently left Williams off his ballot altogether, costing him the award, and concluded that Williams had lost it for his failure to butter up sportswriters.[8] What Kaese did not know was that the writer in question was his own *Globe* colleague, Melville Webb, who had taken offense when Williams berated him in the clubhouse early in the season.

Because Williams rarely made things easier for Boston writers, they liked to think that he created problems for managers as well, and immediately assumed that he would run afoul of Joe McCarthy. But McCarthy well understood that Williams—like Joe DiMaggio—was one of those very few uniquely valuable players whom any manager had to make an effort to keep. "If I can't get along with a .400 hitter," he reportedly commented, "it will be my fault." Leaving aside his new team's greatest strength, he turned to its obvious weaknesses.

McCarthy had moved quickly to improve the Cubs and Yankees when he took them over, and he wasted no time now. The filling of holes had already begun during 1947. In May the Red Sox had attempted to strengthen their catching by acquiring canny veteran and lusty bench jockey Birdie Tebbetts from the Tigers. Although Tebbets had never hit more than .294 or appeared in more than 111 games in a season, the New England native had a reputation as a good handler of pitchers and was

---

7. On this and other episodes from Williams's early career see Williams with Underwood, *My Turn at Bat*.

8. *Boston Globe*, November 28, 1947.

already looking forward to a career as a manager. Then, in June, they had acquired thirty-five-year-old veteran Denny Galehouse, who had begun with the Indians in 1936 and later pitched for the Red Sox, from the St. Louis Browns. Galehouse, who had been one of the aces of the Browns' staff during their pennant year of 1944, had a fine half season in Boston, going 11–7 with an excellent 3.32 ERA. Toward the end of the year he advised manager (and soon-to-be general manager) Joe Cronin regarding other Browns who might be available.

The Browns' brief era of wartime glory was over, and they were rapidly sinking into obscurity and poverty once again. While they had outshone the rival Cardinals until the mid-1920s, during the 1930s they had been the weakest franchise in baseball, their attendance reaching an almost incredible low of 80,922 fans in 1935. In December 1941 the American League had actually been about to approve their transfer to Los Angeles when Pearl Harbor intervened.[9] Helped by their 1944 pennant, they averaged 500,000 fans a year from 1944 through 1946, but fell all the way to last place in 1947. The performance of the team was something of a mystery. Their assets included some more than respectable pitchers, including Galehouse, Jack Kramer, and left-hander Sam Zoldak; shortstop Vern Stephens, a good fielder who consistently drove in 80 to 100 runs a year; and two strong left-handed power hitters, Walt Judnich and veteran outfielder Jeff Heath. Several of these players commanded respectable salaries. With the Browns having finished last and drawn 320,474 customers despite their presence, owner Richard Muckerman and general manager Bill DeWitt concluded that they could do about as well without them.

We have seen that DeWitt discussed one huge deal with Cleveland owner Bill Veeck during the World Series, but without result. Six weeks later, in November, the Browns and the Red Sox made two major deals on consecutive days. The first sent Vern Stephens and pitcher Jack Kramer to Boston in exchange for six undistinguished players and the enormous sum of $310,000 in cash. (With inflation taken into account, the amount of this sale is quite comparable to the one-million-dollar deals floated by Charlie Finley but vetoed by Bowie Kuhn in 1976.) The next day Boston received another pitcher of much less renown, Ellis Kinder, and veteran third baseman Billy Hitchcock in exchange for three more undistinguished players and $65,000. Stephens—one of the two best offensive shortstops in the league—was the key man in the deals. *Globe* columnist Harold Kaese was ecstatic. Dipping into his extraordinary files, he recalled days on which Stephens, a muscular right-handed hitter who stepped to his left and

9. William B. Mead, *Even the Browns* (Chicago, 1978), 33–35.

pulled the ball hard, had destroyed the Red Sox in Fenway.[10] How Stephens and Pesky would split up the shortstop and third base positions was left undetermined. McCarthy reserved the decision until spring training.

A few months later, the Red Sox apparently completed their roster by acquiring thirty-three-year-old left-handed outfielder Stan Spence from the Washington Senators in exchange for journeyman outfielder Leon Culberson and infielder Al Kozar. Over the last five years Spence had established himself as a decent hitter despite the enormous handicap of playing in Griffith Stadium, the worst hitters' park in baseball. He had also been a fine center fielder. Together with Sam Mele, Spence certainly might be expected to take care of right field. While Jones at first and Tebbetts behind the plate could not be counted on offensively, the team seemed much stronger.

Spring training got off to an entertaining start when McCarthy, defusing a possible confrontation with Williams, broke his own coat-and-tie rule and showed up for dinner in the hotel dining room wearing a loud sports shirt. "Hi, Ted, how was the fishing and how's the new baby?" asked McCarthy when Williams arrived for the first morning's workouts. A few minutes later the Red Sox were busily taking batting practice, and Williams had his first clue that he and McCarthy might see eye to eye after all. Within days, McCarthy called the writers over and asked them not to discuss the ticklish question of which established shortstop, Pesky or Stephens, would move to third. He was apparently confident that either one of them could; with the Yankees, he had shifted two minor league shortstops—Joe Gordon and Red Rolfe—to second and third base, respectively. A few weeks into spring training he decided that Pesky would make the switch, and Pesky, although somewhat disappointed, accepted the assignment willingly.

The Red Sox pitching staff presented a large array of uncertain possibilities. The brightest spot was veteran Joe Dobson, a thirty-one-year-old Oklahoman who had improved steadily since joining the team in 1940 and posted his best season during 1947, an 18–8 mark. Mickey Harris, Dave Ferriss, and Tex Hughson, it was hoped, might recover their 1946 form; Denny Galehouse and lefty Earl Johnson might maintain their 1947 performance; and something might be expected from newcomers Kramer, Kinder, and twenty-five-year-old southpaw Mel Parnell, who had had a very difficult year in 1947 both at Boston and Louisville, posting ERAs of 6.35 with the big club and 7.30 in triple-A before breaking a finger and missing most of the year. With five to seven possible starters, McCarthy

10. *Boston Globe*, November 18, 1947.

could adopt the same strategy he had used in New York and spread the workload around generously. With the Yankees he had preferred to use five or six starting pitchers, and rarely had a pitcher near the league lead in starts, complete games, or innings pitched. McCarthy never burned out a good pitcher during his years with the Yankees. In spring training in 1948 he gave most of the work to the more doubtful pitchers on the staff. Denny Galehouse, an ace in the latter part of 1947, had hardly pitched at all when he was tapped to start on Opening Day.

McCarthy's managerial personality had emerged clearly during his fifteen-year reign with the Yankees. He was known for strict rules against card playing, and for demanding that his players focus unremittingly upon the game. His own concentration was ferocious—he would often work out problems on his club smoking alone in a darkened hotel room—and he knew how to make use of almost everything that happened on a ballfield. With his lantern jaw and chunky body, he could be an impressive presence on the field, and although he respected umpires, he also knew how to try to intimidate them in a key game. "God damn you," he told Ernie Stewart on a hot July day in 1943, when Stewart had ejected pitcher Charley Wensloff for throwing his glove in protest, "you didn't put my pitcher out, did you? If you put that pitcher out, I will turn this crowd loose on you. They'll mob you." "Oh no you won't Joe," replied Stewart—no wimp himself—"because I'll give you thirty seconds to get out of here, and if you don't, I'll forfeit the game." But when the game was over, McCarthy told Wensloff, "I don't know what you did to minor league umpires in throwing your glove or anything like that, but you are in the major leagues now and you can't do that. The next time you do that it is gonna cost you five hundred dollars for getting thrown out in a crucial spot."[11]

McCarthy, like Leo Durocher, Earl Weaver, or Billy Martin, was driven by demons demanding him to master every conceivable situation. He had an extraordinary memory, which he tried to use to his advantage on almost every play. Most of his players respected him enormously, and remembered him as an understanding boss. Joe DiMaggio commented that while he never became too close to any particular player, he made them all feel that he was interested in them. He showed remarkable patience with injuries, apparently understanding, as many managers do not, that a player could really be suffering from an injury even if it caused the manager no pain. He almost never criticized players in the press, although he could be sharp-tongued in private when he thought a player was loafing. Like two of his favorite players, Lou Gehrig and Joe DiMaggio, he kept a tremendous

11. Larry Gerlach, *The Men in Blue: Conversations with Umpires* (New York, 1980), 120–21.

amount inside himself. When things went badly he would drink to excess. Even players who admired him knew that he would occasionally fall off the wagon, leaving his coach Earle Combs to run the club for a day or two.

As manager of the Yankees McCarthy had continually fed new young talent into his lineup, but he must have realized rather quickly that the Red Sox farm system lacked the richness of the Yankee organization. Only two prospects really distinguished themselves in spring training: infielder Billy Goodman, who had hit a robust .340 at Louisville but who seemed to lack a position, and catcher Matt Batts, who had hit .260 at Toronto, and who looked like a better backup for Tebbetts than Roy Partee. McCarthy was also saddled with a bonus baby pitcher, eighteen-year-old Chuck Stobbs. Under the then-current rules of baseball, any player signed directly by a big-league club had to spend two years in the majors before going to the minors, and Stobbs was such a player. The winter trades certainly had strengthened the team enormously, however, and gave him a chance to win with the talent available.

In Cleveland, Bill Veeck was equally determined to strengthen his team. It was not without assets. The Indians' most distinguished performer was the most commanding pitcher in baseball, Bob Feller, who had joined them at seventeen in 1936. In the whole history of major league baseball, only a few pitchers have made a comparable first impression, including Walter Johnson and Dwight Gooden, both of whom also reached the majors before the age of twenty. Feller probably had the most stuff of them all. While Ted Williams was playing mock nine-inning ball games against a friend in San Diego, going through thirty to forty at bats every afternoon, Feller was pitching to his father, an Iowa farmer, every afternoon and evening after school and chores, and throwing curveballs into his pillow before going to sleep at night. Before his eighteenth birthday, Feller proved that his blazing fastball and superb curve put him in a class by himself as a strikeout pitcher. In 1936 he struck out 15 batters in his first start, and tied Dizzy Dean's record of 17 in his third. After the season he returned home to complete high school, and his graduation ceremonies were carried on a nationwide radio hook-up. A sore arm had stopped him briefly in 1937, but since then he had carried an astonishing workload. Because his control remained erratic, he threw enormous numbers of pitches. In six full seasons (1938–41, 1946–47), Feller had led the league five times in wins, five times in games started, three times in complete games, five times in innings pitched, six times in strikeouts, twice in hits allowed, and five times in walks. He had pitched no-hitters in 1940 and 1946, and struck out a record 18 batters on the last day of 1939.[12] He had spent the years 1942–45 in the navy.

The first two postwar years of 1946 and 1947 had been eventful ones for Feller. Upon taking over the club, Veeck had encouraged him to pitch every third day for the rest of the season and try for Rube Waddell's record of 343 strikeouts in a year. Feller, who had had ambitions to break many records, knew that he had lost his chance at Walter Johnson's career mark by spending three and one-half years in the navy, and this idea appealed to him. He was successful, breaking the record with 348.[13] He pitched 371 innings during the year, and another 100 in postseason exhibitions. Although Feller's records eventually fell in the 1960s and 1970s, they remain the most impressive ever compiled in context, simply because strikeouts were so much less common in the 1930s and 1940s. When Feller struck out 348 batters in 1946, American League hitters fanned at the rate of 4.2 per game. When Nolan Ryan struck out 383 in 1973, they struck out at the rate of 5.1 per game, more than 20 percent more often.

Early in 1947 Feller had suffered a freak injury on the mound pitching a night game against the Philadelphia Athletics. He had made 10 of the first 11 outs in the game on strikeouts, felt he had the best stuff of his life, and thought he might strike out as many as 20 batters when Barney McCosky came to the plate and catcher Jim Hegan signaled for a curve. Throwing fastballs, Feller had kicked up a small pile of dirt on the mound, and he knew that he would step into it to throw the curve. Fearing to telegraph the pitch or break his rhythm, however, he did not kick it away. He struck McCosky out, but the dirt gave way and he landed hard on his right shoulder. He returned from the injury to pitch almost three hundred innings again, but his strikeouts fell below two hundred for the first time ever in a full season. Still, he appeared fully recovered by the spring of 1948, and remained easily the most famous and effective pitcher in baseball.

Feller's career also brings out an important point about baseball in the 1930s and 1940s: although average players were paid less than one-tenth of what they are today, stars could make a fortune, both on and off the field. Thus, in early 1938, just past his nineteenth birthday, he signed a contract for $20,000—equal to about $160,000 today—for his second full season. He made enough two years later to build his family a large, modern new farmhouse, and reportedly was paid $50,000 in 1940. He also took advantage of numerous opportunities to earn money off the field, both by barn-

12. An excellent source on Feller's early years is Bob Feller, *Strikeout Story* (New York, 1947).

13. While this record was officially recognized for decades, the editors of the *Baseball Encyclopedia* later determined that Waddell had in fact struck out 349 batters in 1904.

storming in the off-season and through endorsements, personal appearances, and books. His telephone rang so frequently that the Indians by 1948 were assigning a member of the staff to room with him on the road, so that another player would not be disturbed. Today, visitors to Feller's home outside Cleveland find that nothing has changed in this respect.

The Tribe's other veteran longtime star was third baseman Ken Keltner. Keltner had been a twenty-one-year-old rookie sensation back in 1938, hitting .276 with 26 homers and 113 RBIs and fielding brilliantly. He remained a fielding standout, best known for the two backhand plays that stopped Joe DiMaggio's hitting streak in 1941, but he had never had another season as good at the plate. In 1946, hampered by injuries, he hit 13 homers in 116 games, and he had finished 1947 with a .257 average, 11 homers, and 76 RBIs.

Owner Bill Veeck was a compulsive trader. He had enormous faith, some of it justified, in his own ability to size up talent and motivate players. He had one major weakness as an operator: his impatience, which as he freely admitted made it difficult for him to invest in the future of a young player. Veeck had made his first big move at the 1946 World Series. Taking advantage of a feud between Yankee owner Larry MacPhail and All-Star second baseman Joe Gordon, he plucked the American League's 1942 MVP from the Yankees in exchange for Allie Reynolds. Despite Gordon's dreadful 1946 season, Veeck appeared to have made a steal. Gordon, an acrobat, was a fine second baseman and right-handed power hitter, while Reynolds was thirty-one, the same age as Gordon, and had failed to replicate two good wartime seasons in 1946. The deal turned out well for both clubs. Reynolds was the Yankee ace during 1947, and Gordon led the Indians with 29 homers and 93 RBIs.

The Indians had a fine scouting system, and two good young players had made their debuts in 1947 as well. Left-handed-hitting Dale Mitchell was one of the few returning war veterans to begin a baseball career in 1946, at the age of twenty-four. He led the Texas League with a .337 average and hit .316 for the Indians in 1947. Slightly less successful was another rookie, lefty first baseman Eddie Robinson, the RBI king of the International League in Baltimore in 1946, who hit .245 with 14 homers in 318 at bats for the Tribe in 1947. The rest of the outfield was a very mixed bag, including big, slow, strong, and strikeout prone Pat Seerey and veteran Hank Edwards. Veeck had made another deal with the Yankees in December 1946, swapping veteran second baseman Ray Mack and young catcher Sherman Lollar for outfielder Hal Peck, whose main distinction was having played for Veeck in Milwaukee, and two pitchers, Al Gettel and Gene Bearden. Bearden, a left-handed knuckleballer, was recommended to

Veeck by his friend Casey Stengel, who had managed Bearden at Oakland after having worked for Veeck in Milwaukee. Bearden spent 1947 in the minors; Gettel had a reasonably good 11–10 season; and Peck hit a decent .293 as a part-time outfielder. Behind Feller, the pitching staff in 1947 featured converted third baseman outfielder Bob Lemon, who went 11–5 as a starter over the second half of the year, and several men who had done fairly well—Al Gettel (11–10), recovering alcoholic Don Black (10–12), Ed Klieman, and Steve Gromek—but not spectacularly.

The 1947 Indians were actually a somewhat better ball club than their 80–74 record indicated. The simple "Pythagorean formula" developed by Bill James relates a team's total runs and runs allowed to its winning percentage by the formula $Runs^2/(Runs^2 + Runs\ Allowed^2)$. Based upon their 687 runs scored and their 588 runs allowed, they should have had a percentage of .577 and 88 wins. This measurement—a team's predicted percentage—is the most accurate measurement of the overall ability of a ball club over a season—more accurate, indeed, than its won-loss record. Thus, in this book, when one club is referred to as superior to another, this is what is meant. In this case, the Indians' eight-win difference indicated a poor record in low-scoring games, which history shows is usually simply a matter of bad luck that is unlikely to continue for two consecutive seasons.

Cleveland's Municipal Stadium helped the Indians' pitchers and hurt their hitters. On the road they were second in the league in runs scored, third-lowest in runs allowed. With Robinson, Gordon, Keltner, Hank Edwards, and Pat Seerey all hitting homers in double figures, they trailed the Yankees in homers on the road by just one, 60 to 61.

As the 1948 season neared, Veeck continued his search for better ballplayers. He got Allie Clark, a right-handed-hitting outfielder, from the Yanks in exchange for pitcher Red Embree. Returning to the Browns after the big St. Louis–Boston deal, Veeck acquired right-hander Bob Muncrief and lefty first baseman–outfielder Walt Judnich for three players and $25,000. Two weeks later, in one of his less impressive deals, he acquired Browns second baseman (and aspiring Hollywood actor) John Berardino for $65,000.[14] Berardino could entertain his teammates on trains with impromptu Shakespeare productions, but his career with the Browns had failed to reveal much major league talent. He became the Indians' only spare infielder during 1948, and was not an asset.

Veeck made two more deals in early 1948. The Indians lacked a center fielder, and Veeck got slim, thirty-year-old Texan Thurman Tucker, a fair

14. Originally the deal called for outfielder Catfish Metkovich and $50,000. Metkovich was returned for an injury, and his value assessed at $15,000.

left-handed hitter, from the White Sox, where Tucker in 1943 had made 399 putouts in just 132 games. Tucker was also one of the very few players in the league who consistently stole bases in double figures. But Veeck's most daring gamble came in April, when he bought right-hander Russ Christopher from Connie Mack for $25,000.

Christopher, six feet three inches and 175 pounds, had a rare heart defect that made him vulnerable to respiratory problems and oxygen deficiency. A good strikeout pitcher and reliable starter during the war, he had become a fine reliever in 1947, going 10–7 with 12 saves and a 2.90 ERA. In the spring of 1948, he got pneumonia. Veeck, who loved taking chances on players with physical or emotional handicaps, offered to buy Christopher. Connie Mack, who combined the image of a saint with the spending habits of Ebenezer Scrooge, allowed himself to be talked into receiving $25,000 for a potentially worthless asset. Christopher recovered, and when the season began in 1948 he was ready to pitch.

The Indians in training camp had an infield comparable in strength to that of the Red Sox. The writers speculated that Hank Greenberg, who had joined the club operation after his release by the Pirates in 1947, might even spell Robinson at first if need be, but Greenberg declared himself through as a player and concentrated on learning the front office end of baseball. At their best, Gordon, Boudreau, and Keltner seemed at least the equal of Doerr, Stephens, and Pesky, although the difference in ballparks almost guaranteed the Sox players superior statistics, and Keltner had had two poor seasons in a row. The Indians' outfield was more confused. Only Dale Mitchell had definitely performed well in 1947. Thurman Tucker was impressing at center, and Doby, with the help of Tris Speaker, was doing much better and had clearly justified the decision to sign him. But Doby and Tucker could be expected to share playing time with right-handers Clark and Seerey and left-handers Judnich, Hank Edwards, and Hal Peck. Boudreau, who loved options, carried seven or eight outfielders all year.

As the team returned to Cleveland to open the season on April 20, Boudreau pronounced it the best he had ever managed. No one, however, picked the Indians to finish first. The more open question, in light of recent events, was whether Lou Boudreau would still be managing the Indians in April 1949. No one could have foreseen how the controversy with Veeck would transform Boudreau, the Indians, and the 1948 American League season.

The Yankee team that had won the pennant in 1947 was built around great but aging veterans of the prewar era. Their first baseman, left-handed

George McQuinn, was finishing up one of the unluckiest careers in base-ball history. Born in 1910, McQuinn had spent the potentially most pro-ductive years of his baseball career trapped in the Yankee farm system behind Lou Gehrig. When he escaped in 1938—just one year before Gehrig's sudden retirement—McQuinn landed in the hot nether regions occupied by the St. Louis Browns. Kept out of military service partly by his age, McQuinn toiled for the Browns while the rest of the league deterio-rated under the impact of war, and was rewarded with a pennant in 1944. He was traded to Connie Mack's Athletics in 1946, released after one year, and re-signed by the Yankees, who, strange to say, hadn't found a long-term replacement to Gehrig yet. He rewarded them with perhaps his best season ever, hitting .304 with 13 homers and 80 RBIs, and actually received several first-place votes in the MVP voting.

Second base was held by Snuffy Stirnweiss, whose major league career had begun as a wartime replacement in 1943, after ulcers kept him out of the army. A right-handed hitter, Stirnweiss had hit over .300 in 1944–45, winning the batting title in 1945 with a .309 average and the league slug-ging percentage crown as well with 32 doubles, 22 triples, and 10 homers for a .476 mark. No other batter has led the AL in slugging with less than a .500 mark since 1915, and Stirnweiss's record in 1946 and 1947, when he failed to reach .260, established him as one of the weakest hitters ever to win a batting title. His fielding statistics were mediocre as well, but at twenty-eight he retained the Yankees' second-base job.

Shortstop Phil Rizzuto, a native New Yorker and a darling of the Italo-American community, had reached the Yankees in 1941, left in 1943 for the war, and quickly reestablished himself in 1946. Rizzuto's reputation has been enhanced by his service for the Yankees and by two .300 seasons at the plate (1941 and 1950, when he was selected the Most Valuable Player), but in 1946–47 he was a .270 hitter with no power and only average strike zone judgment. His fielding statistics were good, but he certainly ranked below Lou Boudreau of Cleveland and the heavy-hitting Vern Stephens of the Browns among AL shortstops. Rizzuto was thirty in 1948. Largely forgot-ten by history, Yankee third baseman Billy Johnson, also thirty, was a solid hitter, with a .285 average, 10 homers, and 95 RBIs in 1947. Like all right-handed hitters, he suffered from playing in Yankee Stadium.

Catching during 1947 had been split between veteran Aaron Robinson and twenty-two-year-old rookie Yogi Berra, who also played some games in the outfield. Berra had hit .280 with 11 homers in just 293 at bats, but doubts persisted about his ability behind the plate, especially after the Dodgers stole five bases against him during the first four games of the 1947 World Series. Another youngster, twenty-two-year-old Bobby Brown, had distinguished himself as a left-handed-hitting utility infielder, hitting .300 in 150 at bats.

The real strength of the Yankees lay in their outfield. Right fielder Tommy Henrich had returned from the war with more left-handed power than ever, posting career highs of 35 doubles and a league-leading 13 triples in 1947, along with 16 homers and 98 RBIs. Officially, Henrich was still only thirty-two in 1948; actually, he was thirty-five, having chopped three years off his age when the Yanks signed him in the 1930s.[15] Leftfielder Charlie "King Kong" Keller, thirty-one, had returned in 1946 to one of his finest seasons, hitting 30 homers and driving in and scoring more than 100 runs, but had fallen victim in 1947 to a serious back injury that required an operation. He was expected to return in 1948. McQuinn, Henrich, and Keller provided the left-handed power upon which the Yankees have depended since the days of Ruth and Gehrig.

The heart of the team, of course, was thirty-three-year-old Joe DiMaggio, center fielder and right-handed hitter extraordinary, and, together with Ted Williams and Bob Feller, one of the three greatest stars in baseball. The quiet first-generation American from the Bay Area had joined the team in 1936 and ushered in the third of the Yankee dynasties. Although badly hurt by playing in Yankee Stadium, the right-handed-hitting DiMaggio had turned in some of the best seasons in American League history before the war. In his second year, 1937, he hit .346 with an amazing 46 homers and 167 RBIs; in 1939, he led the league with a .381 average; and in 1941 he hit safely in 56 consecutive games. DiMaggio's *road game* figures of 27 homers in 1937 and a .413 average in 1939 suggest that he might easily have hit 60 home runs or batted .400 in a more congenial ballpark. In all these respects his career bears a remarkable similarity to that of the young Henry Aaron, who also hit as many as 45 homers and hit as high as .355 in a very poor hitters' park, Milwaukee County Stadium, and who once hit 26 road home runs in a 154-game season. Although DiMaggio had never led the American League in putouts, he was also regarded as an outstanding center fielder. Quiet, totally serious in his demeanor, he was the complete professional.

The Yankee Clipper had had trouble finding his form after the war. He suffered from arm, leg, and back injuries in 1946, and he hit just .290 with 25 homers. Although his statistics for 1947—a .315 average, a career-low 20 homers, and 97 RBIs—were still far below his prewar norms, he barely

15. See Henrich's interviews in Donald Honig, *A Donald Honig Reader* (New York, 1988), 249, and Maury Allen, *Where Have You Gone, Joe DiMaggio* (New York, 1975), 67–68.

beat out Ted Williams for the 1947 MVP award in a very divided vote. Certainly his best years seemed to be behind him in the spring of 1948.

The Yankee pitching staff was undergoing a transition. Of the prewar stars, only Spud Chandler was still active in 1947, and he retired early in 1948. The aces of the staff in 1947 were thirty-two-year-old Allie Reynolds, acquired from Cleveland for Joe Gordon, who finished with a 19–8 record; rookie Frank "Spec" Shea, the "Naugatuck Nugget," who went 14–5; and lefty reliever Joe Page, 14–8 with a 2.48 ERA, to whom future statisticians would eventually award a league-leading 17 saves as well.[16] The legendary thirty-nine-year-old Bobo Newsom had been acquired late in the 1947 season and won seven games down the stretch, but he was released. Right-handers Vic Raschi, Karl Drews, and Randy Gumpert had also made some starts, as had twenty-seven-year-old lefthander Tommy Byrne.

The most sensational Yankee pitching performance of 1947 had been thrown in the World Series by thirty-year-old Bill Bevens. Bevens, with a 7–13 record and a 3.77 ERA, had started the fourth game of the World Series and gone into the bottom of the ninth with a 2–1 lead and a no-hitter. With two out and two on in the ninth, he had surrendered a pinch-double to Cookie Lavagetto that bounded off the right-field wall, glanced off Tommy Henrich's glove, and drove in the tying and winning runs. Bevens had a sore arm in spring training in 1948, but his return was expected within a few months. It never happened. He never recovered, and the Yankees finally gave up on him in early 1949. The ball that Lavagetto hit for a double on October 3, 1947, was the last pitch that Bill Bevens ever threw in a major league game.

The Yankees' statistics were profoundly affected by playing in Yankee Stadium, where poor visibility and an enormous center field (ranging from 415 in left center to 466 in dead center) made it easy to pitch, but difficult to hit. In direct contrast to the Red Sox, the park made their hitting seem less impressive than it was, and their pitching more so. Thus the team ERA of 3.39 led the league in 1947, but on the road the Yankees allowed 326 runs, fourth-*highest* total in the league and the highest in the first division. Their league-leading total of 794 runs scored was all the more impressive under the circumstances, and well over half of them had been scored on the road. Despite their aging lineup and improvements in other clubs, they looked a good bet to repeat in 1948. They had won the 1947 pennant by a full twelve games over Detroit and fourteen over the Red Sox. Weiss made

---

16. The concept of "saves" did not yet exist in 1947.

only one major trade over the winter, but it was a big one. Taking advantage of the poverty of the Chicago White Sox, he acquired Ed Lopat—widely regarded as the best left-hander in the league after a 16–13, 2.81 ERA season for a last-place club—in exchange for lefty Bill Wight, catcher Aaron Robinson, and Fred Bradley. The Yankees now had a reliable left-handed starter, something they had lacked in 1947.

The manager of the Yankees, Bucky Harris, was one of the most widely respected figures in baseball. He had joined the Washington Senators as their regular second baseman in 1920 at the age of twenty-three, and established himself as a good hitter and an excellent fielder. In 1924 Senators owner Clark Griffith created a sensation by making him the Senators' playing manager, and Harris promptly led the team to its only world championship. He was an innovative field general who outdueled the legendary John McGraw in the seventh game of the 1924 World Series. McGraw had been platooning left-handed hitter Bill Terry, who hit .429 for the series. To get Terry out of the lineup in game seven, Harris started right-hander Curley Ogden, but replaced him with lefty George Morgridge after Ogden pitched to the first two batters. McGraw eventually removed Terry from the game, and when Walter Johnson relieved in the ninth with the score tied 3–3, Terry was no longer around to worry him. The Senators, who had tied the game on a double by Harris in the eighth, won the game in the bottom of the twelfth on another double by Earl McNeely.

Harris managed the Senators to another pennant the next year, but lost a close World Series to the Pittsburgh Pirates. His subsequent managerial career had been less distinguished. The Senators could not keep pace with the great Yankees of 1926–28, and Clark Griffith traded Harris to Detroit, where he also became the manager, after 1928. Harris managed Detroit for five years and the Red Sox for one season, and returned to the Senators in 1935 after Tom Yawkey bought player-manager Joe Cronin from Griffith for $225,000. He kept the Senators out of last place, but they remained a bad team until his departure after 1942. He spent one year with the Phillies, and then stepped down after nineteen continuous years as a manager.

Harris was not a taskmaster as a manager, but he was frank in his opinions of ballplayers. A fine fielder himself, he could not abide weak defensive play. Like Ty Cobb, he had contempt for Rogers Hornsby because he did not think Hornsby could catch a pop fly. He could be death on an incompetent umpire, but he backed arbiters up when they had to assert their authority. Years later Ernie Stewart remembered Harris's reaction when he threw out the first player of his major league career, Ben Chapman of the Senators, for calling him a "pretty boy son of a bitch." "Good boy," the manager remarked approvingly when Stewart told him what Chapman had said, and returned to the dugout.[17]

According to Harris's son, Stanley Junior, Harris had resisted returning to managing after 1946, but MacPhail had eventually talked him into it by promising that Harris would succeed MacPhail as general manager when MacPhail left the team. The Yankee team Harris took over in 1947 had more talent than any team he had managed in twenty years, and he did an excellent job calming a turbulent situation and taking them to his second world championship. He spread the workload evenly among no less than seven pitchers, and worked rookies Bobby Brown and Yogi Berra into the lineup well. Harris, like Joe McCarthy, belonged to the pre-1900 Lost Generation, whose members had come up through the school of hard knocks. Those like Harris and McCarthy who had risen to the top of the baseball world had done so by fearlessly relying upon their own judgment, and Harris had repeatedly showed that he still had the courage of his convictions in the recent World Series. In the first game, he set tongues wagging by pinch-hitting for pitcher Frank Shea in the fifth inning with the score 1–1, and was rewarded with a five-run inning and a key victory. In the ninth inning of the incredible fourth game, he ordered Bill Bevens to walk Pete Reiser, the potential winning run, in the ninth with two out, and Lavagetto's double tied the series for the Dodgers. Harris emerged with the world championship, but MacPhail resigned without making good on his promise to get Harris named as the new GM.

In 1948 Harris was in the second year of a two-year contract, but was now working for new management. George Weiss may have seemed steadier than Larry MacPhail, but what Harris did not know was that Weiss was determined to rid the team of every legacy of the MacPhail era. Weiss began by dropping old Bobo Newsom, who had pitched 116 innings with a 2.79 ERA down the stretch in 1947, but who was the antithesis of what Weiss felt a ballplayer should be. Thirty-nine-year-old Spud Chandler, who had also pitched 128 excellent innings, was also at the end of the road. When Bevens turned up with a sore arm in spring training, Harris's pitching staff was about 400 innings short, with only Ed Lopat available to fill the gap. Despite the shortfall in the pitching staff, the New York press generally took an optimistic line as the season opened.

The winter's frantic movement of talent from the second division into the first foreshadowed a much sharper struggle for the flag in 1948. The Detroit Tigers, world champions in 1945 and second-place finishers in

17. Gerlach, *The Men in Blue*, 107.

1946 and 1947, allowed themselves to be left behind. Playing in a good hitters' park, the Tigers in 1947 had, together with the Athletics, one of the two outstanding pitching staffs in the league. Their aces were righty Fred Hutchinson and southpaw Hal Newhouser, who slipped from the spectacular heights he occupied in 1944–46 but still posted a 2.87 ERA, third in the league behind Lopat and Feller. Their strongest hitters were twenty-four-year-old third baseman George Kell, power-hitting left fielder Pat Mullin, center fielder Hoot Evers, and controversial Dick Wakefield, the first big bonus baby, who had never quite lived up to his $50,000 price tag. Except for the loss of Roy Cullenbine, the Tigers were roughly the same club in 1948 as in 1947. Having drawn a record 1,722,590 fans in 1946 and 1,398,093 in 1947, they saw no reason to change. As it turned out, they won only seven fewer games in 1948, but instead of finishing second, they finished fifth.

Connie Mack's Philadelphia Athletics had climbed during 1947 from last place all the way to fifth, 78–76. Eighty-six years old, Mack had not been in a pennant race since the early 1930s, when he reportedly suffered catastrophic losses in the stock market and sold off one of the greatest teams in history, mostly to Tom Yawkey. Mack had never again tried seriously to compete with owners like Yawkey or MacPhail, but frugally enjoyed the image of sainthood that his suits, high collars, clean language, and white hair had polished for decades. A few years earlier, he had confided to umpire Ernie Stewart that he preferred not to make a real run at the pennant. "What I like to do," he told Stewart on a train east from spring training in California, "is keep my ball club in contention from first to fourth place until the first of July. By that time we have made enough money that we can tail off, and with a last-place ball club you don't have to raise anybody's salary. With a first-place ball club everybody wants a raise, so I can make more money finishing last than I can first." Stewart recalled forty years later that Mack, alone among all the club owners in the league, failed to provide umpires with free food and drink between games of doubleheaders.[18] A current Philadelphia anecdote told of a cab driver who took old Connie to the railroad station, received the exact fare in payment, and asked, "Hey pop, what about a tip?" "Certainly," his passenger replied. "Don't bet on the As."[19]

In 1946—the biggest attendance year in baseball history—Mack's lackadaisical attitude enabled his tenants, the Phillies, to draw more fans than his own team. Despite everything, Mack found himself in 1947 with

18. Ibid., 122.
19. Bob Considine, "Mr. Mack," in Charles Einstein, ed., *The Fireside Book of Baseball* (New York, 1956), 53.

an adequate team, with fine pitching and defense. The Athletics allowed the fewest road runs of any American League team, although the Yankees and the Indians, helped by their home parks, allowed fewer overall. The aces of the staff—composed entirely of right-handers—were Canadian Phil Marchildon, a wartime flyer and inmate of a German prison camp; Dick Fowler; Bill McCahan; Joe Coleman; and reliever Russ Christopher, whom Mack was about to sell to Cleveland. They were joined in early 1948 by lefty Lou Brissie, another veteran whose leg had been reconstructed with the help of a metal plate. Mack—often given to sweeping statements for the press—argued during spring training that Brissie would be better than Lefty Grove.

Offensively the Athletics lacked power. Center fielder Sam Champman and shortstop Eddie Joost, an excellent fielder, led the team with 14 and 13 homers, respectively; no one else was in double figures. The rest of the team—first baseman Ferris Fain, second baseman Pete Suder, third baseman Hank Majeski, catchers Buddy Rosar and Mike Guerra, and outfielders Barney McCosky and Elmer Valo—were all line-drive hitters, most of them with fine strike-zone judgment (the A's were second in the league in walks, behind the Yankees). The team had more in common with Connie Mack's first dynasty, the 1910–14 club, than with his powerhouse of the early thirties. Mack played traditionally, ordering sacrifice bunts whenever possible. Coach Al Simmons, a star of the thirties, frequently took over direction of the team when Mack dozed on the bench, and his son, Earle, went on the field to argue with the umpires when the occasion demanded it. Connie was still always ready for hotel-lobby press conferences and comments on other teams, however.

Little, understandably, could be expected from the St. Louis Browns, who had reinforced their cellar status by unloading most of their established players. They completed their fire sale by selling outfielder Jeff Heath to the Boston Braves, thereby laying some claim to have decided not one, but *both* of the 1948 pennant races. Veteran manager Zack Taylor took over for Muddy Ruel as manager. The Browns still had one or two hitters left, including outfielder Al Zarilla and catcher Les Moss, who could post respectable batting averages, but Sportsman's Park was a good hitters' park, and their averages were not worth what they seemed to be. Some of their pitchers were also somewhat better than their St. Louis statistics indicated, and one hurler, Cliff Fannin, turned out to be one of the strongest pitchers in the league.

Clark Griffith in Washington, and the Comiskey family in Chicago, had been in charge of their clubs nearly as long as Connie Mack. The Senators, who had last won a pennant fifteen years earlier but had just missed another one in 1945 and finished fourth in 1946, had slipped to seventh in 1947. Their offense—never robust in vast Griffith Stadium, where any ball hit to left field had to travel more than 400 feet to become a home run—had collapsed on the road as well, scoring just 252 runs away from Washington. First baseman Mickey Vernon, who had beaten out Ted Williams for the 1946 batting title, dropped almost ninety points from his average in 1947. The Senators' pitching staff—including right-handers Early Wynn, Walt Masterson, Sid Hudson, Ray Scarborough, and left knuckleballer Mickey Haefner—was generally dreadful. Griffith Stadium held down their ERAs to respectable levels, but the Senators led the league in runs allowed on the road. The Nats had been lucky to beat out the Browns for last place in 1947, and they were likely to contend for the same honor in 1948. The Senators had a new manager, Joe Kuhel, replacing Ossie Bluege. Griffith was still trying to win, but the cards were stacked against him. He had a large front-office payroll—filled, as Bill Veeck wrote many years later, with relatives whose duties were only barely visible to the naked eye—and a very low population base upon which to draw. Washington was a small southern town of well under one million people in 1948, and suburban Maryland and Virginia were still mostly forest and farmland.

The White Sox were at least as weak. The loss of Rudy York, whom they had acquired from the Red Sox in mid-1947, left forty-year-old shortstop Luke Appling, never known for his power, as the team leader in home runs, with eight. For all that, the team's offense was considerably better than its defense in 1947, scoring more runs on the road than the Senators, the Browns—or the Red Sox. The pitching closely rivaled the Browns' and the Senators', and could certainly be expected to decline now that Ed Lopat had departed to the Yankees. Ted Lyons, who with Luke Appling had constituted most of the franchise during the 1930s and early 1940s, had become the manager in late 1946. Still, the White Sox attendance in 1947 was almost 900,000 fans. As a group, the White Sox fans have been among the most loyal in the whole modern history of baseball, but only rarely has a good team given them the chance to show it.

The choice of the greatest pennant race in baseball history is inevitably a matter of taste. Great races have involved as few as two and as many as four teams. For nerve-racking excitement, nothing, perhaps, can match the two great four-team races in baseball history: the forgotten American League race of 1908—won by the Tigers of Ty Cobb and Sam Crawford by a single game over Cleveland and the defending champion White Sox, with the Browns close behind—and the AL's 1967 campaign, in which the Red Sox, finally breaking loose from the second division, beat out the Twins and the Tigers on the final day, after the White Sox had dropped out only two days previously. But closer inspection dims the luster of these two seasons, simply because none of the teams involved was really very good. The 1908 Tigers won the pennant with just 90 victories out of 154 games, while the 1967 Red Sox won only 92 out of 162. Similar comments apply to an even greater degree to some of the races that have occurred since the advent of divisional play in 1969. Thus in 1972 four out of six National League East teams found themselves in contention on the final day of the season, but the Mets, who emerged victorious with a pathetic 82–80 record, can only be described as the best of a bad lot, and few fans are likely to remember the details of the final week now.

At the other extreme, the great two-team races of baseball history have attracted much more attention. The most famous of all, the 1951 fight between the Dodgers and the Giants that culminated in a three-game playoff won by Bobby Thomson's one-out, three-run homer in the ninth inning of the last game, was in its own way incomparable, and has been the subject of a fine literary treatment.[20] For the last six weeks of the season, that race undoubtedly had everything: a fantastic 37–7 record by the Giants to come back from 13½ games out, fine performances by Hall of Famers like Jackie Robinson, Duke Snider, Pee Wee Reese, Monte Irvin, and twenty-year-old rookie Willie Mays, the presence of Leo Durocher in the Giant dugout, and the incredible denouement. On the other hand, until early August the 1951 season was, frankly, a bore: the Dodgers were running away with it. The Giants also took a little of the luster off their miracle year by losing the World Series to the Yankees in six games, after taking a 2–1 lead. Ten years earlier, the Dodgers and Cardinals had fought two magnificent two-team races, the Dodgers winning by two games in 1941 and the Cardinals returning the favor in 1942, when they posted 106 wins to the Dodgers' second-place record 104. Both races had drama and controversy, and each team featured a couple of Hall of Famers. The same two teams went down to the wire in 1946, forcing the first true playoff in National League history.

Other memorable two-team races include the 1965 battle between the Giants and Dodgers, dominated by Willie Mays, Juan Marichal, Sandy Koufax, Don Drysdale, and Maury Wills (in which the Reds also stayed in contention into the last week), and the 1962 Giant-Dodger battle, which ended in another three-game playoff decided in the ninth inning. While the 1962 race also featured fantastic performances by great players, and

20. Thomas Kiernan, *The Miracle of Coogan's Bluff* (New York, 1975).

while both teams also topped 100 victories, it lost some luster in the last two weeks and during the playoff itself, when ragged play by both teams culminated in the Dodgers' walking in the tying and winning runs in the ninth inning of the last game. The 1949 American League race, in which the Yankees triumphed by one game after taking the two final games of the season from the Red Sox, has justly become the subject of a recent book by David Halberstam. Last, the 1978 battle between the Red Sox and Yankees in the American League East—clearly the greatest since the advent of divisional play—featured tremendous performances by many players (Jackson, Guidry, Rice, Yastrzemski, Tiant) probably destined for the Hall of Fame, a September stretch of phenomenal tension, plenty of controversy, and a dramatic, one-game playoff in Fenway Park that has already been immortalized by Roger Angell and Peter Gammons.[21] But like the 1951 National League race, the 1978 race only got going in August. Until then, it was a Red Sox runaway, and it took a substantial Red Sox collapse, helped by injuries to Butch Hobson and Dwight Evans and the benching of Bill Lee, to allow the Yankees to get back into the race.

The closest three-team races in history include the 1927 National League battle between the Pirates, Cardinals, and Giants; the 1956 National League race, when a great but aging Dodgers team overtook a younger Braves squad on the very last weekend, one day after a power-laden Reds team had fallen by the wayside; and the 1959 race, when the Dodgers and the Braves had to play a playoff, one day after the Giants were eliminated. Here again, however, the three contenders were somewhat less distinguished: the two teams tied for the pennant with just 86 wins each, one of the lowest figures in history. Three other three-team races stand out more clearly.

The first, chronologically speaking, was the most exciting struggle of the dead-ball era, the 1908 fight between John McGraw's New York Giants, the Tinker-Evers-Chance Chicago Cubs, and Honus Wagner's Pittsburgh Pirates. "The National League pennant race in 1908," Bill James has written, "was like the American League pennant race in 1967, only with one of the teams being in New York and another in Los Angeles, and with Fernando Valenzuela or Mark Fidrych being called up by another team in September so he could make four starts against one of the teams that was trying to win the thing, and with one of the key games suddenly erupting into a Pine Tar-type controversy, which necessitates New York making a special trip to Los Angeles for the 162nd game, which Sandy Koufax is to

---

21. Roger Angell, *Late Innings: A Baseball Companion* (New York, 1982), 94–113; Peter Gammons, *Beyond the Sixth Game* (Boston, 1985), 108–61.

pitch against Bob Gibson, with a few odd death threats, riots, attempts to fix the game, and some loose talk about a strike thrown in for good measure."[22] To be more specific, the race ended in a tie because of the incident of "Merkle's boner," forcing the replay of a Giants-Cubs game at the Polo Grounds. The Cubs beat Christy Mathewson—trying for his *38th* victory of the year—4–2, on a triple by Joe Tinker, while Mordecai "Three-Finger" Brown relieved in the first inning and stopped the Giants the rest of the way. The Pirates, meanwhile, finished just one game out, and their 98 wins and .636 percentage are records for a third-place team. This season has already been chronicled, in wonderful fashion, in G. H. Fleming's *The Unforgettable Season*, a selection of newspaper clippings that is one of the very few books to tell the entire story of a season from start to finish.[23] A very similar race occurred in the American League in 1920, when the Cleveland Indians, featuring player-manager Tris Speaker, survived the death of their beaned shortstop, Ray Chapman, to win 98 games and nose out the White Sox by two games and the Yankees (for whom Babe Ruth had his first great year) by three.[24] A cloud, however, shall always hang over this victory, which owed a good deal to the exposure in the last few days of the season of the Black Sox scandal, stripping the Chicago squad of eight of its best players for the last few games.

The 1948 American League race ranks securely with any of these, and can easily be viewed as the best of them all. Four teams were in contention during the first half of the season, and during most of July and August it became the closest four-team race ever, with the top half of the standings reshuffling almost every day. Only three contenders remained as September dawned, and each of them was clearly a great team, easily capable of running away with a pennant in an average year. Joe DiMaggio, Williams, and Feller rank among the greatest players of all time, and the teams' rosters included other future Hall of Famers such as Boudreau, Lemon, Paige, Berra, Rizzuto, Doerr, and managers Joe McCarthy and Bucky Harris. (This, surely, was the only four-team race in which every manager was destined for baseball's highest honor.) Several other stars, including Joe Gordon, Larry Doby, and Vern Stephens, have a strong claim to the Hall, while Gene Bearden had one of the most amazing rookie years in baseball history, and Ken Keltner and Tommy Henrich had Hall of Fame–caliber seasons. The Cleveland infield may have been the best one-season quartet in the history of baseball, and the Cleveland owner was Bill Veeck, another deserved Hall of Famer. The careers of the participants in the 1948 season

22. Bill James, *The Bill James Historical Baseball Abstract* (New York, 1988), 66.
23. G. H. Fleming, *The Unforgettable Season* (New York, 1981).
24. On this race see Mike Sowell, *The Pitch That Killed* (New York, 1989).

span the entire history of organized baseball. Manager Connie Mack of the Athletics had begun his career as a catcher for the Washington National League Club in 1886; Bobby Brown, a twenty-three-year-old infielder for the Yankees in 1948, recently stepped down as the president of the American League.

The year 1948 was a unique one which combined unprecedented fan interest, dramatic changes in several American League clubs, and great individual performances to create what was probably the greatest pennant race of the twentieth century. The best hitter in baseball flirted with a .400 average until sidelined by a freak injury; the best pitcher suffered through a dreadful first half of the season, only to rebound and find himself, on the last day of the season, with a chance to win his twentieth victory and clinch the pennant; the best all-around player in the game turned in his most amazing season despite a crippling injury, and kept his team alive down the stretch; while yet another player won a well-deserved and unanimous selection as the league's Most Valuable Player. With seven games to go, three teams were tied for the lead, and with two games to go, only one game separated them. As Harold Kaese of the *Boston Globe* wrote twenty years later, 1948 was "the season of seasons" and a year to remember. It was both the climax of one era in the history of baseball, and the beginning of another. And even those who lived through it often forget exactly how incredible it was.

3

Out of the Gate

(APRIL 19–MAY 31)

Following a well-established pattern, the season began—as it would end—with the four western clubs of Cleveland, Chicago, Detroit, and St. Louis playing one another, while the eastern Yankees, Red Sox, Athletics, and Senators did the same. The American League had fielded the same eight teams since 1903, clustered in the East along the Atlantic coast and in the Midwest on the shores of the Great Lakes and the Mississippi. In the course of each season, the four eastern teams made four swings around the West, and the four western clubs returned the favor. In between these trips, the eastern and western halves of the league separated into two parts and played among themselves. The defending champion Yankees got off to a good start this year, but three bigger stories dominated the news: a very hot start in Cleveland, the emergence of a Cinderella contender in Philadelphia, and a disastrous start for Joe McCarthy at the helm of the Red Sox.

The Cleveland Indians opened at home on Tuesday, April 20 against the Browns before the largest Opening Day crowd in major league history—73,163. For the sixth time, Bob Feller pitched the Cleveland opener, and for the fourth time he won it, shutting out the Browns 4–0 with just two hits. This was not Feller's best Opening Day performance: in 1940, he had started the season with a no-hitter in Chicago against the White Sox. Cleveland proceeded to win its next five games in impressive fashion against the Tigers and White Sox before dropping its first two at home against the Tigers to conclude its western stay in first place with a 6–2 record and a three-game lead. On the mount, Feller won two starts before failing against the Tigers on May 1, and Bob Lemon also secured two wins against one loss. At bat, two infielders got off to fantastic starts: Boudreau, whose endless string of line-drive extra-base hits raised his average all the way to .519, and Ken Keltner, who hit four homers in the Indians' first four games. They left for their first eastern trip on Monday, May 2.

Back east, the Red Sox began poorly, losing their first three games to the Athletics, including both ends of an April 19 (Patriots' Day) morning-afternoon doubleheader in which 1947's aces, Denny Galehouse and Joe Dobson, lost close games. In the second game, the crowd was struck dumb in the sixth inning when Ted Williams lined a bullet right off Lou Brissie's injured leg, and the pitcher collapsed in a heap. With time called, Williams left first base and ran over to see how badly Brissie was hurt. "For Chrissake, Williams," yelled Brissie from the ground, "*pull* the damn ball!"[1] Boston then repaired to New York for a weekend confrontation with the Yankees, who had begun almost as badly, losing two of three to the Senators in Washington.

At the Yankees' home opener on Friday, April 23 against the Red Sox, Joe DiMaggio received the Most Valuable Player trophy for 1947. To the fans, the press, and even to the two players themselves, every game between the Yankees and the Red Sox was a confrontation between Ted Williams and Joe DiMaggio. The argument over their relative merits raged continually from 1939, when Williams entered the league, through 1951, when DiMaggio left it. Newer statistical techniques make it easier to resolve.

While American Leaguers unanimously regarded Joe DiMaggio as the league's best all-around player, no one disputed Williams's right to the title of the greatest hitter. They were absolutely right. Williams and DiMaggio can be compared systematically by using the Runs Created formula developed by baseball statistician Bill James.[2] The Runs Created formula measures the offensive performance of a team or an individual player according to three factors: the number of times reaching base, the number of total bases, and the total number of opportunities at the plate. The basic formula—(Hits + Walks)/(At bats + Walks) × Total Bases—predicts the number of runs actually scored by a team very accurately. When applied to a player, it gives a good idea of the number of runs for which the player was personally responsible. (More sophisticated versions of the formula, which we shall use here, also include stolen bases, caught stealing, and the number of double plays a player has grounded into, thereby making more outs.) Unlike runs scored or runs batted in, a player's runs created are essentially independent of the performance of the rest of his team.

1. Williams, with Underwood, *My Turn at Bat*, 16.
2. James, *Historical Baseball Abstract*, 276–89.

Joe DiMaggio in 1947 came to the plate 601 times, walking 64 times and being hit by pitches three times. He had 168 hits in 534 official at bats for a .315 average, and 31 doubles, 10 triples, and 21 homers for 279 total bases and a .522 slugging average. His on-base percentage was .391. He stole three bases, was not caught once, and grounded into fourteen double plays. He created a total of 109 runs (his career highs were 173 in 1937, when he had 46 home runs, and 162 in 1941, the year of his 56-game streak).

Ted Williams in 1947 came to the plate 692 times and walked 162, with 184 hits and a .343 average. He was hit by only two pitches, and had an on-base average of .497. His 40 doubles, 9 triples, and 32 homers gave him a slugging average of .615, and although he stole no bases and was caught once, he grounded into just ten double plays. Overall he created an astonishing 186 runs, a figure which he had equaled almost exactly in 1942 (185) and topped in 1946 (188) and in 1941, when he hit .406 (202).

Refinements for the influence of the ballparks the two men played in reduce, but do not eliminate, Williams's offensive superiority. Five-year (1946–50) averages for runs scored inside and outside of Yankee Stadium indicate that DiMaggio would have created 113 runs in 1947 in a neutral park. The same adjustment reduces Williams's total to 168. Their adjusted career highs are 183 for Williams in 1941, and 178 for DiMaggio in 1939.

A further important refinement—also introduced by Bill James—increases Williams's superiority. Every major league team has twenty-seven outs' worth of opportunities to score runs in every game, and each player's contribution must also be evaluated according to the number of those outs he uses up, since every out he makes reduces the opportunities of other players on his team. Williams made fewer outs—359 in 1947 compared to DiMaggio's 380, and 285 in 1941 compared to DiMaggio's 356 in the same year, when they had almost exactly the same number of plate appearances.

Williams also won the argument in the opening game of the Red Sox–Yankees series, going three for five with his first home run of the year and robbing Gus Niarhos of a homer with a fine catch, as lefthander Mickey Harris shut the Yankees out 4–0 for the Red Sox first win of the season. The Yankees evened the series on Saturday behind Allie Reynolds, who beat Joe Dobson 7–2, despite a tremendous solo homer by Williams in the eighth. And Joe DiMaggio had the last laugh on Sunday before 68,021 fans, as his three-run homer in the bottom of the first inning keyed a 5–4 win behind Lopat and Joe Page. The Yanks had reached .500, tying them with the Athletics, who had lost three straight at home to Washington, and the Red Sox were 1–5.

Rain and cold washed out most of the next week's play, but the Red Sox managed a 6–0 win over the Senators behind rookie Mel Parnell and an

11–5 drubbing of the Athletics in Philadelphia. Williams got four hits and his first assist against the Senators, including a double to left field, and opened the scoring against Lou Brissie and the Athletics with a homer to right. "You don't have to pull it that far, Williams," Brissie called to him. Meanwhile, the Yankees got their first look at the Athletics, winning 4–2. The Yanks were 5–3, the Red Sox 3–5, as the two teams settled into Fenway for three more games on Friday, April 30. In the opener Mickey Harris surrendered four Yankee homers and Allie Reynolds got his third win, 6–0. On Saturday, 32,720 fans saw the Red Sox win a classic Fenway Park game, 8–6, as Williams, three for three with two walks, offset a three-run homer by Joe DiMaggio over his favorite target, the Boston left-field wall. The next day Williams tripled and homered for four more RBIs as Joe Dobson posted a 7–1 victory. Joe Page, relieving, drew a nasty roar from the packed Fenway house in the eighth when he gave up homers to both Williams and Vern Stephens and promptly decked Bobby Doerr. The Red Sox could thank Williams for each of their five wins. Now hitting .400, he had been the hitting star of every one.

The surprising Athletics swept a three-game weekend series from the Senators in Washington, putting them among the league leaders as the eastern clubs went home to entertain the Indians, Tigers, White Sox, and Browns. Philadelphia took two games and first place from the Indians on May 4 and 6, but Cleveland rebounded with two easy victories in Washington behind Lemon and newcomer lefty Gene Bearden. Bearden, one of the league's only knuckleballers, became the first Cleveland pitcher other than Lemon or Feller to complete a game, and Larry Doby had three RBIs and three hits, one of them a fantastic home run over the dead-center-field wall in Griffith Stadium. Only Babe Ruth, according to longtime Washington observers, had ever reached this spot. Boudreau, who had used the same lineup and batting order for the first six games of the season, was now switching outfielders and cleanup hitters in almost every game.

Tied with Philadelphia at .667—despite having played three fewer games—the Indians took a Saturday night train to Boston for their first confrontation with the Red Sox. Thanks to Ted Williams and shortstop Junior Stephens, Boston had reached .500 by taking two out of three from the Tigers during the week. On Tuesday, a two-run triple by Vern Stephens was the big blow in a 4–2 win. The next day, Mel Parnell pitched well in his first start in Fenway, but trailed 3–1 in the bottom of the ninth. Williams helped tie the game with a single, and in the top of the tenth, with the bases loaded and one out, he made a fine running catch in left-center and rifled the ball to the plate for a double play. One and one-half innings later, Stephens won the game with a home run into the screen in left.

By his own admission, Ted Williams in his early years with the Red Sox had been an indifferent fielder at best, often losing interest in that rather large portion of a ball game when he was not at the plate swinging a bat. As a Red Sox rookie, he would sometimes practice his swing in left field, prompting shortstop and manager Joe Cronin to yell, "Hey kid, how about practicing a little less of this"—pantomiming a swing—"and a little more of this?"—fielding an imaginary ground ball. But in the spring of 1946, Williams in spring training had stunned his teammate Dom DiMaggio by asking him for advice on his fielding. He had set new career highs for putouts and total chances in both 1946 and 1947, and in spring training during 1948 he had modestly confided to a reporter that he thought himself the most underrated outfielder in the league. His early season fielding had been absolutely sensational. Those like columnist George Will who perpetuate the myth that Williams was a poor fielder have not studied his performance after 1945.

The Red Sox lost the last game of the Tiger series on Thursday, 8–3, behind Ferris and fell back below .500 losing a single game to the lowly Browns on Saturday, 9–4 behind Kramer. Their pitching was entirely at sea. Their seven victories had each been won by a different pitcher—Harris, Parnell, Johnson, Kramer, Dobson, Ferriss, and Kinder. For their first series with the first-place Indians, McCarthy chose Dobson and Kinder for the Sunday doubleheader, and Boo Ferriss for the single game on Monday.

The series matched Williams against the Boudreau shift, which together with Cleveland pitching had held Williams to an average of about .200 in 1947. Nothing, moreover, excited Williams more than the chance to face the most famous pitcher in baseball, Bob Feller, who opened the series on Sunday. Williams homered off Feller, but Keltner replied with two four-baggers of his own, and the second helped win the game in ten innings, 4–1. Impressing more each day, the Indians simply overpowered the Red Sox in the last two games of the series. Keltner's third home run of the day and a monster two-run shot by Larry Doby to dead center overcame one by Williams for a 9–5 win in Saturday's nightcap, and on Monday afternoon Doby doubled and homered again as Cleveland coasted to a 12–7 win.

Keltner's remarkable start was a tribute to Bill Veeck's motivational techniques. Keltner, a man with a ready smile and a massive upper body, enjoyed a drink and a good time—a type that Veeck, who shared these tastes, tended to favor—and in early 1947, Veeck had attempted to give him some incentive to bounce back from a poor 1946 season. He had promised Keltner a $5,000 bonus—equal to perhaps a third of his salary—if he had "a good year" in 1947, defined roughly as a .300 average and 100 RBIs. On Opening Day of 1947, Marsh Samuel, Veeck's public relations director and the Indians' resident statistician, watched Keltner hit two line drives for outs. He marked them in his scorebook with red dots, and continued this practice for the rest of the season. By the end of 1947, both Samuel and Veeck agreed that Keltner had been the victim of an unusual amount of bad luck. Keltner finished the year at .257 with 11 homers and 76 RBIs, but Veeck gave him the bonus anyway, moving Keltner to tears. He had come to camp in 1948 determined to do better, and he was already closing in on his home run total for the entire 1947 season.

Cleveland's five-game winning streak had failed to open up much of a lead because New York and Philadelphia had been chewing up the Tigers, Browns, and White Sox. The Yankees had vaulted right into contention by winning five out of six games against these three clubs and running their record to 11–6. Yankee pitchers had turned in five strong games—one each by Vic Raschi, Allie Reynolds, and Red Embree, and two by Frank Shea. Young Bobby Brown, a 1946 bonus baby who had been a star football player at USC, had hit well while subbing for an injured Phil Rizzuto, winning one game against the Browns with a home run that most observers thought was foul. The Yankees' Sunday game against the White Sox was preceded by the filming of scenes from the forthcoming movie *The Babe Ruth Story*. With retired Yankee great Lefty Gomez playing Washington Senator pitcher Tom Zachary, William Bendix acted out Ruth's 60th homer in 1927 eight times, trying to recapture the Babe's inimitable pigeon-toed trot. Perhaps inspired by Bendix, Keller, Johnson, McQuinn, and Henrich all homered in an 8–0 win behind Shea. The big surprise of the year, however, was the Philadelphia Athletics, who had followed their three wins over the Senators and two over the Indians with three more over the White Sox and Tigers, running their winning streak to eight games to stay in a virtual tie for first.

STANDINGS
Monday, May 10, 1948

Team	Won	Lost	Pct.	Games Behind
Cleveland	11	4	.733	—
Philadelphia	12	5	.706	—
New York	11	6	.647	1
Washington	9	9	.500	3½
St. Louis	6	8	.429	4½
Detroit	8	12	.400	5½
Boston	7	11	.389	5½
Chicago	3	12	.200	8

Cleveland finally came to New York on Tuesday afternoon, May 4, and the Yankees also drew within percentage points of first place as Allie Reynolds became the first pitcher in the league to win his fifth game, beating Lemon, 4–1. They seemed ready to move into first the next night when Joe DiMaggio robbed Boudreau of a triple in the top of the first and welcomed Gene Bearden to New York in the bottom of the inning with a three-run homer. But that game, the whole series, and the Indians' eastern trip suddenly came to an end when a huge rainstorm deluged New York. The confrontation between the two teams was delayed for ten days, until a Sunday doubleheader in Cleveland scheduled for May 23. Meanwhile, the Red Sox beat the White Sox twice in Boston, while in Philadelphia, the remarkable Athletics surged into a 1½-game lead over the Indians with two victories over the Browns.

Over the weekend, the Athletics really got the baseball world's attention by taking a New York series with the Yankees. Vic Raschi won Friday's opener, 3–0, behind homers by Johnny Lindell and Berra, but Philadelphia shocked 69,416 enthusiastic New Yorkers the next day, sweeping a doubleheader 8–6 and 3–1. Sunday's finale was rained out. Connie Mack knew how to wring the maximum interest out of his quick start. In a well-publicized interview, he declared his infield of Fain, Suder, Joost, and Majeski to be superior to the famous $100,000 infield of Stuffy McGinnis, Eddie Collins, Jack Barry, and Home Run Baker—an opinion which the Hall of Fame, to date, has shown no inclination to share. And during the weekend, he purchased thirty-seven-year-old pitcher Nelson Potter from the Browns for $20,000.

Back in Cleveland, the Indians had won two out of three over the same weekend from the White Sox. Bob Feller stopped them 7–1 on Saturday, May 9, for his fourth victory; Boudreau finished the weekend hitting .423; and the amazing Keltner hit two more homers, giving him six in eight games and twelve overall. A half-game behind the Athletics at 13–6, Cleveland now began a nine-game home stand against the eastern clubs. The schedule could not have been better designed to increase the excitement in northern Ohio still further. Visits from the Athletics and the Red Sox would be followed on Sunday, May 23, by a doubleheader with the hated Yankees.

Although the season was only weeks old, it was already emerging quite clearly as the climax of the young career of Bill Veeck. In the whole history of major league baseball, only a few owners, including Larry MacPhail, Branch Rickey, Walter O'Malley, Charlie Finley, George Steinbrenner, and Ted Turner—have had the courage to seize the opportunities offered by changes in technology, society, and baseball itself to increase the appeal of the game. Veeck was also such an owner, and his long struggle to carve out and hold on to his rightful place in the national pastime is one of the most extraordinary stories in American sports.

Veeck's career as an operator, as we have seen, had begun with the Milwaukee Brewers of the American Association in 1941, and he had quickly begun looking for a major league club. Veeck was a visionary in other ways. He had seen plenty of the Negro leagues in Chicago and elsewhere during the 1930s, and he knew that they offered a potentially critical market of both players and customers to whoever showed the courage to open it up. He was also a political liberal with a real egalitarian passion. In 1943, during his third season in Milwaukee, he made a secret, dramatic bid to purchase the bankrupt Philadelphia Phillies, stock them with stars from the Negro leagues, and easily win the National League pennant. In another daring and quite unprecedented move, he enlisted the left-wing Congress of Industrial Organizations (CIO) as his financial backer. The plan collapsed, according to Veeck, because the CIO insisted that he guarantee to play at least one white player at all times, and because Commissioner Landis, when apprised of his plans, immediately arranged for another buyer.[3]

Veeck joined the Marines in late 1943, although he continued to run the Brewers from afar. He refused a commission, and at twenty-nine became the oldest man to undergo basic training at Parris Island. On Bougainville in the South Pacific, his lower right leg was broken by the recoil of an artillery piece, and the injury was complicated by tropical infection. Veeck eventually underwent the first of three amputations in 1947. He spent several hours every day soaking his stump in a bathtub, and began reading at least one book a day. Years later, during his long exile from baseball, he started a new career as a book reviewer, and became an unusually erudite man.

After purchasing the Indians in 1946, Veeck immediately began a new series of giveaways, fireworks, circus acts, and endless rounds of speeches to anyone who would listen in an effort to increase interest in the Indians. The team had a hard core of extremely intense fans and had frequently contended during the late 1930s and early 1940s. It tended to fade late in the year, but had just missed the pennant by a single game in 1940. It played most of its games in League Park, a tremendous hitters' park with a short right-field fence. The Indians of the late 1930s were filled with players like Earl Averill, Hal Trosky, Jeff Heath, and Roy Weatherly, who hit for tremendous averages but never seemed quite able bring home a winner. On

3. Veeck with Linn, *Veeck—as in Wreck*, 14–92, 173–74.

Sundays and in occasional night games the Indians played in huge Municipal Stadium, whose 80,000-plus capacity dwarfed every other park in baseball. Veeck immediately scheduled all the Indians' games there for 1947. He also tried to capitalize upon existing on-field assets and to acquire some new ones.

As we have seen, Veeck had also followed through on his plans to integrate his team, signing Larry Doby in 1947. The move made sense in Cleveland, which had a great tradition of black athletic achievement. Olympic track stars Jesse Owens and Harrison Dillard—the latter now preparing for the 1948 Olympic Games in London—both came from the area, and the Cleveland Browns of professional football's All-American Conference included several black players, led by star fullback Marion Motley. Cleveland fans were more than ready to welcome a black star.

Now, with a first-place team, Veeck was determined to exploit the 80,000-seat capacity of Cleveland's Municipal Stadium to the fullest. Advertising Feller as the starter for the first game of the May 23 doubleheader with New York, he set his sights on the all-time, one-day major league attendance record of 81,841. He arranged special excursion trains and a reduced price for children under twelve, and piled up an advance sale of 57,000 fans. The owner himself, however, would miss the game. His amputated leg had never fully healed—largely, of course, because of the pressure of his nonstop schedule—and he was slated to go into the hospital for another operation late in the week.

Behind more strong pitching, the Indians knocked the Athletics out of first and took a 1½-game lead on Tuesday and Wednesday, May 18–19. Gene Bearden, making his third official start, beat Brissie 6–1, and finally earned himself a place in the rotation, and Feller, pitching with just three days' rest, gave up just one hit during the first eight innings. The hit was a smash by catcher Buddy Rosar off Keltner's glove, and in the press box the Cleveland official scorer discussed changing it to an error, if need be, to give Feller his third no-hitter. Two solid hits in the ninth settled that dilemma and gave the A's a run, but the Indians, with Boudreau getting three more hits to raise his average to .439, won 6–1. Their record was 15–6, and Feller's was 5–2.

They reached 17–7 against the Red Sox, who had continued to thrash around the .500 mark over the last week and came to Cleveland with a record of 11–13. On Thursday the Indians knocked out Mickey Harris in the second inning of the first game, and turned a second-inning, 7–0 lead into a 13–4 triumph behind Lemon. On Friday night, however, Williams went four for four and the Red Sox pounded out eighteen hits and won 11–5. Williams, at .389, still trailed Boudreau by thirty-three points in the batting race, but led Keltner 33–26 in RBIs. On Saturday, Gene Bearden, looking more impressive in every start, stopped the Red Sox on six hits for his third win while the Indians got a total of thirteen hits and won, 7–0.

Cleveland's five wins in six games set the stage perfectly for Sunday's big doubleheader with the Yankees. New York had won three out of five in St. Louis and Chicago to arrive exactly two games behind the Indians. Joe DiMaggio had broken out of a two-week slump with a tremendous series in Chicago. On Thursday he had hit for the cycle, added an extra home run, scored four runs and drove in six as the Yankees won 13–2 behind Vic Raschi, and on Saturday he had homered again in a 10–2 win. The Athletics, meanwhile, had won two of three in Detroit to hang on to second place, half a game ahead of the New Yorkers.

The May 23 doubleheader in Municipal Stadium between the Yankees and the Indians seemed to match the two strongest clubs of the young, exciting season. The Tribe owed its success to the phenomenal performance of its infield. Eddie Robinson was hitting .304 with 20 RBIs, Boudreau had hit .422 with a league-leading 38 runs scored, and Keltner had a .326 average, a league-leading 12 homers and 26 RBIs. While Joe Gordon was hitting just .255 at second, he had 5 homers and 26 runs batted in of his own. Helped by the right-handed power of its infield, the Tribe had yet to lose to a left-handed pitcher. Thurman Tucker, hitting .310, led the outfielders, while Doby had 6 homers and Allie Clark and Pat Seerey had performed well in platoon roles. The team led the league with a remarkable .293 average, and Feller, Lemon, and Bearden had all pitched very well.

The Yankees had also hit well. A platoon of Johnny Lindell and Charlie Keller was hitting a combined .409 (52/127) in left, and McQuinn at first and Johnson at third had hit .328 and .292 with reasonable power. Catchers Niarhos (.344) and Berra (.283) had done well, shortstops Rizzuto and Brown were around .300, and DiMaggio, at .283, was coming on strong. Only Henrich and Stirnweiss had started slowly. On the mound Reynolds led the league in wins, Raschi and Shea had pitched strongly, Page had been sharp in relief, and Lopat, though 2–3, had generally pitched adequately.

Bill Veeck's plans for a record crowd went awry when it began to rain on Sunday morning. The rain eased in time for the games to be played after an hour's delay, and Veeck himself showed up in the third inning in defiance of his doctors' orders, but the crowd came up a little short of the record at 78,431 fans—not one of whom, it is safe to say, ever forgot what they saw that day.

The rivalry between Bob Feller and Joe DiMaggio's Yankees had been a tremendous source of excitement ever since both men entered the American League as rookies in 1936. Fifty-nine thousand Cleveland fans had turned out for Feller's first start against New York in July 1937, when Feller, at age eighteen, had entered the top of the ninth inning with the game tied 1–1. DiMaggio, who already had a double and a triple in the game, came to bat in that inning with the bases loaded and delivered a grand-slam home run on an 0–2 curveball. A few weeks later, in Yankee Stadium, Feller struck out twelve Yankees and went into the ninth leading 5–2, but gave up a three-run homer to Lou Gehrig. He had finally gotten a victory in September 1937 in Cleveland, although Joe D had hit another 400-foot home run.

The Yankees acquired an edge on Feller some time thereafter, according to Tommy Henrich, when they discovered characteristic movements in his motion that gave away whether he was going to throw a fastball or a curve. Despite that, he managed to keep his record at about .500 against them simply because both his fastball and his curve were so overpowering. The feud had heated up again after the war, when a New York writer had suggested in April 1946 that Rapid Robert was through as a great pitcher. Feller responded in Yankee Stadium on April 30, 1946, with perhaps the greatest performance of his career, his second no-hitter.

Now the rivalry was on again, and the pennant might easily be at stake. After Feller got the Yankees in order in the first, Reynolds got an unlucky start in the bottom of the inning when Thurman Tucker beat out a slow roller to Johnson at third and advanced to second when Johnson threw wildly. Reynolds struck out Doby and got Boudreau to ground out to Brown at shortstop, but Eddie Robinson worked him for a walk, and Joe Gordon, for whom Reynolds had been swapped eighteen months earlier, singled to left-center for a 1–0 lead. Keltner, who had not hit a homer since the previous Sunday against the White Sox, now drove the ball into the left-field stands to make it 4–0.

Generations of baseball writers and fans have lionized reputed "clutch hitters" who supposedly saved their home runs for the late innings of close games, and today statisticians actually compute batting averages for late-inning situations. Nothing, of course, matches the drama of a late-inning homer that reverses the outcome of a game—and many such blows were struck during the 1948 season—but the fascination with such hits reflects a misunderstanding of baseball. Runs and RBIs count equally whether they are delivered in the first inning or the ninth, and a hitter who breaks up a 1–1 game with a homer in the ninth could have accomplished the same result in any of his earlier at bats. Far more games are won with three-run homers in the first, which set the whole tone of the game, energize (or quiet) the home crowd, and frequently force the opposing manager to remove his starting pitcher. Usually a 4–0 lead is decisive—but not, as it happened, on May 23, 1948.

Feller sometimes claimed that Ohio native Tommy Henrich was an even tougher hitter for him than DiMaggio, and he walked Henrich in the top of the fourth. One out later, DiMaggio, who had singled in the second, lined a high, inside pitch more than 350 feet into the stands in left to bring the Yankees within two runs. But Feller promptly fanned Berra and Johnson, and the score remained at 4–2 through five innings as Feller continued to dominate the rest of the Yanks.

Henrich walked again with one out in the Yankee sixth, and Keller lined a single to right center to bring DiMaggio to the plate again. Feller pitched him low and away, and the Yankee Clipper hit a drive that shot out of the infield, so low that Lou Boudreau actually leapt for it. The ball rose and rose on a line out into left center, finally coming to rest 465 feet away for three runs and a 5–4 Yankee lead. The ground trembled under Feller's feet as Berra singled to right and Bill Johnson drove the ball deep to center, but Thurman Tucker made a leaping catch against the fence and McQuinn ended the inning by grounding back to Feller. Reynolds, meanwhile, yielded no runs from the second through the sixth innings.

Boudreau pinch-hit for Feller leading off the bottom of the seventh, but Cleveland failed to score. When the new Indian pitcher Bob Muncrief faced DiMaggio with one out in the top of the eighth, Joe D hit his third home run of the game to straightaway left—only the second time in his career that he had ever accomplished this feat. With the score still 6–4 as the Indians began the bottom of the ninth, Dale Mitchell worked Reynolds for a walk, and Boudreau, rigorously playing the percentages, sent lefty Hal Peck, rather than Pat Seerey or Allie Clark, to hit for catcher Jim Hegan. Peck ran the count to 2–0, and Bucky Harris replaced Reynolds with lefty Joe Page. Defying Harris's strategy, Peck singled to left. Reserve catcher Joe Tipton batted for Muncrief and successfully sacrificed the runners along.

The tying runs were on second and third with one out, and Boudreau sent the right-handed Allie Clark to hit for Thurman Tucker. Playing the percentages himself, Page walked Clark to load the bases, and promptly struck out the left-handed Doby on three pitches. Boudreau, 0–4 but still hitting well over .400, came to the plate with the bases loaded.

Joe Page never liked to let the opposition's most dangerous hitter cost him the game. Working carefully amidst the screams of the enormous crowd, he issued Boudreau a walk, forcing in the Indians' fifth run, moving the tying run to third base, and bringing the left-handed Eddie Robinson to the plate. Then Page struck Robinson out on three pitches to end this incredible game.

DiMaggio's fantastic performance had given the first round of 1948's battle between Feller and the Yankees to the New Yorkers. But the Indians came back stongly to divide the doubleheader, 5–1, behind Don Black, and save first place. The split kept the Yankees two games out of first and maintained a half-game lead over the Athletics, who swept a doubleheader against the Browns. Equally important, the Indians had maintained the goodwill of the crowd, who were accustomed to seeing them start well against weaker western neighbors, only to crash against the invincible New Yorkers. But what would echo through the ages was the heroic effort of DiMaggio in game one—the first, but not the last of many critical contests during this year that he appeared determined to win single-handed.

STANDINGS
Monday, May 24, 1948

Team	Won	Lost	Pct.	Games Behind
Cleveland	18	8	.692	—
Philadelphia	19	10	.655	½
New York	17	11	.607	2
Detroit	15	16	.484	5½
St. Louis	12	14	.462	6
Washington	12	16	.429	7
Boston	12	17	.414	7½
Chicago	7	20	.259	11½

Drained, perhaps, by their wild Sunday, the Indians could do no better than a split in Tuesday and Wednesday games with the Senators. Then, as the eastern clubs returned home, they won three out of four in Chicago. Unfortunately, center fielder Thurman Tucker, who was tied for the league lead in runs scored with Ted Williams at 29, broke a finger and was lost indefinitely. Lemon won his sixth game, tying Yankee Allie Reynolds for the league lead, but Feller, surprisingly, lost the opener of a Sunday doubleheader 4–2, dropping his record to 4–4. Back in Cleveland for yet another Memorial Day doubleheader on Monday, May 31, the Indians split with the Browns.

Cleveland lost ground to the Athletics, who finished their western trip with seven wins and just one loss before returning home to face the Yankees. Nearly 30,000 fans jammed Shibe Park on Friday night to see the A's win 5–3. They won again the next day, beating Allie Reynolds 6–5, and came from behind three times to beat the Yankees 6–5 again in the opener of Sunday's doubleheader. And although the umpires called the second game of the doubleheader in the top of the sixth with the Yankees ahead 2–1—much to the disgust of Connie Mack, who may have paid for his own chronic mistreatment of the arbiters—they remained in first place.

On Monday, the A's played a doubleheader against those erstwhile pennant favorites, the Red Sox. Boston was completing one of the worst road trips in the history of the franchise. The season that had begun so hopefully with McCarthy at the helm was now in a shambles.

The Red Sox had left Cleveland on Saturday, May 22, having lost two straight to the Tigers and two out of three to the Tribe. The next day, in Chicago, they lost their third straight doubleheader to the worst team in the league. Wasting fine pitching performances by Earl Johnson in the first game and Denny Galehouse in the second, they lost both games 4–3 in ten innings, with just eight hits in the opener and seven in the nightcap. Two days later in St. Louis, the Browns shelled their old teammate Ellis Kinder for eight hits in four innings and coasted to a 9–4 win behind lefty Sam Zoldak. Williams went three for four with a double and Stephens marked his return to St. Louis with a home run, but it wasn't enough. McCarthy now made a daring move, substituting right-handed infielder Billy Goodman, a line-drive hitter, for slumping Jake Jones at first. The new lineup managed to beat the Browns 5–3 in ten innings on Wednesday behind Dobson, with Stephens driving in three runs—only the second win of a seven-game western trip.

After a long train ride to Washington, the Red Sox lost a heartbreaker on Friday night, 2–1, to Washington pitcher Ray Scarborough, who could handle any club in the league. Mel Parnell pitched well, giving up just six singles and one trip in eight innings, but despite two doubles by Williams the Red Sox got just one run, leaving the bases loaded in the ninth. Things got even worse in Saturday's doubleheader. In the first game, a double and triple by Williams helped Jack Kramer reach the bottom of the ninth inning with a 4–2 lead, but four hits and a walk gave the Senators a 5–4 victory. In the nightcap the Senators knocked out Earl Johnson for a 7–1 lead after eight innings. In the top of the ninth the Sox rallied, battering three pitchers for four runs and bringing Williams to bat with the bases loaded and two out. Pitcher Walt Masterson walked him to bring the Red Sox to within one run, but Stan Spence ended the game flying deep to right center. To top it off, Pesky injured his knee and missed the next six games. Finally, on Sunday, the Red Sox were simply blown out, 8–1, as Denny Galehouse failed to repeat his strong Chicago showing.

A shaken Red Sox club, losers of eleven of their last thirteen games, took the field in Philadelphia for their Memorial Day doubleheader as the Boston press indulged in an orgy of second-guessing. Having tried Goodman, Bobby Doerr, and even Billy Hitchcock in the leadoff spot, McCarthy restored Dom DiMaggio there and returned Jake Jones to first. Joe Dobson, who had won two and lost one on the trip, faced Lou Brissie in the first game and managed to rally the team with a 7–0 shutout, as Williams hit a two-run homer. Lefty Mickey Harris pitched almost as well in the second game, taking a 1–0 lead into the bottom of the sixth, but one hit, three walks, and a balk gave the Athletics the only runs they needed for a split, 2–1. On Tuesday the Red Sox' road trip came to an end on a relatively happy note when Ellis Kinder won 8–1 with the help of two-run homers by Vern Stephens and Bobby Doerr. But the Red Sox found themselves anchored firmly in seventh place, twelve games behind Cleveland in the loss column. The reasons were not far to seek.

Theodore Samuel Williams had played every inning of every game, fielded brilliantly, and hit .382 with 11 home runs and a league-leading 43 RBIs. No other regular, alas, was within one hundred points of him. Junior Stephens had 7 homers, but only 25 RBIs and a .271 average. Table-setters Dom DiMaggio and Johnny Pesky weighed in at .245 and .265 with a total of no home runs, while Bobby Doerr was hitting .255, with 4 homers in 38 games. At first base, Billy Goodman (.250) seemed to be taking over from Jake Jones (.239). Right field was a contest between Mele (.247, one home run) and Spence (.261, three homers). The catchers—Tebbetts and Batts— were hitting relatively well.

The pitching picture was even worse. The Red Sox had scored only 22 fewer runs than the Indians, but had given up 65 more (191 to 126). Only Joe Dobson had shown real consistency, and he was 5–4. As columnist Harold Kaese suggested, McCarthy might easily have contributed to the problem by using so many pitchers. He had given starts to no fewer than nine—Dobson, Galehouse, Ferriss, Harris, McCall, Parnell, Johnson, Kramer, and Kinder—and his starters had been averaging about six days' rest. In part, this was McCarthy's style of managing. Many of his Yankee teams had only one pitcher with more than 200 innings pitched. McCarthy was a percentage manager whose clubs had consistently scored lots of runs. He was content with a steady, consistent pitching staff that would keep his team in ball games, and he tried to keep his hurlers rested. While Boudreau frequently pitched Feller and Lemon on three days' rest and Bucky Harris pitched Reynolds and Lopat with four, McCarthy generally regarded four days between starts as an absolute minimum. It was clear on June 1, 1948, however, that McCarthy had yet to choose even five main starters. The record of the first six weeks suggests that he still regarded Mickey Harris, rather than Mel Parnell, as his ace left-hander, and that Boo Ferriss ranked higher in his estimation than Ellis Kinder.

Last but not least, the Red Sox had been somewhat unlucky. Their 173 runs scored and 191 runs allowed should have given them a .451 percentage; they were actually at .385 (15–24). What accounted for the difference, of course, was their astonishing knack for losing one-run games—two to the Athletics, one to the Yankees, two to the White Sox, and three in a row in the disastrous four-game series in Washington. Losing eight one-run games, they had won just one. The season was only a little more than one-quarter done, but already some observers were nearly ready to write off the campaign. To win 95 games—a very conservative minimum to win the pennant, since both Cleveland and Philadelphia were on a pace to win well over 100—they would have to play at a .700 clip for the rest of the season. To do that, they would have to hit better, pitch better, and play better in the clutch.

As it turned out, they did all that, and more.

STANDINGS
Tuesday, June 1, 1948

Team	Won	Lost	Pct.	Games Behind
Philadelphia	26	12	.684	—
Cleveland	23	11	.676	1
New York	21	15	.583	4
Detroit	19	20	.487	7½
St. Louis	16	17	.485	7½
Washington	17	21	.447	9
Boston	14	23	.378	11½
Chicago	9	26	.257	15½

4

Tightening Up

(JUNE 1–JUNE 28)

On Tuesday, June 1, the Indians began a critical two-week trip east. While Cleveland could generally expect to gain ground whenever the schedule matched them with the Browns, White Sox, and Tigers, they lost their advantage when they had to face the Yankees, Athletics, and Red Sox—and their June schedule featured twenty-seven games against the eastern clubs, half on the road and half at home. It was a rainy June in the East, and in the end the Tribe had to wait until later in the summer to play three of those games. As it was, they established themselves as firm favorites with the help of the most controversial umpiring call of the year.

The trip began badly. Lemon lost a heartbreaker, 2–1, to Ray Scarborough on Wednesday night, June 3, as fleet left fielder Gil Coan manufactured both of the Senators' runs. The next day's game was rained out, and Veeck made a trade, shipping ineffective pitcher Al Gettel and big, slow Pat Seerey to Chicago for outfielder Bob Kennedy. Despite Seerey's power—25 home runs per 154 major league games—the Indians had apparently concluded that his bulk was too heavy a burden to carry in the outfield. For some reason he had never been tried at first, where he might usefully have platooned with Robinson. Bob Kennedy at twenty-eight was a more versatile player than Seerey, with an excellent arm and the ability to play third base as well as the outfield, but he had a lifetime .236 average and had never hit more than six homers in a season. On the same day the Indians also announced that respiratory problems had again driven relief ace Russ Christopher to bed. Friday's game was the tensest pitching duel of the year. Feller and Mickey Haefner pitched eleven innings of scoreless

55

ball, and the Indians did not break through until scoring five runs in the fifteenth for a 5–0 victory.

Cleveland put some distance between themselves and the Athletics with three weekend wins in Philadelphia behind Bearden, Lemon, and Steve Gromek, who won his first start. During the following week, the strain of the pennant race apparently became too much for old Connie Mack. Shaky pitching cost the Athletics two of three games against the Tigers, but they managed to beat the Browns on Friday and Saturday. In the first game of a doubleheader on Sunday, Brissie and Nelson Potter lost a 5–1 lead in eighth, surrendering six runs and losing the game. "Were you doing your best out there?" Mack asked Potter, an ace of the pennant-winning 1944 Browns who had pitched in the majors for ten years. "I paid $20,000 for you and that was my mistake. I don't care how good any player ever was, has been or could be. All I care about is how much good he is now." The A's won the nightcap, but Mack gave both Potter and thirty-eight-year-old Bill Dietrich their unconditional release the next day. The purge left Mack with just five healthy pitchers.

The Red Sox, meanwhile, had begun to show some signs of life. When their home stand began on the evening of Wednesday, June 2, a remarkable 34,303 fans had turned out to watch them try to stay out of the cellar, only to see the lowly Browns beat Mel Parnell 3–1. But they squared the series the next day, 3–2, behind Kramer, and on Friday they swept their first doubleheader of the season behind Dobson and Galehouse, 10–4 and 7–2. Vern Stephens had four hits and four RBIs on the day, the unlucky Galehouse won his first game of the year, and Billy Goodman, apparently settled at first, went four for nine. A Saturday game against the Tigers was rained out. When the Red Sox took them on for a doubleheader on Sunday, Pesky returned to the lineup, and McCarthy now fielded the batting order that, with one change, would carry him through the rest of the season: DiMaggio, Pesky, Williams, Spence, Stephens, Doerr, Goodman, and Tebbetts or Batts. In the first game the Sox trailed 4–2 in the bottom of the eighth, but Stephens tied it with a two-run homer in the eighth and drove in the winning run in the ninth. In the nightcap, Williams, Stephens, Spence, and Doerr demolished five Tiger pitchers on the way to a 12–4 win, the team's fifth straight. Williams went five for eight on the day with a double, a home run, four runs, and three RBIs. He now led the league in batting with .391 and in RBIs with 46—a pace that would give him 161 for the season. Despite winning five of six games, however, the Red Sox still found themselves 19–24, a full ten games off the lead, as the Indians came to town for three scheduled games.

Rain washed out the Red Sox and the Indians on Monday, June 7, while the author of this book celebrated his first birthday in Arlington, Virginia. They met in Fenway Park the next night before another packed house. In a surprise, Boudreau held out Feller on a cold, damp night and started Bearden, who had pitched seven innings and won a game the previous Saturday, to face Parnell on two days' rest. The game included the year's biggest rhubarb—one whose full significance only became apparent much, much later.

With the score 0–0, Johnny Pesky opened the third with a single, but Boudreau made two brilliant plays deep in the hole to preserve the tie. Allie Clark walked to open the fourth, bringing Boudreau to the plate. With a 2–2 count, he sliced a fly down the right-field line. The ball dropped into the tight right-field corner in Fenway, about six rows into the stands. Several fans, interviewed during the game by reporters, affirmed that the ball had crossed the fence in foul territory. According to an AP report—which Boudreau later denied—the Cleveland manager began to turn around and return to home plate when he saw the ball land. Then first-base umpire Charley Berry signaled a home run.

JOHNNY PESKY: It was foul by ten feet.

MEL PARNELL: When Berry signaled a home run, Bill McKechnie, the Cleveland first base coach, burst out laughing. I ran in to Ed Hurley, the plate umpire, and said, "Isn't there anything you can do?" "It's his call," he said.

GENE BEARDEN: It was a home run—sure it was!

Boston had men on base in each of the next three innings but never scored, and Bearden won his sixth game, 2–0. Two decades later, Ted Williams remembered this game as perhaps the most important one of the year.[1] For the third time in a row, Parnell had pitched very well but emerged with a loss, and the Red Sox were now eleven games back. They rebounded two days later, blasting Feller from the mound with eight runs in the bottom of the fourth and winning 15–6. The Indians had split the series, but Feller had now failed to win in four consecutive starts. This time he had been well and truly shelled, and his 5–5 record was becoming a source of concern as the team moved to New York.

The Yankees had passed the Athletics and moved into second place, three games behind Cleveland, with eight wins in eleven games against Detroit, Chicago, and St. Louis. Unfortunately, in the opener against Detroit, Charlie Keller broke his hand making a catch and was lost indefinitely. Bobby Brown continued to hit strongly at second base, but he had

---

1. In one of the very few factual errors in his autobiography, Williams gives the score of this game as 2–1 (Williams with Underwood, *My Turn at Bat*, 168).

apparently not convinced Bucky Harris that he should stay there. In eleven games, Brown had hit .392, raising his overall average to .349, and winning two games with last-inning hits, but he had participated in just three double plays. Rain washed out the rest of the series with the White Sox, setting up a brutal weekend on their next visit in late July. The Yanks could make it into first place if they could sweep their four-game series with the Indians.

Lemon and Raschi opened the series on Friday night, June 10, before almost 68,000 fans. The two teams picked up where they had left off in their May 23 doubleheader and treated the crowd to another hitting show—a pattern destined to continue throughout the season. With the Indians leading 5–3 in the top of the third inning, Yankee catcher Yogi Berra protested veteran umpire Cal Hubbard's calls a bit too vigorously behind the plate, and Hubbard decided to teach the young catcher a lesson and threw him out of the game. A shower of debris delayed the proceedings for ten minutes.

With one out in the top of the seventh and the score 6–6, Judnich grounded to second and was given a single when Brown couldn't keep the ball in his glove. It was a fateful play. Two batters later, Bucky Harris replaced him with Stirnweiss, who remained at second for the rest of the season. Reserve catcher Joe Tipton promptly doubled to clear the bases for a 9–6 lead. Joe Page fanned Boudreau to end the big Indian rally in the seventh inning—incredibly enough, the first time in 42 games that Boudreau had struck out. He still hoped to break Joe Sewell's all-time record of three strikeouts in a season. The game wasn't settled until Feller, relieving, struck out pinch hitter Sherman Lollar with the bases loaded and the score 10–8 in the bottom of the ninth, which Joe DiMaggio had opened with a home run.

The Indians had their biggest day of the year on Saturday as their awesome right-handed-hitting infielders helped sweep the Yankees, 7–5 and 9–4, before another 68,500 fans. The biggest gun was former Yankee second baseman Joe Gordon, who hit three homers and drove in six runs on the day to raise his RBI total to 37. In the first game Gene Bearden failed to hold the Yankees once again, and this time it was Lemon who had to relieve and get Joe DiMaggio with the tying runs on base for the final out.

Feller faced Lopat in the finale on Sunday, June 13, but few of the 49,641 on hand were likely to remember much about the game. It was Babe Ruth Day in Yankee Stadium, and a stooped, wasted Ruth, with cancer eating away his voice and his body, made his farewell speech while his number was retired. A team of Yankee All-Stars drawn mostly from the 1930s played two innings against an older group composed mostly of Ruth's 1923 teammates, brought together to commemorate the first year of operation for Yankee Stadium. (Two of the more famous 1927 aggregation, Lou Gehrig and Tony Lazzeri, were already dead, while another, Earl Combs, was coaching for the Red Sox in Boston.) In a rasping voice, Ruth spoke of his great love for baseball.

Feller carried a 1–0 lead into the bottom of the sixth, when DiMaggio hit a one-out triple against the 415-foot sign in left and Berra followed with his sixth home run to right field to take the lead. In an effort to get a sweep, Boudreau had risked Feller, who had pitched three rough innings in Boston on Thursday and relieved on Friday night. Now, he hit for him in the bottom of the sixth and chose another starter, Bearden, to relieve, even though the Yanks had hit Bearden hard on two previous occasions. Bearden got the side out in the seventh without much trouble, but DiMaggio—who had hit a rained-out homer against him back on May 12—greeted him in the eighth with a 400-foot triple. After two outs, disaster struck when Gordon fumbled McQuinn's grounder and Rizzuto homered for a 5–1 lead. The Indians rallied for two runs in the ninth, but Joe Page closed out another classic by striking out Eddie Robinson once more with two on for the final out. Feller had not pitched badly, but he had lost again. Still, Cleveland's superb 8–3 road trip had established a solid, six-game loss column lead over Philadelphia, and a three-game lead overall. They had become the big story of the season.

STANDINGS
Monday, June 14, 1948

Team	Won	Lost	Pct.	Games Behind
Cleveland	31	14	.689	—
Philadelphia	31	20	.608	3
New York	28	21	.571	5
Detroit	26	25	.510	8
Washington	24	28	.462	10½
Boston	22	26	.458	10½
St. Louis	19	29	.396	13½
Chicago	13	31	.295	17½

Not for twenty-eight years had the Indians actually won a pennant, but local interest in them had never flagged. Their hitters—helped by League Park, where they played most of their home games until 1946—posted impressive averages during most of the heavy-hitting thirties. Helped by Cy Slapnicka, one of the greatest scouts in baseball history, they had come up with a number of genuine stars during the late 1930s and early 1940s, including Feller (1936), Keltner (1938), and Boudreau (1939). They also had a habit—one which persisted into the 1960s—of starting the season with a rush, only to fade during the summer. And well before the era of Bill Veeck, they had a history of bitter controversies, which the three daily papers—the *Plain Dealer,* the *Press,* and the *News*—reported in loving detail.

Thus, the history of the Indians during the 1930s included the stories of the signing of Feller in 1936, at the age of sixteen, by Slapnicka, who originally penned his name to a minor league contract, and the subsequent controversy later that year, when Judge Landis, the commissioner of baseball, accused Slapnicka of fraudulently controlling Feller's contract from Cleveland while shuffling him between two minor league teams. Landis threatened to declare Feller a free agent and set off a bidding war, but eventually relented when—according to Feller—Bob's father threatened to sue baseball in court. Six months later, Landis did free Tommy Henrich, another Cleveland signing. Landis believed absolutely in the maintenance of strong minor leagues, and fought throughout his tenure against the majors' growing tendency to turn them into training grounds.[2] Other big stories of the prewar period included pitcher Johnny Allen's 15-game winning streak in 1937, which he lost on the very last day of the season, and the night of July 17, 1941, when Ken Keltner made two great plays and stopped Joe DiMaggio's incredible hitting streak at 56 games before 67,468 fans. The biggest prewar story of all, however, involved the season of 1940.

In the cold light of history, the Indians of 1940 do not emerge as a particularly good team. Their hitting was mediocre at best, and their pitching and defense lacked depth. But they got a fantastic 27–11 season from Bob Feller—one of the two greatest seasons ever turned in by a twenty-one-year old pitcher[3]—and, when the Yankees got off to a terrible start, found themselves in the midst of a hot pennant race with the Detroit Tigers. Meanwhile the team's manager, Oscar Vitt, had angered the players with frequent criticisms, both public and private. The climax began when Vitt went to the mound to remove highly respected veteran pitcher Mel Harder and asked him when he was going to start earning his salary. The players decided to try to seek Vitt's removal, and a delegation led by Harder and Johnny Allen, and including Feller—but not rookie Lou Boudreau—met with team president Alva Bradley, a prominent local businessman who had never claimed to know much about baseball. Bradley reacted noncommittally.

2. After the Henrich incident, another Cleveland player who had been held in the minors for years presented himself at Landis's office and asked for the same treatment, but the commissioner declined, pleading an informal statute of limitations. That player was Denny Galehouse, now with the Red Sox.

3. The other was achieved by Vida Blue in 1971.

The meeting took place on June 13. "Paris fell to the Germans on June 13," wrote Cleveland newspaperman Franklin Lewis some years later, "but you never would have suspected it from the front page of the next morning's *Plain Dealer.*" Sportswriter Gordon Cobbledick broke the story, and it became the story of the year. The Indians' players immediately apologized, but they became indelibly known as the Cry Baby Indians. The stands filled with diapers, baby bottles, and other infantile paraphernalia in every other American League city for the rest of the season. Things got worse when they lost to the Tigers on the last weekend of the season, finishing with just 89 victories. While statistics show both the Tigers and the third-place Yankees to have been far superior teams, the fans naturally blamed the players' outburst for the narrow defeat. Vitt lost his job a few weeks later.

Franklin Lewis of the *Cleveland Press* had been left out of the original "cry babies" story, but he more than made up for that with a random remark after the season, while speculating about Vitt's successor. "If Clark Griffith owned the Indians," he wrote, recalling Bucky Harris's selection as manager of the Senators in 1924 at the age of twenty-seven, "he would put Boudreau in charge of the team even if he were only twenty-three years old." The idea went nowhere then, as Bradley selected veteran manager Roger Peckinpaugh, but one year later, after Peckinpaugh was fired, Boudreau talked himself into his appointment as the youngest manager in baseball history.

The advent of Bill Veeck in 1946, of course, was the next big story in Cleveland baseball. In 1946 the team began playing all its games in Municipal Stadium, and in 1947 Veeck moved the fences in somewhat to increase home run hitting. As 1948 began, the Indians' organization was becoming one of the strongest in the league. Their farm system included such future stars as Al Rosen and Ray Boone, and with Veeck poised to make new forays into the Negro leagues and Latin markets, the Indians were set to contend for years to come.

The Indians were holding on to first place on merit. They were a truly great team, built—like every great team—around a core of tremendous hitters. They had fortunately managed to combine three excellent infielders in their thirties—Boudreau, Gordon, and Keltner—with two fine young outfielders, Mitchell and Doby, and a fine supporting cast. Their main weaknesses to date included their second-line pitching—only Lemon and Feller had been consistently effective, and Feller, obviously, had been slipping—and their inability to hit consistently at home, in Municipal Stadium. While Bill Veeck planned to do something about the pitching, the players would have to handle the problem of the stadium themselves.

The heart of the 1948 Indians was their three veteran right-handed infielders, Joe Gordon, Lou Boudreau, and Ken Keltner, who for that one season—together with Eddie Robinson—probably made up the greatest infield of all time. Boudreau, at thirty, and Keltner, a year older, were having by far the finest seasons of their careers, while Gordon was turning in another in a long series of brilliant campaigns. Boudreau had hit .300 three times, topped by a wartime figure of .327 which won him the 1944 batting title. At the halfway mark of 1948, he was hitting .355, his eight home runs were only three shy of his career high, and his 54 RBIs gave him a fine chance to top 100 for only the second time in his career. Keltner, who in eight full seasons had never managed to duplicate his 1938 rookie figures of 26 homers and 113 RBIs, was threatening to top 26 homers before the All-Star break, and Joe Gordon was having another one of his customarily great years despite his low batting average. Gordon hit over .300 only once in his career—in 1942, when his .320 average, with 18 homers and 103 RBIs, won him the MVP over triple crown winner Ted Williams—but he showed consistently good power and on-base average, despite playing his whole career in two ballparks—Yankee Stadium and Municipal Stadium— that did not favor right-handed hitting. At the All-Star break the Indians would lead the league in batting average and, on a per-game basis, in runs scored, and the infield was mainly—although not solely—responsible. Catcher Jim Hegan—never an offensive standout—was suffering through a dismal first half of the season, but he was destined for the best offensive season of his career.

The offensive accomplishments of first baseman Eddie Robinson, Gordon, Boudreau, and Keltner during 1948 have never been matched. Even with Robinson playing only 131 games, the four starting infielders eventually finished the year with a total of 432 RBIs. This total is not a record for an infield—the Detroit Tigers quartet of 1934 (Hank Greenberg, Charlie Gehringer, Billy Rogell, and Marv Owen) drove in 462 runs. But the Tigers played in a league in which runs were about 8 percent more frequent than in 1948, and they played in a good hitters' park, while the Tribe played in a bad one. Both as a percentage of their team's runs and as a percentage of the league's runs scored, the Cleveland total was superior. The same holds true in relation to the amazing 1931 Yankees, whose infield (Lou Gehrig, Tony Lazzeri, Lyn Lary, and Joe Sewell) drove in 440 runs, helping the team set the all-time record of 1,067 runs scored in a season, and the 1938 Red Sox quartet of Jimmy Foxx, Bobby Doerr, Joe Cronin, and Pinky Higgins, who drove in 455 of their team's 902 runs.

This, however, was only part of the Cleveland infield's value. All four players were among the top two or three in the league defensively. Keltner led the league's third basemen in assists for the third time in his career in 1948, although he barely trailed Bill Johnson and Hank Majeski in total chances per game. Boudreau finished second in the league in both putouts and assists for shortstops, and led in double plays with 119. Gordon finished third in the league in assists. Robinson led the league in fielding percentage for first basemen. Keltner, Boudreau, and Gordon all had outstanding defensive reputations, and their statistics fully justify them. They were especially valuable behind Lemon and Bearden, who threw so many ground balls.

While the infielders came from the generation of the late 1930s, the team had also come up with two of the finest outfielders of the postwar generation. One, Dale Mitchell, finished the first half with a fine .306 mark, one he was destined to improve by a full thirty points by the end of the season. Mitchell is another player whose reputation has been shaped by circumstances. He is remembered today, if at all, mainly for having struck out to end Don Larsen's perfect game in the 1956 World Series, but his statistics suggest that as a hitter he may have been the equal of Wade Boggs, who will probably wind up in Cooperstown. Because of the war, Mitchell did not even enter professional baseball until 1946, the year of his twenty-fifth birthday, when he led the Texas League in hitting and went up to the Indians to stay. Boggs, by contrast, entered professional baseball at twenty-one and took four years to make the majors. Mitchell proceeded to accumulate a .315 lifetime average in seven seasons as an Indians regular before becoming a part-timer in 1954, at the age of thirty-three. And while Boggs has had a longer career—for which diet and conditioning may be largely responsible—the large difference in their lifetime averages could easily be accounted for by the difference between Fenway Park and Municipal Stadium. Mitchell also averaged more than 50 walks a year, a fine figure for a leadoff hitter, and in 1949 he hit 23 triples, the highest figure in either league since the introduction of the lively ball.[4] Had Mitchell played in Boston, Detroit, or Philadelphia, he would have been an annual contender for the batting championship.

The remainder of the outfield picture was, to say the least, confused. While Larry Doby had pretty firmly established himself in the lineup by the All-Star break, Mitchell was the only man who had consistently started. The remainder of the outfield playing time had been shared among no less than six players: Thurman Tucker, Hank Edwards, Allie Clark, Walt Judnich, the departed Pat Seerey, and the recently arrived Bob Kennedy. It was in the outfield, indeed, that Lou Boudreau had most thor-

4. Earl Combs of the Yankees also had 23 triples in 1927.

oughly indulged his penchant for hunch-playing, to the continuing frustration of Bill Veeck and his new assistant, Hank Greenberg.

Managing a baseball team presents an extraordinary variety of intellectual and emotional challenges. Every game presents the manager with dozens of minute-to-minute decisions, beginning with the making out of the lineup card and the selection of the starting pitcher, and continuing throughout the game as different situations present different options. Every team is made up of twenty-five proud, talented, highly competitive athletes, some of whom will disappoint the manager's expectations at any given moment. Meanwhile, every good manager knows, or learns, that baseball is fundamentally a game of *long-term* percentages, in which superior talent will prevail over time if only it is given a chance to do so. No matter how brilliant, far-seeing, or just plain obsessive a manager may be, much of the game will always remain beyond his control, and even a .666 manager will end one-third of his days on a low note. And baseball is a game of such complexity that one can nearly always imagine something that might have been done differently, some move that might have been made that would have turned a defeat into a victory. The manager, moreover—unless he happens, like Boudreau, to have been a playing manager—has no physical outlet for his frustrations. It is hardly surprising that so many great managers have been heavy smokers, drinkers, gamblers, or misanthropes.

Boudreau himself had had a relatively relaxed, but not necessarily useful, introduction to managerial life during the war years, when good players were hard to come by. Now, thanks to Veeck's moves, he had numerous options to work with, and, thanks to his winter controversy with Veeck, he was frantic to bring home a winner. Emotionally Boudreau had the advantage of being a player, but he suffered from other disadvantages of youth. He simply could not accept the fundamental limitation of managing a baseball team: the impossibility of controlling every specific event. His desire to stay on top of every situation had led him, in 1946 and 1947, to begin calling pitches from shortstop, an experiment which he finally abandoned early in 1948. At the most critical moments of ball games, when the game was on the line in the late innings, he would sometimes remove either a pinch-hitter or a relief pitcher in the middle of an at bat. And during 1948, he could not bring himself to leave his lineup or his batting order alone.

Boudreau handled his lineup during the first half of the season like a gambler trying a series of systems. He used exactly the same lineup and batting order during the six-game winning streak that opened his season—

Tucker (cf), Doby (rf), Boudreau, Gordon, Robinson, Clark (lf), Keltner, and Hegan—but began fiddling with it after the team's very first loss. In the first week of May he began platooning Allie Clark and Pat Seerey against left-handers and Dale Mitchell and Doby against righties, batting Mitchell fifth or seventh and leading off with Thurman Tucker against all types of pitching. Then, in late May, Tucker was injured and Pat Seerey was traded to Chicago for light-hitting Bob Kennedy. Mitchell became the leadoff man, with Walt Judnich going into center field and batting third against right-handers, followed by Gordon and Keltner, who had taken over the league's home run lead in May while batting seventh much of the time. A new lineup—Mitchell, Hank Edwards, Boudreau, Eddie Robinson, Judnich, Gordon, and Keltner—took over first place by one-half game on June 5, and with Doby injured, it remained the left-handed platoon for the next eleven days, with Bob Kennedy leading off and Allie Clark batting second against left-handers.

Doby replaced Edwards in the left-handed platoon after coming back on June 17, and Boudreau continued to try various bizarre combinations against left-handers, leading off with Berardino at first in place of Robinson against Hal Newhouser on June 29, and following him with Bob Kennedy, himself, Clark, Gordon, and Keltner. Doby was benched again in early July, with Mitchell, Edwards, and Judnich playing against right-handers, and Berardino took over first base from Eddie Robinson again in the last six games before the All-Star break. The power hitters constantly shuffled around the lineup, with Robinson juggled between cleanup and seventh. All told, Boudreau used thirty-one different batting orders in the Indians' first sixty-four games. No single combination lasted for as long as two weeks.

In retrospect, the two most questionable shifts made by Boudreau were the substitution of Berardino for Eddie Robinson, who was destined for a fine career as a power hitter, and his failure to make a firm commitment to Larry Doby. His frequent lineup changes and frantic late-inning moves were still driving his bosses, Bill Veeck and Hank Greenberg, to distraction, but Veeck was sticking to his resolve not to interfere or criticize. And in retrospect, it remains an open question whether the manager's constant juggling of his lineup and batting order helped or hurt the team. Like Dick Williams's many moves with the 1972 Oakland A's—including his decision to use four different second basemen in every game—it shows a tendency to look too hard to find an edge every day, rather than to let percentages prove themselves out over a whole season. Today, fantasy league owners generally learn how futile it is to juggle their roster in an attempt to avoid players' slumps, and older managers like Joe McCarthy obviously knew this in 1948. Yet Boudreau's use of six outfielders kept all his gardeners interested, and all of them but Judnich were hitting reasonably well as the first half of the season drew to a close.

The pitching situation was somewhat clearer, but not altogether satisfactory. The brightest star was Bob Lemon, who had started nineteen games, winning thirteen and losing seven, in his first full season as a major league pitcher. Feller, however, was rapidly becoming a source of concern, as he failed repeatedly to hold leads. Knuckleballer Gene Bearden was slowly emerging as a reliable starter, running his record to 7–3 by the All-Star break, and Russ Christopher had done well in relief. Beyond them, however, the picture deteriorated quickly. Don Black had won only twice in his first six starts; Bob Muncrief had been inconsistent; and Steve Gromek had hardly been given a chance. The Indians had played fewer games than any of the contenders, and the burden of making them up would weigh upon them more heavily during the next few months. Beginning on June 15, when they would entertain the Red Sox in Cleveland, they were scheduled for sixteen games in fourteen days against the four eastern clubs, followed, after one day off, by fourteen games in thirteen days against the West.

The Indians needed a pitcher, and, more specifically, a left-hander. Behind Bearden they had only Bill Kennedy, with a 1–0 record but an 11.45 ERA in six games. St. Louis and the Browns beckoned once again. After staying near .500 for the first six weeks of the season, the Brownies were rapidly sinking despite some excellent hitting from outfielder Al Zarilla and rookie third baseman Bob Dillinger. Their two best pitchers were right-hander Cliff Fannin, who at twenty-four was one of their most valuable remaining properties, and twenty-nine-year-old Sam Zoldak, who had managed to keep his ERA below 3.50 during his last two seasons with the Browns, but had now gotten off to a poor 2–4 start with an ERA of almost 5.00.

In Cleveland on June 15, two hours before the trading deadline, Veeck announced the acquisition of Zoldak. While the Browns diminished their chances of finishing respectably with this last round of their long-running fire sale, no one could argue that they had failed to receive adequate compensation. The price was pitcher Bill Kennedy and $100,000, a tremendous sum. Only seventeen months earlier the Detroit Tigers had sold Hank Greenberg, the American League home run and RBI champion, to the Pirates for just $75,000. But Veeck was playing for high stakes, and felt he knew exactly what he was doing. "Zoldak wasn't worth $100,000 or even $50,000 to a team fighting for third place," Veeck wrote years later. "He wasn't worth $20,000 to a team in the second division. But at that moment, with that team I had in Cleveland, he was worth whatever I had to pay."[5] Veeck still had one more pitching move in mind, but he kept it to himself for the moment.

While going all out for the pennant, Veeck was laying the foundations for a strong future in the decade to come. During 1948 and 1949 he signed two more fine black players, Cuban Minnie Minoso and Luke Easter. He also plucked Mickey Vernon and Early Wynn, each of whom had a disastrous 1948 season, from Washington after 1948 in exchange for Eddie Robinson and Joe Haynes, a journeyman pitcher who happened to be Clark Griffith's son-in-law. Meanwhile, the Cleveland scouting system and farm system—now under the direction of Hank Greenberg—continued to turn out excellent talent. Pitcher Mike Garcia, shortstop Ray Boone, and third baseman Al Rosen all reached the Indians briefly late in 1948, and Boone and Rosen eventually took over for Boudreau and Keltner, while Cuban Bobby Avila appeared not long after to replace Gordon. In the early fifties the system contributed Al Smith, Herb Score, and Rocky Colavito, as Hank Greenberg took over as general manager and continued Veeck's intensely competitive (and pro-integration) practices. Greenberg also finally screwed up his courage and made the move Veeck had hoped to make, replacing Lou Boudreau with Al Lopez as manager in 1950.

By 1951 the Indians were contenders again, and they gave the Yankees a run for their money in each of the next six seasons. Luck, alas, was rarely with them. They finished second in five of those seasons by margins of 5, 2, 8½, 3, and 9 games. They won again only in 1954, when they recorded a record 111 victories. After another brief decline, they became contenders again in 1959, finishing second, but disaster struck when Frank Lane, who had replaced Greenberg after 1957, traded Colavito for Harvey Kuenn. (The Indians compounded the mistake spectacularly five years later by giving up two great prospects, Tommie Agee and Tommy John, to get Colavito back.) Lane had previously shipped young outfielder Roger Maris to Kansas City, from whence he went, inevitably, to the Yankees. The Indians rapidly began a decline that was not reversed until the 1990s.

On the day Zoldak joined the team, the Red Sox arrived for three games in Municipal Stadium, 11½ games off the pace. While the Indians played in New York, Boston had split two heavy-hitting games with Chicago on

---

5. Veeck with Linn, *Veeck—as in Wreck*, 150.

Friday and Saturday in Boston. Another rain-out on Sunday set up a brutal three-day, five-game set between the two clubs in July. The big story, once again, was Williams, who on Friday had two doubles to left field, a single, a bases-loaded walk, and seven RBIs, raising his average to .395, and two more hits on Saturday (.398). The team would have to do much better out west to have any hope of getting back into the race.

A well-rested Mel Parnell got some revenge for his unlucky 2–0 defeat against Cleveland when the Indians opened their big home stand against the East on Tuesday night, June 15, winning 7–3 over Lemon. Pushing his staff again, Boudreau sent Feller against the Sox on Wednesday, just two days after he had pitched six innings in New York, against Joe Dobson. Keltner, always at his best against the Red Sox, put the Tribe on the board in the fifth with his 15th homer, but in the seventh, two-run homers by Williams and Doerr—both to left field—keyed the Red Sox' 7–5 victory. Williams's single, two doubles, and home run raised his average to .408. "I would like to stay up there, of course," he told reporters after the game, "but I will settle for .350 right now." "You will be over .400 in September," said Vern Stephens, whom Williams credited for getting him better pitches to hit. "It's possible," replied Williams. The AP put out a "What's Wrong with Feller?" story around the country after the game. No one seemed to know. Neither Don Black nor Denny Galehouse lasted very long in the wild series finale, which the Indians came back to tie 3–3 and 6–6 before Dom DiMaggio and Williams drove in the last two winning runs to secure a shocking sweep over the league leaders.

The Red Sox immediately tried to show that their sweep was no accident. After a rain-out on Friday, they continued their scoring binge in Detroit, beating the Tigers 9–7 behind Kramer on Saturday, June 19, and 8–3 behind Parnell, who finally won twice in a row, the next day. Williams's average reached .411, and Stephens closed out the scoring in the ninth with a three-run homer. They beat the White Sox 11–6 with fifteen hits on Tuesday night and waited out a rain-out on Wednesday. They lost the opener of Thursday's doubleheader 3–1 and fell behind 5–1 in the nightcap, but one homer by Dom DiMaggio and two by Williams led them to an 8–5 comeback win.

While the first two months of the season had featured a number of outstanding hitting performances, Williams's now dwarfed them all. His 15 homers trailed Joe DiMaggio and Keltner by just one, and he led the league with 65 runs batted in and a batting average of .417. He had also walked 62 times in 54 games—a pace which would give him 177 on the year and break Babe Ruth's all-time record of 170. He had reached base 152 times in 268 plate appearances, an unbelievable average of .567.[6] Had it not been for some freak mishaps, there is no telling what the Splendid Splinter might have done over the 1948 season. A year like Rogers Hornsby's 1922 season—.401, with 42 homers and 152 RBIs—was well within reach. Even Joe McCarthy, who had seen plenty of Williams since 1939 and could well remember the feats of Hornsby, Ruth, and Gehrig, was awed by the experience of watching him every day. "If I could hit like you," he told Williams quietly on the bench, "I'd play for nothing. I'd play this game for nothing."[7]

The Red Sox lost again in St. Louis on Friday, June 25, but swept a doubleheader with the Browns on Sunday to go 9–2 on their swing through the West. Dobson, winning his ninth, and Boo Ferris, who won his first game as a starter since May 4, did the pitching, and Williams hit a three-run homer and kept his average at .415. In the second game, McCarthy finally put Stephens, who now had 54 runs batted in in 59 games, in the cleanup spot, dropping Stan Spence to fifth. The Sox' lineup was set, and with the sole exception of Doerr, every one of them was pounding the ball. Obviously all this was most encouraging, but the team had not yet achieved more than respectability. Their overall record was still only 31–28 as they headed to New York to face the Yankees on June 29. They were still only in fourth place, though with the help of their eastern brethren, they had drawn within 5½ games of the league-leading Indians, who had not rebounded from the Red Sox' sweep a week earlier.

Following the sweep, the Indians had won three out of four on the weekend of June 19–21 from Mack's Athletics, sans the discarded Bill Dietrich and Nelson Potter. Despite losing two games and outfielder Barney McCosky in Detroit, Philadelphia still trailed by only five games in the loss column. They gained a game on Friday as Lemon, in relief, gave up two runs to lose 5–4, but the Indians squared the series 4–0 on Saturday. Only 15,000 fans showed up for that game, but on Sunday, interest in the Indians overflowed. To the amazement of all, including Bill Veeck, 82,781 fans flooded in to see Feller and Lemon pitch a doubleheader, breaking the all-time single-day attendance record of which the rain had deprived the Indians four weeks earlier. Feller, now 5–7, went down 3–0 when Eddie Joost and Sam Chapman homered, but Boudreau, desperate for a complete game, left Feller in. The Indians finally broke through and went ahead 4–3 in the bottom of the seventh, and Feller made the lead hold up. Lemon followed in the second game with a four-hit, no-walk shutout, his best

6. Harold Kaese column, *Boston Globe*, June 18.
7. Williams, with Underwood, *My Turn at Bat*, 163.

outing by far in the month of June. The Indians' lead was up to 3½ games—the highest it would get for the remainder of the year.

STANDINGS
Monday, June 21, 1948

Team	Won	Lost	Pct.	Games Behind
Cleveland	34	18	.654	—
New York	32	23	.582	3½
Philadelphia	33	25	.569	4
Boston	27	26	.509	7½
Detroit	28	28	.500	8
Washington	25	32	.439	11½
St. Louis	21	32	.396	13½
Chicago	17	33	.340	17½

Cleveland now had to defend that lead in four midweek games against the Yankees, who came in once again with Joe DiMaggio on a hot streak. New York had split two games in Chicago on the previous Tuesday and Wednesday, and the Yankees split the first two games of their series in St. Louis as well. Then Joe DiMaggio, who had only one home run in the previous two weeks, broke loose in Sunday's doubleheader. In the first game he opened the scoring with a two-run shot in the first, and the Yanks were never headed in a 4–2 win behind Raschi. In the second game DiMaggio broke a 2–2 tie in the eighth with another homer, and hit yet another in the ninth, his 15th, giving the team a 6–2 win and himself six RBIs on the day. The Yankees, 4–2 on the trip, had gained 1½ games on the Tribe, and came into Cleveland again on Monday evening, June 21, in second place, 3½ games back.

Almost 50,000 fans showed up on Monday, the night after Ohio fans had broken the all-time single-game record, to see Bearden face Reynolds in the first of four games. The game was tied at one in the fourth when DiMaggio, to whom Bearden clearly presented no mystery whatever, hit his fourth home run in three games over the right-center-field fence. The Yankees proceeded to hammer Bearden and Gromek, scoring in each of the last four innings of a 13–2 romp. Sam Zoldak, the $100,000 beauty, got his first start the next night against Frank Shea, who lately had suffered from an underdose of run support, and Thurman Tucker, recovered from his finger injury, started in center for the first time since late May. Zoldak gave up just eight hits, Joe DiMaggio's 16th homer in the eighth, tying Keltner, was a solo shot, and the Indians squared the series, 5–2.

Lopat and Don Black staged a tight pitching duel in the third game, as Keltner's 17th homer in the seventh tied the game at one. Black was still pitching in the top of the twelfth when Lindell singled, and Boudreau allowed him to load the bases for northern Ohio native Tommy Henrich, who broke out of a long slump with a grand-slam home run, giving New York a 5–1 victory and a 2–1 lead in the series.

A split would maintain the Indians' lead at a comfortable 3½ games, and Boudreau had his ace, Feller, to face the red-hot Vic Raschi. This time Feller stopped the Yanks cold the first time through the order, but in the fourth Lindell touched him for a two-run homer. Feller gave up another home run to Lindell in the fifth, and another to DiMaggio—his 17th—in the ninth. Although they had men on base in almost every inning, the Indians repeatedly failed to get the big blow, hit into three double plays, and emerged with a 4–0 loss. Once again, as in so many years past, the Yankees had come into town and humiliated the Indians, taking three of four and moving to within a game and a half.

The Indians' travails were not finished. Over the weekend of June 25–27, they managed just a split in four games with the lowly Senators, with Lemon and Bearden both taking losses. The Tribe finished their home stand with a disturbing record of six wins and nine losses. Their problems boiled down to one word: hitting. They had averaged just .247, with 11 homers in 15 games, compared to 52 in their previous 45. Keltner had gone just 8 for 48 (.167), with 3 homers but only 7 RBIs; Robinson had gone 10 for 52, with 1 homer and 6 RBIs; and Gordon hit .216, although he had hit 4 homers and driven in 14 runs. Only Boudreau himself had held steady at .363, and he had scored just 8 runs and driven in 2. The Indians' right-handed power was less effective in Municipal Stadium than in most parks on the road, and they simply did not get enough base hits there. Their outfield situation remained extremely unsettled, all the more so since Doby, who had gotten some big hits, had sprained an ankle against the Senators, while Tucker's finger had begun to hurt again. They remained in first place despite a 15–15 home record, thanks to an amazing 21–7 mark on the road.

Both the Yankees and the Athletics had taken advantage of the Tribe's split with the Senators. The Yankees lost the opener of a three-game set in Detroit, 4–2 against Newhouser, but took the next two games behind Reynolds and left Tommy Byrne. Johnny Lindell, now a full-time player owing to Charlie Keller's broken hand, had raised his average to .326, with 10 homers. Only Bobby Brown had a higher average, and Brown was sitting on the bench. The Yanks' 9–4 western trip did not match the Red Sox' 9–2, but it still brought them within one game of the Indians. That,

however, was good enough only for third place. The Athletics had rebounded from their poor showing in Cleveland, taking seven out of eight
games from the Browns and the White Sox. Their series in St. Louis began
rather inauspiciously, as they blew an 8–5 lead in the bottom of the ninth to
lose 9–8. But they won the last three games of the series—two of them by
single runs—and beat the White Sox in Chicago four times over the weekend of June 25–27, winning 4–1, 4–2, 6–5, and 6–2. Despite mediocre
hitting, Connie Mack's precipitous release of Potter and Dietrich, and an
injury-ridden pitching staff, the A's seven-game winning streak left them
just one game behind the Indians. They had a 23–6 record against the
Senators, Browns, and White Sox, compared to 15–7 for the Indians and
20–8 for the Yankees.

Now the Indians had a chance to fatten their lead against the weaker
clubs in the two weeks before the break, while the eastern clubs chewed
each other up again. During those two weeks, they added another man to
their roster—one of the most famous ballplayers in the history of baseball.

STANDINGS
Monday, June 28, 1948

Team	Won	Lost	Pct.	Games Behind
Cleveland	37	21	.617	—
Philadelphia	40	26	.606	1
New York	37	25	.597	2
Boston	31	28	.525	6½
Detroit	29	32	.500	9½
Washington	24	34	.439	13
St. Louis	23	37	.396	15
Chicago	18	39	.340	18½

5

Enter Leroy

(JUNE 29–JULY 12)

As the first half of the season drew to a close, the Indians rebounded from their disastrous home stand with a 9–4 swing around the West. Meanwhile, they put three of the biggest stories of the year—each involving a pitcher destined for the Hall of Fame—onto the nation's sports pages.

Arriving in Detroit for a three-game series after the conclusion of their home stand against the eastern clubs, the Indians now rebounded dramatically and brilliantly. Feller had begun with a superb performance against Hal Newhouser, striking out eight and allowing just one run through eight innings. The next night, Bob Lemon, the twenty-seven-year-old Californian whose 10–6 record marked him as the real ace of the Indians' staff, capped his first full half-season as a pitcher with a no-hitter, the only one of the year. A remarkable athlete, Lemon had entered organized baseball at age seventeen in 1938 and played five years in the minors as an outfielder/third baseman. After three years in the navy, he had become a relief pitcher in 1946, appearing in 32 games, and a starter in mid-1947, turning in an excellent 11–5 record and 3.45 ERA. Only twice was Lemon's masterpiece seriously threatened. In the bottom of the first, with Cleveland leading 1–0, third baseman George Kell just missed a double down the left-field line, and in the fourth, Kell forced Mitchell to make a leaping catch against the left-field screen.

The rest of the week, however, confirmed the Indians' continuing need for more pitching. On Thursday, Muncrief, Gromek, Zoldak, and Christopher failed in a 9–4 defeat in Detroit. On Friday, July 2, in St. Louis, Don Black, Klieman, Gromek, Lemon, and Christopher barely managed be-

73

tween them to hold the Browns to six runs, but Boudreau, Keltner, and Gordon enabled the Indians to win an 8–6 victory to stay one-half game ahead of the Athletics. On Saturday, homers by Boudreau and Robinson gave Feller an 8–2 win. A July 4th doubleheader in St. Louis was rained out, giving the Indians nine games to make up, and guaranteeing tremendous pressure upon their pitching staff. They had played six games fewer than the Athletics and three fewer than the Yanks—but the same number as the Red Sox, who seemed to need pitching at least as badly.

The team returned to Cleveland for a July 5 doubleheader against the Tigers in a highly charged atmosphere. Cleveland baseball writers, as we have seen, had a tradition of creating controversies, and on July 1, beat writer Harry Jones of the *Plain Dealer* had dropped another explosive ingredient into the biggest season since 1940, the year of the "Cry Baby Indians." An unidentified veteran player, he reported, had blamed the team's poor home record on the behavior of the fans.

> "I can speak for just about the whole ball club," he said. "I travel with them and I live with them and I know what they all talk about. We just don't play the same kind of ball at home that we do on the road, simply because of the fan reaction there. . . .
>
> "We're not trying to alibi," the player continued, "we're simply facing facts. On the road, win or lose, we're a better ball club, because the pressure isn't there. Not that we mind pressure, but when you get booed at every move-ment [sic], then it gets a little rough.
>
> "A pitcher throws two or three balls in a row and the crowd hollers: 'What's the matter with him? Get him out of there.' A hitter takes swing and misses and they holler: 'Sit down, ya bum!' But the payoff is when they start yelling to get the ball game over and start the fireworks when we're behind.
>
> "I don't think the crowd reaction has ever been this bad before. It was not good in '46 and it got worse this year. . . .
>
> "I think it's worse in Cleveland than in any city in the American League and I think everyone on the ball club will agree with me," the player said. "Philadelphia would be a close second. It's even worse in Cleveland, this overexcitement and booing, than it is in Boston and it usually gets pretty bad there.
>
> "Look at Pat Seerey. He's playing pretty good ball at Chicago, much better than he would in Cleveland. In fact, he always was a better ball player on the road than he was at home. And he was always a good hitter in the spring until he got to Cleveland and had to take that chatter from the fans. . . .
>
> "I know this, when we were at home the last time, if I heard it once, I heard it a dozen times, the players were saying, 'I wish to hell we were on the road.'"

Because of the turnover since Veeck took charge, the Cleveland roster actually included very few "veteran players" who, like the speaker, had been playing since 1946: Boudreau, Hank Edwards, Hegan, Feller, a few other pitchers, and Keltner. The third baseman was the most likely suspect, partly because he liked to loosen his tongue after games in local watering holes. The mystery was never cleared up, but the damage had been done. Veeck, who firmly believed in the customer's right to dissent, defended the fans and thanked them publicly for their support, but the 59,042 who showed up were determined not to be deterred by the anonymous veteran.

The first game left the fans happy enough. Keltner's 18th home run— tying DiMaggio again—a two-run homer by Gordon, and a three-run triple by Dale Mitchell gave Lemon a comfortable 6–2 win. The scoreboard showed the Athletics and Yankees losing the first games of their doubleheaders, and the fans hoped to see the Tribe open up some distance. Boudreau, playing a hot hand, chose Zoldak for the second game instead of Bearden, who hadn't pitched in eight days. Zoldak shut the Tigers out for five innings, but Detroit closed the score to 4–3 in the eighth, and Boudreau brought in Feller. Rapid Robert, who never liked to relieve, gave up two walks and a three-run homer by Pat Mullin. Boos cascaded around Feller and Boudreau as the manager removed his ace. Hal Newhouser relieved to preserve the 7–5 win, and the Indians failed to gain.

Under the circumstances, manager Lou Boudreau was not surprised the next morning when Veeck telephoned and asked him to come to the park early to bat against a kid pitcher who might shore up the Indians' staff. Boudreau found Veeck and Hank Greenberg waiting for him when he emerged onto the field in his uniform. "Where's the kid?" he asked. Veeck pointed into the almost empty visiting dugout. Recognizing the man he saw there, Boudreau quailed in amazement.

The man who walked out of the dugout had been pitching for a living since 1926, when Larry Doby was in diapers and Bob Feller was six years old. He had pitched well over a hundred games a year for much of the next twenty-two years, and his name—Leroy "Satchel" Paige—was a household word in major American cities, in hundreds of small towns, and all over the Caribbean, Mexico, and the northern tier of South America, where baseball, not soccer, is king. Over the years he had rarely failed to give an excellent account of himself in games against teams of barnstorming major leaguers, including Dizzy Dean, Joe DiMaggio, and Bob Feller. He had also toured the country playing semipro nines, advertising himself as the world's greatest pitcher, and guaranteeing, on pain of forfeiture of his appearance money, to strike out the first nine men. He had pitched, and won, a game in the Dominican Republic, before General Rafael Trujillo and his police, when defeat might have meant jail, or worse. (The game decided a

series between Paige's team, recruited on behalf of Trujillo, and one organized by the general's leading political rival, who apparently hoped to
destroy the Dominican dictator's mystique by fielding a better ball club.)
While no one had any idea of his total income from baseball, it may easily
have exceeded that of any other player to date except Babe Ruth. Being a
firm believer in the good life, however, he had not saved a great deal of it,
concentrating—like Ruth—upon living each day as it came.

Paige's skill was legendary. No less an authority than Dizzy Dean, after
losing a thirteen-inning, 1–0 decision to him in front of a team of major
leaguers in early 1934, had pronounced him the best pitcher he had ever
seen. Another witness to that game was sixteen-year-old Bill Veeck. Paige
was reputed to have struck out Rogers Hornsby five times in a single game,
and Charlie Gehringer three. In 1937 the right arm that had blazed fastballs by so many batters developed a sharp pain, and a doctor, after a brief
examination, told him that he was through. But a year or two of rest cured
him, and he had begun to fill ballparks all around the Americas again. He
had pitched games against Bob Feller as recently as the winter of 1947–48,
and Feller, whom Veeck had consulted before bringing him to Cleveland,
had given him a strong recommendation. He was a gangling six feet, three
and one-half inches tall, wore size twelve shoes, and weighed about 180
pounds. According to the best available evidence, he was exactly one day
shy of his forty-second birthday when Veeck presented him to Boudreau
for his first major league tryout.

Paige had never yet pitched in a major league game, despite all his
experience against major leaguers, for one reason and one alone: he was
black. He was not a politician or a crusader, he had made more money and
enjoyed more celebrity status than most major leaguers, and he seemed to
think of himself simply as Satchel Paige, world's greatest pitcher, rather
than as a representative of his race. As he recounted much later in his
autobiography, *Maybe I'll Pitch Forever,* he had reluctantly passed up an
offer of $500 to pitch a game for the Chattanooga Lookouts in the white
Southern Association—provided that he paint his face white. His manager
had talked him out of it, Paige wrote, but "I think I'd have looked good in
white-face. [And] nobody would have been fooled. White, black, green,
yellow, orange—it don't make any difference. Only one person can pitch
like me." Still, Paige had been devastated two years earlier when his Kansas
City Monarchs teammate, Jackie Robinson, rather than himself, had become the first black player signed by organized baseball. His performances
had done as much as anything else to encourage discussion of adding black
players to the majors, and he felt he deserved the honor. Now Veeck was

giving him a chance to prove, unequivocally, after all these years, how good he really was.[1]

Boudreau immediately agreed to catch Paige for a while, and then to bat against him. Trying to assert his authority, he suggested that the pitcher begin by jogging all the way around the ballpark to loosen up. This request violated Paige's principles. He owed his durability, as he frequently explained, to the strict observance of a set of six rules, the first of which commanded him to avoid running at all times. Like Henry IV of France, however, Paige was not about to risk his chance on a point of conscience, and he jogged about seventy-five yards before returning to announce that he was ready. Boudreau got behind the plate, and Paige threw perhaps fifty pitches, 90 percent of them for strikes. Boudreau, at this moment the second-leading hitter in baseball, picked up a bat and tried, futilely, to make a solid hit. "Don't let him get away, Will," he told Veeck. "We can use him."[2]

When Veeck announced the signing the next day, most of the press reaction reflected the enormous reputation that Paige had built up over the last twenty years. New York writer Tom Meany argued that this was a far more exciting event than the signing of then-unknown Jackie Robinson, since Paige was already a legendary figure. Cleveland writer Gordon Cobbledick suggested that the wisdom of the decision boiled down to one simple question: How much did Paige have left? In Boston, Dave Egan— a political liberal—lauded Veeck, blasted the Red Sox front office for allowing Paige to get away, and pointed out that he had called for signing the great pitcher a full year earlier. On the whole, reaction had relatively little to do with the color line; it could be compared, perhaps, to the nation's excitement in 1970, when a Supreme Court decision finally cleared the way for the undefeated Muhammad Ali to resume his career and take on undefeated Joe Frazier for the heavyweight championship. The exception, alas, was the hidebound editor of the *Sporting News,* J. G. Taylor Spink. "Veeck," he wrote in an editorial, "has gone too far in his quest for publicity."

> To bring in a "rookie" of Paige's age casts a reflection on the entire scheme of operation in the major leagues. To sign a hurler at Paige's age is to demean the standards of baseball in the big circuits. Further complicating the situa-

1. Two outstanding sources on Paige's life are Leroy (Satchel) Paige, *Maybe I'll Pitch Forever* (as told to David Lipman) (New York, 1961)—the quote is on 37—and one of the greatest articles in the history of American sportswriting, Richard Donovan, "The Fabulous Satchel Paige," in Einstein, *The Fireside Book of Baseball,* 75–95.
2. Veeck with Linn, *Veeck—as in Wreck,* 187–88.

tion is the suspicion that if Satchel were white, he would not have drawn a second thought from Veeck.[3]

Spink's reasoning, as Veeck pointed out years later, was specious: if Paige were white, he would in all probability have finished his major league career some years earlier with around 300 wins, and would now have been awaiting his election to the Hall of Fame. Only actual competition would test the truth of Spink's assertion that the signing was simply a publicity stunt. Veeck certainly did not see it that way. Stunts, he had proved, drew people to the ballpark, but a pennant would draw many more. The Indians needed more pitching, and he had taken advantage of an untapped source. With the Indians still shy of both relievers and starters, Paige was bound to get his chance pretty quickly, and he intended to make the most of it.

On the very evening of Paige's tryout, the Tigers blasted Muncrief again in a 9–0 rout. Berardino had to replace Eddie Robinson, who had wrenched his knee, at first base, and the fans booed the team heavily again. Things improved dramatically on Wednesday and Thursday, July 7 and 8, as Feller and Bearden pitched 10–2 and 14–1 complete game victories against the lowly White Sox. Dale Mitchell, now the regular leadoff man, went six for ten; Boudreau's four hits raised his average to .364; Gordon went four for nine; and Keltner hit his 20th homer in less than half a season and drove in four runs. Feller's victory raised his record to 9–9, while Bearden got his first win in almost a month, making him 7–3. Both Doby (ankle) and Robinson (knee) were out through the All-Star break the following week, but the Indians faced nothing more arduous than three games with the lowly Browns, a single night game on Friday and a Sunday doubleheader.

Lemon, coming off two straight wins against the Tigers, started on Friday evening, but promptly gave up three runs in the first, and trailed 4–1 when Boudreau pinch-hit for Lemon in the bottom of the fourth. In the top of the fifth, Satchel Paige strode in from the bullpen for his first appearance in the major leagues. Plate umpire Bill McGowan, universally acknowledged as the best arbiter in the American League, allowed photographers onto the field to take pictures of Paige's warmups.

Browns first baseman Chuck Stevens, the first batter to face Paige in a major league game, lined his second pitch sharply into right for a single. In succeeding months, Paige made such a habit of allowing the leadoff man to reach base that Veeck began to suspect him of doing it on purpose, but here it was cause for concern. A sacrifice moved Stevens to second, but Paige promptly retired the next two batters. He repeated the same pattern in the

3. Quoted in ibid., 189.

next inning, giving up a leadoff single which center fielder Judnich played into a double, but retiring the side without a run. Boudreau pinch-hit for him in the bottom of the inning with Doby, whose ankle allowed him to hit but not run, and Doby's single made the score 4–2. The Indians could manage just one more run, however, and the Browns won 5–3. Paige entertained the crowd with a variety of motions, including a dramatic hesitation pitch, but the Indians lost another game off their lead to the Athletics, who beat the Red Sox on the same evening.

Trying to wind up the first half of the season on a winning note, Boudreau went with Feller in the first game of Sunday's doubleheader and came back with Lemon, who had pitched four innings on Friday night in the nightcap. These were not only the last games before the All-Star break, but also the last games the Indians would play in Cleveland until July 27. The Tribe staked Feller to a 2–0 lead in the bottom of the first on homers by Mitchell and Hank Edwards. He did not give up a hit until the sixth, but homers in the seventh and ninth gave Cliff Fannin a 3–2 victory and dropped his record below .500 again. In the nightcap Boudreau's gamble paid off, as Lemon found form and finished his first half with a 5–0 shutout, his thirteenth win. The split gained a game on the Yankees, who lost, and kept pace with the Athletics, who split with the Red Sox, and the Indians finished the first half with a one-half-game lead.

A last controversy erupted on the same day. Boudreau had another reason for starting Feller and Lemon on short rest. Bucky Harris, the manager of the American League All-Star team, had picked both men for the squad, and both of them, having pitched nine innings on Sunday, could reasonably claim an exemption from much duty in St. Louis on Tuesday against the National League. Veeck, however, had decided to go even further in Feller's case. Believing that Feller needed a rest, he bluntly told him to skip the game. As Feller explained almost thirty years later, he hesitated to risk withdrawing, but he gave in when Veeck promised to take the blame. On Saturday, July 10, the papers had carried the story that Feller had withdrawn from the game on his own responsibility.

Based on his 1948 record—nine wins, ten losses, and a 3.57 ERA— Feller's qualifications for the game were doubtful. But he was still one of the biggest attractions in baseball, and the fans certainly expected to see him on the AL roster. Bucky Harris immediately made the most of the situation, announcing that he would never again select Feller for the squad and proposing that a penalty be levied against players who defaulted on their obligations to the fans by withdrawing from the game. This was a clever psychological ploy, since fans around the league were bound to express their agreement when Feller next pitched against them. Killing two birds with one stone, Harris also tapped Joe Dobson of the Red Sox to replace him, thereby potentially weakening another rival club.

In a new statement, Veeck belatedly took responsibility for Feller's decision and stated bluntly that Bob's main job was to win games for the Indians. But the damage was done, and Feller was bound to hear more boos, especially from the rabid, unforgiving Cleveland fans, if he could not right himself during the eastern trip after the All-Star break. More important were the views of manager Boudreau. Having proclaimed through April and May that the Indians would win the pennant, he had now amended his statement. They would win the pennant, he said, if Feller returned to form.

It was never easy for the eastern clubs to gain any ground when the schedule matched them against one another, and the Red Sox faced an especially daunting task as they arrived in Yankee Stadium for the first of three on the evening of Tuesday, June 29. Despite their brilliant 9–2 western trip, they remained 6½ games out, with a mere 31–28 record and three teams to overtake. Their pitching situation was only marginally clearer than in the first two months of the season. Dobson (9–5) and Kramer (6–3) had firmly established themselves as the aces of the staff, but McCarthy had still made no firm choices among Dave Ferriss, Denny Galehouse, Mickey Harris, Mel Parnell, and Ellis Kinder. Parnell, 2–5, had been extremely unlucky, while the rest had all mixed a few good outings with a good many bad ones. Following Yankee Stadium tradition, McCarthy opened with the left-hander Parnell. The Yankees on the other hand had at least had three solid starters—Raschi (9–1), Reynolds (8–3), and Lopat (5–5), while Shea's 3–8 record owed a great deal to poor run support, and Joe Page had generally been effective in relief.

As it turned out, the Yankees won the three-game series, as Lopat shut Boston out 7–0, beating Parnell, and the Bronx bombers won a 10–7 slugfest in the finale. The red-hot Vern Stephens won the second game for Boston with a home run and five runs batted in en route to a 7–3 victory, with Kramer ending Raschi's seven-game winning streak. The stocky shortstop, sometimes called "Shoulders," had suddenly come into his own. Known for stepping into the bucket, he was a dead pull hitter with the strength to reach the left-field seats in Yankee Stadium. Stephens had driven in 28 runs on the road trip, a third of the runs scored by the whole team, and his total of 60 RBIs trailed only Williams's 69 and Joe DiMaggio's 67.

Returning home on Friday evening, July 2, the Red Sox dropped two of three to the Athletics. Lou Brissie gave up just six hits to win the opener 4–2, and got a little revenge against Ted Williams, who went just one for four and dropped his average all the way down to .399. On Saturday the Sox went down again, 8–2, although Williams got two hits in three trips to get back to .402. The A's had now won ten out of their last eleven games, while the Red Sox had lost four out of five, dropping their record to .500 again.

Sunday's game, pitting Kinder against Scheib, once again raised the question of whether a man in his late eighties could manage a baseball team. The Red Sox finally began hitting, but the A's tied the game in the seventh inning, 5–5, on a two-run homer by shortstop Joost. The bottom of the inning began quietly with a walk to Williams and a single by Spence off reliever Charlie Harris. Harris then walked both Stephens and Doerr, forcing in the lead run, and Billy Goodman singled in two more for an 8–5 lead.

Connie Mack, having won the series already, facing a doubleheader with the Senators the next day, and still working with eight pitchers in the wake of his great purge, decided to let Harris suffer through the inning and kiss the game good-bye. He apparently wanted to make an example of Harris, who had enjoyed himself a bit too much the previous evening. Eight batters and one out later, with the score now 14–5, Mack finally had to remove Harris and bring in Bill McCahan. He did little better, and by the time Williams made the third out in his third at bat of the inning, Boston led 19–5. Still, the Red Sox had dropped a full eight games behind the Indians, while Philadelphia had closed to just 1½ out, tied with the Yanks, who had matched them with two wins in three games against the Senators before heading to Boston for a July 5 doubleheader. Joe DiMaggio now trailed Williams in RBIs, 72 to 69. He had done a phenomenal job of making his hits count—69 RBIs on just 79 hits, compared to 72 on 93 for Williams. Despite their fine hitting and pitching, the Yanks seemed unable either to sweep a series or climb all the way into first place.

STANDINGS
Monday, July 5, 1948

Team	Won	Lost	Pct.	Games Behind
Cleveland	41	24	.631	—
New York	41	27	.603	1½
Philadelphia	42	28	.600	1½
Boston	33	32	.508	8
Detroit	32	36	.471	10½
Washington	31	37	.456	11½
St. Louis	25	40	.385	16
Chicago	21	43	.328	19½

The country celebrated the Fourth of July with an extra day off on Monday, the fifth, and the Yankees returned to Fenway Park leading the season series, 5–4. Needing another winning streak to get back in the race, the Red Sox got going with three tough, exciting wins over the New Yorkers on Monday and Tuesday. In the second game of Monday's doubleheader, Galehouse—who had saved the opener, 7–4, in the ninth—came in again in the ninth with the game tied 7–7 thanks to a homer by Doerr. After Galehouse retired the Yankees, Matt Batts opened the bottom with a single. After fouling off two bunts, Galehouse bravely succeeded with two strikes. Racing for first in an attempt to give his team three chances to win the game instead of two, he hit the base awkwardly, fell, separated his left shoulder, and missed the next three weeks of the season. But his daring paid off, as Dom DiMaggio singled Batts home for an 8–7 victory and a sweep. Galehouse, who had a win and a save on the day, had enjoyed pitching against the Yankees since coming into the league and had won many big games against them, including a shutout for the Browns in the final week of the season in 1944 that had helped to clinch the pennant. In the series finale, the Red Sox scratched out two runs and Dobson won his tenth victory, 2–1. The series sweep moved the Red Sox within two games of the Yankees in the loss column, but they were still seven games behind the surging Indians—*and* the Athletics, who had taken two out of three from the Senators while Boston swept New York, and moved into second place.

Philadelphia remained in second after splitting Wednesday and Thursday games with the Yankees. The Yankees concluded the first half of the season with two wins in three games in Washington, leaving them in third place, 3½ games behind the Indians. More disturbing was the condition of Joe DiMaggio, who missed the last two games of the series. Officially he had a sore right heel; actually it was clear that his right heel had a bone spur which would eventually require surgery, just as his left heel had in 1947. DiMaggio hit and ran with a very upright posture, which some later speculated had put tremendous pressure on his back and his heels throughout his career. DiMaggio's two days off, in the midst of the pennant race, gave Bucky Harris a reasonable pretext for removing him from the starting All-Star lineup in St. Louis on Tuesday, July 13. Another great star would also miss the game—and therein lay an extraordinary tale.

During the Red Sox' last week, their pitching did not allow them to sustain the momentum they had built up in their three-game sweep of the Yankees. Homers by Doerr and Stephens gave Dave Ferriss a 6–2 lead over Washington before a packed Fenway Park on Wednesday evening, July 7, but the fans suffered through a five-run ninth in which Ferriss, Parnell, and Joe Dobson all failed to hold the lead and lost the game. Parnell, his luck finally changing, emerged with his fourth win the next night, 4–1. Williams, who had five hits in the two games, now had an average of .394. His

Ted Williams, the 1946 MVP and 1947 Triple Crown winner, with new teammate Vern Stephens, acquired by the Red Sox from the St. Louis Browns before the 1948 season. (Sporting News/Archive Photos)

Former Yankee manager Joe McCarthy, who took over the Red Sox in late 1947, looks on as his star player, Ted Williams, takes batting practice during spring training. (UPI/ Corbis-Bettmann)

Although overshadowed by his older brother, the Red Sox' Dom DiMaggio was the superior center fielder of the two, by far the best in the American League. (Sporting News/Archive Photos)

The three aces of the 1948 Red Sox staff: Mel Parnell, Joe Dobson, and Jack Kramer. (*Boston Herald*)

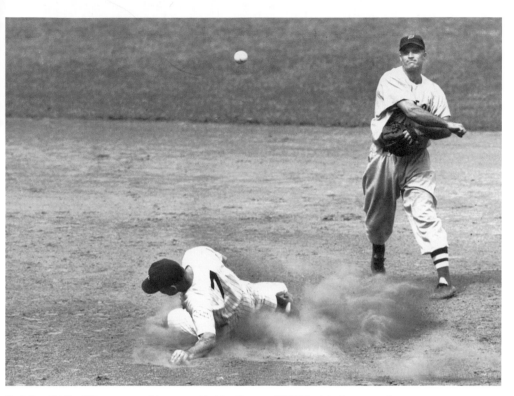

Red Sox Hall of Fame second baseman Bobby Doerr. (UPI/Corbis-Bettmann)

Vern "Junior" Stephens—an outstanding defensive shortstop as well as a slugger—crosses the bag to complete a double play. (UPI/Corbis-Bettmann)

Manager Bucky Harris (*center*) of the world champion New York Yankees with two newly acquired pitchers, Ed Lopat (*left*) and Red Embree (*right*), in spring training, 1948. (Sporting News/Archive Photos)

Joe DiMaggio, the Yankee Clipper, connecting in Fenway Park, his favorite visitors' venue. (American Stock/Archive Photos)

Ohio native Tommy Henrich was an even tougher hitter for ace Cleveland pitcher Bob Feller than Joe DiMaggio. (Sporting News/Archive Photos)

Brilliant, fun-loving, erratic Yankee reliever Joe Page, one of the heroes of the 1947 World Series. (Sporting News/Archive Photos)

Youthful catcher Yogi Berra had a difficult year behind the plate until August 1948. (Sporting News/Archive Photos)

Three of the most influential owners in American League history: Clark Griffith of the Washington Senators, Connie Mack of the Philadelphia Athletics, and young Bill Veeck of the Cleveland Indians. (Cleveland State Library)

Two canny businessmen, Bob Feller (*left*) and Bill Veeck, celebrate the "extortion" of Feller's big 1948 contract. (Cleveland State Library)

Shortstop-manager Lou Boudreau doing what owner Bill Veeck thought he did best.
(Cleveland State Library)

Perhaps the greatest infield of all time: third baseman Ken Keltner, shortstop Lou Boudreau, second baseman Joe Gordon, and first baseman Eddie Robinson, who together drove in 432 runs in 1948. (Cleveland State Library)

Both Satchel Paige, the old master, and Larry Doby, the youngster who first integrated the American League, played critical roles in the 1948 pennant race. (Sporting News/Archive Photos)

72 RBIs and 65 runs scored both led the league, and his 16 homers trailed only Keltner and Joe DiMaggio. The Boston press had unanimously lauded his play, although Dave Egan could not resist pointing out that he had driven in just three runs in the eight-game home stand, and accused him of the obscure sin of "protecting his batting average." He had played every inning of every game. But by the time the Red Sox reached Philadelphia on July 9 for their last four games before the All-Star game, Williams had suffered, without even knowing it, a serious injury.

During the six-hour train ride from Boston to Philadelphia that day, Williams was standing in the middle of a coach when Sam Mele came down the aisle. A rabid boxing fan, the Splendid Splinter often blew off steam by sparring playfully with teammates in the manner of Sugar Ray Robinson or Joe Louis. "Where do you think you're going, Mele?" said the grinning, gangling Williams, blocking the path like Little John. Mele smiled, squared off, and the two outfielders began exchanging light punches. One hit Williams under the ribs, and as he recalled twenty years later, it felt "funny."[4]

That night, the Red Sox took a 4–0 lead into the bottom of the seventh behind Kinder (3–4), only to watch Kinder and Johnson surrender six runs. Boston went ahead again with three runs in the top of the eighth, and Joe Dobson, making his fourth appearance in three days, took a 7–6 lead into the bottom of the ninth but lost 8–7, the second game in three outings that Boston had let slip in the very last inning. Stephens, with a 4–4 night, raised his average to .314 with 70 RBIs, but Williams went 0–4 and complained of a sore rib cage. That night, he could hardly draw a breath. Mele's punch had damaged a ligament.

Like most good managers, Joe McCarthy had a well-developed sense of the difference between unavoidable misfortune, which must be accepted, and avoidable misfortune, which it was the duty of his players to prevent. He was furious. Had he known that Williams was going to miss thirteen games, he would have been more so. It was surely not a coincidence, moreover, that Wally Moses, not Sam Mele, replaced Williams in left field and in the third spot in the order the next day.

The Sox did not miss Williams on Saturday, July 10, as homers by Stephens (his 17th) and Doerr (his 15th) gave Kramer his seventh straight victory. In the wild opener of Sunday's doubleheader, Boston blew an 8–6 lead in the bottom of the ninth yet again, but won in the tenth, 9–8, on Dom DiMaggio's two-out single. In the nightcap, the Sox fell behind 6–1 as the Athletics bombed Mickey Harris, started a comeback with a three-

4. Williams with Underwood, *My Turn at Bat*, 163–64.

run homer by the torrid Pesky, but lost 6–5 when blue laws forced the Athletics to stop the game at six o'clock on Sunday, before the completion of the eighth inning.

As usual, the three eastern leaders had fought each other to a virtual standstill. The Athletics emerged from the two-week struggle with an 8–6 record, while the Yankees went 7–7 and the Red Sox 8–7. Both Philadelphia and New York finished the first half of the season four games behind Cleveland in the loss column. The Red Sox had a full seven games to make up. And because of rain-outs at home, Boston would begin the second half with sixteen games in eleven days against the western clubs, culminating in three with Cleveland.

STANDINGS
Monday, July 12, 1948

Team	Won	Lost	Pct.	Games Behind
Cleveland	45	28	.616	—
Philadelphia	48	32	.600	½
New York	44	32	.579	2½
Boston	39	35	.527	6½
Detroit	39	37	.513	7½
Washington	34	42	.447	12½
St. Louis	28	45	.384	17
Chicago	23	49	.319	21½

The true measure of a ball club over a full season is its ability to score and prevent runs. To paraphrase Napoleon, the gods of baseball favor the big battalions—and the big battalions are the teams that can regularly and decisively outscore their opponents. In addition—despite Connie Mack's famous, utterly illogical dictum that pitching is 75 percent of the game— clubs can much more easily outscore their opponents by assembling a superior offense than a superior defense. One can demonstrate in many ways that hitting skill varies more than pitching skill, and we shall eventually see that the vast majority of the most valuable players of the 1948 season were hitters, not pitchers. In 1948, as in most of the years of the late 1940s, the variance among teams' runs scored was greater than the variance in their runs allowed, when park effects are taken into account.

A great team, in short, is nearly always built around a core of great hitters, capable of creating runs well in excess of the average, and a pitching staff perhaps *slightly* superior to the average. What confuses the issue, in 1948 and in almost every baseball era, is the relatively greater success of teams that play in pitchers' parks, such as the Oakland Athletics of the early 1970s, the New York Mets of the late 1980s, the Los Angeles Dodgers in several eras, the Cleveland Indians of the late 1940s and early 1950s, the Baltimore Orioles of the 1970s, and above all, the Yankees. The reason these teams always seem to have outstanding pitching staffs is that their parks reduce run production, making an average pitcher look like a good one. On the other hand, their hitting—which generally looks good, but not great—is truly great, despite statistics that appear only slightly above average. Teams like the Yankees or the Oakland A's rarely lead their league in runs scored overall, but frequently lead it in runs scored on the road. In every year that the Yankees have fought for the pennant with the Red Sox— 1948, 1949, 1950, 1977, and 1978—the New Yorkers have outscored the Red Sox on the road, often by a substantial margin.

To improve their record, moreover, teams need to improve their run production significantly. The Pythagorean formula—which as we have seen predicts a team's winning percentage with the equation ($Runs^2/(Runs^2 + RunsAllowed^2) = PCT$)—confirms this. The 1948 Red Sox, with 907 runs scored and 720 runs allowed, had a Pythagorean percentage of .613, very close to their actual winning percentage. A win in a 154-game season was worth .0065 percentage points, so that to win four more games they would have had to reach a percentage of .639. The Pythagorean formula shows that to have done this, they would have needed to score fifty additional runs—more than ten runs for each additional victory. Because of the workings of the laws of probability which the Pythagorean formula expresses, it also requires more and more runs to improve as a team gets better. To the Detroit Tigers, roughly a .500 team in 1948, fifty runs would have been worth five or six additional victories, but to the .613 Red Sox they would have been worth only four victories.

Because twenty-seven outs are not enough consistently to manifest hitting superiority, however, superior teams will play a certain percentage of close games. Often such games occur because bad weather, poor visibility, or a ballpark like Griffith Stadium in Washington make it very difficult for *anyone* to score more than two to three runs in nine innings. When this happens, the outcome of a ball game becomes much more doubtful. On the average, therefore, a superior team is much *less* likely to prevail in a one-run game than in a game decided by a substantial margin of superiority. It is not very common for a team to win a pennant by winning a large percentage of their one-run games, although two very famous teams—the 1951 miracle New York Giants, and the 1969 Mets—have done so. More often, a fluke run of one-run games can vault a mediocre team into contention, or keep a superior one out of first place for much of the season.

The records of the four contenders at the All-Star break generally reflected their ability level, with one major exception. On the Saturday before the All-Star game the Indians and the Yankees had the most impressive offensive record in the league. The Yankees led the league with 387 runs scored and the Indians were just behind with 386, but the Indians had played four fewer games. They also led the league in batting average, the Indians hitting .275 and the Yankees .272, and in home runs, with 77 each. These were extraordinary achievements, since the two teams played in parks that decreased run production by 6 to 12 percent. Both teams had scored more runs on the road than at home. Neither team, however, had won as many ball games as they should have. The Indians at the All-Star break had scored 400 runs and given up only 273, for a Pythagorean percentage of .682. Their actual percentage of .616 was about five games worse than this, and their 2–7 record in one-run games exactly accounted for the difference. This was in turn related to their poor hitting in Municipal Stadium, where five of the one-run losses had taken place. They had scored more than one-half a run per game less in Municipal Stadium, where their averages were much lower and they depended almost entirely on the home run, than on the road. In addition, Bob Feller had pitched three of the one-run losses, in part because he was allowing home runs at a prodigious rate, and because Boudreau had left him in a number of games until he lost a lead. As Boudreau himself had remarked, Feller had to pitch better for the Indians to win the pennant.

The Yankees' record was also somewhat inferior to what it statistically should have been. With 394 runs scored and just 281 runs allowed, the Pythagorean formula would have predicted a winning percentage of .663. Their actual percentage was only .584—a difference, at this point in the season, of about six wins. The reason, once again, lay largely in their 11–10 record in one-run games. Their pattern, however, was exactly opposite to the Indians'. The Tribe had been losing one-run games at home; the Yankees had been losing them on the road. They had a 20–19 record on the road and a 24–13 mark at home, largely because of one-run games. At home the Yankees had a 9–3 record in one-run games; on the road, their record was 2–7.

The problem lay in the Yankees' pitching, and in the problems of one pitcher in particular. Yankee Stadium was a good pitchers' park for two reasons: it had poor visibility and fairly spacious foul territory for its time, lowering batting averages, and its huge power alleys made it difficult to hit a home run unless one could pull the ball sharply. Any reasonably good pitcher could do well there, but Yankee pitchers inevitably faced more trouble on the road. The most homebound pitcher on the staff was left-handed relief ace Joe Page, whose record of 2–4 included two home wins and three road losses—all of them by one run—against the Athletics, White Sox, and Red Sox. Page was the Achilles' heel of the Yankee staff so far, and his weakness inevitably cost the Yankees ball games because he was used as the relief ace. Bucky Harris's relatively lenient style may have contributed to the problem. Page did not spend evenings in his hotel room reading on the road, perhaps contributing to his failures in road games.

While the Yankee offense was one of the most effective in the league, the lineup showed room for improvement. DiMaggio led the regulars with an even .300 average on the last weekend before the All-Star break, with Lindell close behind at .295 and 12 homers, Billy Johnson at .279, and Stirnweiss, Berra, and McQuinn bunched around .270. Henrich, however, was stuck at .246 with 9 homers, and Rizzuto had dropped out of the Sunday averages with a mark of less than .224. The most interesting problem for Bucky Harris was Bobby Brown, the team's leading hitter at .327 and one of its most productive offensive players. Brown was obviously a better hitter than Stirnweiss or Phil Rizzuto, and he was slightly superior offensively to Bill Johnson. But Brown had a bad defensive reputation—a reputation which his statistics do seem to justify. In addition, Stirnweiss and Rizzuto were both established veterans, and Rizzuto in particular had been a darling of the New York fans for eight years. Harris stayed with them despite their poor hitting.

Meanwhile, the Athletics, 48–32 at the break, had managed to stay in second place in exactly the opposite way. Their 385 runs scored and 354 runs allowed should theoretically have given them a percentage of .545, but their actual percentage was .600 because they had an 18–9 record in one-run games, accounting for almost 40 percent of their victories. They had won two one-run decisions against the Indians, three against the Yanks, three against the Red Sox, two against the Senators, three against the White Sox, and four against the lowly Browns. Not only had they scored just enough runs to win, but they had done so against the worst teams in baseball. Philadelphia had a combined 26–8 record against the Senators, the Browns, and the White Sox. The Indians had a 20–9 record against those teams, the Yankees 24–10, and the Red Sox just 15–13.

Seven games behind in the loss column, with three clubs ahead of them and Ted Williams injured, the Red Sox had a very long row to hoe as the first half of the season came to a close. Their runs scored (398) and runs allowed (339) totals were marginally better than those of the Athletics, but their Pythagorean percentage of .580 was well behind that of the Yankees and the Indians. Because of their disastrous string of close losses in April and May, their actual record still trailed their projected record by about four games. They would in any case have to improve their overall record, scoring more runs and allowing fewer of them, to challenge the Indians and the Yankees. Some evidence suggested that they might indeed do this. After a slow start, Junior Stephens had enjoyed an incredible six weeks in June and early July, finishing the first half with 17 homers, 74 runs batted in, and a .300 average. Johnny Pesky and Dom DiMaggio, at .273 and .266, had improved, and could be expected to get much closer to their lifetime averages. Bobby Doerr might also do somewhat better. New first baseman Billy Goodman had gotten his average all the way to .313, although he had yet to hit a homer. Stan Spence, at .206, certainly could improve. The pitching also showed signs of stabilizing, with Jack Kramer, Joe Dobson, and Mel Parnell pretty well established as the mainstays of the staff, but Denny Galehouse was hurt and Mickey Harris and Boo Ferriss had failed repeatedly. And with sixteen games scheduled in the first eleven days after the break, the pitching staff had no more time left in which to recover.

The American League won the All-Star game, 5–2, even though the injured Williams—whose home runs had already won two games for the AL in 1941 and 1946—and Joe DiMaggio each made only a token appearance. Boudreau, DiMaggio (pinch-hitting), and Vic Raschi drove in the runs, while Stan Musial homered for the NL. In retrospect, however, Williams made the most memorable observation. "The guy on your team who impressed me most, Blackie," Williams said to Cincinnati pitcher Ewell Blackwell, "is that kid Bobby Thomson of the Giants. I realize he struck out but he looked to me like a real good hitter. He stands up there nicely and takes a good cut. He's gonna be a terrific ball player some day."

"That's mighty high praise because no one studies hitters more intently than Thumping Theodore," wrote columnist Arthur Daley of the *New York Times*. Three years later, Thomson proved Williams right with the most dramatic swing of the bat in baseball history.

6

The Streak

(JULY 15–JULY 26)

STANDINGS
Thursday, July 15, 1948

Team	Won	Lost	Pct.	Games Behind
Cleveland	45	28	.616	—
Philadelphia	48	32	.600	½
New York	44	32	.597	2½
Boston	39	35	.527	6½
Detroit	39	37	.513	7½
Washington	34	42	.447	12½
St. Louis	28	45	.384	17
Chicago	23	49	.319	21½

The baseball schedules for 1948 had been drawn up by a Boston attorney, Clement Schwerner. Mr. Schwerner, who did not lack a sense of drama, had taken the predictions of the press to heart and matched the Red Sox and the Yankees on the last two weekends of the season. Meanwhile, his schedule for the month following the All-Star break could not have been better designed to put pressure on the Indians in their quest for their first pennant in twenty-eight years. The second half began with the eastern clubs entertaining the western, and because of rain-outs on earlier trips, the Indians had four games each with the Athletics, Senators, and Yankees, and three with the Red Sox. Immediately thereafter, the western clubs would return home to entertain the East, and Cleveland would play twelve games, including four each against the Red Sox and the Yankees. All told, the Indians were scheduled for twenty-seven games in twenty-five days, most of them against other contenders.

For Lou Boudreau, opening on July 15 with a doubleheader in Philadelphia, the schedule meant more starts for Steve Gromek, who had started only once during the first half; new acquisition Sam Zoldak, Veeck's "$100,000 pitcher"; and, possibly, Satchel Paige. The Indians also desperately needed Bob Feller to return to form. Gromek teamed with ace Bob Lemon for the doubleheader. Boudreau also announced that Mitchell and Doby would play regularly in left and center, while Hank Edwards and Allie Clark platooned in right.

A crowd of 35,199, huge by Philadelphia standards, saw the Indians' hitters get off to a good start in the first game of the doubleheader as Gromek coasted to a 6–1 win. In the second game, Bob Lemon had to leave the game leading 4–3 after Pete Suder's relay throw hit him in the head. Boudreau brought in Paige to protect the one-run lead against the second-place club. He gave up a game-tying homer to Majeski, but eventually emerged with his first major league win, 7–5, with the help of a solo homer by Keltner—number 25—and a two-run shot by Doby. The sweep gave Cleveland a 2½ game lead.

Bob Feller took the mound the next night against Lou Brissie to thunderous boos. Taking Bucky Harris's criticisms to heart, the Philadelphia crowd hung banners from the upper deck reading "Back to the Farm" and "Feller the Quitter." Feller failed to make it through the bottom of the first as five hits, a walk, an error by Gordon, and a sacrifice fly gave the Athletics five quick runs, and Bob Muncrief took over as the fans booed again. Lou Brissie served up Keltner's 22nd homer, a three-run shot, but coasted to a 9–4 win. The next day, Saturday, the Athletics squared the series and moved back to within one-half game when Joe Coleman shut the Indians out 5–0 on just six hits, beating Zoldak.

As the Tribe moved on to Washington for four games in the next three days, Boudreau announced that Feller would start the second game of Sunday's doubleheader in place of Paige, whom he had tentatively penciled in to make his first start. "It is fresh, green dollars to stale, moldy doughnuts," the acerbic Dave Egan wrote in Boston, "that old Clark Griffith, who hires Venezuelans and Cubans but can't quite bring himself to hiring American Negroes, wanted Lou Boudreau to start Satchel Paige yesterday in Washington for the sake of added gate receipts."[1] Egan was right, and Griffith repeated his request on the Indians' last visit to Washington.

1. *Boston Daily Record,* July 19.

Washington's Griffith Stadium was the toughest park in the league for the Indians to play in. Its left-field fence—an incredible 405 feet away down the foul line—took away most of their right-handed power, and they never seemed to get out of Washington without a real battle. Bearden had to pitch brilliantly in Sunday's first game, giving up just seven hits in eight innings en route to a 2–1 win. The second game gave the 28,631 fans in attendance their money's worth. Although Feller pitched fairly well, he gave way to Christopher in the seventh trailing 3–2. The Indians took a 4–3 lead in the top of the eighth, but Eddie Yost doubled off the left-field wall in the bottom of the ninth and scored with two out to tie the game. The teams battled until the twelfth, when a triple by Dale Mitchell started a two-run Indians rally and Zoldak, in relief, got the win.

Monday evening's game was even better. With Lemon on the mound, the game began well for the Tribe when Gordon hit a three-run homer in the first, his 18th, giving him 75 runs batted in. But Lemon and Ed Klieman gave up five runs in the third, and the Tribe trailed 6–3 in the top of the sixth. A three-run triple by Jim Hegan tied the game 6–6, but Hegan was called out by rookie plate umpire Joe Paparella trying to score on Joe Tipton's fly for the last out of the inning. Russ Christopher and Satchel Paige held the Senators scoreless in the sixth, seventh, eight, and ninth, but the Indians could not take the lead. Paige gave up a bloop double to Bud Stewart to open the bottom of the tenth, and after Mark Christman was passed intentionally, Boudreau brought in Zoldak to pitch to left-handed Mickey Vernon. Vernon flied deep to right, where Allie Clark could not prevent Stewart from advancing to third with one out.

Boudreau now sent in Gromek to pitch to the right-handed Buddy Kosar, and replaced Judnich with Doby in center and Clark with Bob Kennedy in right. Kennedy had one of the strongest arms in the league, and despite the low probability of a fly ball to right, Boudreau was looking for the best possible chance of saving the game. Kosar obliged with a long fly to right center. Kennedy raced back and to his right, actually outrunning the ball, and caught it moving *toward* the infield. As Stewart took off from third with the run that would win the game, Kennedy cut loose for the plate. The throw was perfect, and Hegan tagged out Stewart for the third out, ending the inning.

The top of the eleventh began with Gromek grounding to short, but Mitchell, who had 31 hits in his last 76 at bats (.408), got his fourth hit of the day. Doby, back in the lineup, forced Mitchell at second, but beat the relay, sprained ankle and all, and stole second. Kennedy, continuing his heroics, singled him home for the lead run. With one out and one on in the bottom of the eleventh, Yost doubled down the right-field line, but a quick pickup by Kennedy held the runner at third and preserved the Indians' 7–6 lead. Bearden, the sixth Indian pitcher—and third from the starting rotation—replaced Gromek, and purposely passed right-handed pinch hitter Tom McBride. Weak-hitting Carden Gillenwater flied to short left where Mitchell made the catch and fired to the plate as Earl Wooten tried to score. For the second inning in a row, umpire Joe Paparella called a Senator runner out to end the inning—and, this time, the game. Boudreau had used nineteen players, but not even his severest critic could claim, this time, that he had made too many moves.

Don Black, virtually the only Tribe hurler not to have worked during the first three games, lost a 2–1 finale on Tuesday to Ray Scarborough, who had beaten Lemon 2–1 in early June. Winning three out of four, the Indians headed for New York with a very tired pitching staff. Lemon, Paige, and Zoldak had all pitched in two of the four games, while Christopher, Bearden, and Klieman had each appeared in three.

The Indians needed their three wins out of four to stay one full game ahead of the Athletics, who had resumed their domination of the weaker western clubs with three wins out of five over the White Sox in a pair of doubleheaders on Sunday and Monday and a single game Tuesday. Their loss in the very first game of the series occurred when Chicago's Pat Seerey, the big, slugging outfielder whom the Indians had traded for Bob Kennedy, turned in the rarest hitting feat in baseball, hitting four home runs in eleven innings for a 12–11 win. To this day, only nine players since 1900 have homered four times in one game, four of whom—Chuck Klein, Seerey, Mike Schmidt, and Bob Horner—accomplished the feat in extra innings.[2] Asked to comment, Bill Veeck expressed his sorrow at letting Seerey go, and predicted that he might become an all-time great. In the era of the DH he certainly might have, but he was destined for a short career. Bob Kennedy, of course, made the trade look somewhat better with his heroics on Monday evening.

Another big story broke on Tuesday. The American League office in Chicago announced the suspension of Bill McGowan, the most respected umpire in the league.

Umpiring, as well as stars like Feller, DiMaggio, and Williams, probably had something to do with the superior popularity of the American League. The junior circuit's twelve umpires followed the tradition of league founder Ban Johnson and controlled play with an iron hand. Thanks to men like Bill Summers, Cal Hubbard, and Red Jones, serious rhubarbs were far less common than in the National League, where only a few of the arbiters had

---

2. The others were Lou Gehrig, Gil Hodges, Joe Adcock, Rocky Colavito, and Willie Mays.

the courage to control Leo Durocher. McGowan had been umpiring in the American League since 1925, when Clark Griffith of the Senators had discovered him in spring training and persuaded the new American League president, Will Harridge, to jump him all the way from the middle minors to the AL. McGowan, alas, was the kind of eccentric, towering personality who would never reach the major leagues today. He was both a diabetic and a compulsive gambler—on horses, not baseball—but on the field he dominated the proceedings from start to finish and enjoyed the complete trust of players and managers. He had established his authority by refusing to take anything from anyone, and therefore almost never had a serious argument. He was also technically superb, especially behind the plate calling balls and strikes. The esteem McGowan enjoyed, as well as the arbiter's prickly personality, is reflected in comments by a much younger fellow umpire, Joe Rue, many years after McGowan's death.

> I got off on the wrong foot with Bill McGowan. After the first game I worked with him in Detroit he said, "You haven't asked me for any advice, Joe. I guess you're one of those kind who knows it all. You call your balls and strikes like some punk from the Eastern League." I said, "Bill, I want to tell you something. I've been umpiring for a good many years. I was purchased by this league for more money than you ever knew existed. I've been calling balls and strikes the same way wherever I've been, and I'm pretty goddamn good. You're supposed to be the ace of umpires; but to me you're a pain in the ass, and if I ever ask you anything, it will be over my dead body." But I have to say this: McGowan was the best umpire in the league.[3]

After the third game of the Cleveland-Washington series, in which McGowan was the crew chief, Senator manager Joe Kuhel officially protested that after Kennedy had thrown out Ed Stewart at the plate in the bottom of the tenth, McGowan had thrown a baseball at Stewart when he began arguing with plate umpire Joe Paparella. On Thursday night, McGowan had thrown his ball-and-strike indicator at pitcher Ray Scarborough after Scarborough had shaken his head at some of the arbiter's calls.

American League president Harridge aroused the most conflicting feelings among the umpires who worked for him. Joe Paparella regarded him almost as a father, while Ernie Stewart, whom Harridge had fired in 1945, felt that he was not up to his job. "Mr. Harridge," he said many years later, "was not a joy to the umpires."

> He was not stern enough with the ballplayers; he did not know baseball; he didn't even attend games. He'd come to the office as secretary to Mr. Ban

3. Gerlach, *The Men in Blue,* 71. For other comments on McGowan, see 101–3.

Johnson, and when Mr. Johnson died suddenly, then Mr. Mack fronted for Mr. Harridge and got him (he called him his "boy") to be president of the American League. Mr. Harridge was an old lady; he was not a pleasure to work for. He didn't back you strongly enough, he was critical of you, and he listened to stories.[4]

Eighteen months earlier, Harridge had fired Stewart—widely regarded as the best young umpire in the league—after Stewart, following the suggestion of baseball commissioner Happy Chandler, had written his fellow umpires to ask for suggestions on improving their working conditions.[5] Now Harridge responded to Kuhel's protest by suspending McGowan. Subsequent events proved, however, that McGowan had not lost his stature as the league's leading umpire.

In New York, the Indians' next stop, the Yanks had been knocked out of the headlines during the All-Star break by one of the biggest stories in the history of New York sports: the move of Leo Durocher, for nine years the manager and symbol of the Dodgers, to their hated rivals the Giants. Like Boudreau, Yankee manager Bucky Harris had to worry about his pitching. His aces, Allie Reynolds and Vic Raschi, had each won ten games, but both had shown signs of fading in early July. Ed Lopat had done well, but Frank Shea and Joe Page had been erratic, and young Tommy Byrne, a wild but often overpowering lefty, had lost three in a row before the break.

Opening the second half in third place, three full games behind the Indians, the Yankees had taken two of three from the Browns on Thursday and Friday, winning 4–2 in the opener of their Thursday doubleheader behind Frank Hiller and 4–0 on Friday behind Lopat. They lost the nightcap on Thursday when Browns third baseman Bob Dillinger went four for six with a triple and five RBIs, and ace Cliff Fannin held on for a 10–4 victory against Allie Reynolds. New York slipped a little further off the pace against the Tigers. In a packed Sunday doubleheader, Hal Newhouser beat Raschi in the opener, 5–3, but the Yankees won an abbreviated nightcap behind Tommy Byrne, 12–4. Monday's game was washed out, and the Yanks dropped a heartbreaker on Tuesday. Reynolds gave up just four hits during the first eight innings, but with the score 1–1 in the ninth, Snuffy Stirnweiss dropped a pop fly from George Kell, and Hoot Evers got his second game-winning hit of the series, a single. Joe D went 0–4, making him 1–20 in his last six games. The Yankees, with three wins and three losses since the break, trailed the Indians by 3½ as they entertained them for a doubleheader on Wednesday afternoon, July 21, before 67,133.

4. Ibid., 110; for Paparella's comment, see 144.
5. Ibid., 123–27.

Behind Muncrief, the Indians took a 3–1 lead off Ed Lopat as Boudreau drove in all the runs with a homer and a sacrifice fly, but Joe DiMaggio tied the game with his 20th home run in the bottom of the third. Then the Yankees pulled away, as Bill Johnson, Phil Rizzuto, and Cliff Mapes also homered to make the final 7–3. It was Muncrief's third straight loss, and Boudreau dropped him from the rotation. Steve Gromek faced Frank Hiller in a wild nightcap. Doby reached base and scored in the first inning for the second straight game, but Henrich tied the game with his 10th homer in the bottom of the inning. The teams traded runs again in the third, and Dale Mitchell drove in two with a double in the fourth for a 4–2 lead, driving out Hiller and bringing in Joe Page. New York retaliated again in the bottom of the fourth, as a two-run double by Henrich, an error by Gordon, and a single by DiMaggio gave the Yankees four runs and a 6–4 lead. McQuinn's 10th homer helped bring the score to 8–4 in the fifth. Facing the Yanks for the first time, Satchel Paige enthralled the crowd, setting down Henrich, Berra, and DiMaggio in order in the bottom of the sixth. And in the top of the seventh, five Indian hits earned them three runs and closed the gap to 8–7.

Bearden and Christopher struggled through the seventh, and the top of the eighth inning began with Clark's single to left. Boudreau sacrificed, Gordon walked, and Keltner singled in the tying run. Boudreau sent Berardino up to hit for Robinson, who never hit Joe Page well, and Harris countered by bringing in Karl Drews. Boudreau, countering again, sent up Judnich to hit for Berardino and Walt walked to load the bases. Then catcher Jim Hegan broke up the game with a grand-slam home run to left field. The Yankees got two men on base in both the eighth and ninth but did not score, and Russ Christopher got the 11–7 win. Once again Boudreau's moves had worked like magic, and the Tribe had salvaged a split.

Feller faced Raschi in the rubber game on Thursday evening, June 22, having lost three of four previous starts against the Yankees and failed twice since the break. Charlie Keller returned to the Yankee lineup in left for the first time since June 1, and 68,258 patrons greeted Feller with a torrent of boos when he took the mound. With Boudreau scoring one run and driving in another, Feller took a 2–0 lead into the bottom of the second, but Henrich's two-run homer promptly tied the game. The torrid Mitchell answered that with a homer in the top of the fourth, but in the bottom of the inning, two walks helped load the bases, and the incomparable DiMaggio hit a grand slam into the left-field seats for a 6–3 lead. Joe D now had four homers and a triple in Feller's four starts against the Yankees. Breaking out of his slump with 8 RBIs in three games against the first-place Tribe, the Yankee Clipper regained the league lead with 82.

The Indians were far from dead. Boudreau opened the bottom of the sixth with a single, and two hits by Keltner and Hegan, an error and a passed ball brought the Tribe to 6–5 against Byrne. Paige replaced Feller in the sixth and captivated the huge crowd by holding the Yanks for two innings without a run, striking out DiMaggio. But the Indians wasted a Boudreau triple in the top of the seventh and stranded runners in the eighth and ninth, and Byrne finished with a 6–5 win that gave the Yanks a 2–1 edge in the series. In the locker room, Boudreau asked Feller if he would like to take some time away from the club. Feller, now 9–12, declined.

Losing two out of three, the Indians stayed just one-half game ahead of Philadelphia, which split two games with the Browns. Cleveland now headed for Boston for the last three games of their road trip. Twenty-four members of the roster took the train; the twenty-fifth, Satchel Paige, who generally moved according to his own clock, failed to make the station, and flew up instead, incurring his first major league fine at the hands of Boudreau. The Indians' pitching staff had turned in only one complete game during the eleven-game road trip. And in Boston, the Tribe encountered the hottest team in baseball—a club that had suddenly found itself, despite the absence through injury of its greatest star.

The Red Sox' home stand against the western clubs featured no less than sixteen games in the eleven days following the midseason break—four each with the Tigers and Browns, five with the White Sox, and three with the Indians. They had to play five doubleheaders, including two day-night doubleheaders, an innovation pioneered by Branch Rickey in Brooklyn and adopted, to the disgust of Dave Egan, by Tom Yawkey and Joe Cronin to wring the maximum possible cash benefits out of the postwar attendance boom. Ted Williams, meanwhile, was still nursing his sore side. Joe McCarthy penciled in Kramer, Parnell, Dobson, and Kinder for the series against the Tigers, but after that he would not be able to avoid some reliance on second-line pitchers. As Dave Egan had pointed out over the All-Star break, the Red Sox—still seven games behind—could not afford as much as one really bad week if they hoped to make a real run for the pennant.

The Sox got off to a fine start against Fred Hutchinson of the Tigers on the afternoon of July 15, rapping out twelve hits for a 13–5 victory behind Jack Kramer. In the night game, Mel Parnell turned in one of the pitching gems of the season, beating Dizzy Trout 3–1 in just one hour and twenty-two minutes. Parnell yielded six hits, walked none, and had a two-run double in the third. Stan Spence had three hits and three runs on the day in the third spot, where he had replaced Williams. Despite the sweep, the

Sox still trailed the Indians, who swept the Athletics on the same day, by seven games.

MEL PARNELL: I was always a fast worker. I figured that if I worked quickly, my defense would have an easier time staying on their toes. And I always enjoyed working against a fast worker like Dizzy Trout.

Joe Dobson got off to a rocky start against young Art Houtteman the next afternoon, and the Red Sox went into the bottom of the sixth trailing 3–1. After Pesky doubled to left to open the inning and Spence walked, McCarthy ordered Stephens to sacrifice. The ploy worked when Doerr singled to tie the game, 3–3. Boston tallied one more in the seventh on a Dom DiMaggio double, and another in the eighth when Stephens hit his 18th homer to left center. Dobson yielded just seven hits, and the Red Sox picked up a game on the Indians, losers in Philadelphia, to trail by six. But Boston failed to capitalize on another Cleveland loss the next day, when Virgil Trucks held them to just four singles in a 3–1 defeat. Ellis Kinder took the loss.

On Sunday, July 18, McCarthy sent his two biggest disappointments, Dave Ferriss and Mickey Harris, to face the Browns in a doubleheader. Form held, and Ferriss left the opener in the third trailing 4–0. But Earl Johnson pitched five good innings of relief, and the Red Sox—led by Spence, Goodman, and Tebbetts—scored six runs each in the fourth and sixth innings to win the game 12–5. Harris started out even worse in the second game, giving up four runs in the first, but McCarthy had to stay with him. Trailing 5–3 in the fifth, the Sox erupted for another four-run rally keyed by Dom DiMaggio's triple, and hung on for a 7–6 win and a sweep. Johnny Pesky had five hits on the day, and Harris finally got his second win—his first since April—against seven defeats. The Indians swept the Senators, but the two great come-from-behind victories kept Boston six games out.

Mel Parnell took the mound on Monday night against the Browns on just three days' rest and turned in another gem, winning 4–1. His teammates scored their runs in the bottom of the first when Pesky singled, Stan Spence doubled, Vern Stephens was intentionally walked, and Bobby Doerr delivered a grand-slam home run. It was Parnell's fourth victory in six starts at night, and his sixth overall. Like Bill Lee and Bruce Hurst, Parnell was a ground-ball pitcher, and this enabled him to overcome the normal left-hander's disadvantage in Fenway Park. On this occasion Red Sox infielders had eleven assists. The Sox kept pace with the Indians, who beat the Senators.

A Tuesday afternoon crowd of less than ten thousand fans saw Jack Kramer run the Red Sox' winning streak to four the next day against his old Brownie teammates with an 8–3 win. Once again the team had to come from behind, scoring four runs in the bottom of the fifth with the help of a three-run double by Tebbetts. The win gave the Sox a 7–1 record since the break, and left them five games behind the Indians, who lost in Washington. Now Boston had to face the White Sox for five games in three days.

With Dave Ferriss penciled in to start game two of Wednesday's day-night doubleheader against the White Sox, McCarthy needed a strong showing from Joe Dobson in the opener. He got it, as Dobson allowed just six hits and one run, and a double and a triple by the hot Doerr led the way in a 3–1 victory before 7,148 fans. In the nightcap Ferriss failed once again, leaving in the second inning in favor of Earl Johnson, and the home team trailed 6–0 as they began the bottom of the third against lefty Frank Papish. Papish promptly opened the door by walking the bases loaded, and Doerr cleared them with a double. When Mele followed with a two-run homer, Boston had pulled within a run. But the White Sox grabbed a 9–6 lead in the top of the seventh and carried a 9–7 margin through eight and one-half.

The bottom of the ninth began with a single by Stan Spence, his fourth hit on the day. Chicago manager Ted Lyons brought in forty-three-year-old sidearm reliever Earl Caldwell, who promptly got Vern Stephens to fly out to right. Caldwell then hit Bobby Doerr, however, and Sam Mele doubled to right, driving in Spence and scoring Doerr after the White Sox mishandled a throw to tie the game. Billy Goodman was intentionally walked to bring up rookie second-string catcher Matt Batts, and Batts lifted a sacrifice fly to right to win the game. Tex Hughson, who pitched a perfect inning in the top of the ninth, got the win, his first. It was the third time in the home stand that the Red Sox had come from behind to win, and the doubleheader split between the Yankees and Indians in New York moved Boston into a tie for third with New York, 3½ games behind Cleveland.

A crowd of 18,250 turned out on Thursday afternoon for another doubleheader. Denny Galehouse had finally recovered from his separated left shoulder, and McCarthy tapped him for the first game and Kinder for the second. The well-rested Galehouse pitched a five-hit shutout, walking only one man, and a two-run homer by Stephens led the way to a 3–0 victory. In the nightcap Stephens just missed another home run in the first inning when his RBI single hit the top of the left-field wall, and Ellis Kinder was racked for three runs in the second. Spence walked again in the third, and Stephens got another home run over the wall, his 20th, to tie the game at three. With 83 runs batted in, Stephens took over the league lead from Joe DiMaggio, who had just finished destroying the Indians in New York. A two-run single by Sam Mele in the fifth gave the Red Sox a 5–3 victory, as Kinder finished strongly for his first win since July 4. The Indians' defeat in New York brought the Red Sox to within two games of the lead, one-half game ahead of the Yankees and one behind Philadelphia. Boston had won eight straight.

McCarthy could have tapped Parnell for the series finale with three days' rest on Friday, but he preferred to save all three of his aces for the weekend series with the Indians—a series that had suddenly acquired awesome significance. Mickey Harris took the mound, and another face returned to the Red Sox lineup at last. "That collective groan heard around the American League today was touched off when Ted Williams returned to the Red Sox lineup and participated in a 13–1 humiliation of the Chicago White Sox," the UP reporter wrote that afternoon.[6] Williams went two for four with a double and three RBIs. His .388 average still led Boudreau—steady at .357—fairly comfortably, but he now trailed teammate Stephens by 9 RBIs, 83 to 74, and lagged six home runs behind Keltner. The Red Sox' three-game weekend set with the Indians—featuring a rare Saturday twin bill that would allow the Tribe to catch a night train home to Cleveland on Sunday—offered them a chance to go all the way into first place. Indeed, any one of four clubs—the Indians, A's, Red Sox, or Yankees—could find themselves in first at the end of the weekend.

STANDINGS
Saturday, July 24, 1948

Team	Won	Lost	Pct.	Games Behind
Cleveland	51	33	.607	—
Philadelphia	54	37	.593	½
Boston	51	36	.586	1½
New York	49	35	.583	2
Detroit	43	45	.489	10
Washington	38	48	.442	14
St. Louis	30	52	.366	17
Chicago	27	58	.318	24½

Bob Lemon and Sam Zoldak faced Jack Kramer and Mel Parnell on Saturday before a packed house of 34,129. Looking for a right-handed edge, Boudreau benched Robinson and substituted Berardino in both

6. *Cleveland Plain Dealer,* July 25.

games. Lemon, who had failed to finish his starts in Philadelphia and Washington, got a rude awakening in the bottom of the first, when Dom DiMaggio singled, Pesky singled, and Williams doubled to left field. A sacrifice fly by Doerr and a single by Goodman gave the Red Sox a 3–0 lead. But on a hot day in Fenway, with the Indians playing the Red Sox, a 3–0 lead in the first was not worth very much. In the top of the second Berardino hit the left field wall, but DiMaggio threw him out at second. Umpire Bill Summers, realizing the importance of the occasion, allowed Berardino to bump him during the subsequent argument. Kramer promptly walked Hegan, and Lemon got himself right back into the ball game with a home run. Mitchell, who was winding up an almost unbelievable road trip, singled; Doby—feeling at home in Boston once again— singled to center; and Hank Edwards doubled them both home for a 4–3 Indian lead.

In the bottom of the second, a lack of consistency among the umpires cost the Red Sox dearly. When plate umpire Johnny Stevens called Pesky out on strikes, the Red Sox third baseman—remembering Berardino's protest in the top of the frame—protested himself. "The goddamn ball was two inches outside," he said, and Stevens gave Pesky the first heave-ho of his five-year career. McCarthy, enraged by the inconsistency, scrambled onto the field and was ejected as well. This was serious, since American League rules barred both men from both ends of the doubleheader. "I'm sorry, Joe," Pesky said, as they walked down the runway toward the clubhouse. "That's all right, son," McCarthy replied typically, "just don't let it happen again." McCarthy spent the rest of the day in the runway under the stands, within earshot of the Red Sox dugout, and Billy Hitchcock replaced Pesky. Both sides threatened in the third and fourth innings, but no one scored.

Trailing 4–3 in the top of the fifth, Kramer walked Gordon and Berardino and gave up a single to Keltner to load the bases. Coach Del Baker, now running the club, brought in Ferriss, who suddenly rose to the occasion, fanning Hegan and retiring Lemon on a fly to right. In the bottom of the inning the Red Sox tied the game 4–4 on a hit, an error by Joe Gordon, and a double by Billy Goodman. But when Tebbetts grounded to Keltner with men on second and third, Keltner managed to trap Mele between third and home, and Boudreau, alertly covering third base, tagged out Goodman trying to advance to third to end the inning.

Mitchell opened the top of the sixth with yet another base hit, and managed to break up a possible double play when Doby grounded to Stephens. Hank Edwards followed with a double to center, but Dom DiMaggio managed to make a quick pickup and hold the speedy Doby on third. After Ferriss walked Boudreau intentionally, Gordon made a bid to break the game open with a drive to deep left, but Williams made a fine leaping catch against the wall, and only Doby scored from third. The Red Sox outfield had saved at least three runs, and Ferriss escaped down just 5–4.

Double plays bailed both teams out of trouble during the next two innings, and the Indians still led 5–4 in the bottom of the eighth. Goodman led off with a walk, but the Indians retired the next two batters, Goodman advancing on Ferriss's grounder. Then Dom DiMaggio singled Goodman home to tie the game. Hitchcock promptly beat out an infield hit, and Ted Williams singled in Dom D for a 6–5 lead. Russ Christopher relieved and got the side out, but the damage was done.

Berardino and Hegan grounded out to start the top of the ninth, and Allie Clark hit for Christopher. Joe McCarthy—still stationed in the runway—followed the situation through Mickey Harris, who relayed him information from the dugout.

"Who's up?" yelled McCarthy.

"A pinch hitter, Allie Clark," replied Harris.

"Tell Dave to sidearm him," screamed McCarthy, who was proud of being able to remember every hitter's weakness—"tell him to sidearm him."

"Okay," replied Harris, and Earl Combs passed on the signal.

"Did he get it?" yelled McCarthy. "Did he get the signal?"

"Yeah," shouted Harris. "Tebbetts got it. The first pitch was a strike. Clark missed it."

The crowd roared, and Harris reported a second strike. Loud groans erupted around Fenway, however, as Clark took the next two pitches for balls.

"Come on, Dave," moaned McCarthy, "get him, boy, with that sidearm."

A tremendous shout erupted. "Strike three, swinging," screamed Harris. "He got him."

"Good boy, Dave. That's the way to do it," shouted McCarthy, and the reputedly dour manager took off his hat and danced a little jig.[7] The Red Sox had won, 6–5, and trailed Cleveland by one-half game.

Parnell and Zoldak both pitched brilliantly during the second game, which was 0–0 going into the top of the fourth. Then Gordon walked, Keltner doubled, and Berardino delivered a sacrifice fly for a 1–0 lead. The action was tense for the next three innings, as both sides dazzled on defense. Parnell retired Gordon with two on in the top of the seventh, and after the stretch, the Red Sox finally got to work.

Dom DiMaggio opened with a walk, and after Hitchcock flied out, Williams again came through with the key hit of the game, doubling off the

7. *Boston Globe*, Sunday, July 25.

left-field wall for a 1–1 tie. Boudreau relieved Zoldak and brought in Feller to pitch to Stephens and Doerr. Feller had relatively little respect for Stephens—"an All-American out," he says today, "he had a blind spot"— and he got Junior to line out to Mitchell in left for the second out.

Boudreau now ordered Feller to walk Doerr, who had always hit him well, at one time breaking up a no-hitter. Disaster followed. Feller threw four more balls to Sam Mele, loading the bases. He threw two more to Goodman, and Boudreau replaced him with Christopher. He completed the walk, forcing in the lead run, before Tebbetts flied out to end the inning. The Red Sox had scored twice with just one hit—Williams's double to left field. Feller never liked to relieve, and one cannot help wondering why Boudreau had not turned to Christopher at once. Parnell faced only seven batters in the last two innings, and a most unlucky Sam Zoldak took the loss. The Red Sox completed the doubleheader sweep, 2–1, and passed the Indians in the standings.

A remarkable performance by the Athletics against the Tigers in Philadelphia kept Boston in second. Trailing 6–3 in the eighth inning, the Athletics scored five runs to take over first place. In New York, meanwhile, 30,012 fans saw the Yankees split the first of two doubleheaders with the White Sox. Frank Shea returned to favor with 6–2 victory in the first game, but the Yankees lost a killer in the second. Trailing 4–2 in the bottom of the ninth, the Yankees scored two runs to tie the game, but Page and Randy Gumpert promptly gave up four Chicago tallies in the top of the tenth. Bucky Harris fined Joe Page after the game, effectively confessing his mistake. During 1947, Harris and Larry MacPhail had paid the flamboyant Page a $250 bonus every two weeks, provided that Page curtailed his off-field activities and stayed in shape. Over the winter, George Weiss had abandoned this arrangement in favor of a generous $20,000 contract for the star reliever. Page's habits had apparently deteriorated, and he was not the reliable stopper he had been during 1947.

It was possible, as the day's action started on Sunday, July 25, for the four leaders to finish the day within a half game of one another. In Philadelphia, the Athletics split with the Tigers, but could stay in first place if Cleveland beat the Red Sox. In New York, Joe DiMaggio took matters into his own hands, going three for three in the first game to key a 5–3 win behind Ed Lopat, and adding a triple, two home runs, and three RBIs in the nightcap as Raschi won 7–3, his second victory in four days. Joe D's 86 RBIs now led Junior Stephens by one. It was Bill Johnson day, and Johnson responded with a three-run homer in the second game. The pair of weekend doubleheaders witnessed a remarkable display of durability by catcher Gus Niarhos, who caught three of the games and part of the fourth. Bucky

Harris was struggling to keep a good lineup on the field. Yogi Berra, who had split a finger in the last game against the Indians, sat out the whole weekend with injuries, and Johnny Lindell had still not recovered from an infection. Bobby Brown and Cliff Mapes filled in the outfield.

The game that would decide the league lead in Boston paired Joe Dobson, 3–1 against the Indians and 12–6 overall, against Steve Gromek, who had done so well on the first two legs of the Cleveland road trip. Gromek got off to a rocky start in the bottom of the first when Pesky doubled, Williams walked, and Bobby Doerr hit a two-run triple. The 2–0 lead held up for the rest of the game thanks to an amazing performance by Dom DiMaggio.

The Little Professor's heroics began in the second, after Boudreau had singled and Keltner had walked. Berardino sent a long drive to left-center which DiMaggio had to backhand against the wall, saving at least one run. In the next inning, with one out, he made another fine play off Steve Gromek, whereupon Dale Mitchell singled to right. Ted Williams chimed in with a fine catch off Doby in the sixth, and Doby answered with a good catch off Billy Goodman with a man on in the bottom of the inning.

Trailing 2–0, Satchel Paige made his Fenway Park debut in the bottom of the seventh. He got Dobson on a short fly to Dale Mitchell, whereupon Dom DiMaggio hit the second major league homer off Satchel, a screen shot to left field to make the game 3–0.

DOM DIMAGGIO: It was his hesitation pitch. I had seen him use it throwing in practice, and I made up my mind that I would not get out ahead of it. Sure enough, he stepped and stopped dead, but I held my stance and hit the ball over the fence. I looked over at him as I was trotting around the bases and he was scratching his head.

Paige got Pesky to foul out, and faced Ted Williams for the first time in a big-league game. He worked the count to two and two, and after the next pitch the Splendid Splinter appeared to begin to throw his bat away in disgust. But the umpire called it a ball—pitchers often complained that the umpires valued Williams's judgment more than their own—and Williams eventually walked. Stephens flied out to Doby to end the inning. Boudreau hit into a double play to end a Cleveland threat in the eighth, and Dom DiMaggio robbed Gordon of a double to start the ninth, as Dobson completed the shutout.

The Red Sox' 3–0 victory gave them a sweep of the Indians, a winning streak of twelve, fifteen wins out of their last sixteen games, and first place. The winning streak was more a tribute to their pitching and defense than to their hitting. The only consistent hitting star of the home stand was Bobby

Doerr, who had 19 RBIs in the sixteen games. Stephens had only 9 RBIs, and his total of 84 now trailed Joe DiMaggio by 1. Williams, of course, had returned just in time to play a key role in the sweep of the Indians and raise his average back to .391, but the other regulars' averages had stayed about where they were. Meanwhile, Dobson, Kramer, and Parnell had eight wins between them; Ferriss, Harris, Kinder, and Galehouse had each turned in one key performance; and Earl Johnson had pitched well in relief. Sam Mele had also hit well, but Stan Spence had gone back into right field on the last game of the home stand. Although Spence was still hitting only .215, McCarthy apparently appreciated his superior power, his walks, and his defense. Billy Goodman, hitting .313, was definitely established at first. Table-setters DiMaggio and Pesky were still hitting only .260 and .279, but Pesky had scored 64 runs and DiMaggio 69 to put them among the league leaders.

The excitement was all the greater in Boston because the Braves were in first place as well, marking the first time since 1916, as Dave Egan noted, that both Boston clubs had led their league for as much as a single day. Egan did not, however, pass up another opportunity to needle Yawkey, Cronin and company, who had made no move to integrate the team. The Fenway faithful, he noted, had given Larry Doby and Satchel Paige several big ovations over the weekend. "On every possible occasion," he wrote a few days later, "the public hereabouts seizes the opportunity to stand up and be counted in favor of participation of Negroes in organized baseball."[8] Larry Doby himself enjoyed his visit: he was now hitting an even .400 against Red Sox pitching. In response, Joe Cronin said that Red Sox scouts had failed to turn up any Negro League players of major league caliber. The Sox front office did make a move as the western trip began, buying the contract of forty-three-year-old right-hander Earl Caldwell from the White Sox, and Egan quickly mocked Caldwell—who had pitched in five games for the Philadelphia Phillies in 1928—as the Red Sox' answer to Satchel Paige. The move, alas, exemplified the peculiar mixture that made up the Red Sox in the late 1940s: a fine team, a brilliant manager, and an inept, bigoted front office.

The Red Sox team that emerged during the last two weeks of July 1948 stayed together, with very few modifications, for the next three years, continuing to contend for the American League pennant. It had taken half a season for Joe McCarthy to put together a team of enormous strengths, but one never quite the equal of either the Indians or the Yankees. Still, the per-

8. *Boston Daily Record,* July 28.

formance of the Red Sox under McCarthy fully justifies Bill James's assessment of the lantern-jawed Irishman as the greatest manager of all time.[9]

When McCarthy took over the Red Sox in the fall of 1947, it was the third time that he had taken the helm of a well-financed ball club that had fallen upon hard times. In each case, he had worked quickly to reshape the club—a style reminiscent of Whitey Herzog or Dick Williams, who also have a philosophy of what makes a winning ball club and waste no time in implementing it. In 1926 McCarthy had taken over the last-place Chicago Cubs, once one of the premier franchises of the National League. It was the first big-league opportunity for McCarthy, who had never played in the majors, and he moved quickly, unloading two aging stars, shortstop Rabbit Maranville and pitcher Grover Cleveland Alexander, and acquiring a new center fielder and shortstop, Hack Wilson and Jimmy Cooney. Wilson was acquired from the minor leagues after the Giants demoted him temporarily and then failed to put him back on their major league roster, to the fury of John McGraw. The Cubs moved all the way to fourth in 1926. The team acquired the valuable but unhappy Kiki Cuyler from the National League champion Pirates for virtually nothing after the 1927 season and finished third, only four games behind St. Louis, in 1928. The next year the acquisition of Rogers Hornsby from the Braves for four players and a large sum of cash gave the Cubs the pennant, as their runs scored jumped from 714 to 982 in a single season. They barely failed to repeat in 1930, despite the emergence of Gabby Hartnett, because Hornsby broke his foot and was lost for the season. Oddly enough, McCarthy was fired in the last week of the season and Hornsby got his job.

McCarthy moved straight to the Yankees, who had lost two successive pennants to the Athletics and finished third, sixteen games off the pace, in 1930. He immediately shifted Ben Chapman from third base to the outfield, put Joe Sewell at the hot corner, and made twenty-one-year-old Lefty Gomez the ace of his staff. The team improved by eight wins and set the all-time record for runs scored in 1931—a record that has never been broken—but still trailed the Athletics by thirteen games. Twenty-one-year-old Frankie Crosetti became the shortstop in 1932, Red Ruffing hit his stride on the mound, and the team improved thirteen games and won the pennant and world championship in 1932. But the pitching staff faded again the next year, and Babe Ruth, Tony Lazzeri, and Earl Combs began to decline. The Yankees slipped by sixteen games and finished behind Washington in 1933. McCarthy continued to promote young players, and

9. Bill James, *The Bill James Guide to Baseball Managers* (New York, 1997), 149.

finally got back on top in 1936, when Joe DiMaggio joined the team. During the next six years he added Tommy Henrich, Joe Gordon, Charlie Keller, Phil Rizzuto, and Bill Johnson, and the Yankees won seven pennants in eight years, failing only in 1940. The Yankee farm system and the Yankee scouts, led by Paul Krichell, Bill Essick, and Joe Devine, discovered and developed this remarkable stream of talent, but McCarthy deserves the credit for using it. He also shifted Red Rolfe from shortstop to third base and Joe Gordon from shortstop to second in order to get them into the lineup in 1935 and 1938.

After quitting Larry MacPhail and the Yankees in disgust in 1946 and retiring for eighteen months, McCarthy had taken over the Red Sox—another team that had just slipped badly—in late 1947, with full authority to make trades. Once again he had used it—and Tom Yawkey's bankroll—acquiring Junior Stephens, Jack Kramer, and Ellis Kinder from the Browns, and Stan Spence from the Senators. And once again, in the first few months of the season, he had strengthened his lineup by shifting two shortstops to new positions: Johnny Pesky, the incumbent, to third base, and rookie Billy Goodman to first. For all that, the team had begun the year disastrously, as we have seen, because Ted Williams alone had gotten off to a good start at the plate, and because of confusion regarding the pitching staff. In retrospect, the hitting problems in the first half of the season seem to have reflected difficulties experienced by the players in adjusting to McCarthy's offensive philosophy.

McCarthy had cut his managerial teeth in the late 1920s and 1930s, the greatest hitting era in baseball history. To judge from the Yankees' statistics, he had begun in 1936 to focus more upon the importance of getting on base—something which until 1935 had largely taken care of itself, with Babe Ruth and Lou Gehrig walking more than 100 times a season. Rookie Joe DiMaggio walked only 24 times in 1936, but the walk totals of most of the other regulars increased between 50 and 100 percent. The team walk total increased from 604 to a league-leading 700, and the Yankees scored a league-leading 1,065 runs. They led the league in walks in four of the next five years. It took McCarthy one more year, apparently, to turn to the problem of his own pitchers' bases on balls. Yankee pitchers allowed 663 walks in 1936, the second-highest total in the league, but only 506, the second lowest, the next season. They continued to post totals in the lower half of the league for the rest of the McCarthy era.

The team McCarthy took over in Boston had walked 666 times in 1947, with Ted Williams accounting for an astonishing 162, almost one quarter of the total. McCarthy and his coaches apparently began ordering the rest of the team to take more pitches, and Johnny Pesky, in particular, remembers that he was no longer allowed to hit on 2–0 and 3–1 counts. It seems likely that the need to adjust to a new hitting rhythm partly accounted for the poor starts of Pesky, Dom DiMaggio, Stephens, and Doerr—but not, of course, Williams, who needed no instruction in taking pitches. By late July, however, the Red Sox had adjusted to McCarthy, and by the end of the year the results were dramatically apparent.

Dom DiMaggio, who had topped 74 walks only once in four full seasons, drew 101 walks in 1948, a new career high, and followed with 96 in 1949 and 82 in 1950. Pesky improved his career high from 72 to 99, and followed with 100 the next year. Bobby Doerr improved his career high from 67 to 83 in 1948, and followed with 75 in 1949. Junior Stephens's 77 walks were also a career high, and he increased it to 101 in 1949. Stan Spence's 82 walks were just shy of his 1943 high of 84, but he played in only 114 games. Birdie Tebbetts's career high went from 39 walks to 62, and he duplicated that figure the next year. Billy Goodman walked 74 times. Walks were the key to the Red Sox' 1948 offensive season. Despite the advantage of playing in Fenway Park, they trailed both Cleveland and New York in batting average and in home runs. But they walked 823 times, compared to 646 for the Indians and 623 for the Yankees, and thereby managed to lead the league in runs scored with 907, compared to 857 for the Yankees and 840 for the Indians.

The Red Sox of 1948–1950 were a great offensive team, but of a very particular kind. They did *not* have great power, and led the league in home runs only once, in 1949, with a relatively low total of 131. They were one of the greatest long-sequence offenses ever assembled, adept at stringing together base hits and walks—especially, of course, in Fenway Park, which apparently had the best visibility of any ballpark in the league. They were vulnerable, however, in pitchers' parks, and especially vulnerable in cool weather, which makes it much harder to string hits together and which probably also contributed to their annual slow start. The importance of home runs increases as hitting as a whole decreases, and the Red Sox did not have great home run power. And with the exception of Williams, none of their hitters was quite as good as they seemed to be. As a group, Williams, Stephens, and Doerr were inferior to Boudreau, Gordon, and Keltner or to Joe DiMaggio, Henrich, and Berra in 1948, and Doby and Mitchell were probably slightly superior to Dom DiMaggio and Pesky, as well. Fenway Park contributed substantially to the averages of most of the Red Sox.

The Red Sox pitching staff, of course, was less distinguished. Of all the pitchers on the 1948 staff, only Mel Parnell, sore-armed Tex Hughson, and perhaps Dave Ferriss were ever truly outstanding hurlers. Dobson, Kramer,

Galehouse, Earl Johnson, and Harris had been good pitchers, but never great ones. Still, under McCarthy's tutelage, they made the most of what they had. They, too, quickly assimilated his thinking about the importance of a walk. The 592 walks they issued were nearly the fewest in the league (Detroit hurlers walked just 589), while New York hurlers walked 623 and Cleveland pitchers 646. With the exception of Mel Parnell, no Boston pitcher had great stuff, but they forced the opposition to earn their way on base. And when the ball was put in play, the Red Sox pitchers had the help of what was probably the league's best defense.

In his always evocative but frequently inaccurate book *Summer of '49*, David Halberstam frequently refers to the Red Sox' poor defense. In fact, Boston's defense was excellent, certainly superior to the Yankees'. Dom DiMaggio consistently outperformed his brother in center field, even though many balls that Joe could catch in Yankee Stadium bounced off the left-center-field wall in Fenway Park. Ted Williams by 1948 had become an outstanding left fielder, and Stan Spence had been a fine center fielder. Pesky was just learning his way at third in 1948, but his statistics show him to have been every bit as good as the Johnson-Brown combination the Yankees fielded. Billy Goodman was a fine athlete at first. Above all, however, Halberstam's claim reflects a misreading of the ability of two shortstops, Phil Rizzuto and Junior Stephens.

Phil Rizzuto captured the hearts of Yankee fans from the moment he burst upon the scene in 1941. Only five feet six inches tall and (maybe) 150 pounds, and a local boy to boot, he was a natural crowd favorite. He was also a perfect gentleman on the field and off, and he has been a consistently entertaining broadcaster for the last forty years. A long campaign secured his election to the Hall of Fame in 1994. Yet a cold look at his statistics suggests that he was, at best, the third-ranking American League shortstop of his generation, both offensively and defensively.

Rizzuto hit .300 twice—in 1941, his rookie year (.307), and in 1950, when he had a truly extraordinary season and hit .324. His lifetime average is a mediocre .273 and his slugging percentage a below-average .355. He hit 62 career home runs, about 4 for every 154 games. Bill James's *Historical Abstract* rates him as a dead-average offensive player over his career, but James's method probably slightly overrates players who played for good defensive teams. Rizzuto, in short, was not an offensive asset to the Yankees over the length of his career, although he was an asset in 1941 and 1950.

Defensively Rizzuto enjoyed a tremendous reputation, partly because his small size made him look so quick. Halberstam in *Summer of '49* makes the remarkable claim that Rizzuto probably lowered Yankee pitchers' earned run averages one run per game, implying that he singlehandedly saved the

Yankees 154 runs per year. This is the kind of claim that no one who has ever spent a few hours with fielding statistics would make about anyone, much less Rizzuto, whose statistics show him to have been a good shortstop, but not the best of a fine collection of contemporaries. Rizzuto never led American League shortstops in assists, showing a career high of 445 in 1942. Boudreau led the league three times and topped Rizzuto's career high five times, posting totals of 475 and 483 in 1947–48. And Junior Stephens posted the highest assist totals of all: 494 in 1947, 540 in 1948, and 508 in 1949. Stephens, in other words, had an extra assist, compared to Rizzuto, every two or three games. Rizzuto had higher putout totals, but statistics suggest that this was because Stephens deferred to Pesky and Doerr on popups. "I thought I was more agile than Stevie," says Johnny Pesky, "but he had a better arm. Maybe that was why McCarthy decided to play him at short and me at third." Statistics indicate that Pesky hit the nail on the head.

Stephens in 1948–49, in short, was at least as good a shortstop as Rizzuto, and he was considerably more valuable offensively because of his tremendous power. The same was true of Boudreau. Stephens, Boudreau, and Rizzuto were almost exactly even in total chances per game in 1947–49. The leader—by a substantial margin—was Philadelphia shortstop Eddie Joost, who may have been the best of all defensively and who was certainly far superior to Rizzuto offensively. For six seasons—1947–52—Joost averaged 118 walks and 18 home runs a year, more than making up for low batting averages. Phil Rizzuto, in the late 1940s, was the fourth most valuable shortstop in the American League. And over his career, Junior Stephens was a much better player.

Stephens, indeed, led the league in assists in both 1948 and 1949 by a large margin, and hit brilliantly for three years. Defensively he was one of the two anchors of a great defensive club (Dom DiMaggio was the other). Remarkably, while Stephens led all shortstops in assists, DiMaggio set a new American League record for outfield putouts—a truly amazing feat. Fielding statistics are powerfully affected by the tendencies of pitching staffs, which are now known to differ widely in their percentage of ground balls and fly balls allowed. The league leader in outfield putouts and the league leader in infield assists usually reflect the tendency of their staffs, and for this reason they almost never come from the same team, as they did in 1948. Indeed, this happened on only two other occasions between 1946 and 1981.[10] The Red Sox' defensive strategy under McCarthy was to throw the ball over the plate and let the opposition hit it. It would not have

10. The teams involved were the 1959 and 1965 White Sox, and in both cases the outfielders involved—Jim Landis and Ken Berry—led the league with unusually low totals for putouts, far below Dom D's 504.

succeeded so well had the Red Sox not enjoyed outstanding defense—no better, perhaps, than the Indians' of 1948, but superior to the Yankees'.

McCarthy's emphasis upon strike-zone judgment was simply one aspect of a remarkable knowledge of the percentages of baseball. While he was not a garrulous manager like Leo Durocher or Earl Weaver, he frequently amazed even veteran players by introducing points that they had never heard of in ten years or more of professional baseball. In spring training, after making a relay throw that just missed a runner at the plate, Junior Stephens was amazed when McCarthy told him he should have thrown the man out. "What did I do wrong?" asked the well-armed shortstop. "You went out too far," McCarthy explained. "Let the outfielder throw the ball into you. *Your* throw has to be accurate."[11] He also told his number-seven hitter *never* to try to stretch a single into a double, because the opposition would nearly always pitch around the number-eight hitter (usually Birdie Tebbetts, who had a little power) to face the pitcher with a man on second.

McCarthy did not hound players. He disliked hearing them discuss anything but baseball at the ballpark, but he expected them, as professionals, to know how to behave and how to play the game. He set an example by paying so much attention to the details of his own job, and most players responded by focusing upon theirs. He also understood the importance of psychology. He rarely announced his choice of starting pitcher before game day, either publicly or privately, because he did not want his pitchers to lose any sleep. And he apparently understood, when he joined the Red Sox, that the Boston players were worried about his comparing them to the Yankees. Birdie Tebbetts in particular thought he might suffer in comparison with Bill Dickey, but McCarthy's first words to him put him at ease. "Johnny Murphy said I should rely on you," said the manager, referring to his former Yankee relief ace, who was now working for the Red Sox. Similarly, he told the writers that it was up to him to get along with Ted Williams. He had seen enough of Williams from 1939 through 1946 to know that Williams's approach to baseball was every bit as serious as his own. With the Red Sox, the two men frequently found themselves alone in the locker room late in the afternoon, the last men to leave the ballpark.

It was clear to many at the time—and it is much clearer now—that the 1948 Red Sox were not the equal of the 1948 Indians, or even of the 1948 Yankees. The Indians had five future Hall of Famers (and Gordon and perhaps Doby should join them), while the Red Sox had only two, Williams and Doerr, and were clearly superior to Cleveland at only one position, left field. As Bill James has argued, Bobby Doerr was not the equal of

11. *Boston Herald*, April 6, 1948.

Joe Gordon at second, certainly as a hitter. Junior Stephens's 1948 season was not the equal of Boudreau's (although he was more valuable offensively over his whole career), Pesky did not match Keltner's phenomenal figures for 1948, and Eddie Robinson in 1948 was probably more valuable than Billy Goodman. Lemon, Bearden, and Feller were also certainly superior to Parnell, Kramer, and Dobson. Dom DiMaggio was a very fine player in 1948, but Larry Doby, even then, was only just behind.

Few managers ever got more out of a ball club than McCarthy did the Red Sox in 1948. The team's real problem did not relate to the players on the field, but to the organization as a whole. The well of minor league talent was almost completely dry. The Red Sox triple-A farm club in Louisville was going nowhere, and the whole farm system seems to have included only one really fine prospect, Walt Dropo, a heavy-hitting first baseman who did not reach the club until 1950. The team was built almost entirely around players signed in the late 1930s—Williams, Pesky, DiMaggio, and Doerr— and around recent acquisitions through trades. Eddie Collins, who had just stepped down as general manager, had failed to pick up much new talent during the war, and Cronin, his replacement, was destined to do even worse. Of the three contenders, the Red Sox had by far the weakest bench. The lack of a broader talent base not only made it more difficult for them to contend with the Yankees and the Indians, but also promised the rapid disintegration of the franchise during the 1950s.

From 1946 through 1961, when Carl Yastrzemski joined the Red Sox, it is fair to say that Walt Dropo was the only outstanding—or potentially outstanding—offensive player that the Red Sox organization ever produced. The mishandling of Dropo, in retrospect, seems almost incredible. A right-handed-hitting first baseman who was fully six feet, five inches tall and weighed 220 pounds, Dropo was not even signed to organized baseball until 1947, when he was twenty-four years old. After a very impressive 87 games at Scranton in the Eastern League, he was promoted to Louisville in early 1948, but dropped to Birmingham in the Southern Association after only 28 games. In retrospect, the Red Sox might have been better off to bring him up and give him, rather than Billy Goodman, a shot at first base. Dropo played briefly with the Red Sox in 1949 and finally reached them for almost a full season in 1950. He hit .322, with 34 homers and 144 RBIs, one of the greatest seasons ever by a rookie. But the beginning of 1951 found him back in the Pacific Coast League, and in 1952 he was traded to the Tigers.

Besides Dropo, the best hitters the system produced were Goodman, who averaged over .300 through 1956, and third baseman Frank Malzone. But despite Goodman's .354 batting title in 110 games in 1950, neither of these players was more than a marginally valuable hitter. They typify the many players whose average has been raised to the .280–.310 level in Fenway Park, but who would be average at best anywhere else. Malzone had a little power; Goodman had none at all. The Red Sox system turned out other players like Jimmy Piersall, Ted Lepcio, Sammy White, and Dick Gernert, whose averages were boosted to respectability by Fenway Park, but who could not really help the team win. Joe Cronin in 1953 also managed to pluck a real star, Jackie Jensen, from his father-in-law Clark Griffith's Washington Senators in exchange for pitcher Mickey McDermott and outfielder Tom Umphlett. Meanwhile, Ted Williams, despite numerous injuries and almost two more years of military service, remained one of the greatest players in the league, and the team did come up with some effective pitchers. With Williams's help, they managed to stay around .500 for most of the 1950s before collapsing completely in the early 1960s. By the time this writer arrived in Boston for college in the fall of 1965, Fenway Park was drawing less than five hundred fans to some games.

The failure of the scouting system was compounded, of course, by Yawkey and Cronin's refusal to sign any black players. Dave Egan was already goading them to do so in 1948, and Jackie Robinson had actually had a Red Sox tryout before his signing by the Dodgers, but Yawkey and Cronin—together with most of the American League owners, except Bill Veeck—behaved as though integration were a fad that would eventually go away. The racial climate in the Boston area was far more tolerant than it later became—Mayor Curley, in particular, enjoyed the support of the local black community, and as Egan pointed out, Satchel Paige and Larry Doby got very warm receptions in Fenway Park—but the team leadership was unmoved until 1959, when they brought up Pumpsie Green. Earl Wilson, a fine black pitcher, was traded after five seasons in the early 1960s, and promptly became a twenty-game winner in Detroit. The first black offensive players of any distinction to come up through the system were George Scott and Reggie Smith, who together with Yastrzemski finally brought the team a pennant again in 1967. Both Scott and Smith eventually spent their most productive years in other cities. Racism continued to hurt the Red Sox through the 1980s.

The chronic tendency of Boston writers and Red Sox fans to blame the moral or physical defects of their players for setbacks is utterly misplaced. Indeed, as we shall see, the team figures for the year showed the Red Sox to have been a clutch team, one that got more runs out of their accumulated walks and hits than could normally be anticipated. Their problems—like the problems of every Red Sox team since the 1920s—could be traced directly to the front office. Meanwhile, the fans of New England were privileged to have seen their team post the hottest streak of the season and put itself into the thick of the pennant race. And from late July through the first week of October, there was never a dull moment.

STANDINGS
Monday, July 26, 1948

Team	Won	Lost	Pct.	Games Behind
Boston	54	36	.600	—
Philadelphia	56	38	.596	—
Cleveland	51	36	.586	1½
New York	52	37	.584	1½
Detroit	44	45	.494	9½
Washington	39	50	.438	14½
St. Louis	32	53	.376	19½
Chicago	28	61	.315	25½

7

Midsummer Madness

(JULY 27–AUGUST 8)

As all eight American League teams boarded westbound trains on the late afternoon of Sunday, July 25, the heaviest pressure lay, once again, on the Cleveland Indians. Having lost a 3½-game lead during their eastern trip, they now returned home to face the eastern clubs yet again. With the Red Sox, Yankees, and Athletics set to feast once again on the White Sox and Browns, another 6–9 Cleveland home stand against Boston, Washington, New York, and Philadelphia, such as they had experienced in June, could leave the Indians in a desperate situation. For American League fans, all four daily box scores would have a critical significance for at least the next two weeks.

The streaking Red Sox began their trip with more bad news on the injury front. In Sunday's game with the Indians Steve Gromek had hit Ted Williams in the knee with a pitch, and soreness kept him on the bench when the team reached Detroit for a Tuesday night game. A record night crowd of 54,609 saw Kinder beat Hal Newhouser 8–0. But the Red Sox' thirteen-game winning streak finally came to an end the next day, as Dizzy Trout shut them out and the Tigers battered Denny Galehouse, Dave Ferriss, and nineteen-year-old Chuck Stobbs for eighteen hits in a 13–0 rout. The next night Williams returned to the lineup and doubled to left while Jack Kramer, pitching strongly, won his tenth game in a row for a 12–3 record. The 8–1 win put a full half game between the Red Sox and the Athletics, with New York and Cleveland another 1½ games behind, as Boston headed to Cleveland for a four-game weekend series.

Meanwhile, the Indians' 6–8 eastern trip had left them fighting the

Athletics for second place in three games in Cleveland. The trip was a very bad omen. Only a year earlier, Bob Feller, in his autobiography *Strikeout Story,* had noted repeatedly that eastern trips—especially the third eastern trip—had traditionally been disastrous for Cleveland pennant hopes, and this one fit the pattern all too closely. Their pitching remained a problem. Gromek appeared on his way to a fine second half and Zoldak had continued to pitch well, but Lemon was obviously showing the effects of leading the league in innings pitched during the first half of the season. Bearden had been relegated to middle relief, and Feller, facing overwhelmingly hostile fans for the first time in his career, had suffered three more bad outings on the eastern swing. Offensively there were some bright spots. Mitchell had hit a Hornsbyan .424 (28 for 66) since the All-Star break to raise his average to .332, Gordon had pounded the eastern pitchers at a .436 clip, and Boudreau's average was steady at .351.

Boudreau had announced that Ed Klieman would make his first start of the season on Tuesday evening, but as veteran *Cleveland Plain Dealer* beat writer Harry Jones explained to his readers the next morning, Lou sprang a surprise on the Athletics and the fans.

> Bob Feller (and not Ed Klieman) was the Cleveland Indians' starting pitcher before 60,260 astonished spectators at the stadium last night, and though he didn't help much, Feller (not Klieman) was the winning hurler as the tribe moved into second place in the American League, two percentage points ahead of the defeated Philadelphia Athletics.
>
> A surprise, last-minute choice of Manager Lou Boudreau, Feller (not Klieman) lasted long enough to post his 10th victory of the season as the Indians rallied to gain a 10 to 5 verdict in a contest in which Klieman (and not Feller) was billed as the starting pitcher.
>
> But Feller (not Klieman) was cheered by the crowd as he took the mound at the start of the game, cheered as he never has been anywhere this season. The cheers turned to jeers, however, as Feller (not Klieman) left the mound shortly after the Athletics' Sam Chapman tied the score in the fifth by clouting a grand slam homer.
>
> The Indians came back after that damaging blow to score four runs in the sixth inning and another in the seventh, and so it was Klieman (not Feller) who was applauded at the finish, for the bespectacled relief twirler, taking over in the seventh, blanked the As the rest of the way.
>
> The victory went to Feller because he was lifted for a pinch hitter during the sixth-inning assault on Phil Marchildon, the third Athletic flinger. Phil suffered most of the Indians' 15-hit barrage, which included Ken Keltner's 23d home run and Joe Gordon's 19th of the season.[1]

1. *Cleveland Plain Dealer,* July 28.

Indeed, although Feller was in trouble in every single inning, the Indians in their turn had one of their best hitting games in Municipal Stadium, with fifteen hits, including three for Clark, two each for Mitchell, Gordon, and Robinson, and a two-run single for Doby. Two days later, the papers reported that Feller had visited A. L. Austin, a Cleveland osteopath who had cured Feller of an arm injury back in 1937.

The next afternoon witnessed another one of those bizarre plays which inevitably take place during any baseball season, but whose significance can become legendary in a tight pennant race or in postseason play. Allie Clark's fourth homer gave Lemon a 2–0 lead over Dick Fowler, and Lemon held a 3–2 lead in the top of the eighth inning when two Athletics reached base with two out. The inning appeared to be over when outfielder Don White lifted a fly to short left center.

Dale Mitchell and Larry Doby converged on the ball—Mitchell moving more slowly, but Doby running at top speed. The sun was over the stands between home and third base, and Doby was looking almost right at it as the two Philadelphia runners dashed for home. At the last instant, he cut in front of Mitchell to make the play, but lost sight of the ball. As the newspapers reported the next day, the ball struck him squarely on the head and fell safely.

> LARRY DOBY: The ball did not hit me in the head. The sun blinded me and I didn't see it, but it actually hit the bill of my cap. Of course, it made a better story to say it hit me in the head.

The Indians' dugout collapsed in laughter, but two runs scored and Philadelphia took the lead. Doby just missed a home run to deep center in the bottom of the ninth, and the Athletics won and moved back into second.

The blown fly ball was the severest test that Doby had to face in the first full season of a long, historic, and difficult career. As an all-sports star in Paterson, New Jersey, in the early 1940s, Doby had dreamed of playing big-time college football, where black Americans already participated. Drafted into the army during the Second World War, he worked out with several minor and major leaguers who told him he certainly had the ability to play. Returning, he joined the Newark Eagles of the Negro National League, where his teammates included Monte Irvin. The signing of Jackie Robinson in 1946 changed everything, of course, and Doby initially heard that the Dodgers might sign him as well. But Veeck had apparently contacted Branch Rickey in early 1947 and suggested that the Indians sign Doby to integrate the American League instead. Doby joined the Indians directly from Newark in early July 1947, just three months after Robinson's big-league debut.

Doby's first year was extremely difficult. At twenty-three, he was a much better long-term prospect than Robinson, who was five years older, and as a powerful left-handed-hitting second baseman, he had a chance to become an all-time great. With Gordon, Boudreau, and Keltner on the team, however, he—like Robinson with the Dodgers—had no chance of playing his regular position—or any position in the infield—any time soon. Worse, Boudreau resented him somewhat because Veeck had not consulted him about the signing. During the whole of the second half of 1947, Doby appeared in just 29 games—only 6 of them in the field. "It was the most frustrating time of my life," he says today, "because I wasn't playing. This had never happened to me before. I would much rather have been playing in triple-A, or even at Newark."

Doby's relations with many teammates were difficult as well. About ten of them declined to shake his hand when he was introduced around the locker room. When he went on the field for the first time in Chicago, he stood alone for perhaps fifteen minutes before Joe Gordon offered to play catch. Today, Doby remembers Gordon, Jim Hegan, and Bob Lemon as the most helpful among his teammates, and adds that Keltner was "always friendly." Others never warmed to him, but by early 1948, about half of those who had refused to shake his hand were gone. Most helpful of all, perhaps, was the Indians' coach and former National League manager, Bill McKechnie. "You know," he told Doby late in the year, "with Gordon and Boudreau and Keltner on this team, there's no room for you in the infield. I think next year we'll try you in the outfield."

Doby had never played the outfield, but in the off-season he bought a new book by Tommy Henrich, *How to Play the Outfield,* and virtually committed it to memory. Legendary Indian center fielder Tris Speaker had also worked with him in spring training. With his great speed, he had rapidly adjusted during 1948, and had already made a number of spectacular catches while establishing himself as an excellent hitter.

McKechnie was the first man to speak to Doby when he reached the dugout after his disastrous blunder. "Now we'll see if you're the major leaguer we think you are," he told him.[2] "Forget it, boy," said coach Muddy Ruel—using a form of address common for young white players, however insensitive it may have been. "It was probably my fault," Tris Speaker graciously told the press. "I told him in spring training that the center-

2. Boudreau with Fitzgerald, *Player-Manager,* 177–78.

fielder should take everything he could reach." As it turned out, Doby rebounded immediately, and went on to a great season and a fine career.

Doby inevitably had more trouble with teammates. "I was used to a team concept," he says, "and I could never socialize with my teammates after the game"—partly because of segregation in many cities, but partly, apparently, because of his teammates' attitudes. Although Paige was officially his roommate, Doby rarely saw him and never felt close to him. On the rare occasions when he was in their room, Paige enjoyed cooking catfish on a portable cooker, emitting a Deep South odor that Doby's New Jersey nostrils did not find congenial. Certain opposing pitchers, including the Red Sox' Joe Dobson and Dave Ferriss, also knocked him down frequently. But what made Doby's whole career so much more difficult than those of Jackie Robinson, Willie Mays, Roy Campanella, and Henry Aaron was a broader problem that became the tragedy of the American League.

The American League had been the superior league since the 1920s, making it—as Doby remembers—"the more exclusive club." It was no accident that maverick Bill Veeck had been the man to break the color barrier. In the National League, after Robinson's elevation to the Dodgers had led them straight to a pennant, Rickey had immediately added Roy Campanella and Don Newcombe, and the crosstown Giants had countered with Monte Irvin and Hank Thompson in 1949 and Willie Mays in 1951. Not coincidentally, the Dodgers and the Giants became the major players in every pennant race from 1951 through 1954, joined in 1955–56 by the Braves (with Henry Aaron and Billy Bruton) and the Reds (with pitcher Brooks Lawrence and sensational rookie Frank Robinson). What happened in the American League, alas, was very different.

In the last few weeks of 1947, while Doby was sitting on the Indians' bench, the St. Louis Browns also signed two black players, Willard Brown and Hank Thompson, who later starred with the Giants. The Browns dropped the two players and the experiment, however, before 1948. In 1948 Veeck, as we have seen, added Paige, and the next year, he signed the black Cuban Minnie Minoso and Luke Easter. By 1950 Veeck was gone, and Minoso was traded to the White Sox. But the two other leading franchises in the league—the Yankees and the Red Sox—resolutely refused to enter the market for black players. In both cases, key individuals played critical roles.

Ironically, Larry Doby remembers today that Ted Williams and Dom DiMaggio always treated him warmly, as did much of the Boston press and the crowd at Fenway Park. As we have seen, leading columnist Dave Egan campaigned repeatedly for the integration of Boston baseball. Owner Tom Yawkey and general manager Joe Cronin, however, steadfastly maintained an all-white team, although they occasionally gave spring training tryouts to black players. And in New York, Yankee general manager George Weiss was perhaps the most outspoken bigot of all. Before the 1952 World Series, over drinks with reporter Roger Kahn, Weiss said the Yankees would "never" get black players, because boxholders from Westchester wouldn't want to "sit with niggers."[3] With Mickey Mantle, Yogi Berra, and Whitey Ford on his team, Weiss managed to win pennant after pennant without tapping the black market until 1955, when he added the great catcher-outfielder Elston Howard. Until 1966, the only other black regular on any of the Yankee teams Howard played on was Latin third baseman Hector Lopez (1959–61). And by 1966, with Berra gone and Mantle and Ford in terminal decline, the team had fallen out of contention.

The Red Sox, meanwhile, refused to add any black player until 1959, when they settled on the very inadequate Pumpsie Green. The only American League team that aggressively pursued black talent in the late 1950s was the Washington Senators, who by the time they left for Minnesota in 1961 had acquired Lennie Green, the fine shortstop Zoilo Versalles, and catcher Earl Battey. The Twins in 1964–65 added Tony Oliva, Mudcat Grant, and Sandy Valdespino and succeeded the Yankees as pennant winners.

By that time—1965—the only starting black position players in the rest of the league were Don Buford and Flynn Robinson of the White Sox; Paul Blair of the Orioles; Willie Horton of the Tigers; Leon Wagner of the Indians; Howard of the Yankees; and Felix Mantilla of the Red Sox. National League lineups, by contrast, included Maury Wills, Willie and Tommy Davis, John Roseboro, and Lou Johnson of the Dodgers;[4] Willie Mays, Willie McCovey, and Jim Ray Hart of the Giants; Donn Clendenon, Roberto Clemente, and Willie Stargell of the Pirates; Frank Robinson and Vada Pinson of the Reds; Henry Aaron and Mack Jones of the Braves; Tony Taylor, Dick (then known as Richie) Allen, and Alex Johnson of the Phillies; Bill White, Curt Flood, Bob Gibson, and Lou Brock of the Cardinals; Ernie Banks and Billy Williams of the Cubs; and Walter Bond and Jim Wynn of the Astros. The only National League team without a black starter was the Mets, run by general manager George Weiss. The National League had at least eleven future black Hall of Famers, while the American League did not have a single one. The All-Star game had become an annual National League victory party.

Within this broader context, Larry Doby remained, for the whole of his

3. Roger Kahn, *The Boys of Summer* (New York, 1972), 164. Kahn in 1972 discreetly referred to Weiss as the third-ranking Yankee executive.

4. Johnson actually replaced Tommy Davis, who broke his ankle early in 1965.

thirteen-year career, what Jackie Robinson was for only two or three years: an outsider. Doby had to endure the further humiliation of the arrival of relatively light-skinned, straight-haired Latin players like second baseman Bobby Avila, who regarded themselves—and who were accepted in many restaurants—as white. The league as a whole never fully accepted him. When the Indians won the pennant in 1954, beating the Yankees by eight games, Doby was clearly their outstanding offensive player, but he lost the MVP vote to Yogi Berra, whom he outperformed in every offensive category except batting average. One can hardly escape the conclusion that race deprived him of the honor. In 1958, Doby passed another milestone when he became the first black player to start a fight with a white player. Charging the mound after Yankee Art Ditmar hit him with a pitch, he decked Ditmar with a left hook that writer Shirley Povich compared with Sugar Ray Robinson's. Doby was ejected from the game, but Ditmar was not.[5]

In 1948, Doby was simply one element of the greatest pennant race of all time, who overcame the obstacles he faced and made a decisive contribution to his team. As the fourth-best hitter on the team, in a league filled with immortals, he received much less press attention than Robinson—already the Dodgers' leading star—the year before, and race was almost never mentioned in most stories about the pennant race in the mainstream press. In retrospect, however, the American League's racial attitudes were the single most important factor in the league's decline over the next twenty years—and the decline of the stronger league contributed to the overall decline of baseball.

The Indians' opening loss dropped them back to third, still 1½ games out, as the Athletics moved back into a virtual tie with the Red Sox. The Yankees remained only percentage points behind the Indians, having split a pair with the Browns, losing 4–0 to tough Cliff Fannin and winning 4–0 behind Frank Shea. Lindell and Berra were still missing from the lineup. As the weekend began on Friday, July 30, the pressure fell squarely upon the first-place Red Sox and Indians, who faced each other for four games in Cleveland while the Mackmen moved on to Detroit and the Yankees to Chicago.

A total of 59,862 paying customers settled into their seats to watch Bearden face Parnell as the series opened on Friday evening. The Red Sox had failed to score against Bearden in eighteen previous innings, but quickly broke his spell in the top of the first when Dom DiMaggio and

---

5. In fairness, pitchers in this head-hunting era were almost never ejected for throwing at batters.

Pesky walked, Williams singled for a run, and Bobby Doerr hit a two-run homer, his twelfth of the month, for a 3–0 lead. But in the bottom of the frame, two walks, two fielding blunders, and four hits chased Parnell, and McCarthy waved in Galehouse with two on, one out, and six runs in.

Since losing a heartbreaker on opening day against the Athletics, Galehouse had had a strange season. He had had three more good outings as a starter, most recently a shutout of the White Sox in Fenway on July 22, but had also been dealt with rather harshly by the Senators, the Indians, and, only two days before, the Tigers. This time he began by walking Doby intentionally to load the bases, and Clark obediently spanked the ball off Galehouse's glove to Doerr, who started an inning-ending double play and ended the nightmare inning.

It was not a night for young left-handers. Bearden left in the top of the second after giving up three more hits and a run, but Don Black managed to end the rally with the Indians leading 6–4. Robinson doubled home Keltner in the bottom of the third to make it 7–4, but another double to left-center by Williams scored DiMaggio and Pesky in the top of the fourth and closed the gap to 7–6. Boudreau brought in Satchel Paige to face the Red Sox for the second time, and Paige retired Stephens and struck out Bobby Doerr to end the inning. Paige and Galehouse retired the side in order in the fifth, but in the sixth Pesky's sacrifice fly scored DiMaggio, who had doubled and advanced on Clark's wild throw, and tied the game 7–7.

Paige gave up the last run of the game in the top of the seventh on three singles. Denny Galehouse faced only thirteen batters in the last four innings, giving up just one run in 8⅔ innings for an 8–7 win. Although Paige gave up just two runs—one unearned—compared to Bearden's four and Black's two, he took his first loss of the year. The thirty-six-year-old Galehouse had proven that he could still turn in an excellent performance against a contending team, and McCarthy never forgot it. The surging Red Sox increased their lead to three games over the Indians and one and one-half over the Athletics, whom the Tigers pounded 17–2. And in Chicago, the Yankees lost a game despite Henrich's second grand slam of the year, when Reynolds was knocked out of the box and the bullpen failed in an 8–6 loss. After finishing the first half at .255, Henrich had now hit .403 since the break to bring his average up to .285, with 3 homers and 17 RBIs in the bargain.

One would have thought that the tension could not have increased after Friday night's thriller in Cleveland, but it did. With Feller facing Dobson on Saturday afternoon, both teams scored in the first inning again, and Cleveland held a 2–1 lead through five. Then came four of the wildest innings of the year. In the top of the sixth Feller hit Dobson in the wrist with the bases loaded and gave up a two-run double to the sizzling DiMaggio before leaving in favor of Klieman. Keltner promptly cracked his 24th homer in the bottom of the inning to tie the game, 4–4. A double by Stephens and three walks gave Boston the lead in the top of the seventh, but Boudreau singled and Hegan homered to regain the lead 6–5 in the bottom of that frame. A half-inning later, Russ Christopher relieved with DiMaggio and Pesky on base, and Stephens delivered his 21st home run, good for an 8–6 lead and the league lead in RBIs, with 87. Mitchell's triple and Keltner's single drew within one in the bottom of the eighth, but forty-three-year-old Earl Caldwell got the side out, and Dom DiMaggio drove in an insurance run with a bunt single in the top of the ninth.

The bottom of the ninth began well for Cleveland, as pinch hitters Thurman Tucker and Hal Peck doubled and walked. McCarthy took out Caldwell and brought in Mel Parnell, who had pitched the first inning of the previous night's game, and Boudreau now made one of the moves that drove Bill Veeck to distraction. Larry Doby was one for three on the day and had gone three for five against Parnell one week earlier, but Boudreau sent up Berardino to pinch-hit for him, and Johnny flied out. But Allie Clark singled to score Tucker and send Peck, the tying run, to third. Boudreau called the hit-and-run with Mitchell at the plate, and when Mitchell grounded to second, Doerr had to go to first, allowing Peck to score the tying run. Then Parnell walked Keltner intentionally and struck Gordon out to send the game into extra innings.

Steve Gromek and Parnell allowed no runs until the bottom of the eleventh, when Parnell had to face Keltner again with two out and the winning run on second. Once again McCarthy ordered him passed intentionally to face Gordon, and this time Gordon singled to center, scoring Tipton with the winning run. Coming from behind three times, the Indians had closed to within two games of the lead on the eve of Sunday's doubleheader. The Athletics climbed to within a half-game of the lead in Detroit, winning 4–3. In Chicago, Henrich had another big game and the Yankees won Lopat's ninth straight game, 4–2, as Lindell finally returned. Luke Appling, the forty-one-year-old White Sox shortstop/third baseman, also had three hits, raising his career total to 2,501.[6] The *New York Times* reported that another great shortstop, fifty-eight-year-old Dave Bancroft—who had played against Bucky Harris in the 1924 World Series—was also at the game. Bancroft was currently the manager of the Chicago

6. Appling had another full season ahead of him, and had he not missed almost two full wartime seasons he would undoubtedly have passed 3,000 hits. He was deservedly inducted into the Hall of Fame in 1964.

Colleens, "one of the teams in the girls' hardball All-American League"—the league now made famous by the movie *A League of Their Own.*

STANDINGS
Sunday Morning, August 1, 1948

Team	Won	Lost	Pct.	Games Behind
Boston	57	38	.600	—
Philadelphia	58	40	.592	½
Cleveland	53	38	.582	2
New York	54	39	.581	2
Detroit	46	48	.489	9½
Washington	40	54	.426	16½
St. Louis	34	55	.382	15
Chicago	31	64	.326	26

With both bullpens exhausted, Lemon and Zoldak for Cleveland and Kinder and Harris for Boston had to come up with good performances. As it turned out, the Indians' superior pitching depth showed. A two-run homer by Larry Doby and a two-out pop-up that dropped among three Red Sox infielders helped Cleveland score five runs in the first, and by the top of the third Kinder was gone and the Indians led 8–0. But the Indians suffered a costly injury when Stan Spence flied deep to right and Hank Edwards—now the regular right fielder against right-handed pitching—leapt against the fence to make the catch and separated his shoulder. He was lost for the season—the third time in his career that he had injured himself making a catch. Lemon became the first Indian hurler to throw a complete game since July 15, eighteen games ago, and finally got his fourteenth win against five losses.

The second game was delayed twenty-five minutes by a shower in the bottom of the first, with the score 0–0. It was still 0–0 when Boudreau walked with one out in the bottom of the second, and Robinson advanced him to third with a single to left. Hegan, catching his second game of the day, struck out, bringing Zoldak to the plate with two out.

Lou Boudreau—at the top of his game as a player, and managing by far the strongest team he had ever had—was going all out to bring Cleveland its first pennant in twenty-eight years, keep his job as manager, and show up Bill Veeck. Speed was not one of Boudreau's many assets as a ballplayer. He had had trouble with his ankles ever since breaking one of them in his first full season, and they pained him so much that he did not expect his playing career to last much longer. But now, watching Mickey Harris check him at third, look at first, hesitate, and deliver a strike to Zoldak, it occurred to Boudreau that he might be able to steal home for the first time in his career. He signaled his intention to coach Bill McKechnie, who winked back.

With a weak hitter at bat and two out, the steal of home—as John Thorn and Pete Palmer argued in *The Hidden Game of Baseball*—is a much-neglected percentage play.[7] Zoldak's chances of keeping the inning alive were less than one in five, so that even a one-in-three chance of success would justify Boudreau's attempt. Lou almost didn't get the chance, as Harris got a quick second strike, and then threw a ball. Boudreau took off on the next pitch, a high and inside delivery that catcher Matt Batts had to reach for. The play was close, but Bill Summers called Boudreau safe. Batts leapt to his feet in protest, momentarily forgetting about Eddie Robinson on first and allowing him to take second.

During the last three days, Joe McCarthy had had to endure Stephens's costly error on a double-play grounder on Friday night, two terrible base-running blunders by Birdie Tebbetts and Earl Caldwell on Saturday, and two botched pop-ups in the first game of the doubleheader. Boudreau's theft of home was too much. Charging onto the field, McCarthy raged alternately at Summers and Matt Batts, while Batts also insisted that he had blocked the plate. Summers—who later had to endure a similar protest from Yogi Berra and Casey Stengel after Jackie Robinson stole home in the first game of the 1955 World Series—held firm. McCarthy was careful not to be ejected, but at one point he turned and kicked the ground in frustration.

What turned the incident into a cause célèbre back in Boston was the imaginative vision of one Boston writer, who reported that McCarthy had actually kicked Batts. It took another two days for the story to reach the Red Sox on their next stop, and denials by McCarthy and Batts never really caught up to the original story. In any case, the score was 1–0 when McCarthy finally returned to the dugout.

MATT BATTS: Mickey Harris took a long time winding up, and he threw a high pitch. I had to go up for it and come down to tag him. I really thought he was out. I forgot to call time.

McCarthy came out raging. "God damn it," he said, "call time out! Tag him!" "It wasn't my fault," I said. "The pitch was too high." He was kicking dirt, kicking the plate. He didn't kick me.

A couple of days later McCarthy called a meeting and apologized. "I haven't exactly gone crazy," he said, "and if I was going to kick anybody in the

7. John Thorn and Pete Palmer with David Reuther, *The Hidden Game of Baseball* (New York, 1984), 158–59.

butt I'd pick on somebody else, because Matt Batts would get up and kick the shit out of me." I told him not to worry, that he didn't have to apologize.

With Gordon hitting a two-run homer, the Indians led 6–0 when Williams hit his 17th home run in the top of the ninth with no one on—his first home run since his rib injury early in July. Three outs later, Zoldak had his revenge for his unlucky loss to Mel Parnell one week earlier. After losing four in a row to the Red Sox, the Indians had snapped back with three consecutive victories, as only Galehouse of the Red Sox pitchers had managed to contain them. Helped by heavy hitting and Boudreau's shock theft of home, the Indians had squared the season series with Boston at nine wins apiece, ending the Red Sox' seven-day reign as league leaders.

Indeed, as the four teams moved toward a virtual tie, the Red Sox, having started Sunday in first place, dropped all the way down to fourth, while the Indians earned nothing more than a tie for second. In Detroit the Athletics kept first place with a 4–2 victory. And in Chicago, Vic Raschi and Tommy Byrne swept the White Sox, 8–2 and 7–5, behind a combined twenty-three Yankee hits, including two-run homers by DiMaggio and Billy Johnson. Unlucky Phil Rizzuto hurt himself again, and Frankie Crosetti substituted for him in the first game and Brown in the second. Yogi Berra finally returned to catch the second game. The sweep left the Yankees in a virtual tie for second with the Indians, just one game away from the top—the closest to the lead they had been since the very first day of their season, when they had trailed the Athletics by half a game. Joe DiMaggio, with six runs batted in in the last two days, regained the lead from Junior Stephens, 90 to 87.

With Philadelphia, Cleveland, New York, and Boston fighting for the lead, the schedule guaranteed that two of the contenders would be facing each other every day, with the exception of those days on which Cleveland faced Washington. After the usual Monday day off, the Tribe opened a two-game set with the Senators on the evening of August 3, but Boudreau now found another way to increase the general excitement by giving Satchel Paige (1–1) his first major league start. Bearden and Gromek were also available, but the Indians had to play fifteen games in twelve days beginning on August 5, and Boudreau needed to find out exactly what Satch could do, and for how long. The Cleveland fans obviously shared Boudreau's curiosity, and the biggest night crowd in baseball history, 72,434, showed up to see Paige face Early Wynn, the Senators' ace, who was enjoying a wretched season.

Paige began poorly, surrendering two walks and a triple in the first, but escaped down 2–0 and held Washington scoreless into the fifth. Hegan finally homered to take the lead in the bottom of the sixth inning, and Klieman pitched the eighth and ninth after the Indians had stretched their lead to 5–3. Paige emerged with his first win as a starter, and expressed his willingness to do as much duty as required after the game. Keltner, with three hits, raised his average all the way to .302. The next morning's papers showed that Satchel had pitched the Indians into first place for the first time in ten days. In Chicago the A's had lost a heartbreaker, 2–1, and in Detroit, Frank Shea pitched the Yankees to a 15–3 victory behind homers by McQuinn, Henrich, and Berra. And in St. Louis, the Red Sox turned the race into a virtual four-way tie for first with a 15–8 rout of the Browns. Jack Kramer had to leave the game in the third inning with a sore shoulder, but was still credited with his eleventh straight win and thirteenth overall. Williams hit his 19th home run, and Stephens's 3 RBIs raised his season's total to 90, just one behind Joe DiMaggio.[8] All four contenders had now won eighteen more games than they had lost, and a total of .006 separated them in the standings. A week later, the *Sporting News* reported that the standings were the closest in history for this point in the season.

STANDINGS
Wednesday Morning, August 4, 1948

Team	Won	Lost	Pct.	Games Behind
Cleveland	56	38	.596	—
New York	57	39	.594	—
Boston	58	40	.592	—
Philadelphia	59	41	.590	—
Detroit	46	50	.479	11
Washington	40	55	.423	16½
St. Louis	35	57	.387	19½
Chicago	31	65	.333	25

On Wednesday, rain-outs in Chicago and Detroit and a day off in Cleveland gave the Red Sox a chance to move back into first by winning in St. Louis. They scored six runs in the top of the first, but for the second time in a row, Mel Parnell failed to make it through the first inning, giving way to Kinder after only one-third of an inning as the Browns actually took a 7–6 lead. Kinder eventually went into the bottom of the ninth with an 8–7 lead,

---

8. The two men would finish with more than 130 RBIs each if they could maintain their current pace. They eventually exceeded that figure by a total of 32 RBIs.

but three singles and a walk gave the Browns two runs and the victory, and the Red Sox fell all the way to fourth place instead.

Boston tested McCarthy's nerves again the next day, blowing yet another early lead. Two hits by Williams helped build up a 7–1 margin in the fifth, but the Browns scored five times on three walks by Dobson, *two* errors by Stephens at shortstop, and a fly by Hank "Bow-Wow" Arft that became a triple when Williams—still limping from his injured knee—could not reach it. With the score tied at 8–8 in the top of the ninth, Stephens singled in the winner to keep the Sox just one game out. The Red Sox pitching staff, which had performed so well in Fenway, was collapsing on the road. The team had scored 31 runs in three games against the Browns, but won only two of them. The Browns were amazed by the amount of batting practice the Red Sox put in. While the St. Louisians contented themselves with a bunt and four swings every day, McCarthy's Red Sox took at least twice as many.

In Chicago, the Athletics vaulted themselves from third place back into second with a doubleheader sweep. In Detroit, Allie Reynolds turned in a fine game against Fred Hutchinson to hold the Yankees in third with a 2–1 victory. Reynolds, who needed help from Joe Page in the ninth, got his eleventh victory against five losses after a full month's drought. His problems since the All-Star break suggested that he, like Bob Lemon, had been worn out by his great first half. And in Cleveland, Bearden beat Ray Scarborough, 3–0, on three homers—two by Jim Hegan, who had an amazing knack for making his rare round-trippers count, and one by Bearden himself. The win kept the Tribe on top of the standings by .002, although they were technically one-half game behind both the Yankees and the Athletics. The game, however, temporarily cost the Indians the playing services of Lou Boudreau, who hurt his shoulder, side, and ankle in a collision at second base. It was not certain when he could return to the lineup, and the Indians now faced a very hot Yankee club for four crucial games.

The last weekend of the eastern clubs' third trip west offered a real opportunity to the Athletics and Red Sox, who faced the Browns and the White Sox for three and four games, respectively, while the Yankees and the Indians slugged it out head to head. The Athletics lost a 2–1 heartbreaker to the Browns' Bill Kennedy on Friday but rebounded smartly on Saturday and Sunday, winning 7–1 behind Brissie and 7–5 behind Fowler. Their domination of the weaker clubs had continued, given them a combined 26–8 record against the White Sox and the Browns, compared to 14–5 for the Indians, 24–9 for the Yankees, and 23–12 for the Red Sox.

Nothing came easily for the Red Sox, who opened their series in Chicago on Friday without Ted Williams, who finally acknowledged the seriousness of his injured knee and sat out the game. Trailing 1–0 in the top of the sixth, Boston broke through when Junior Stephens hit his 23rd home run with two on, giving him a league-leading 95 RBIs. But Pat Seerey answered in the bottom of the seventh with a three-run shot of his own off Galehouse, and the Red Sox trailed 4–3 in the ninth. With one out in the top of the ninth, Tebbetts singled, and McCarthy sent up Ted Williams to hit for Galehouse while inserting Wally Moses—certainly no greyhound himself—to run for Tebbetts. With the White Sox outfield swung around to the right, Williams blooped the ball to left-center, and Moses took off for home. The bulky Seerey ran, ran, ran—and made the catch, flipping the ball to second to double up Moses and end the game. The Red Sox fell 1½ games off the pace the next day when left-hander Al Gettel gave up just four hits on the way to a 5–1 victory over Mickey Harris. Joe McCarthy faced his most serious pitching crisis of the season. Jack Kramer was recovering from a sore shoulder that had forced him out of his last start, Dobson's wrist was sore, having been struck in Cleveland a week earlier by Bob Feller's pitch, and Parnell had followed his three wins in ten days during the big home stand with two dreadful outings and a loss in relief.

Parnell finally returned to form, getting his eighth victory and his first win in two weeks in the first game of Sunday's doubleheader, 8–1. The second game was a 1–1 struggle through ten innings, and an error and a bad throw by Dom DiMaggio allowed the White Sox to score the winning run in the eleventh. Losing three out of four to the wretched White Sox dropped the Red Sox 2½ games off of the pace. While they had won nine of eleven on their last western trip, this one ended at 6–8. The pitching staff had simply collapsed after winning fifteen games in eleven days at home, managing just three complete games in fourteen outings—one each by Kinder, Kramer, and Parnell. With three more games in New York and four in Washington, their flirtation with the flag could easily be over by the time they got home.

The four-game weekend series between the Yankees and the Indians was the biggest of the season. Six weeks earlier, the Yankees had wrecked the Tribe's June home stand with three victories out of four, and they could probably take over the lead if they could repeat that performance. Having won six of their first eight in this home stand, the Indians had to try to maintain that pace in order to remain in first. The Yankees came into Municipal Stadium with a new hurler on their roster. A week earlier, the *Times* had reported that Bucky Harris was pressuring George Weiss to call up twenty-three-year-old Bob Porterfield from Newark, where Porterfield had a 15–6 record and a league-leading 1.91 ERA. Weiss had refused to bring Porterfield up and pay him a major league salary, and a frustrated Harris had bet his coach, Chuck Dressen, twenty dollars that the general manager would never call him up. "Never lost a bet more cheerfully in all my life," said Bucky, as he paid Dressen off—while Weiss prepared for the last laugh.

Bob Feller, who opened the series on Friday before 71,258 fans, had finally gotten his tenth victory against the Athletics ten days before, but he had not pitched a complete game since July 11 or a complete game victory since July 7, and he had won none and lost four against the Yankees, who had repeatedly touched him for home runs. His opponent Ed Lopat, by contrast, had won nine straight, and was 2–1 against the Indians. Only one regular from the two teams was absent, but that was Lou Boudreau. Feller quickly went down 3–0 in the first two innings, surviving the first when Doby caught DiMaggio's bid for a two-run homer right at the fence. But the Indians scored twice in the second, and Allie Clark—enjoying a tremendous home stand as the regular right fielder—tied the game with his tenth home run in the third, as Feller settled down. With two on and one out in the Indian fifth, Lopat walked Hegan intentionally to face Feller with the bases loaded. Feller, who had a lifetime batting average of well under .200 and a total of three home runs, managed to drive one of Lopat's junk balls through the middle and into the outfield for two runs and a 5–3 lead. The Tribe increased its lead to 6–3 in the bottom of the sixth, and a three-run homer by Gordon, his 21st, made it 9–3 in the bottom of the seventh.

Feller might have had an easy complete-game victory but for the absence of Boudreau. Berardino kicked a double-play ball with one out in the eighth, and after a walk and Stirnweiss's two-run double, Boudreau waved in Klieman, his new relief ace, and Feller left the mound to a tremendous ovation. Cleveland hearts sank when Henrich singled for two more runs and cut the lead to 9–7, but Keller flied out, and DiMaggio came up just a little short once again when Dale Mitchell caught his drive against the left-field fence. Trailing 9–7, the Yankees threatened again in the ninth, but Christopher got the last out with two men on base. It was the Indians' sixth straight win, and Feller raised his record to 11–12. The Athletics' defeat gave the Indians a half-game lead.

On Saturday, before more than 66,000 fans, Vic Raschi turned in one of the most brilliant pitching performances of the season, shutting the Indians out on four singles, walking just two, striking out seven, and running his league-leading record to 14–4. Lemon also pitched well, but was beaten by Joe DiMaggio, who finally broke out of his slump, driving in three runs on two doubles and stealing home on the front end of a double steal for the

Yankees' last run. His 93 RBIs trailed Junior Stephens by two. Henrich, continuing his tremendous hitting, had two hits and two runs scored, and the Yanks closed to within .002 of the Indians. The series and the league lead would ride on Sunday's twin bill.

Boudreau was still on the bench when the Indians and the Yankees squared off for their Sunday doubleheader before 73,484. For the second day in a row, Boudreau decided to rest Allie Clark, who had hit very well throughout the home stand, and replace him with early-season regular Thurman Tucker, who took over center field while Larry Doby moved back to right. He chose his new second-half stalwarts, Sam Zoldak and Steve Gromek, to face Frank Shea and Yankee phenom Bob Porterfield. With the Athletics playing just one game against the Browns, either team could move into first place by sweeping the doubleheader, and the Yankees seemed determined to do so. Scoring two runs each in the fourth, fifth, and seventh, they chased Zoldak and took a 6–1 lead into the bottom of the seventh.

As the huge crowd sat down from an anxious stretch, Shea walked Keltner but got the first two outs. Then Johnny Berardino, who had made a costly error, atoned for some of his sins and awakened the crowd with a home run into the left-field seats. A moment later, Eddie Robinson sent his 11th homer—and his first in many weeks—into the right-field stands to cut the Yankee lead to 6–4. Jim Hegan promptly singled to left, and a routine runaway suddenly turned into a managerial battle of wits. Boudreau sent left-handed Hal Peck to bat for Klieman, Harris countered with lefty Joe Page, and Boudreau substituted Allie Clark for Peck. Clark promptly walked on four pitches, and Dale Mitchell grounded the ball deep into the hole at short, where Rizzuto could not make a play. The bases were loaded, the Indians trailed 6–4, and Boudreau turned over his hole card. With Thurman Tucker—0–7 for his last two games—due up next, the shortstop-manager walked out of the dugout with a bat in his hand himself. The Boy Manager was giving himself a chance to strike a blow every bit as memorable, and every bit as significant, as the three tremendous home runs hit by Joe DiMaggio to win another Yankee-Indian battle back in May, or his own theft of home against Boston just a week earlier.

DiMaggio's strength was his power; Boudreau's, his bat control and discipline. Playing the percentages, he managed to spank Joe Page's pitch up the middle for a ground-ball single that brought the crowd roaring to its feet and tied the game, 6–6. Page got the side out, but Boudreau promptly called on another ace in the hole, as Satchel Paige ambled in from the bullpen to open the next frame. The great hurler quickly retired two batters, and Doby threw out Rizzuto trying to stretch a single into a double.

With two out and one on in the bottom of the eighth, Eddie Robinson came to the plate. On May 23—the day DiMaggio had rocked the Indians with three homers—Page had struck out Robinson with the bases loaded to save the game. Now Robinson got his revenge, homering off Page for an 8–6 lead. Boudreau brought in Christopher to get the last out in the ninth, but Paige got the win, his third. He had not allowed a run in three outings against the Yankees. The Indians had assured themselves of a split of the series, but they needed another win to be sure of remaining in first place.

Bob Porterfield, who was just a few days' shy of his twenty-fourth birthday, completed a two-year rise through the ranks of professional baseball with his start in the second game. After three years in the 82nd Airborne Division during the war, he had gone to work for his father in his hometown of Radford, Virginia, in the western part of the state. In early 1946 he and his brother organized a semipro team and challenged the local Class D minor league farm club. He struck out the last nine men and was offered a contract. A few months later he was purchased by Norfolk, a Yankee farm club in the Piedmont League, and one season later an outstanding campaign at triple-A Newark earned him a shot in the majors.

His major league debut started out as impressively as his minor league one: he did not allow a hit during the first four innings. Steve Gromek did exactly as well. With the score still 0–0 in the bottom of the fifth, Eddie Robinson hit his third homer of the day over the right-field fence. The Yankees tied it rather luckily on an unearned run in the bottom of the sixth. It was still 1–1 in the bottom of the seventh when Joe Gordon beat out a hit to deep short. A bunt, a walk, a single by Hegan, and a line drive from Hal Peck that glanced off Porterfield's pitching hand and forced the rookie to leave the game in favor of Tommy Byrne gave Cleveland the lead. Klieman shut out the Yankees over the last two innings for a 2–1 win and a doubleheader sweep. Boudreau, Paige, and Eddie Robinson were the heroes of the day. Like Lou Brissie, Robinson had almost lost his career as a result of the war, when he seriously injured a leg. He had come to spring training in 1946 with his leg in a brace, but recovered his strength and made the club. Then he spent most of 1946 playing in Baltimore, in the International League, to be near his baby daughter, who died of cancer during that year. He had a solid 14 home runs in 318 at bats during 1947, but he had never completely won Boudreau's confidence, and Boudreau had lifted him for Berardino at various times during the year. On this day he had delivered three homers in one of the season's biggest doubleheaders.

The double loss dropped the Yankees two games off the pace, and gave the Indians a tremendous 9–3 home stand—6–2 against Boston and New York—compared to 6–9 in their previous home stand against the eastern clubs. Gromek, Zoldak, and Paige had turned in some fine pitching performances, Klieman had been strong out of the bullpen, and even Feller had eked out a difficult win against his Bronx tormentors. Above all, they had hit, averaging seven runs a game in Municipal Stadium. Boudreau and Dale Mitchell had slumped, but Gordon had hit .298 with three homers and ten RBIs during the twelve games, Keltner had sizzled at .344 with two homers and six runs batted in, and Doby, recovering from his dreadful blunder, had made his hits count for eight RBIs. The biggest heroes of all were Eddie Robinson, who had hit .395 with three homers, and unsung Allie Clark, who hit .387 with three homers and seven RBIs against the Athletics, Red Sox, and Senators before Boudreau unaccountably benched him against the Yankees.

Boudreau and Keltner were in the midst of easily the greatest seasons of their careers. The same was not true of Gordon, who had had one season (1942) that was better, and at least two others (1947 and 1939) that were nearly as good. Gordon was one of the outstanding players of his time. The *Sporting News* named him the outstanding second baseman in the major leagues six times—1939–42 and 1947–48—and he beat out triple crown winner Ted Williams for the MVP in 1942. He hit .300 only once, but walked an average of 79 times per season and hit an average of 26 home runs—more than half of them on the road. His career offensive won-loss percentage, as measured by Bill James, was .619—considerably higher than those of Red Schoendienst (.521), Frankie Frisch (.591), and his contemporary Bobby Doerr (.578), all of whom are in the Hall of Fame. Gordon, most unjustly, has not yet been elected, even though the *Sporting News* selections and MVP voting indicate that his contemporaries regarded him as superior to Doerr.

Gordon was also an outstanding personality on the Indians, where he was finally earning what he was worth. In five years with the Yankees, culminating in his MVP season in 1942, he had managed to get his salary all the way up to $11,000 per year, but he had more than doubled that figure now. During 1948 he and Boudreau were the steadiest hitters on the team. He hit only .260 over the first half of the year, but piled up 17 homers and 67 RBIs, and his average climbed during the second half of the season. Alone among the Indians, he had both won and lost pennant races before. The Indians would not have been anywhere near first place without him.

There was more good news for the Indians as they prepared for a western trip. Now it was their turn to fatten themselves against the weaker western clubs, while the other contenders ate each other up. Both the Yankees and the Red Sox had just one more scheduled game in Municipal Stadium. The

Tribe had one more long eastern swing to make late in August, but 40 of their remaining 53 games were scheduled against the Browns, the White Sox, the Senators, and the Tigers—including their last eight games of the season. Bill McKechnie, who had been playing and managing for more than forty years, had noticed the significance of the schedule months earlier, and never failed to bring it up to reassure his young boss. "Don't worry, Louie," he told Boudreau—"we're going to back in."[9]

Bill Veeck was well on his way to a record of his own. With almost two months left in the season, the Indians had drawn an incredible 1,719,305 paying customers at home and broken their old record—set the previous year—by almost 200,000. Municipal Stadium held more than 80,000 people, but it was clear from reaction around the Cleveland area during the Yankee series that the Indians could have sold considerably more tickets had they had more room. Cleveland patrons telephoning early in the week had been incredulous to learn that no reserved seats remained. Veeck issued a public statement, pointing out that fans in other parts of northern Ohio tended to plan further ahead, and warning the local clientele that they had better buy their seats in advance too. The Indians had drawn their 1.7 million fans in just 42 home dates—an average of almost 41,000 per game. With 23 more home dates left, they seemed very likely to break the all-time record of 2,265,512 set by the Yankees in 1946. They were not alone. The Yankees' pace was not far behind, and the Red Sox—with a park of about half the capacity of the Yankees'—were selling out almost every evening or weekend game. The three-year postwar baseball boom was peaking both because of the historic pennant race and because 1948, unlike 1946 or 1947, was a phenomenal year for hitting, which invariably stimulates attendance. Ted Williams had won the triple crown in 1947 with a .343 average, 32 homers, and 114 RBIs, but none of those figures looked good enough to lead the league in 1948. Williams was keeping his own average around .380, DiMaggio and Keltner had neared 30 homers, and Stephens and DiMaggio were close to their 100th RBI in the first week of August. While Williams had been the only American League hitter to top 100 RBIs in 1947, now at least ten players had a chance to do so, including DiMaggio, Henrich, Gordon, Keltner, Boudreau, Stephens, Doerr, Hank Majeski, and Williams himself.

Four teams had played brilliantly to produce a magnificent four-team race. Three of them, as it turned out, were destined to play even better from here on out. The Indians on Monday, August 9, found themselves in first

9. Boudreau with Fitzgerald, *Player-Manager*, 179.

place by half a game with a winning percentage of .606. Had they merely maintained that percentage for the rest of the way, they would not even have finished second.

STANDINGS
Monday, August 9, 1948

Team	Won	Lost	Pct.	Games Behind
Cleveland	60	39	.606	—
Philadelphia	63	42	.600	½
New York	59	42	.584	2½
Boston	60	44	.577	3
Detroit	49	52	.485	12
Washington	42	60	.412	17½
St. Louis	39	60	.394	20
Chicago	35	68	.340	25½

8

Satchel the Magnificent

(AUGUST 9–AUGUST 23)

While the competition may have eased somewhat for the Indians in mid-August, the pace increased. As the eastern clubs headed home on Monday, August 9, Cleveland began a daunting western trip of ten games in seven days, including two single games against the Tigers, consecutive double-headers in St. Louis on Wednesday and Thursday, and four games in Chicago over the weekend. Having initially announced that Satchel Paige would make his second start in the series opener against Detroit, Boudreau in the wake of Paige's relief win had to alter his plans, and tapped Bearden and Feller for the Detroit series. A crowd of 56,369—many of whom had hoped to see Paige—broke the Detroit night attendance record set by the Red Sox and the Tigers just two weeks earlier, and saw Bearden manage a 5–3 win with the help of Robinson's three-run homer, his third in two days. But the next day Feller failed to win his twelfth victory, losing 7–3. The Tribe remained barely in first.

Surprisingly, they could do no more than continue their .500 pace in a pair of doubleheaders in St. Louis on Wednesday and Thursday, August 11 and 12. In the opener on Thursday, Bob Lemon cruised to a 7–0 lead after 4½ innings, but Paige had to come in with the score 7–4 in the seventh and save Lemon's league-leading fifteenth victory. Boudreau finally returned to the lineup and went four for nine on the day to hike his average to .346. But the Browns shelled Bob Muncrief—making his first start in three weeks—and Ed Klieman in the second game, winning 12–4. On Friday afternoon, the Browns battered their old teammate Zoldak with nine hits in less than four innings for an 8–4 victory. Fresh out of rested pitchers, Boudreau

135

started Bearden in the nightcap with just two days' rest, and the game was one of the most remarkable and least dramatic of the season. The Indians scored nine runs in the top of the first, four in the third, two in the fourth, four in the fifth, three in the sixth, three in the seventh, and one in the eighth. Feller—getting some between-start exercise—took over in the bottom of the eighth with a 26–1 lead, and held off the Browns to finish the game at 26–3. The *Baseball Encyclopedia* has not credited him with a save.

The box scores for these two games reveal some interesting aspects of baseball in 1948. The two teams combined for sixty hits and forty-one runs, but the pitchers consistently threw the ball over the plate, walking just ten and striking out only ten during the two games. As a result, the 12–4 first game took just one hour and forty minutes, and the 26–3 nightcap an amazing two hours and twenty-three minutes. The same doubleheader would surely take at least seven hours in the 1990s. Leaving for a four-game series in Chicago, the Indians had once again dropped out of first place.

As Joe McCarthy took the train from Chicago on the evening of August 8 to meet his old team the Yankees, his season was at a crossroads and his pitching situation was critical. The Sox had eleven pitchers on the staff, compared to ten for the Indians and nine for the Yankees, but eighteen-year-old Chuck Stobbs simply traveled with the club because of the bonus rule, and McCarthy lacked confidence in Tex Hughson. Earl Caldwell, the front office's only contribution, was a doubtful quantity, and Dave Ferriss and Mickey Harris had both failed repeatedly. Now McCarthy's aces, Jack Kramer and Joe Dobson, were both suffering from injuries, and Mel Parnell had failed in two of his last three starts. McCarthy tapped Jack Kramer, hoping that his sore shoulder had recovered since his last start in St. Louis, to face Ed Lopat to start the three-game set on Tuesday before 67,691 fans.

It was Bucky Harris, not McCarthy, whose pitching plans received a rude shock in the very first inning when Pesky's hard grounder struck Lopat in the groin, and the pitcher collapsed in agony. After a few minutes he decided to leave the game, and Harris brought in Frank Hiller. Williams, bad leg and all, tripled for a run, Hiller walked three men, and Harris gambled and brought in his wildest pitcher, Tommy Byrne. By the time Byrne finished the inning, the Red Sox led 4–0. Led by Joe DiMaggio, who had gone just 9 for 50 on the western trip, the Yankees pecked away and tied the game 4–4 in the bottom of the seventh. After McCarthy relieved Kramer with Hughson, DiMaggio singled to left, and two runs scored when Williams booted the ball. But in the top of the eighth, the Red Sox, helped by four walks by Byrne and reliever Raschi, a two-run single by

Dom DiMaggio, and a ground rule double by Junior Stephens into the left-field stands, took a 9–6 lead. Lefty Earl Johnson survived the ninth when Dom DiMaggio robbed Henrich of at least a double with a fine catch, and the Red Sox passed the Yankees with a gutsy victory as Stephens took over the RBI lead from Joe DiMaggio, 97 to 96.

With Dobson hurting, McCarthy chose Galehouse, who had turned in a tremendous 8⅔ innings of relief against the Indians in Cleveland just eleven days earlier, to face a well-rested Allie Reynolds. Reynolds was on top 2–1 with one out in the Yankee fourth when third baseman Bill Johnson—a right-handed pull hitter—crossed up the Red Sox defense with a 400-foot shot to right-center field. Dom DiMaggio took off with the crack of the bat, running perhaps 100 feet into right center and leaping high at the last second to catch the ball in his gloved hand and complete the most remarkable outfield play of the season. The crowd rose to its feet and gave him a one-minute standing ovation.

Dominic DiMaggio was known as the Little Professor for his glasses, but he might just as easily have earned the same name for his approach to outfielding. He stood only five feet, nine inches tall and weighed less than 170 pounds, but he was one of the fastest players in the league, and he had developed his own approach to center-field play. To begin with, he played shallow, giving him a much better chance at bloops and pop-ups. Second, he was perhaps the only center fielder in the history of the game who always stood sideways to the plate as the ball was pitched instead of facing it, enabling him to get a quicker break backward. All outfielders are encouraged to do this, but contemporary press accounts make clear that DiMaggio did so to a far greater extent than any other. He studied the hitters, positioned himself carefully, and, like all great outfielders, reacted to every pitch thrown by the pitcher before the batter had even decided to swing. He had established his credentials as a center fielder in 1940, his rookie year, in two amusing incidents involving Red Sox shortstop and manager Joe Cronin.

DOM DIMAGGIO: The first exhibition game I ever played at center was against the Reds. Ernie Lombardi was up. Joe Cronin used to tell you where guys would hit the ball, and he liked to move you around the outfield. He waved me back, and back, and back, until I was almost standing up against the fence. I thought to myself, "this is crazy," but I did it.

Lombardi hit a high pop-up over Cronin's head. Cronin started back for it, and then gave up. I came running in and took it on the bounce. I didn't say anything—just lobbed the ball in to him.

A few weeks later, on Opening Day, we were playing the Senators. Cecil Travis came up. He was a left-handed hitter and a notorious left-field hitter.

Cronin moved me over, and over, and over, until I was almost shaking hands with Ted Williams. I even said, "Hi, Ted."

Travis hit the ball over Bobby Doerr's head at second into right-center. The pitch was on the inside part of the plate, and I had already started running that way, so I managed to cut it off. I turned around, and I saw Travis jockeying between first and second. Doerr had come out into short right field to take the relay, but Cronin was figuring on the ball going to the wall and was just standing at shortstop with his back to me. There was no one to throw to at second. Finally, someone got his attention, and he took the throw at second.

That was the last time Cronin ever moved me around on the field.

Because he played shallow, and because of his ability to make a break on a ball literally before it had even been hit, Dom DiMaggio could convert bloopers into outs, yet still make a play on a sliced shot like Billy Johnson's that looked uncatchable as it left the bat. More significant, despite playing half his games in the relatively small Fenway Park outfield, he had finished first or second in putouts for a center fielder in every one of his four full seasons, and twice led the league in assists. His arm did not have an outstanding reputation—unlike his brother Joe's—but like many smaller outfielders, he apparently more than made up for any lack of strength by getting to the ball so quickly.

DiMaggio was now in the middle of his finest defensive season. He eventually finished 1948 with 13 assists—second in the league—and an all-time American League record of 503 putouts. That record—and a corresponding record for total chances accepted—stood for twenty-nine years, until 1977, when Chet Lemon of the White Sox, whose schedule gave him seven extra games, managed to make 512 putouts. Career highs in putouts for a season for other center fielders include Tris Speaker, 423; Joe DiMaggio, 441 (also in 1948); Larry Doby, 411; Duke Snider, 382; Mickey Mantle, just 372 (in only 145 games); and Willie Mays, 448. Only Richie Ashburn consistently posted defensive totals in the range of Dom DiMaggio's 1948 season.[1] DiMaggio was, in short, one of the two or three finest center fielders in the history of the game. It is generally forgotten that it was an injury to Dom DiMaggio—a twisted ankle he sustained after doubling in two runs in the top of the eighth inning of the seventh game of the 1946 World Series, forcing him to leave the game—that enabled Enos Slaughter to make his famous dash from first to home on Harry Walker's hit to left-center in the bottom of the eighth. The Red Sox unanimously agree that he

1. In his *Historical Baseball Abstract*, Bill James suggests that Ashburn may have been helped by his ballpark and pitching staff: see 397–98.

would have reached the ball much more quickly and held Slaughter at third, as he did many times on hits off the center-field wall at Fenway.

MATT BATTS: As an outfielder I would take Dom DiMaggio over Joe DiMaggio—of course, I saw much more of Dom. He was a super center fielder and I never saw anybody any better, even Willie Mays or Mickey Mantle. I never saw anybody who could break forward or back as well as he could.

LARRY DOBY: I think Dom DiMaggio was at least the equal of Joe DiMaggio as an outfielder. Of course, he didn't have the New York media working for him.

As a hitter, DiMaggio was a model of consistency who in 1948 was in the midst of one of his finest seasons. His lifetime .298 batting average is very good; his lifetime on-base percentage of .380 is outstanding. He hit only .285 during 1948, but drew a career-high 105 walks. A venerable baseball myth holds that smaller players tend to tire easily, but DiMaggio in 1948 was enjoying a great second half, hitting .301 as opposed to just .252 at the All-Star break. He did not miss a single inning of the entire season. He had good line-drive power, averaging 41 extra-base hits for every 154 games over his career, and finished 1948 with 40 doubles, fourth in the league. Leading off in every game, he drove in a remarkable 87 runs. He was a skilled bunter, and one of the leading base stealers in the league.

JOHNNY PESKY: I thought Dominic was the perfect ballplayer.

Dom DiMaggio's great catch kept the Yankee lead at 2–1, and Boston took a 3–2 lead in the top of the seventh on Pesky's triple, Williams's walk, Stephens's sacrifice fly, and singles by Doerr and Goodman. Williams in the top of the seventh padded the lead with a home run to left field, his third opposite-field round-tripper of the season, and Matt Batts drove in the last Red Sox run. Meanwhile, Galehouse shut out the Yankees for the last six innings on just five hits and one walk for his fifth win against six losses. Porterfield, whose hand injury had not turned out to be serious, was scheduled to face Dobson or Parnell in Thursday's finale, but rain washed out the final day of the series. The Red Sox' two-game sweep had dropped the Yankees into fourth place, three games out of first, while bringing them within two of the top.

The Red Sox had gained on the Indians, but the amazing Athletics had won two of three over the Senators, good for a record of 65–43, a winning percentage of .602, and a half-game lead in first place. They were a team of good average hitters with fine on-base percentages, including Elmer Valo

(.322), Barney McCosky (.327), and Eddie Joost and Ferris Fain, who were hitting only .250 and .251 but eventually finished the year with 119 and 113 walks, trailing only Ted Williams in that category. Hank Majeski, meanwhile, had more than 80 RBIs, rivaling Keltner as the league's most productive third baseman. Dick Fowler and Joe Coleman had been excellent of late, and Lou Brissie had pitched well as a starter and reliever. Their record was still far superior to what might have been expected from their totals of runs scored and allowed, and reflected their remarkable talent—or good fortune—for scoring runs when they would do the most good. They had a 36–14 record against the Senators, Browns, and White Sox.

Connie Mack, aged eighty-six, still wore his famous high collar and managed from the dugout, waving his famous scorecard at his fielders and, on occasion, shaking it at umpires. He could no longer remember his players' names or maintain his concentration over the full length of a game, and coach Al Simmons, a veteran of Connie's great 1928–32 teams, frequently had to disregard his signs and give the team instructions on his own. ("You used better judgment than I did, Al," Connie would sometimes admit.) He was also as cheap as ever. Reporter Bob Considine, doing a long piece on him for *Life* in late July, had discovered that he had not yet installed a telephone line between the home dugout and the bullpen in Shibe Park, forcing coaches to use a bizarre set of signals to indicate what pitcher should warm up—pantomiming shoveling coal for Joe Coleman, or picking flowers for Dick Fowler, whom Connie referred to as "Mr. Flowers." (During the course of a long interview, Connie consistently referred to Considine as "Mr. Constantine.")[2] And for whatever reason, he had not managed during the whole first four months of the season to arouse the kind of excitement prevailing in Cleveland, in Boston, and in New York. Fewer than ten thousand fans had showed up on the last night of the series with the Senators.

The Athletics were a fine club, but they lacked the power to compete with the three teams over whom they enjoyed a momentary ascendancy. More than half of their remaining games pitted them against the other three contenders, including nine straight over the next ten days against the Yankees and the Red Sox. Few people really believed they would be on top in September, and such in fact was not destined to be the case. Yet we must pay tribute to this remarkable aggregation of gutsy pitchers, fine fielders, and line-drive hitters, which, on the morning of Friday the thirteenth of August, 108 games into the season, led the most remarkable pennant race in the history of major league baseball.

2. Considine, "Mr. Mack," in Einstein, *Fireside Book of Baseball*, pp. 54–56.

STANDINGS
Friday Morning, August 13, 1948

Team	Won	Lost	Pct.	Games Behind
Philadelphia	65	43	.602	—
Cleveland	63	42	.600	½
Boston	62	44	.585	2
New York	60	44	.577	3
Detroit	50	54	.489	13
St. Louis	42	62	.382	16
Washington	43	62	.426	16½
Chicago	36	69	.343	27½

The stage had been set for an unusually well-attended Friday evening of baseball in Chicago's Comiskey Park earlier in the week, when Lou Boudreau had announced that Satchel Paige would start the game. The Chicago public had already witnessed many of Paige's fabulous exploits, partly because the Negro leagues' All-Star game usually took place there, and the *Chicago Herald-American* had further increased interest by serializing his life story. The White Sox had quickly sold out every reserved seat, the first time in more than a decade that this had taken place. On Friday, a gigantic crowd showed up at the ticket windows and bought up the unreserved and bleacher seats several hours before the game was due to begin. The crowd was thoroughly integrated, moved less by racial pride than by the chance to see one of the most fabulous gate attractions in the history of baseball.

What happened as game time approached has happened perhaps half-a-dozen times in the history of baseball. Patrons with and without tickets jammed the surrounding streets, forcing Bill Veeck, among others, to leave his cab several blocks from the stadium. When Veeck reached the park, he pleaded with the elderly Mrs. Charles Comiskey to make a virtue of necessity and simply open up the park to all comers. She declined to do so, and the crowd took matters into their own hands and literally broke down the gates. Thousands streamed in, to be followed, shortly thereafter, with thousands more holders of reserved and box seat tickets who found their seats occupied.

The official attendance of 51,013 was about ten thousand higher than any other White Sox crowd during 1948, and just shy of the all-time Chicago record. Those present at the game agree that this was an underestimate of ten to twenty thousand people, including thousands who remained under the stands throughout the game. The crowd did not, however, threaten the field itself, and the game began on time, after Satchel accepted a trophy from the *Chicago Herald-American* as "one of America's most famous athletes" and shook hands with heavyweight champion Joe Louis.

The game, of course, was not merely an exhibition of a legend, but, like all games now, a critical contest. Indeed, Paige, making his second start, had a chance—for the second time in a row—to pitch the Indians back into first place. The great artist rose to the occasion. During the first four innings exactly one White Sox reached base—future Hall of Famer Luke Appling, who singled with two out in the first. Cleveland did not score until the fifth, when Doby tripled and scored on Hegan's sacrifice fly. The White Sox got one runner on in each of the next three innings, but that was all. The Indians scored four more runs and Paige had his fourth victory, a 5–0 shutout, after just one hour and fifty-four minutes. Even against the worst team in the league, it was an outstanding performance. The next day the Indians jumped off to a four-run lead behind another second-half star, Steve Gromek, and survived a scare in the ninth when Russ Christopher struck out big Pat Seerey with two on and two out to preserve a 4–2 victory.

In Sunday's packed doubleheader, Boudreau sent out Feller—making his third start in ten days—and Lemon, making his third start in nine days, to finish the road trip. Boudreau's triple and Doby's three-run double got the Indians off to a three-run first-inning lead, and Feller, who allowed eleven Chicago hits but walked only one, brought his record to 12–13 with a 6–2 victory. Boudreau was the hitting star again in the nightcap, as Lemon coasted to an 8–0 victory, Cleveland's fifth straight. With two of the eastern contenders battling each other to a standstill over the weekend, the Indians suddenly found themselves with a 1½-game lead.

Boudreau, who went 7 for 10 during the doubleheader, had now gone 19 for 46 (.413) with 11 RBIs since returning to the lineup in St. Louis eight games previously, hiking his average all the way from .344 up to .361, potentially within reach of Williams, who had dropped to .377. Mitchell did almost as well on the road trip, hitting .408 (20 for 49) to hike his average all the way to .336. It was the second straight road trip in which Mitchell had topped .400. And with six more home games against the Browns and White Sox during the next week, the Indians seemed poised to increase their lead.

While the Indians were sweeping the White Sox, the Yankees entertained the first-place Athletics for four games. Their two consecutive home losses to the Red Sox had left them three games out, and they had to make a surge soon to make much of an impression upon the race. They began well on Friday night, falling behind 5–0 as the Athletics chased Porterfield, but rallying against lefty Lou Brissie for eight runs in the bottom of the eighth before 60,745 fans. The next day, against right-handed pitching, Bucky Harris unveiled some major lineup shifts designed to improve the team both offensively and defensively.

Since the All-Star break the Yankees had continued to score runs at an impressive clip of almost six per game. The man most responsible for this result was Old Reliable Tommy Henrich, who over the last month had hit .374, with 4 homers, 24 runs batted in, and a remarkable 27 runs scored in 25 games, giving him 80 on the year, just 2 behind Dom DiMaggio's league-leading total. Other good hitters over this stretch included third baseman Bill Johnson (.304, but only 3 homers and 12 RBIs) and Charlie Keller (.302). Joe DiMaggio had managed to accumulate 23 more RBIs during these 25 games, although he had fallen into a woeful slump during the last six games with the Indians and the Red Sox. Johnny Lindell had only just returned to regular action after his long illness, and Yogi Berra had hit well but missed eight games with injuries.

First and second base were Bucky Harris's two offensive weaknesses. At first, thirty-nine-year-old George McQuinn had hit just .203 over the last month, with 2 homers and 10 RBIs, and Harris had apparently decided that he had reached the end of the road. Stirnweiss at second had hit a miserable .216. Defensively, Harris was still not satisfied with Berra, and Gus Niarhos was hitting a very respectable .280. Meanwhile, the team's leading hitter, Bobby Brown (.313), had come to bat just 29 times in 26 games. On Saturday, George McQuinn sat down, signaling the end of his career, and Harris replaced him at first with Henrich, who had played some first base in 1946. Berra moved to right field, where he had already played a few games, and where he could concentrate on his hitting. Gus Niarhos became the regular catcher, and Bobby Brown replaced Bill Johnson at third base against right-handed pitching. Meanwhile, Harris began agitating for the promotion of a young right-handed-hitting outfielder, Hank Bauer, to platoon with Berra in right, or perhaps to spell Lindell against left-handers should his injury and illness problems persist.

The changes behind the plate, at first, and in right field had an almost immediate impact. The substitution of Brown for Johnson was more questionable, since Johnson's superior power largely made up for Brown's higher average, but the Golden Boy had hit too well to keep out of the lineup. Harris could have gotten considerably more offensive punch by inserting Brown at second or at shortstop instead, but this he declined to do, refusing to risk a suspect fielder in the middle of the infield. In retrospect, of course, Harris's most interesting decision was the move of twenty-three-year-old Yogi Berra—destined to be the greatest catcher of his generation, and perhaps of all time—from behind the plate in favor of Gus Niarhos, who was four years older and far more experienced. Doubts about Berra's ability behind the plate had surfaced during the previous October's World Series, when the Dodgers had stolen five bases against him, but base thievery had not played a significant role in any of the Yankees' recent games. As Craig Wright has recently made clear, however, a catcher can have a powerful effect upon his pitchers' performances, partly by influencing umpires' calls.[3] A look at the Yankee box scores for the previous month of the season indicates that Harris had, in fact, recognized a real pattern in his team's performance.

During that month, Berra had caught 12 full games, and Niarhos 9. With Berra behind the plate, Yankee pitchers had averaged 5.3 walks and 3.8 strikeouts per game. Pitching to Niarhos, they had walked just 3.7 batters per game and struck out 3.9. The difference was reflected in runs allowed: 4.4 per game with Berra at catcher, and just 2.6 with Niarhos behind the plate. Last, five wild pitches or passed balls had occurred with Berra at catcher, while Niarhos had not allowed a single one. Part of Yogi's difficulties, apparently, was technical, while another part probably had to do with relations with the American League umpires. Bill McKinley remembered him thirty-five years later as "[not] a bad guy, but a pest. He was always turning around, saying something. . . . I think he did it not knowing what he was doing." Joe Paparella remembers him today, with a touch of sarcasm, as "not only a great catcher, but a great umpire."[4] Cal Hubbard, one of the senior umpires in the league, had seen fit, a few months earlier, to throw him out of the game for arguing balls and strikes. Bucky Harris, a veteran of almost thirty years in professional baseball, had seen something, and as always, he had the courage of his convictions. Berra moved to right field.

The new lineup rapped out seventeen hits and got Vic Raschi his fifteenth win, 14–3, on Saturday, August 14, as DiMaggio, with a home run and four RBIs, regained the home run lead from Keltner, 25 to 24, and the RBI lead from Junior Stephens, 102 to 100. The win moved the Yankees within a half-game of the Red Sox and 1½ of the Athletics, but they still trailed the Indians by three full games. But the Athletics showed 72,468 Sunday fans that they were far from dead. Six times in a row they had lost the first game of a series and come back to square it or win it, and now they made it seven. Joe DiMaggio tied the first game 2–2 with his 26th home run in the bottom of the ninth, but the Athletics took the lead in the tenth, 5–4, and Brissie stopped yet another Yankee rally after Joe D had tripled.

3. Craig R. Wright and Tom House, *The Diamond Appraised* (New York, 1989), 22–51.
4. Gerlach, *The Men in Blue,* 138, 166, and interview with Joe Paparella.

Henrich opened the scoring with a first-inning solo homer off Bill Mc-Cahan in the nightcap, but in the top of the second poor fielding by Henrich and DiMaggio enabled the Mackmen to send home four runs on just one hit, and Philadelphia won 5–3. The Athletics remained in second place, 1½ games behind the Indians, who swept the White Sox. The Yankees suddenly found themselves five full games off the pace, and the New York papers began to despair.

The Red Sox, meanwhile, finished their road trip with four games in Washington, where they had lost four straight back in May. Parnell took the mound on Friday and continued to rebound with another win, his ninth, 6–2, as Dom DiMaggio, the hitting star of the whole western swing, doubled and singled. Joe Dobson did less well on Saturday in his first start since Bob Feller's pitch had struck him on the right wrist two weeks earlier, falling behind 3–0 in the sixth, but Earl Johnson took over and the Red Sox rallied for four runs in the top of the eighth, including Stephens's 100th RBI, and moved into second place, 1½ games behind the Indians. Kramer fell behind again the next day, 5–1, against tough Ray Scarborough, and this time a ninth-inning rally featuring Williams's 20th home run fell one run short. In the nightcap Ellis Kinder and Mickey Harris failed to hold leads of 4–0 and 7–4, but Dobson relieved and eventually escaped with an 8–7 win, behind Spence's three-run blast. Having pulled their record for the road trip up to 10–9, Boston finally headed for home trailing the Indians by 2½ games.

STANDINGS
Monday, August 16, 1948

Team	Won	Lost	Pct.	Games Behind
Cleveland	67	42	.615	—
Philadelphia	67	45	.598	1½
Boston	65	45	.591	2½
New York	61	46	.570	5
Detroit	52	55	.486	14
Washington	44	65	.404	23
St. Louis	42	62	.402	23
Chicago	36	73	.330	31

The American League played no games on Monday, August 16, as the teams traveled to new home cities in the East and West, but every morning newspaper in the country had a baseball headline on its front page the next day, and at least two extra pages of baseball coverage inside. On the evening of August 16, at about eight o'clock, Babe Ruth had died of cancer of the throat at the age of fifty-three.

Ruth's illness had been well known all year, although he had never been told that he had cancer, and the nation's obituary writers had had ample time to prepare for the passing of one of the most famous men in American history. The *New York Times* obituary took up an entire page of the front section, and another page was devoted to the listing of Ruth's many records and box scores of three games: his first game as a pitcher for the Boston Red Sox in 1914; the last game of the 1927 season, in which he hit his 60th home run of the year; and the third game of the 1932 World Series, in which he reputedly called his home run to center field off Chicago Cubs pitcher Charlie Root. Obituaries, columns, and editorials unanimously hailed the Babe for restoring interest and confidence in baseball after the disastrous Black Sox scandal, and changing the nature of the game with his home run power.

The era of straight-arrow journalism had not yet really begun, and the obituaries discreetly portrayed Ruth as the lovable, accessible, often irresponsible, sometimes hot-tempered, undisciplined and sensual man that he was. They noted that he was a gambler (though never, as far as anyone has ever discovered, on baseball), that he enjoyed spending sprees (although, as his biographer Robert Creamer has confirmed, he made some very wise investments and enjoyed a most comfortable retirement), and that he could rarely, if ever, remember a name: men under forty were invariably "Kid," while their seniors rated the title "Doc." But like many politicians, he was always ready to acknowledge an old acquaintance who approached him on the street, only to turn to a companion and remark, "I don't think I ever saw the son of a bitch in my life."

Ruth's background was hardly the stuff of which middle-class myths are made. The *Times,* trying to put some legends to rest, quoted Ruth himself on the Baltimore children's home, St. Mary's Industrial School, where he had landed at the age of seven, learned to play ball, and remained until joining the Baltimore Orioles, one of the great minor league teams of all time. It was, said the Babe, "a training school for orphans, incorrigibles, delinquents, boys whose homes had been broken by divorce, runaways picked up on the streets of Baltimore, and children of poor parents who had no other means of educating them. I was listed as an incorrigible," said the Babe, who once confessed to writer Grantland Rice that he had twice made off with the till from the saloon his father kept, "and I guess I was."

The obituaries detailed his early, brilliant career as a pitcher with the Red Sox; the decision by Red Sox general manager Ed Barrow to switch him to the outfield to take advantage of his remarkable power in 1919; his sale to the Yankees; and his role in the founding of a new dynasty and the construction of Yankee Stadium, "the House that Ruth built." They then described his physical collapse in 1925, apparently from a digestive ailment, and his confrontation with Yankee manager Miller Huggins, who prevailed in an all-out war that ended when owner Jake Ruppert fined Ruth $5,000— easily the equivalent of $50,000 today. Subsequently the Babe began taking better care of himself, and led the Yankees to four more pennants in 1926– 28 and 1932. He also enjoyed several incredible performances in World Series, culminating in the mythical (probably in every sense) "called shot" against the Cubs.

The later stages of Babe's career were somewhat painful owing to his feud with Joe McCarthy, whose job he demanded after the 1934 season, and the subsequent frustration of his desire to become a manager. When the announcement was made on the day after his death that he would lie in state in Yankee Stadium, more than one New Yorker remarked bitterly that it had taken his demise to get him back into the House that Ruth built. But as late as the spring of 1948, he had remained active in baseball, always willing to provide a quote. In one of his last interviews he had defended Bucky Harris's decision to put Pete Reiser, the winning run, on base in the ninth inning of Bill Bevens's near no-hitter in the 1947 World Series. Reiser, he said, was a home run hitter, and deserved the respect Harris had shown him.

In the forty years since his death Ruth has lost his two most famous records—one, his 60 homers in a season, to an elongated schedule, and the other, his 714 career homers, to an athlete who combined comparable skill with far greater durability and care for himself.[5] The Babe's colossal stature, however, has not diminished. He still holds several major single-season records, including runs scored (177 in 1921), walks (170 in 1923), and slugging average (an unbelievable .847 in 1920). Perhaps the simplest and most striking measure of his enduring superiority, however, was published by Bill James in 1986. James's table of all-time home run hitters showed that Ruth hit 46 homers for every 162 games played. Second was Ralph Kiner, with 41, with Harmon Killebrew third at 38 and Jimmie Foxx, Hank Aaron, Lou Gehrig, and Ted Williams tied at 37.[6] On a per-game basis, Ruth as a home run hitter was 9 percent better than the second-best player who ever lived, and almost 20 percent better than Henry Aaron. In track

5. Although Aaron hit home runs at a slower rate than Ruth, we now know that his production suffered early in his career from playing in Milwaukee County Stadium, where homers are hard to come by. Playing in the Polo Grounds, Wrigley Field, or Crosley Field in Cincinnati, Aaron could easily have hit more than 60 homers in a season sometime during the late 1950s.

6. Mike Schmidt, then still active, retired in a tie with Foxx, Aaron, Gehrig, and Williams.

and field, such superiority would translate into holding the world mile record by about twenty seconds. Ruth enjoys this margin of superiority over players who played in his era and in every other, and over players who played in ballparks easier to hit home runs in than his. (In his years in Yankee Stadium, Ruth hit virtually the same number of home runs at home and on the road.) Not only as a personality, but as a home run hitter, Ruth remains utterly incomparable. The editorials of August 17, 1948, proclaimed that there would never be another like him, and the last forty-nine years have borne out their claim.

While Ruth lay in state in Yankee Stadium, the Yankees went to Washington for a midweek three-game set to try to start to make up their five-game deficit. Bucky Harris began the series with Porterfield, who so far was on his way to establishing some sort of rookie record for bad luck. During the 14⅔ good innings he had pitched against the Indians and the Athletics, his teammates had scored a grand total of one run. This time the game was scoreless until the third, when Henrich, continuing his fantastic second half, delivered a grand-slam home run over a temporary fence in center field that had been put up around some fireworks scheduled to go off after the game. It was his fourth grand slam of the season, tying a record held by Frank "Wildfire" Schulte, Babe Ruth, Lou Gehrig, and Vince DiMaggio. He had picked excellent moments to hit them, beating the Indians 5–1 with the first one in the twelfth inning in Cleveland on June 23; tying the Athletics at 5–5 in the bottom of the seventh on July 7 and allowing the Yankees to win the game in the next inning; and taking a 6–4 lead against the White Sox in Chicago in the seventh inning on July 30, in a game the Yankees eventually lost 8–7. This blast put this game out of reach, and Porterfield coasted to an 8–1 win, his first major league victory.

The Yankees won a five-inning, rain-delayed game the next evening behind Raschi, 4–1, as Raschi tied Bob Lemon with sixteen wins. Joe DiMaggio missed a plane and had to get a 2:00 A.M. train from Union Station to New York, where he served as a pallbearer at Ruth's funeral. Allie Reynolds, who had won just one game in the last month, took the mound on Thursday afternoon in quest of his elusive twelfth victory against Early Wynn. He fell behind 1–0 before DiMaggio returned from New York in time to enter the game in the third inning, but the Yankees promptly scored six runs in the top of the fourth, keyed by a three-run triple by new third baseman Bobby Brown.

The Yankees' first three-game sweep of the season suggested that Harris might have found a winning combination. They gained a game and one-half on both the Red Sox and the Athletics, who divided a pair in Boston after their Tuesday game was rained out. On Wednesday, Denny Galehouse evened his record at 6–6 with his fourth consecutive strong performance, scattering eight hits en route to a 10–2 win, while Williams's three hits raised his average back to .381. But on Thursday Philadelphia knocked out Joe Dobson in the seventh and battered the whole Boston bullpen for good measure. The A's avoided the loss of a series for the seventh straight time with a 10–3 win and hung on to second place as they returned home for four more games with New York.

The Indians, meanwhile, made short and sweet work of their two-game home set with the Browns on Tuesday and Wednesday, August 17–18, even though Joe Gordon missed both games with a twisted ankle. Bearden won his fourth consecutive start and his twelfth victory overall, an 8–0 shutout, and Zoldak repeated the feat, 3–0, on the next night. Cleveland pitchers now had three shutouts in a row, going back to Lemon's seventh whitewash of the season against the White Sox in the second game of Sunday's doubleheader. Allie Clark scored all the runs in the Indians' 3–0 victory and raised his average to .324 on the year. Interest in the Indians had become all but uncontrollable. An amazing 55,858 fans saw the game against the Browns on Tuesday night, and 33,227 on Wednesday afternoon. Boudreau now guaranteed that Friday night's crowd against the White Sox would be even larger. Satchel Paige, he announced, would pitch against them for the second time in a week.

STANDINGS
Friday Morning, August 20, 1948

Team	Won	Lost	Pct.	Games Behind
Cleveland	69	42	.622	—
Philadelphia	68	46	.596	2½
Boston	66	46	.589	3½
New York	64	46	.582	4½
Detroit	53	55	.491	14½
St. Louis	43	66	.394	25
Washington	44	68	.393	25½
Chicago	36	74	.327	32½

It looked on Friday, August 20, as if the Indians might emerge from the weekend in command of the pennant race. As the Yankees went to Philadelphia for four games and a tired Red Sox pitching staff hosted the Senators for four more, a well-rested Indians club with three straight shutouts to its credit had four games against the miserable White Sox in Cleveland. The Tribe had to leave for Boston on Monday to face the Red Sox for three games, but their lead could easily be safe by the time they got there.

Friday's action began in Boston, in a rare Friday afternoon double-header necessitated by an earlier rainout. Desperately needing two complete games, Joe McCarthy opened with Mel Parnell—who had pitched two innings in Tuesday's rained-out game with the Athletics—against Ray Scarborough. Parnell and the Red Sox began shakily, surrendering four runs in the first two innings with the help of errors by Pesky and Spence, while Scarborough held the Red Sox to eight hits and one run in the first eight innings. Since their last home stand, however, the Red Sox' confidence in their ability to win in Fenway had become almost unlimited.

Leading 4–1, Scarborough retired pinch hitter Wally Moses and Dom DiMaggio to open the bottom of the ninth. Pesky doubled to left, however, and Scarborough walked Williams, one for three on the day, to bring Vern Stephens—six for his last fifteen—to the plate. The remarkable shortstop drove Scarborough's very first pitch into the left-field screen to tie the game.

On first base, Williams leapt into the air, clapped joyously as he rounded the bases, waited to greet his teammate at home plate, lifted the stocky shortstop off his feet and carried him halfway to the Red Sox dugout. An inning later, Stan Spence led off with another home run, and Earl Johnson had his fifth win in relief—an extraordinary, critical victory. In the second game, Jack Kramer (13–4) surrendered single runs in the first two innings, and then joined his mates in a thirteen-batter, seven-run bottom of the third, highlighted by Dom DiMaggio's grand-slam home run over the left-field wall. Williams and Bobby Doerr homered in the fifth to make it 10–2, and Kramer coasted to a 10–4 victory. Williams, three for six on the day with three runs scored, raised his average up to .385. The sweep assured the Red Sox of gaining half a game on the Indians no matter what happened in Cleveland, and started the home stand off on the right foot.

The game between the White Sox and the Indians at Cleveland began with a party in the open area behind the center-field fence, thrown by Bill Veeck for Governor Thomas J. Herbert and four hundred Ohio mayors to thank the citizenry of the Buckeye State for their unprecedented support. The climax of the well-catered affair was a four-layer cake with two baseballs mounted on top, which was served while a vaudeville act played in the outfield for the benefit of the fans. The largest night crowd in the history of baseball, 78,382, jammed their way into baseball's biggest ballpark to see Satchel Paige go for his fifth victory against Bill Wight. An official total of 201,829 patrons—67,276 per game—had now attended Paige's last three starts.

Both Paige and Wight rose to the occasion, giving up just one hit apiece during the first three innings. A great throw by Doby got Paige out of a jam in the fourth, and in the bottom of the inning, singles by Boudreau, Keltner, and Doby gave the Indians a run. With the score still 1–0, Pat Seerey began the seventh by driving Doby up against the 380-foot sign in left-center to catch his deep fly. Then Paige retired the last nine White Sox in order for a 1–0 win, giving the record-breaking crowd everything they could have asked for. It was Paige's second straight shutout and the fourth straight by Indians pitchers. Indian hurlers had hung up 39 consecutive scoreless innings, just two short of the major league record mark of 41 held by the 1903 Indians, who had accomplished the feat when runs were much harder to come by. The Indians kept their four-game loss column bulge over the Red Sox.

"I should be working on percentage," Paige mused after the game. "It sure wasn't like this in Kansas City.

"Just threw fast balls out there. When a pitch is working I keep using it. Came up with my first curve balls in the eighth and threw three in a row for that strikeout.

"I'm getting back in shape," he remarked, as he started toward the showers. "Guess I didn't go nine innings for six years before this season, but I'm feeling better every game. Fact is I was faster tonight than I've been all season—even thought I was a little too fast on that pitch to Seerey the way it came back. He's the strongest boy I've ever seen hit a ball. If he could have pulled that one it would have been in the upper deck.

"Some day I'd like to see that Seerey hit a straight fast ball that he knew was coming. My guess is that he's the only guy around that might put one into the bleachers.

"I want to thank you, Roomie," said Paige, turning toward Doby. "Just was playing him deep and was back in plenty of time," Doby replied. "My back was right up to the fence when the ball hit my glove."[7]

J. G. Taylor Spink of the *Sporting News* received a telegram after the game.

PAIGE PITCHING—NO RUNS, THREE HITS. DEFINITELY IN LINE FOR THE SPORTING NEWS ROOKIE OF THE YEAR AWARD. REGARDS. BILL VEECK.[8]

How old was Paige? The question on everyone's mind received some small but far from decisive clarification in an incident that hit that papers that weekend. His performances had brought a great many witnesses out of the woodwork, including several who claimed to have seen him pitching

7. *Cleveland Plain Dealer,* August 21.
8. Veeck with Ed Linn, *Veeck—as in Wreck,* 189.

professionally in 1920. Satchel, whose promoter's instinct was much too acute actually to settle the matter, had guffawed at that, and publicly offered to pay five hundred dollars to anyone who could prove that his career had begun before 1927. As it turned out, his memory had failed him. A Cleveland fan turned a Tennessee relative loose in the library, and the avid researcher promptly turned up a clipping showing that Paige had pitched for the Chattanooga Black Lookouts in 1926. Paige earned some more publicity by paying up.

And how good was he? "How can you rate him?" umpire Bill Summers asked writer Gordon Cobbledick ten days later in Washington. "There are few better pitchers in baseball today. Maybe there aren't any. And there are few with more stuff." "The old boy's around the plate all the time and calling balls and strikes for him's a breeze," echoed his colleague Art Passarella. "I was behind the plate in that shutout he worked in Chicago and I never had an easier game in my life."[9]

Satchel was enjoying his entrance upon the big-league stage in more ways than one. His following in every city included several attractive women, for whom he frequently had to request extra visiting-team tickets. "I'm not married," he explained to the Indians brass, "but I'm in great demand." (One young lady failed to receive her tickets because she called not under the name of Juanita, which Paige had left, but as "Mrs. Satchel Paige.") His brilliance was putting more and more pressure on the Indians' competitors.

On Saturday, August 21, in Fenway Park, Ellis Kinder, who had failed to hold the Senators a week earlier, tried again. He fell behind 3–0 in the first inning, but this was Fenway Park, and solo homers by Stephens and Doerr in the second and third innings and a grand slam by Stephens in the fourth gave Boston a 6–3 lead. Kinder squandered the lead again, surrendering three more runs in the top of the sixth, but the Red Sox seemed to have slipped into the same groove they had found during their late July home stand: when they had to, they could score almost at will. DiMaggio, Pesky, Doerr, and Goodman hit safely for three runs in the bottom of the eighth, and Johnson retired the side in the ninth for his second victory in two days. Stephens, with 3 homers and 8 RBIs in the last two games, had raised his totals to 26 and 112 on the year, momentarily tying Joe DiMaggio in four-baggers and taking the league lead in RBIs by 7. The stocky shortstop, whom Dave Egan was promoting for Most Valuable Player, had eclipsed his previous career highs of 24 homers and 109 RBIs with six weeks left in

9. *Cleveland Plain Dealer,* August 31.

the season. More important, the Red Sox had battled back from behind to win once again.

MATT BATTS: When we were five or six runs down in the seventh inning, we knew we were going to win.

The Red Sox' efforts would be of little use, however, if the Indians—winners of eight straight—could continue their current pace in Cleveland. With Gordon still out of the lineup, Bob Lemon broke the major league team record for consecutive scoreless innings in the third, and doubled home Berardino for a 1–0 lead in the fifth. The Tribe right-hander was having an amazing season, shooting for his league-leading seventeenth victory and eighth shutout, and hitting like the converted outfielder he was. He finished the game with a .333 average—29 for 87—with 6 doubles, 5 home runs, and 18 runs batted in.

The Indians finally got another run in the eighth, and Lemon entered the ninth inning with a 2–0 lead. Then, incredibly, the White Sox stunned the crowd with a walk and two home runs by Aaron Robinson and Dave Philley to take the lead, and the Indians went down in order in the bottom of the ninth. To have lost both their shutout streak and their winning streak in a matter of minutes was a shocker, but the Tribe still had a three-game loss column bulge over the Red Sox and Yankees. With Feller and Bearden scheduled for tomorrow's doubleheader, they figured to finish the home stand in good shape.

In Boston, Joe McCarthy stuck resolutely to his pitching philosophy on Sunday. Dobson, Parnell, Kramer, and Kinder had pitched during the last three days, and Galehouse had just three days' rest. Thus, although Mickey Harris had not won a start in a month, McCarthy gave him the ball, and he allowed just five hits and two walks as he went the distance for a 4–1 win behind a two-run homer by Bobby Doerr. It was his 22nd, a new career high. The Red Sox had now won 23 out of their last 25 home games, while the Senators, paying the price for playing in a hot league, had lost nine games in a row.

In Cleveland, 57,747 fans turned out to watch the Indians conclude their home stand, with Feller (12–13) and Bearden (12–2) going against the White Sox. Gordon finally returned to the lineup in the first game, while Boudreau held Clark—perhaps the Indians' best all-around hitter at home—out of the whole doubleheader in favor of Hal Peck and Thurman Tucker. In the top of the fourth inning of the opener, successive errors by Ken Keltner and Larry Doby helped the White Sox to a 2–1 lead, and Chicago got four more off Feller and Klieman in the sixth and two more in the ninth, as the Indians stranded base runner after base runner en route to an 8–1 defeat. In the second game, the Indians got a run in the second when Thurman Tucker hit his first home run of the year, and loaded the bases in the bottom of the second. But the umpires' bizarre failure to invoke the infield fly rule on Boudreau's pop fly behind shortstop allowed Luke Appling to drop the ball and turn a double play while Bearden scored. Down 2–0, the White Sox struck back with a two-run double by Appling and a two-run homer by the relentless Pat Seerey that gave them a 4–2 lead. The rest of the game was a nightmare for the Indians, who put the leadoff man on in the fourth, fifth, and seventh innings but could not score. In the bottom of the ninth, Thurman Tucker grounded out to begin the inning, but Eddie Robinson singled to center and Walt Judnich, pinch-hitting, drew a walk to bring the winning run to the plate. Allie Clark, finally given a chance, batted for Bearden and singled in Robinson to bring the Indians within one. Lefty Frank Papish took the mound to face Mitchell and Doby. Mitchell struck out for only the tenth time of the whole season. Papish threw one strike to Doby—hitting .274—and Boudreau, feeling the strain, removed the left-handed hitter in favor of Berardino, hitting .206. He popped out to end the game.

The Indians had dropped three straight, at home, to the Chicago White Sox. With just one home run and ten runs overall in their last five games, their lead over the Red Sox—3½ games on Friday morning—was down to just one-half game. And as luck would have it, they now had to repair directly to Boston to open a three-game set on Tuesday night, with first place the prize. Boudreau indicated on Sunday that Gromek would open the series against the Red Sox.

Nor was this all. In Philadelphia, the Yankees had won three straight over the Athletics—6–2 on Friday behind Lopat (12–7), 6–0 on Saturday behind Porterfield, who finally got some run support, and 10–0 on Sunday behind the hot Vic Raschi, who took over the league lead in victories from Lemon with seventeen. Bucky Harris's new lineup had won nine times in eleven games, and the third-place New Yorkers trailed Cleveland by only two games, just one in the loss column. They now faced their last extended home stand of the season, eighteen games in just fifteen days against the White Sox, Indians, Tigers, Browns, Senators, and Athletics. The Athletics, having dropped six of their last nine games, found themselves a full game behind the Yankees in fourth place. Those two preseason favorites, New York and Boston, were knocking on the Indians' door.

In Boston, where the fans had not enjoyed such a pennant race in thirty-three years, fans desperately sought tickets for the biggest series of the season to date. Even a heat wave that pushed temperatures into the nineties could do nothing to dampen the almost intolerable excitement. The Red Sox, who had swept into first place against the Indians just one month before, now had a chance to do exactly the same thing again. And on Tuesday morning, the papers informed the Fenway faithful of another sensational development. Lou Boudreau had decided not to use Steve Gromek that night after all. The Indians would try to hold on to first place on Tuesday evening behind Leroy Paige.

STANDINGS
Monday, August 23, 1948

Team	Won	Lost	Pct.	Games Behind
Cleveland	70	45	.609	—
Boston	70	46	.603	½
New York	67	46	.593	2
Philadelphia	68	49	.581	3
Detroit	54	57	.486	14
St. Louis	45	67	.402	23½
Washington	44	72	.379	26½
Chicago	39	75	.342	30½

9

Rising Sun in the East

(AUGUST 24–SEPTEMBER 7)

As the dusk settled over Boston on Tuesday, August 24, huge crowds milled about on Jersey Street outside Fenway Park, desperately hoping to see Joe Dobson—still looking to end his long victory drought—face off against Satchel Paige. An estimated 20,000 fans had to go away disappointed and hear the game on the radio, while 34,172 paid their way in.

Dobson got the Indians in order, and Paige, working with only three days' rest, entranced the huge crowd by setting down DiMaggio, Pesky, and Williams without the help of his outfield. His personal streak of scoreless innings ended in the bottom of the second when Doerr singled and Goodman doubled him home, but hits by Mitchell, Clark, Boudreau, and Keltner gave the Indians a 3–1 lead in the top of the third. Satchel finally proved he was human in the bottom of the inning, however, when he slipped and hit Dobson and gave up a triple to DiMaggio and singles to Williams and Stephens. Boudreau, showing less patience than McCarthy, replaced him with Gromek, the man whom he had originally planned to start. "No excuses," said Paige after the game. "They just got to my fast ball before I had a chance to set up my other pitches."[1] Gromek got the side out with the score 3–3, and Cleveland and Boston found themselves in yet another epic struggle.

The tie lasted exactly two more batters, as a triple by Larry Doby and a sacrifice fly by Eddie Robinson gave Cleveland the lead again in the top of the fourth. The Indians started the top of the fifth with two more singles by

1. *Boston Herald*, August 25.

Mitchell and Clark. Boudreau ripped the ball toward left again, but Pesky, diving, managed to knock it down, and an alert Stephens grabbed it, gunned it to second, and retired Clark as Mitchell slid into third. Keltner, next up, ripped the ball high and deep down the left-field line. Williams, running at full tilt, brought the crowd to its feet with a fine catch, but could not prevent Mitchell from scoring. Gordon followed with a fly ball to deep left, but Williams backed up against the wall and caught it for the third out. Five Indians had hit the ball hard, but great defense had held them to just one run, holding their lead to 5–3.

McCarthy pinch-hit unsuccessfully for Dobson in the bottom of the seventh, but Dom DiMaggio, batting with two out, drove Gromek's pitch into the screen to come within one. The Indians made that up in the top of the eighth, when Keltner and Gordon singled off Earl Johnson and Keltner eventually scored on a wild pitch. The crowd's spirits rose in the bottom of the eighth when Boudreau fumbled Stephens's grounder to allow him to reach first. When Doerr singled to left—his third hit on the night—Boudreau relieved Gromek with Ed Klieman. Stan Spence sacrificed the two runners into scoring position, and Boudreau repeated the defensive move that had worked so spectacularly back in July in Washington, putting Bob Kennedy in right field to try to prevent Stephens from scoring on a fly. Instead, Goodman lifted the ball to left, not deep enough to score the run. But Birdie Tebbetts, batting with two out, atoned for his failure to block the wild pitch in the previous inning with a two-run single to tie the game 6–6. McCarthy, playing for a tie at home, let Earl Johnson bat, and he grounded out for the third out.

Dale Mitchell promptly opened the top of the ninth with a double, but held third when DiMaggio made a quick pickup on Kennedy's single to center. With three right-handers coming up, McCarthy called on sore-armed Tex Hughson, and Boudreau hit his first pitch for a double to right to score a run and take the lead again, 7–6. Keltner followed with a single for his third RBI on the night, but Boudreau held at third. McCarthy replaced Hughson with the only man he had left, forty-three-year-old Earl Caldwell, and the sidearmer got Joe Gordon and induced Doby to hit a grounder which Doerr and Stephens turned into a double play. Leading 8–6, the Indians needed just three outs to extend their lead back to 1½ games—but this was Fenway Park, where Junior Stephens had erased a three-run ninth-inning deficit only four nights before.

Dom DiMaggio led off the ninth and completed his cycle of extra-base hits with a double to center. Pesky followed with a single to right, and DiMaggio prudently held at third to bring Williams to the plate with two on and none out. Boudreau waved in Gene Bearden to pitch to the greatest hitter in baseball. With the crowd on its feet, Williams flied to deep left, and DiMaggio held at third again as Mitchell made the catch.

Bearden often had trouble with right-handed power hitters, and Boudreau brought in Russ Christopher to pitch to Stephens and Doerr. Stephens had homered off Christopher in Cleveland on July 31; he had tied a game in the ninth four days previously; and he had three homers in his last four games. Every fan in Fenway wondered whether he could possibly do it again. The answer, incredibly, was yes. The stocky shortstop cracked Christopher's first offering into the screen in left-center for his 27th home run and the ball game, sending the crowd into a delirious frenzy and the Red Sox back into first place.

The Red Sox' victory—the most dramatic of the season—combined all of the team's strengths and weaknesses: remarkably timely hitting, tremendous power at shortstop, great defense, and a shaky bullpen. Stephens's fourth home run in four days gave him 114 RBIs in 117 games, and put him back in the league lead over Joe DiMaggio. And although his season was hardly finished, this home run was without question the most dramatic blow of his 1948 season—the first of three of the most remarkable seasons that any shortstop ever had.

Stephens, a California native, had entered professional ball at age eighteen and reached the St. Louis Browns in 1942, at the age of twenty-one. Over his first four years with the Browns he averaged exactly 20 homers and 90 runs batted in per season, hitting in the .280–.290 range. He was undoubtedly the most valuable player on the pennant-winning 1944 Browns, but lost the league award to Hal Newhouser of the second-place Tigers. Apparently helped by a cooperative St. Louis draft board, he made it all the way through the war untouched, leading the league in RBIs in 1944 and homers in 1945. He had subpar seasons in 1946 and 1947, but McCarthy and Cronin had willingly paid big money to bring him to Boston at the age of twenty-seven. He had started slowly, but three incredible months had now turned him into a legitimate MVP candidate. During the next three years, he put up some of the most remarkable offensive numbers of any shortstop who ever played the game.

During the 1948, 1949, and 1950 seasons, Junior Stephens averaged 624 at bats, 117 runs scored, 178 hits, 30 doubles, 5 triples, and 33 home runs. He created approximately 120 runs per season, or about 110 runs per season with an appropriate adjustment for Fenway Park. Only three other shortstops—Honus Wagner, Arky Vaughn, and Ernie Banks—ever created runs at that rate over three consecutive seasons. In one other respect, furthermore, Stephens is incomparable. Over these three years, he drove in an *average* of 147 runs per season—137 in 1948, 159 in 1949, and 144 in 1950.

In both 1949 and 1950 he shared the league lead with teammates—Ted Williams in 1949, when the two of them established a post-1945 record that still stands, and Walt Dropo in 1950. Ernie Banks, by contrast, averaged 128 RBIs during his three peak seasons (1957–59). Over a short period, Stephens ranks among the top five or six shortstops in history offensively, and we have already seen that he ranked among the best defensively as well.

One other aspect of Vern Stephens's play deserves some mention: his durability. He has acquired a reputation of a high liver who spent every night on the town, but this is refuted by Pesky, his roommate, and by his performance in 1948–49, when he did not miss a single game. In 1948 Stephens would not be able to maintain the pace he had set through mid-August, when he had 118 RBIs in 116 games (though he did maintain almost exactly that pace all the way through 1949), and his offensive statistics did benefit from circumstances. He was, however, a great player for three years—even if, as we shall see, he was some distance away from being the AL's best shortstop overall in 1948.

"So we lost one," said Joe Gordon, the steadiest and most experienced player on the Indians, after Tuesday night's thriller. "We'll lose some more. But this is one club we can beat." The Indians proved him right on the next afternoon, with 30,745 on hand to watch Bob Lemon face Denny Galehouse, who had stopped the Indians cold over 8⅔ innings of relief three weeks before in Cleveland. This time the Tribe knocked out Galehouse in the top of the second with five hits and four runs. Dave Ferriss did no better, and Lemon allowed just four hits en route to a 9–0 shutout, his finest performance of the year next to his no-hitter. Doby delivered three hits, including another triple off the center-field wall and a homer to right, and was rewarded with a knockdown from Shaw, Mississippi native Ferriss. The Indians regained their half-game lead and tied the season series between the two clubs at ten wins each.

LARRY DOBY: I did have good luck in Fenway Park!

The rubber game was Cleveland's last in Boston. Given the choice between Feller, who hated Fenway and had pitched there only once this season, and the left-hander Bearden, who had shut the Red Sox out twice but failed against them in his last outing, Boudreau picked Bearden and saved Feller for the Yankees. McCarthy continued to rest Kramer, whose arm was apparently suspect, and pitched Parnell with five days of rest, as the two young left-handers faced each other for the third time of the year.

Bearden survived a rocky first when Williams lined into a double play, but went down 2–0 in the third. Hegan's triple off the wall in left made the score 2–1 in the top of the fourth, but a double by Stephens and a single by Spence regained the Sox' two-run lead in the bottom of the inning. But the Indians made the score 3–2 in the sixth when Doby hit the wall yet again for a double and tallied on Parnell's wild pitch, and they tied the game in the top of the eighth on Keltner's double and Bob Kennedy's pinch double. With one out in bottom of the eighth, Pesky beat out a beautiful bunt down the third-base line, and Williams, pulling Bearden for the second time of the afternoon, drove the ball into right for a single. Stephens popped out, but Bobby Doerr drove Bearden's pitch into the screen for a 6–3 lead. A two-run triple by Tebbetts off Christopher made it 8–3, and the Red Sox took the rubber game and first place, 8–4.

The Indians outscored the Red Sox 21–18 in the three-game series, but lost two of the three games. Boudreau, going 5 for 16 in the series, was now hitting .367, while Williams, who went just 3 for 12, fell to .375. Doby, 6 for 13 on the series, was now hitting .388 against Red Sox pitching, including four doubles, two triples, and five of his total of ten home runs. Keltner had six hits on the series, but his home run drought continued. He had hit twenty homers in the first half of the season, and just four since the All-Star break. The Red Sox, moreover, had seized the lead just as the schedule was turning their way again. They now faced six games in six days against the White Sox, Browns, and Tigers, while the Indians had eight games in six days against the Yankees, Senators, and Athletics.

The Yankee club that the Indians had to face in a doubleheader on Friday, moreover, was playing the best ball of any team in the league. In terrible heat, the Yankees had taken three out of four from the White Sox during the week, including a complete-game victory from Porterfield. They had gained 2½ games on the Indians and a half-game on the Red Sox, and the three teams were tied in the loss column at 47. New York seemed to have the best-functioning pitching staff, and Bucky Harris had his three aces, Raschi (17–5), Reynolds (13–6), and Lopat (12–8), ready to face the Indians. The Athletics, meanwhile, seemed finally to be dropping out of the race. They lost two games to the Tigers in Philadelphia to run their losing streak to five before rebounding with a victory on Thursday.

Bob Feller's season and his career were still very much in doubt as he took the mound to open Friday's doubleheader against Raschi. Since eking out his first victory over New York against four losses, 9–7, in Cleveland three weeks before, Feller had won only once in three starts, and his record had fallen to 12–14. Boudreau devised a new lineup for the occasion, featuring Judnich batting second and Doby batting sixth, while Harris fielded the new left-handed lineup, which had won six straight games. Before 61,529 Friday afternoon fans, the Indians blew several offensive

STANDINGS
Friday Morning, August 27, 1948

Team	Won	Lost	Pct.	Games Behind
Boston	72	47	.605	—
Cleveland	71	47	.602	½
New York	70	47	.598	1
Philadelphia	69	51	.575	3½
Detroit	56	58	.491	14
St. Louis	46	69	.400	23½
Washington	46	73	.387	26½
Chicago	40	78	.339	30½

opportunities in the first few innings, while the Yankees broke the ice in the bottom of the second on a single by DiMaggio and a triple by little Phil Rizzuto. Keltner's 25th home run tied the game in the top of the fourth, and Feller, getting stronger, retired six out of seven Yankees in the fifth and sixth. Then the Indians took a 3–1 lead in the seventh, chased Raschi, and won 8–1. Feller had allowed the Yankees just five hits, shutting out their left-handed threats Berra and Henrich and allowing Bobby Brown just one single. Bill McGowan, the plate umpire, told Gordon Cobbledick that he had believed earlier in the year that Feller was through, but that he had never seen him pitch better than in this game.[2] It was the best news Boudreau had gotten on the trip.

Having started Paige on three days' rest in Boston and relieved him with his original choice Gromek, Boudreau inexplicably pitched Gromek in the nightcap, less than three days after he had pitched almost five innings against the Red Sox on Tuesday evening, and gave Zoldak, who had not started for ten days, yet another day of rest. The choice went badly, and after Gromek gave up DiMaggio's 29th home run and singles by Berra and Lindell to open the fourth inning, Boudreau replaced him with Ed Klieman. Rizzuto's double made it 4–0, and the rest of the game was an agony of frustration for the Indians, who got two hits in the fifth, three hits in the seventh, and three hits in the eighth, but emerged with just one run. Reynolds's fourteenth victory gave New York a split.

In a battle of left-handers, Zoldak faced Lopat in the rubber game on Saturday, and Larry Doby opened the scoring in the top of the second with his 11th home run, a solo shot. It was the team's 123rd home run of the year, a new club record. But New York tied it in the second, and the Indians again squandered some chances. Zoldak *twice* managed to bunt into double

2. *Cleveland Plain Dealer,* August 29.

plays while attempting to sacrifice, and a great catch by Joe DiMaggio off Boudreau probably saved a run in the sixth. Gordon finally made it 2–1 in the eighth.

After the Tribe loaded the bases but failed to score in the top of the ninth, Zoldak confessed himself too tired to finish the game. Satchel Paige had pitched four times against the Yankees without allowing them a run, including the ninth inning of the second game of Friday's doubleheader. But to the amazement of the press box, Boudreau tapped Bearden, who had yet to have a good outing against New York, to try to save the game. To make matters worse, Joe DiMaggio, who had hit him like a batting practice pitcher, was leading off the bottom of the ninth.

Bearden solved the DiMaggio problem by plunking him with a pitch to open the inning. He then threw two balls to Yogi Berra, and Boudreau panicked and replaced him with Klieman, who hadn't had a good outing in weeks. Klieman completed the walk to Berra, and Bobby Brown, batting for Bill Johnson, sacrificed the runners into scoring position. With none out, Boudreau ordered Klieman to walk Rizzuto to load the bases. Charlie Keller hit for reserve catcher Ralph Houk, and Klieman walked him to force in the tying run. Cliff Mapes batted for Lopat and grounded to Gordon. Gordon flipped to Boudreau for the force, but Boudreau's throw to first was late, and Berra scored to end the game. The Indians had now scored 33 runs and given up 28 on their road trip, but lost four of six games and fallen from first to third place, behind the Yankees. After the finale in New York, which gave the Yankees an 11–10 edge in the season series, Harry Jones of the *Plain Dealer*, who had generally avoided second-guessing the Boy Manager, reported that all the writers had questioned the use of Bearden and Klieman, rather than Paige, in the ninth. The pennant and Boudreau's job were obviously on the line again.

Back in Boston, the Red Sox made the most of the opportunity presented by the Yankees-Indians series as they faced Chicago. On Friday afternoon, Jack Kramer failed again in another bid for his fifteenth victory, but Denny Galehouse—annihilated by the Indians two days earlier—relieved in the fourth and allowed just two runs en route to his seventh victory. Williams's monstrous 22nd home run keyed the 9–4 win, and a brilliant throw by Williams helped cut off a White Sox rally. "The classy Dennis Galehouse," as the *Boston Herald* called him the next day, had pitched very well in four of his six starts since the All-Star break, and followed both of his bad outings with fine wins in long relief. On Saturday, Ellis Kinder (5–7) pitched one of his best games of the season, winning 6–2. The Red Sox' victories opened up a 1½-game bulge over the Yankees and a two-game lead over the Indians. Meanwhile, the Athletics had run off a new four-game winning streak with a sweep of the Browns to come within a game of the slumping Indians. Perhaps, indeed, they were not out of things yet.

The East Coast heat wave finally broke on Saturday evening, and when the dust had lifted after Sunday's doubleheaders, the standings were unchanged. In Boston, where the Red Sox faced the Browns, Joe Dobson got his fourteenth victory after a five-week drought, 10–2, behind a three-run homer by Williams and a grand slam by Tebbetts, but the Browns ripped Mickey Harris and Earl Johnson and coasted to a 12–4 win in the nightcap. A much worse piece of news was to come. Bobby Doerr, who had not missed a game all season, pulled a hamstring muscle and was lost indefinitely. Veteran Billy Hitchcock replaced him. In New York, Bob Porterfield took a 6–3 lead into the eighth inning against Detroit, but homers by Dick Wakefield and Pat Mullin gave the Tigers a 9–6 win. During the game, a bullet off the bat of Joe DiMaggio took a bad hop toward third base, broke George Kell's jaw, and put him out for the rest of the season. The nightcap was one of the weirdest, wildest games of the year. With the Yankee pitchers hurling one complete game after another, Joe Page had had no work for about two weeks, and Harris penciled him in as the starter. Page squandered a 9–0 lead in the fifth and the Yankees, falling behind 10–9, were most fortunate to pull out an 11–10 victory on Bill Johnson's home run, as Raschi, Lopat, and Reynolds all had to relieve. Having started his ace reliever, Harris had relieved with his three ace starters. And in Washington, the Indians surged briefly back into second as Bob Lemon turned in yet another shutout, 6–0, but blew another game and fell back to third when Boudreau tried to protect a lead with Klieman and Bob Feller, rather than Paige or Christopher, and Walt Judnich somehow managed to let a 328-foot fly go over his head for three Senator runs and a 3–2 loss.

The Red Sox rested on Monday, and Bill Veeck acceded to a request from Clark Griffith and started Satchel Paige in a night game in Washington, drawing 28,058—the largest crowd of the year. Once again Satchel came through, giving up seven hits, just one walk, and losing a shutout only in the eighth inning. The biggest threat to Paige came from his nervous stomach, which filled with gas in the eighth inning. Lacking the bicarbonate of soda Paige asked for, Bob Lemon gave him an aspirin, and the placebo effect coaxed out a much-needed belch. Boudreau injured his thumb, and Gordon—who had come to the majors as a shortstop, and who still liked to claim playfully that he was the best shortstop in the American League—took over for the last few innings, with Berardino going to second. The Indians pulled to within a game and a half of the idle Red Sox, but the Yankees easily kept pace.

In New York, Frank Shea, facing Hal Newhouser—who had amassed a remarkable 15–10 record for a fifth-place club—turned in the greatest performance of his career, giving up just one walk and one hit, a single by Newhouser himself in the third inning, en route to a 3–0 victory, the Yanks' thirteenth in their last fifteen games. The Yankees' and Indians' victories brought them within 1 and 1½ games of the Red Sox, respectively. While the Indians concluded their trip with two games against the Athletics, the Yankees faced the Browns for two in New York, while the Red Sox went against the Tigers twice to conclude their long home stand.

STANDINGS
Tuesday Morning, August 31, 1948

Team	Won	Lost	Pct.	Games Behind
Boston	75	48	.610	—
New York	73	48	.602	1
Cleveland	74	50	.597	1½
Philadelphia	73	53	.579	3½
Detroit	59	60	.496	14
St. Louis	47	73	.392	26½
Washington	47	77	.379	28½
Chicago	42	81	.341	33

On Tuesday and Wednesday, the Red Sox completed a home stand almost, if not quite, as brilliant as their 15–1 set in July. On Tuesday night a packed house of 33,310 watched Mel Parnell beat the Tigers 8–4, and on the next day, Jack Kramer, who had pitched only two innings in the last ten days, finally returned to form with a 10–1 triumph over Virgil Trucks. The Red Sox finished their home stand with a 12–3 mark, and this time it was the hitters, rather than the pitchers, who could take most of the credit. Dom DiMaggio hit .419 and scored 17 runs in 15 games, and catcher Birdie Tebbetts, enjoying his best-ever season at the plate, hit .333 with one home run and 15 RBIs. Goodman and Pesky also hit over .300, while Doerr hit four homers and drove in 13 runs before his injury, and Stephens added four homers and 17 RBIs. Williams had three homers and 11 RBIs, raising his total to 102, but his batting average for the home stand was a relatively unimpressive (for him) .317, and his overall mark slipped to .368, trailing Boudreau in the batting race for the first time since May. The starting pitching had been somewhat shaky, but Johnson and Galehouse had come up with critical relief performances, and Kramer's win offered some hope for the future. The schedule did as well. The Sox had only a five-game road trip during the next seven days, allowing their pitchers to accumulate some rest before opening three games against the Yankees back in Fenway on Wednesday, September 8.

On the same Tuesday and Wednesday, the Yankees tried to keep pace against the Browns, whose hitters had suddenly come to life. On Tuesday night, with 41,335 fans on hand, homers by Keller and Henrich against Yankee-killer Cliff Fannin rolled up a 10–4 lead behind Reynolds and Page. The top of the ninth, however, became a nightmare.

Les Moss doubled to open the frame, and when Eddie Pellagrini followed with a grounder to third, Bobby Brown muffed it. Page got another pinch hitter out on a pop-up for the first out, but Bob Dillinger and Al Zarilla—the Brown's best hitters—promptly singled for two runs to close the gap to 10–6. Jerry Priddy, next up, grounded toward Brown, who turned a potential inning-ending double play into a two-base error that scored two more runs and made the score 10–8. The Golden Boy's defense was always suspect, and this was probably the worst inning of his whole career. Whitey Platt promptly drove a single off Rizzuto's glove and the Browns were within one run. Harris left Page in to pitch to left-handed-hitting outfielder Dick Kokos.

"At this crucial moment," Joseph Sheehan of the *New York Times* wrote, "Dick Kokos rifled a screaming liner down the right center-field alley. The ball rolled to the fence, with Joe DiMaggio and Larry Berra in frantic pursuit and Platt racing around the bases for all he was worth.

"Catching up to the rebounding ball as Platt was rounding into third, DiMaggio whirled and threw it to George Stirnweiss. As Freddy Hofmann, coaching at third, wildly waved Platt on, Stirnweiss whipped the ball to the plate. Stirnweiss' throw was perfect and even though he was bowled over backward by Platt's desperate slide, Gus Niarhos tagged the runner out."[3]

Pandemonium broke loose, but the Yankees still had one batter to retire, and Kokos, the tying run, had made it all the way to third on the play. Bow-Wow Arft, going for the Yankees' weak spot, hit a shot to Brown at third. Brown fumbled it, reached for it, fumbled it again; picked it up on the third try, and gunned it to Henrich at first for the final out.

The Browns jumped out to a 4–1 lead next day on homers by Al Zarilla and Les Moss. Zarilla, third baseman Bob Dillinger, and veteran second baseman Jerry Priddy were all hitting .300, and the Browns had climbed up to sixth place. The Yankees chipped away with the help of a rare home run by Stirnweiss and a triple by Henrich, but trailed 4–3 in the bottom of the ninth. Cliff Mapes, batting for Raschi, opened the ninth with a double, but

3. *New York Times*, September 1.

Stirnweiss struck out trying to bunt. Brown, 0–4 on the day, grounded out for the second out. Henrich came to the plate.

Since the All-Star break, Tommy Henrich had been the best hitter in the American League. Over his last 51 games he had hit .360, with 76 hits, *53 runs scored*, 12 home runs, and 44 runs batted in. He was apparently enjoying his shift to first base, where his hitting had if anything accelerated. This time he managed to drop a fly ball in front of Zarilla in right-center that went for a double and tied the game. The game remained tied until the bottom of the twelfth, when Yogi Berra hit a solo homer for the ball game and the Yankees' fourth straight win.

Of all the Yankees involved in Harris's lineup shift, Berra seemed to have benefited the most. In 21 games since his move to right field on August 14, he had hit .418, with 3 homers and 20 RBIs, to raise his average over .300. One source of concern was Joe DiMaggio, who still shared the league lead in RBIs with Vern Stephens at 118, but had gone just 3 for 17 in five games against the Tigers and the Browns. He, however, was known to hit better on the road than in Yankee Stadium, and the Yankees now had only six more home games left. For two days, they had been within reach of first place, but Red Sox victories had kept them one game back.

The Indians, meanwhile, finally dropped the Athletics out of the race with two victories. A well-rested Bearden got his first win in two weeks and thirteenth overall with the help of three RBIs and a great catch by Boudreau on Tuesday. Several omens on Wednesday night suggested that Cleveland's luck was finally changing. Ken Keltner hit a three-run triple in the first, Joe Gordon emerged from a slump with his 24th homer in the eighth, and Bob Feller finally evened his record at 14–14 with an 8–1 victory, striking out nine batters. The Athletics fell 5½ games behind, and the Indians concluded their road trip at 6–5. But for the second time in a

STANDINGS
Thursday, September 2, 1948

Team	Won	Lost	Pct.	Games Behind
Boston	77	48	.615	—
New York	76	49	.608	1
Cleveland	76	50	.603	1½
Philadelphia	73	55	.570	5½
Detroit	59	62	.488	14
Washington	49	77	.389	28½
St. Louis	47	75	.385	28½
Chicago	42	83	.334	35

row they had lost the league lead during an eastern trip, and had to try to regain it out west. Moreover, they had to play six games in six days in St. Louis and Chicago, returning home only after Labor Day.

The Red Sox express continued to roll in Philadelphia over Labor Day weekend, as Joe McCarthy's practice of keeping his starting pitchers rested paid some impressive dividends. On Friday night, September 3, Joe Dobson ran his record to 15–7 with his best performance of the last six weeks, shutting the Athletics out on just four hits en route to a 2–0 win. The next day, behind Kinder, the Red Sox won again 5–3. Mel Parnell was now available with four days' rest, but McCarthy chose Galehouse to oppose tough Dick Fowler on Sunday. Galehouse did not pitch badly, but lost a 3–0 lead when Hank Majeski singled in a run in the fifth and belted a two-run homer in the seventh to tie the game. Dave Ferriss pitched well in relief, however, and in the top of the tenth Williams doubled to left—his fourth hit of the day—and scored the lead run when Hitchcock singled. Ferriss made the lead hold up for a 5–4 victory and a sweep of the series.

The beat went on in Washington, where the Red Sox took their Labor Day doubleheader behind Parnell and Kramer to sweep a road trip for the first time all year. In the first game they romped to a 12–1 lead and coasted to a 14–6 victory as Parnell ran his record to 12–6. They needed a gem in the nightcap, and Jack Kramer provided it on four days' rest, giving up only four hits and walking one en route to a 2–1 victory and a 16–4 record. The Red Sox' five-game road streak was all the more remarkable because Bobby Doerr was still absent from the lineup, and Junior Stephens—although he had yet to miss an inning—was reported to be ill. They had won seven games in a row, and seventeen out of their last twenty. Yet they needed every single win to avoid losing ground to the Yankees, whose weekend featured an incredible performance by the greatest Yankee of them all.

After Ed Lopat retired the Senators in the first inning of a Yankee Stadium doubleheader on Friday, Joe DiMaggio started things off with a three-run homer in the bottom of the inning, and hit a solo shot later in the game as the Yanks won 6–2. In the nightcap, he hit another three-run, inside-the-park homer in the bottom of the sixth when his Texas leaguer went through Ed Stewart, giving him three homers and seven RBIs on the day. Having started the day tied with Junior Stephens at 118 RBIs, he finished with 125 and 32 home runs. The double win put the Yankees within a half-game of the Red Sox, although they still trailed by one in the loss column.

Bob Porterfield took the mound on Saturday, hoping to pitch the Yankees into first place. His luck ran out, as he surrendered five runs in three innings and left the game trailing 5–0, but the Yankees exploded for five runs in the bottom of the fourth and four more in the fifth to go ahead 9–5, and Byrne held on for a 9–7 victory. Berra, with four RBIs, and Joe D, with two more, led the way. Henrich came to bat with the bases full and a chance to break his jointly held record of four grand slams in a season twice, and missed the record by a few feet in the fifth when his drive down the right-field line went foul. Porterfield's failure, in retrospect, was all too understandable. He had done everything Harris could have expected since his call-up on August 6, winning four and losing just one, but he was now the second most heavily worked pitcher in the American League. With 178 innings pitched at Newark and 52 with the Yankees, his total of 230 was greater than any American League hurler except Lemon, who had pitched 251 innings. Reynolds was leading the Yankees with only 196. In fact, Porterfield's subsequent career suggests that the strain of the 1948 season was too much for the young hurler's arm. He threw just 74 innings in 1949 and 28 in 1950, before recovering with the Washington Senators and turning in several fine seasons in the early 1950s.

Reynolds got his sixteenth victory on Sunday, as DiMaggio hit his 33rd homer and fourth of the weekend in the second. In the bottom of the sixth, with the score 3–3, he proved again that he had entered the kind of zone where nothing can go wrong. Washington pitcher Sid Hudson tried to slow him down with a brushback pitch, and as he ducked away the ball hit his bat and sailed over the head of Mickey Vernon for a double to right. The double started a three-run rally, and strong relief by Joe Page preserved the 5–3 win. On the eve of Labor Day, both the Yankees and the Red Sox had won nineteen of their last twenty-two games.

The Yankees had a new face in the lineup as they took the field for their home Labor Day doubleheader against Philadelphia: outfielder Hank Bauer, a twenty-six-year-old rookie, who had hit .305 with 23 home runs and 100 RBIs at Kansas City. Charlie Keller's back was apparently deteriorating again, and Bucky Harris—who had been seeking Bauer's call-up for weeks—planned to play the rookie in left field against right-handers, and sit down Yogi Berra and put Bauer in right against left-handers. Bauer came through with three hits in the opener, and Vic Raschi won his eighteenth victory against six defeats. But the Athletics rebounded in the nightcap, dropping the Yanks and Lopat 6–2 behind Joe Coleman. Their winning streak over, the Yankees dropped two games behind the Red Sox in the loss column, and 1½ over all, with three games in Fenway next on schedule. The Labor Day crowd of 72,859 raised the Yankees' attendance to 2,243,235, leaving them only 60,000 fans shy of their all-time record set two years earlier, and making them almost certain to break it in their three remaining home games against the Red Sox on the next-to-last weekend of the season.

The Indians arrived in St. Louis for a Friday doubleheader on September 3 trailing the Red Sox by two games in the loss column, but bookies still made them 7–5 favorites to take the pennant, with the Red Sox 8–5 and the Yankees 11–5. As Gordon Cobbledick explained to his readers, the odds made sense: of the Indians' remaining 28 games, 23 of them involved second-division clubs (nine with the Tigers, seven with the Browns, four with the White Sox, and three with the Senators), with three against the Athletics and just one each against the Yankees and Red Sox. Meanwhile, the Yankees and Red Sox would have to play a majority of their games on the road, and had eight more dates against each other.

Boudreau sent two well-rested pitchers, Bob Lemon and Sam Zoldak, against the Browns' two left-handers, Bill Kennedy and Joe Ostrowski. Lemon came up with his third consecutive shutout in the opener, giving up just six hits and walking one and cruising to a 7–0 win, his league-leading nineteenth victory. Lemon had now pitched 260 innings in his first full year on the mound, allowing just 191 hits and walking 102. But Zoldak did not have it in the second game, and Al Zarilla's home run keyed the Browns to a 4–2 victory. The Tribe thus lost a half-game to the Red Sox and a full game to the Yankees.

On Saturday night, September 4, Satchel Paige started against the Browns and drew 16,754, one of the largest crowds of the year in St. Louis. With Paige on the mound, the Indians had now drawn the largest single-game crowds of the year in St. Louis, in Chicago (August 13), and in Cleveland (August 20, the largest night crowd ever). Without Paige, they had also drawn the season's largest crowds in Philadelphia (37,900 on June 6) and in Washington (29,554 on June 4), and the largest crowd in history, 82,781, for their June 20 doubleheader with the A's. Their three-date total of 188,081 with the Yankees on August 6–8 was also a record. Paige led 2–0 in the bottom of the fifth, but a barrage of St. Louis hits scored three runs and knocked him out. With Christopher and Klieman relieving, the Indians tied the game in the top of the seventh, when they loaded the bases but scored just one run. It remained at 3–3 until the bottom of the tenth, when a double, two walks, and a two-out single by twenty-two-year-old Ned Garver, relieving, gave the Browns the victory. The Indians' last game in St. Louis was rained out on Sunday, and re-scheduled as part of a doubleheader in Cleveland the next weekend. The Cleveland hitters were showing the effects of a two-week road trip, and the twelve runs they scored in three games yielded only one victory. They had dropped 3½ games behind the Red Sox—four in the loss column—and three games behind the Yankees.

After a three hundred-mile train ride, Feller and Bearden tried to stop the team's skid in Chicago Labor Day doubleheader. The hitting drought continued in the first game, which rain delayed for almost an hour. While Cleveland finally scratched out one run in the sixth after missing numerous opportunities, the White Sox scored three off Bearden in the second and third. In the eighth, Boudreau grounded out with two on and two out, and in the ninth he sent reserve catcher Joe Tipton to bat for Doby with two out and the bases loaded against lefty Frank Papish. Tipton struck out and the Indians lost, 3–1.

Bob Feller pitched a seven-inning shutout in the second game, which was then called for darkness. It was a good thing that he did, as the Indians managed just three hits and one run themselves en route to a 1–0 victory. They completed their last big road trip with a record of eight wins and eight losses—adequate in most seasons even for a pennant winner, but disastrous this year. Having left home two weeks earlier leading the Red Sox by a half game and the Yankees by two, they now trailed the Yankees by three games and the Red Sox by 4½—five in the loss column. Boudreau's handling of the pitchers in Boston and New York, Keltner's slump, and a general power shortage in St. Louis and Chicago had brought the Tribe to their lowest point of the entire season. Their weakness in close games was becoming a scandal: they were now 9–17 in one-run ball games.

Although the schedule still favored the Indians, they would have to play very well to take advantage of it. Eighteen of their twenty-three remaining games were scheduled against second-division clubs—although nine of them were against the dangerous Tigers—while the Yankees and Red Sox had to play one another five more times. All but three of their remaining games would take place at home, but they still had a better record on the road than at Municipal Stadium. Gordon Cobbledick noted that the Tribe would need to go a superb 17–6 to finish with 95 wins. One wonders what he would have said had he known that 95 wins would *not* have been enough to win. Writing for Tuesday's paper, Cobbledick began listing reasons for the Tribe's failure, and another paper quoted Veeck to the effect that "only a miracle" could give the Indians the flag. The Yankees and the Red Sox were in the driver's seat, and as luck would have it, they would open a three-game set in Fenway on Wednesday.

Whatever the fate of his team and his job as a manager, Lou Boudreau was clearly in the midst of one of the most amazing seasons in baseball history. Just how amazing it was has not become clear until very recently, when his home-road statistics were compiled. Boudreau had hit .393 on the

Indians' road trip (24 for 71), raising his average from .363 to .366. He was challenging Ted Williams for the batting title despite the handicap of playing in one of the more difficult average parks in the majors. In fact, Boudreau on the year had hit only .311 in Municipal Stadium—and an astonishing .406 on the road. He was destined to maintain this pace for the remainder of the season. Boudreau in 1948, in short, may have hit as well as any player in the history of baseball.

STANDINGS
Wednesday Morning, September 8, 1948

Team	Won	Lost	Pct.	Games Behind
Boston	82	48	.631	—
New York	81	50	.618	1½
Cleveland	78	53	.695	4½
Philadelphia	74	59	.556	5½
Detroit	62	64	.492	14
St. Louis	49	77	.394	30½
Washington	49	83	.371	34
Chicago	44	86	.338	38½

The four teams that had fought over the lead during the first five months of the season, and the fans who had flocked to see them in absolutely unprecedented numbers, had already experienced far more than an average season's worth of excitement. Controversies and changes in Boston, Cleveland, and New York had kicked things off nicely even before the season began, and the first half of the campaign had featured the Cinderella performance of the Athletics, Joe DiMaggio's amazing three-homer game in Cleveland, Ted Williams's flirtation with .400, the Red Sox' collapse in May, and Ken Keltner's remarkable home run barrage, as well as the apparent eclipse of Bob Feller and the controversy over his withdrawal from the All-Star game. The second half had kicked off with the Red Sox' remarkable home winning streak, bringing the four contenders into a virtual tie that lasted for weeks. Boudreau and Williams had continued their duel for the batting title, Junior Stephens was turning in a Hall of Fame campaign, Bob Lemon had emerged as a truly great pitcher, Tommy Henrich had done the best hitting of his life, and Satchel Paige had established himself both as a physical marvel and a gate attraction such as had not been seen since the heyday of Babe Ruth, whose death had also hit the headlines. The season would have ranked as a classic had the Red Sox, Yankees, or Indians run away with the rest of the campaign—but none of them did.

The 1940s were the greatest decade in history for pennant races. The National League had wonderful races in 1941, 1942, 1946, 1948, and 1949; the American League had fine struggles in 1944, 1945, 1948, and 1949. The 1948 American League race was the greatest of them all. Why this should be so is a question that we must go beyond the confines of baseball to answer. The players of 1948 had lived through an era of struggle at home and overseas—a struggle over far weightier matters than the American League pennant. Their whole adult lives had taken place amidst heroic undertakings, and they had proved themselves equal to history's most difficult tasks. And the same qualities that had gotten them through the Depression and the Second World War fitted them uniquely to fight out the most dramatic struggle in the history of baseball.

Since the beginning of recorded history and myth, a sequence of generational types has appeared and reappeared through the ages, leading tribes and nations through great national crises.[4] In the *Iliad,* the Greeks who fought Troy included the old prophet, Nestor; the middle-aged commander, Agamemnon; and the youthful hero Achilles, who faced off against his Trojan counterpart Hector. The aging prophet Moses led Israel out of Egypt, railed against the apostasy of next-elder Aaron, and left Joshua's younger hero generation to complete the work of conquering the Promised Land. In the *Star Wars* trilogy, the young heroes Luke and Leia prevail by following the wisdom of the prophet Obiwan Kenobi, with the help of the older, more cynical loner Han Solo. And the United States in the great crisis of the second quarter of the twentieth century showed exactly the same pattern: the elder leadership of Franklin Roosevelt, Henry Stimson, and George Marshall; the command of hardened, capable middle-aged generals like Patton, Bradley, and Eisenhower; and the heroism of a particular generation of youth, the GI generation, born roughly between 1901 and 1924, carefully nurtured during a difficult era, employed by the programs of the New Deal, and then drafted by the millions to fight the Second World War.

The same pattern also had determined the development of twentieth-century baseball. After the catastrophe of the Black Sox scandal, the game in the 1920s and 1930s recovered its health under the stern, uncompromising leadership of Kenesaw Mountain Landis, an older member of FDR's generation. The commissioner's death in 1944 had turned the leadership of the game over to a new generation that would handle the challenges of the 1950s and 1960s much less well. Meanwhile, in the 1930s, a new crop of

---

4. See William Strauss and Neil Howe, *Generations: The History of America's Future, 1584 to 2069* (New York, 1991), and *The Fourth Turning: An American Prophecy* (New York, 1997).

young stars—including nearly all the key figures in this book—had reached the American League determined to leave their mark on history. Bob Feller before the war dreamed of breaking Walter Johnson's records for lifetime wins and strikeouts; Ted Williams arrived in Boston determined to be the greatest hitter of all time; and Joe DiMaggio played every game as if determined to establish himself on the level of Cobb and Ruth.

As it turned out, destiny had chosen these men and their contemporaries for a bigger task, the Second World War. That war, in which Feller served nearly four years and Williams and DiMaggio three apiece, deprived them of any chance for lifetime records. Yet prior to the war, Williams and DiMaggio had each, in the single season of 1941, accomplished feats that have never since been equaled: Williams's .406 average and DiMaggio's 56-game hitting streak. Feller followed suit in 1946 with 348 strikeouts, a record which would probably still stand as well had not conditions in the early 1960s changed to favor pitchers drastically and given Sandy Koufax, and then Nolan Ryan, an edge.

Now the war was over, and the nation's ballparks had once again become the great arena of American struggle. And the GI generation—which included every regular on the contending American League teams but two, Billy Goodman and Yogi Berra—was showing nearly the same endurance, fortitude, and willingness to put themselves on the line day after day as the soldiers of the recent war. Even players like Vern Stephens and Lou Boudreau, who for various reasons had missed the war, showed these qualities during the season, in which Boudreau coped with the pain of his ankles and Stephens did not miss a single inning of a single game. Bucky Harris and Joe McCarthy, meanwhile, had emerged as the Patton and Eisenhower of the campaign, leaders from another generation whose experience helped them deploy their troops in the most effective way possible. Cleveland presented an interesting anomaly. Heroic ages often bring young men to positions of unusual responsibility, and in Cleveland, both the team manager and even the team owner, as well as the players, belonged to the same GI generation.

The huge crowds that flooded every game, meanwhile, undoubtedly were also composed largely of other former GIs and their wives, who, after enduring the Depression and the war, were taking advantage of a long-delayed opportunity to enjoy life. And while many of these couples had already given birth to one postwar child, the combination of the baby boom and television had not yet gone far enough to keep them at home on weekends and evenings. They had earned a good time, and they meant to enjoy it. Their contemporary Bill Veeck made it even easier for them by providing a "nursery"—what we would now call a day-care center—at Municipal Stadium. And on the field, their contemporaries provided them with one of the greatest spectacles in the history of American sport.

The heroic spirit, as we shall see, carried the three main contenders through the entire last month of the campaign and established the 1948 American League season as the most exciting in the history of baseball. No collapse played any part in this race: the three contenders improved their record after September 1, posting a combined 61–30 record from September 1 through the end of the season. September saw the recovery of Bob Feller, a remarkable winning streak from Gene Bearden, a nail-biting attempt by Bucky Harris to hold a pitching staff together, critical performances by the also-rans in the race, and, in the last two weeks, a series of changes of fortune that kept fans in all three cities on an emotional roller coaster. It finished with three teams in a dead-even tie for first with nine days to go, and three in contention on the last Saturday of the year. Only one team could win the pennant, but all played their parts in an unparalleled drama which is nearly as enthralling now, fully fifty years later, as it was at the time it took place.

On September 8, with the Red Sox two games in front, the Yankees came into Fenway Park for three games, while the Indians, home in Cleveland, tried desperately to remain in the race against the Tigers. Boston seemed perhaps on the verge of putting the race away. And the Red Sox might actually have done so, had not the greatest star of them all managed to defy a crippling injury and strike blow after tremendous blow through what gradually emerged as the most amazing month of his entire career.

10

The Great DiMaggio

(SEPTEMBER 8–SEPTEMBER 23)

STANDINGS
Wednesday Morning, September 8, 1948

Team	Won	Lost	Pct.	Games Behind
Boston	82	48	.631	—
New York	81	50	.618	1½
Cleveland	78	53	.695	4½
Philadelphia	74	59	.556	5½
Detroit	62	64	.492	14
St. Louis	49	77	.394	30½
Washington	49	83	.371	34
Chicago	44	86	.338	38½

On Wednesday, September 8, with grandstand tickets going for $40 a pair on Jersey Street, a Boston writer entered the Yankee clubhouse before that night's game and discovered Charlie Keller and Tommy Henrich in a lively argument about the plot of a recent movie. Queried, Henrich cheerfully explained that professionals had to keep loose. The 33,775 fans who paid their way in found that neither the Yankees nor the Red Sox could have been much looser: the teams played their entire three-game series like warriors who simply could not be beaten. The pitchers for the opener were red-hot: Joe Dobson, fresh from two complete-game victories, and Frank Shea, who had followed up his one-hitter against the Tigers with a complete-game win against the Senators five days before. Bobby Doerr was still out of

175

the lineup for the Red Sox, and Bauer remained in left field in place of Keller for the Yanks.

Snuffy Stirnweiss wasted no time in the top of the first, rapping Dobson's first pitch off the left-field wall for a single. Hits by Henrich, Bauer, Joe DiMaggio, and Bobby Brown followed, and the Red Sox came to bat in the bottom of the inning trailing 4–0. Not to be outdone, Dom DiMaggio singled to left to start the bottom of the first, and Johnny Pesky doubled to right-center, sending him to third. An overanxious Ted Williams sent a checked-swing grounder toward third base for an out, but Dom DiMaggio scored. Stephens struck out for the second out, but Wally Moses—subbing for Stan Spence in right—scored Pesky with an infield single. The two-out rally continued as Billy Goodman singled to left, and Birdie Tebbetts tripled over Joe DiMaggio's head in center to tie the game. Billy Hitchcock promptly singled Tebbetts home, and Dobson started the second inning with a 5–4 lead.

With the Indians fading, this three-game series could easily mean the pennant. Gambling, Bucky Harris took out Shea for a pinch hitter in the top of the second and replaced him with Allie Reynolds, who would otherwise have started on Thursday or Friday. Reynolds and Dobson settled down, and runs became harder to come by. Dom DiMaggio gave Boston a two-run lead with an RBI single in the fourth. But Yogi Berra answered with a solo homer in the top of the sixth to make the Sox' lead 6–5, and the Yankees tied the game at six in the seventh before Earl Johnson relieved and got Berra to end the inning.

Joe Page relieved Reynolds in the bottom of the seventh, and Dom DiMaggio doubled off the left-field wall on an 0–2 pitch, his third hit of the night. Pesky promptly sacrificed him to third. Williams—hitless on the night—sent a grounder to second, and when Stirnweiss failed to get Di-Maggio at the plate, the Red Sox led, 7–6. Now Stephens singled to left, and the crippled Bobby Doerr—batting for Wally Moses—walked to load the bases. Another walk to Goodman brought in another run, Harris removed Page, and Boston scored twice more for a 10–6 lead.

Earl Johnson retired the Yankees in the eighth, and the Red Sox entered the top of the ninth still leading by four runs. Henrich, leading off the ninth, was robbed of extra bases by Dom DiMaggio near the right-center-field bullpen. Bauer made the second out. Joe DiMaggio—two for four on the night—lined the ball viciously at Pesky. The ball glanced off the leaping third baseman's glove, and he reached up and grabbed it with his bare hand to end the game and give the Red Sox a 10–6 victory and a three-game loss column lead over the Yankees.

On the same evening in Cleveland, 43,707 fans turned out to see the

Indians try to stay in the race against the Tigers. Bob Lemon, holder of a 28-inning scoreless streak, was looking for his fourth straight shutout and twentieth victory against Fred Hutchinson. Boudreau, typically, began the home stand with a new lineup, batting Doby third for the first time all season and inserting Judnich at first in place of Eddie Robinson. Lemon was staked to a 3–0 lead, but walked the bases loaded and gave up two runs in the fourth. Doubles by Judnich and Hegan ran the Indians' lead to 7–3 in the bottom of the fifth. Dick Wakefield homered in the sixth, and Paige relieved a tired Lemon in the seventh and retired the side still leading, 7–5.

Paige walked two batters in the top of the eighth. With one out and a 2–0 count on Jimmy Outlaw—a decent hitter with no power—Boudreau suddenly relieved Paige and inserted Ed Klieman. The Indians were continuing to unravel, and Boudreau—not to put too fine a point on the matter—was panicking. Klieman—who had made three bad appearances during the Indians' road trip—completed the base on balls and promptly surrendered a two-run single. Zoldak relieved Klieman and retired the next batter, but the game was tied, 7–7.

With the Indians inches away from falling out of the pennant race, Zoldak dueled Art Houtteman from the eighth inning through the eleventh. After the Indians had missed scoring chances in the eighth, ninth, and tenth, Doby singled again, Gordon walked, and Keltner sacrificed in the bottom of the eleventh. After Boudreau was purposely passed to load the bases, Judnich bounced to second, and Doby scored the winning run on a wild throw to the plate. All this merely enabled the Indians to stay five games behind the Red Sox in the loss column. They had finally won a one-run decision after losing six of them in a row.

On the next afternoon in Boston, Porterfield tried to rebound from his bad outing in Washington, while Ellis Kinder—preferred, this time, to Galehouse—went for his third victory in a row. Once again the Yankees started quickly, as triples by Henrich in the first and Niarhos in the second gave them a 2–0 lead, and Henrich, Berra, and DiMaggio combined for another run in the third. McCarthy, patient as ever, let Kinder hit for himself with one out in the bottom of the third, and Kinder walked.

Porterfield now collapsed, walking Dom DiMaggio and Pesky to load the bases for Williams, who had yet to make an impact in the series. The shift was on, and less than ten feet separated second baseman Stirnweiss and first baseman Henrich, but Williams ripped the ball between them for two runs. Stephens singled for another run, and Wally Moses doubled in the lead tally and chased Porterfield. Tommy Byrne walked Goodman, threw two balls to Tebbetts, and gave way to Eddie Lopat in mid–at bat, as Harris called on another starting pitcher. Lopat was no better, and the unstoppable Red Sox eventually scored eight runs in the inning en route to a 9–4 win. Williams, with two hits on the day, regained the batting lead over Boudreau, .367 to .365, while Stephens, with his 122nd RBI, moved to within seven of Joe DiMaggio. The Red Sox had now won 24 of their last 28 games, taking them from fourth place, three games behind the Indians on August 9, to first place, 3½ games *ahead* of the Yankees, on September 10. The absence of Bobby Doerr had hardly affected them, their pitching had been excellent, and their offense was unstoppable. They had now beaten the Yankees seven straight times.

"It becomes more and more apparent," Red Smith wrote in the next morning's *New York Herald Tribune*, "that this Boston ball club is a McCarthy ball club, and if there is higher praise in the language it does not come to mind at the moment. . . . Ted Williams never has been as good a ball player as he is right now. . . . Junior Stephens is having the most terrific season of his life. Birdie Tebbetts never has approached his performance of this summer. Bobby Doerr, currently injured, has excelled all his former standards of fielding excellence."[1]

Taking the field against the Tigers that evening, the Indians had to win again just to stay five games behind in the loss column. The pitching matchup was a classic: Bob Feller, seeking his fourth straight win and sixteenth overall, against Hal Newhouser, who had rebounded from a slow start and now sported a record of 16–11. Veeck had designated the evening as Ken Keltner Night, and the third baseman received a car, $1,000 bank accounts for each of his sons, and a variety of other gifts before the game began.

Feller was good, but Newhouser was even better. After the Tigers put together a run in the third for a 1–0 lead, Newhouser repeatedly retired Boudreau, Gordon, and Keltner with men on base. Boudreau finally removed Feller for a pinch hitter in the bottom of the seventh, after the Indians had loaded the bases with one out on singles by Doby and first baseman Judnich and a slow roller by Hegan. The move worked when Bob Kennedy hit a sacrifice fly to tie the game, but Newhouser got Mitchell to end the inning.

Ol' Satch relieved Feller and got the Tigers out in the top of the eighth, and Gordon singled in the lead run in the bottom of the frame for a 2–1 lead. Needing just three outs to close out a victory, Paige opened the ninth by giving up a double to George Vico. He got the next two outs, but then his magic failed him, and a single by Johnny Lipon scored the tying run.

---

1. *New York Herald Tribune*, September 10.

When he walked the next batter, Boudreau brought in Zoldak to pitch to left-handed hitter Dick Wakefield.

Dick Wakefield had been the first big bonus baby signed by a major league team. The Tigers had paid him $50,000 to sign in 1941—about $500,000 today—and despite an excellent rookie season in 1943, the fans had never forgiven him for it. Now, with two men on, he drove the ball deep to right center, and with the whole season at stake, Allie Clark made a running one-handed catch to end the inning in a 2–2 tie. The unbearable tension continued through the tenth, eleventh, and twelfth innings, as both teams failed to score. After two quick outs in the bottom of the thirteenth, Keltner walked; Thurman Tucker, who had replaced Doby in center field, singled to center; and Eddie Robinson, a late-inning replacement for Judnich, singled to score Keltner for a 3–2 victory. The Indians were still alive, as Zoldak got his second straight win in relief.

Earlier in the day, an intriguing three-paragraph letter had appeared in the afternoon *Cleveland Press*. The author, inspired by Ken Keltner Night, and by suggestions circulating for a Bill Veeck Night, had a suggestion of his own.

> A night to end all nights.
>
> Now they want a "Bill Veeck Night." It's a good idea, but here's another suggestion. Let's have a "Joe Earley Night."
>
> I pay my rent and my landlord spends it on things that keep business stimulated. I keep the gas station attendant in business by buying gas regularly. I keep the milkman in clover by buying milk. He uses trucks and tires and as a result big industry is kept going. The paper boy delivers the paper, wears out a pair of shoes occasionally and the shoemaker wins. My wife keeps a grocer and a butcher (don't we all) in business and the department stores as well.
>
> A lot of people depend on me (and you) so let us all get together, and send in your contributions for that new car for "Good Old Joe Earley Night."
>
> Joe Earley, 1380 Westlake Ave.[2]

Earley's letter struck a resonant chord among *Press* readers, and the paper reported two days later that Joe had received numerous replies and many small amounts of cash. But the most interested reader of all, of course, was Bill Veeck, who recognized a fellow promotional genius. Within hours of the letter's appearance, he was planning to take Joe up on his suggestion.

A mere 9,008 fans turned out on Friday afternoon to see if the Indians could continue to hang on, and this time the Tribe finally broke loose.

2. *Cleveland Press,* September 9.

Bearden was superb, pitching a no-hitter for four innings, and as often seemed to happen with Bearden on the mound, the Cleveland hitters finally came to life. Boudreau and Keltner delivered three hits each, and Gordon's 25th homer—moving him one behind Keltner and two behind Vern Stephens—helped run the final score to 10–1. The Indians still had to play four games with the Browns over the next two days, with Gromek their only rested pitcher, but they were still alive. Meanwhile, Boudreau— three for four on the day—raised his average to .369 and took a two-point lead over Williams.

A much bigger game took place in Boston, where the Red Sox went for a sweep of their series against New York. With the Yankees traveling to Washington after the game the contest was scheduled for the afternoon, but 27,329 showed up despite the opening of school to see Vic Raschi (18– 6) try to beat the Red Sox for the first time in his entire career. To oppose him, Joe McCarthy departed from his normal practice and chose Jack Kramer (16–4), pitching on just three days' rest, instead of Galehouse or Parnell. With a four-game bulge in the loss column, McCarthy apparently felt that one more victory over the Yankees might put them down for the count. The Red Sox had won nine straight games, giving them a 45–13 record—a .776 percentage—since the All-Star game.

Tommy Henrich, capping his remarkable second half with a great series in Boston, greeted Kramer in the top of the first inning with a two-run homer. But Ted Williams drove in Dom DiMaggio in both the first and third to tie the game, 2–2. Meanwhile, Jack Kramer was living off his defense. A great throw by Billy Hitchcock got Bobby Brown out at the plate in the second, and in the third, Wally Moses robbed Henrich of a home run, falling into the right-field stands as he caught his long drive.

The Yankees finally broke through in the top of the fifth as Stirnweiss and Henrich led off with singles, Joe DiMaggio doubled off the top of the left-field wall for a run, and Brown's sacrifice fly eventually scored Henrich and gave the Yankees a 4–2 lead. In the bottom of the inning Junior Stephens hit a shot to third with Pesky and Williams aboard, but Bobby Brown snared it and started a 5–4–3 double play. The Yanks scored two more runs in the sixth, and chased Kramer in favor of Ferriss.

Trailing 6–2 in the bottom of the sixth, the Red Sox did it again. Two singles and a walk loaded the bases, Hitchcock singled in two runs, and Stan Spence, pinch-hitting for Ferriss, singled in another run and sent Hitchcock to third. Bucky Harris made a surprise move, bringing in Frank Shea, victim of the Red Sox just two days earlier, to try to save a one-run led. Shea began by inducing Dom DiMaggio to ground back to him and tagging Hitchcock between third and home. Pesky flied out to center for the second out, and Spence advanced from second to third. Williams made a bid for the lead with a shot toward right, but Henrich made a fine catch to preserve a 6–5 lead.

After Earl Johnson gave up no hits in two innings, Jake Jones pinch-hit for him in the bottom of the eighth and walked. Dom DiMaggio doubled—his third hit of the day—and Pesky's sacrifice fly tied the game. But Shea got Williams out to escape with a 6–6 deadlock. The Yankees did not score in the top of the ninth against forty-three-year-old Earl Caldwell, and Shea got the Red Sox in the bottom of the inning. The crowd sat enthralled, counting on the Red Sox for the one more run that might put the flag in their pocket.

Caldwell—who had been signed to get right-handers out with his side-arm delivery in crucial situations in Fenway—opened the top of the tenth by walking Niarhos. Then a sidearmer got away, and he hit Frank Shea to put two men on with none out. Recovering, he struck out Charlie Keller, who pinch-hit for Stirnweiss. After walking the left-handed Henrich—two for five on the night—to load the bases, he struck out Hank Bauer. With twenty-eight thousand fans looking on in terrified excitement, Caldwell had loaded the bases and retired two men without a single ball having been put into play. The key play of the inning was the pitch that hit Frank Shea, thereby bringing red-hot Joe DiMaggio—the league's leader with 33 home runs and 130 RBIs—to the plate with two out, the bases loaded, and a chance to get the Yankees back into the pennant race.

"I would rather be anybody in the world than Earl Caldwell right now," said a writer in the press box.

DiMaggio fouled off the first pitch. Then Caldwell threw a fastball on the inside corner, perhaps a fraction or so off the plate, and Joe D swung and drove the ball high and deep down the left-field line. The crowd gasped, then sighed with relief as the ball landed a few feet foul. On second base, Frank Shea's heart sank. He well knew the tradition that a batter who hit a barely foul home run had missed his chance, and would not hit another.

Two balls ran the count to 2–2. Then Caldwell threw a curve on the low, outside part of the plate. DiMaggio swung again, and made contact.

DiMaggio was known around the league for his amazing line drives. Back in May, Lou Boudreau had jumped after one that found its way into the bleachers in Cleveland, and Bucky Harris's son Stanley remembers shagging flies during batting practice in Griffith Stadium with DiMaggio at the plate, and moving in for a line drive toward left-center that kept rising and rising until it landed in the bleachers more than 400 feet away. This ball was hit to dead center, toward the bleachers to the right of the flagpole 420 feet away in Fenway Park. It rose, rose, and cleared the fence for a grand-slam home run and a 10–6 lead. Only Larry Doby had previously reached that spot during the season. A shaken Red Sox team quickly yielded two more singles and an error for another run, and Shea set them down easily in the bottom of the tenth. The Red Sox' winning streak was over, their lead over the Yankees was back down to 2½ games, 3 in the loss column. Boston still had a commanding position, but Joe DiMaggio and Cleveland's miraculous victories on Wednesday and Thursday had kept the race alive.

Although Joe DiMaggio's batting average was still just .303, he was now in the midst of one of his greatest seasons. He led Junior Stephens by 7 homers and 12 RBIs, and his RBI total of 134 was already the second-highest of his career. In the field he was on his way to a career-high 441 putouts, although he also finished with 13 errors and the lowest fielding average (.972) of his entire career. And he was doing it all despite a serious, painful injury.

DiMaggio's upright style of batting and running and the intensity of his play had put tremendous pressure on his heels for perhaps fifteen years. He had had an operation on his left heel after the 1947 season, and had apparently put more pressure on his right heel, which had developed a painful bone spur. His pain was so obvious that the club had announced, falsely, that he was suffering from a charley horse. His real injury was much more serious and would need off-season surgery.

Because DiMaggio had such an impressive bearing, and because of his unfailingly calm demeanor on and off the field, only his play gave a clue to his unmatched pride and competitiveness. He bitterly resented enemy fielders who took hits away from him—including, according to his friend the restaurateur Toots Shor, his own brother, with whom he once canceled a dinner date after Dominic robbed him of two extra-base hits in a game in Yankee Stadium.[3] He told a friend years later that often, when the team arrived in St. Louis after a twenty-four-hour train ride, he would make sure to get a good night's sleep because the few thousand people in the stands the next day might include someone who would never see him again. While Ted Williams played to live up to his own standards, DiMaggio also played to live up to the public's. He had more trouble handling failure than Williams, and his constant effort to live up to the image he had created for himself took a heavy toll. Only a few weeks earlier, he had allowed a remarkable glimpse of his inner self to emerge during the train ride home

3. Allen, *Where Have You Gone, Joe DiMaggio*, 41. This is by far the best of the many books on DiMaggio.

from the Yankees' third western trip. The incident is remembered by Stanley Harris, then a student at the University of Virginia, who had made the trip with the team:

STANLEY HARRIS: That night, I had dinner with DiMaggio. When the train stopped in Pittsburgh, we got out to buy a paper. As always, he was immediately mobbed by fans and had to sign some autographs. As we got back on the train, he looked at me.

"You're in college, right?" he said.

I said yes.

"Playing college baseball?" I nodded.

"I'd give anything to trade places with you," he said.

During the last week, DiMaggio had won three of the Yankees' games almost singlehandedly. Thanks to him, the Yankees were still in the race— and with five more games against the Red Sox, their fate was in their own hands. The Yankee Clipper had performed the most spectacular feats, but he was not doing it alone. Henrich was contributing nearly as much. His record since July 16 now included an average of .366, with 63 runs scored in 56 games, 13 homers, and 51 RBIs. Brown had slumped somewhat, but Berra was hitting strongly. The weak spot in the Yankee lineup was leadoff, where Stirnweiss had slumped from .272 in mid-July to .257, with 80 runs scored compared to Henrich's league-leading total of 115.

The Yankee pitchers, however, were showing the strain of pitching a long season with an average of three days of rest. Porterfield, in particular, had now pitched more than 230 innings, and had failed to complete three out of his last four starts. Harris apparently trusted only Joe Page among his relievers, and was increasingly turning to starters to finish games. But overall, the Yankees had an outstanding 23–8 record since Harris had introduced his new lineup on August 13, a .742 pace. A few weeks earlier, Harris had estimated that 95 games would win the pennant, and his team would need just a 13–7 record to reach that goal. But like Gordon Cobbledick, Harris had underestimated the pennant race; 95 games would not even be good enough to finish second.

The Red Sox schedule for the weekend had originally called for two single games against the Athletics, but a rain-out had forced them to add another. The front office, seeking to make up for the relatively small size of Fenway Park by scheduling as many separate home games as possible, had scheduled another day-night doubleheader for Saturday. Commercially the decision was a short-term success—21,415 fans paid their way into the first game, and 34,002 into the second—but Tom Yawkey and Joe Cronin showed very questionable judgment. A day-night doubleheader was hardly the way to keep the team fresh, especially since they had to head west for the last time on Monday.

McCarthy's men kept the pressure on on Saturday with another sweep. A well-rested Denny Galehouse handled the Athletics well in the first game, escaping from jams with the help of five double plays, while Williams led another strong attack as the team coasted to a 9–1 victory. The night game was scoreless for 4½ innings, until Dom DiMaggio continued an amazing second half with a two-run triple in the bottom of the fifth. In 62 games since the All-Star break, the leadoff hitter had led the team with 50 RBIs, compared to 46 for Stephens, 45 for Doerr, and 30 for Williams. Parnell loaded the bases leading 2–1 in the ninth, but Ferris Fain bounced into a 1–2–3 double play to end the game and give the Red Sox eleven victories in twelve games.

The Sunday crowd of 29,100 fans pushed the Red Sox' total attendance for 1948 to 1,438,426 and broke their all-time record set the previous year. The Red Sox managed to amass a 3–1 lead after six, as Williams made two excellent catches to keep Joe Dobson (15–7) in the game. But the Athletics tied the game in the seventh, went ahead in the eighth, and scored six runs off three Boston pitchers in the ninth to win, 10–4. Having won four out of six against New York and Philadelphia, the Red Sox left for Chicago and their last western trip on Sunday evening.

Boston's one loss shaved a half-game from their lead. On Saturday, Joe DiMaggio hit his 35th homer, Henrich had three hits, and the Yankees handed the Senators their eleventh straight loss in Washington, 6–3, behind Allie Reynolds, now 16–6. The next day, a worn-out Bob Porterfield confirmed the message of his last two starts, giving up a walk and three hits for a 3–0 Senator lead in the first. In the top of the second, the bottom of the Yankee batting order came through smartly, and one run was in with two men on when Porterfield's turn came to bat. Bucky Harris sent up Maryland native Charlie Keller, whom he had benched more than a week earlier, and Keller delivered a three-run pinch homer over the right-field wall for a 4–3 lead. The forgotten man of the Yankee pitching staff, left-hander Tommy Byrne, took over in the bottom of the second and gave up just three hits during the last eight innings as the Yankees won, 10–5, in the Senators' last home game. The Yankees cut the Red Sox' lead to just two games and headed west for the last time, beginning with a single game in Cleveland on Tuesday.

The Indians, meanwhile, tried to sustain their momentum in two consecutive doubleheaders against the Browns, who had moved into sixth place behind some fine hitting by Al Zarilla, third baseman Bob Dillinger, and second baseman Jerry Priddy. The Browns' team batting average was all the way up to .270, fourth in the league behind the Indians, Yankees, and Red Sox. With Gordon, Keltner, and Boudreau doing most of the damage, Steve Gromek (8–3) got a 4–1 win in the opener. The second game featured yet another new Cleveland batting order, with Tucker in center and Judnich on first batting sixth and seventh, and Boudreau sent Lemon back out only two days after he had failed against Detroit. This gamble succeeded as Keltner, with four RBIs on the day, ran his season's total to 101, and Lemon got his twentieth victory, 9–1.

The entire Cleveland club was pulling out all the stops in its desperate efforts to climb back into the race. According to Veeck, Marshall Bossard, one of a distinguished family of groundskeepers, was now stationed inside the scoreboard in every game to signal the opposing catcher's signs to Cleveland hitters at crucial moments. (In a bizarre indication of Doby's still-equivocal status, no one ever told him about the signaling.) Boudreau had taken another extraordinary step, barring writers from the locker room after games in order to avoid any embarrassing incidents. Since reporters in the 1940s still recognized their own obligation to describe what had happened on the field, rather than rely on players and managers to do it for them as they do today, he got away with it, but one of the three Cleveland papers retaliated by establishing a daily column to evaluate his managerial decisions. Other guest columnists in the papers included former Cleveland greats Cy Young, Tris Speaker, Elmer Smith, and Bill Wambsganss, the last three the heroes of the team's one other pennant winner in 1920. The writers had never regained the team's trust since Harry Jones's piece in June, in which he had reported a veteran player saying that the team would rather play away than at home.

In the midst of the excitement, however, another rumor began to surface: that Bill Veeck would sell the Indians to a syndicate headed by his assistant, Hank Greenberg, and buy the Chicago White Sox. Cobbledick threw cold water on the rumor, and Veeck denied it, repeatedly and vehemently, during the last month of the season. But although the details of the rumor were false, the gist was true. Veeck was planning on selling the team.

The reasons were not altogether clear, even to Veeck. On the one hand— as he explained almost fifteen years later in his autobiography—his marriage had definitely collapsed, and he would have to sell the team to raise cash for his divorce settlement.[4] Sources on the team, however, believed

4. Veeck met his second wife, Mary Frances Ackerman, after filing for divorce in 1949. They were married in 1950 and remained married until his death in 1986.

that the Jacobs brothers—Veeck's concessionaires, the owners of Sports-service—would gladly have lent him all the money he might have needed, and Veeck admitted that another motive was at work. Win or lose, even he could not top the show he had put on in Cleveland in 1948. Especially if he won, he would have no way to go but down, and it was his nature to go on looking for new challenges. He suffered another awful shock in mid-September when Harry Grabiner, the man who had helped him arrange the purchase of the Indians and run the club, had a stroke in the office before his very eyes, and lapsed into a coma. Despite the denials, Veeck probably already knew that this would be his last full season in Cleveland.

Boudreau had two of the greatest pitchers who ever lived for the double-header of Sunday, September 12: Paige, who had not started for more than a month, and Bob Feller, who had pitched a full seven innings just three days earlier against the Tigers. Paige was less dominant than in the previous month and Boudreau relieved him with Zoldak in the fifth, and Zoldak was credited with the eventual 5–3 victory, his third relief win in Cleveland's latest six-game streak. In the nightcap Keltner delivered a two-run double in the bottom of the first to raise his RBI total to 103, and Feller himself singled and scored on Mitchell's two-out double in the second for a 3–0 lead. But the Browns scored twice in the third, and after Ned Garver replaced Browns starting pitcher Blackie Schwamb, Cleveland runs suddenly became harder to come by. Feller and Garver dueled one another through the fourth, fifth, sixth, and seventh without a run, and Al Zarilla touched Feller for a solo homer in the seventh to tie the game. Both Garver and Feller left the game during the ninth inning, in which both teams threatened but failed to score. Bearden relieved, and the Indians wasted scoring opportunities in the tenth, eleventh, and twelfth, and the day came to an end and the 55,616 fans in attendance went home when the umpires stopped the game on account of darkness. League rules did not allow teams to turn on their lights to finish day games.

The Indians had closed to within three games of the Red Sox, but the tie was a disaster. They had wasted a fine outing from Feller and lost a day off, since the game had to be replayed the next day. Having used Gromek, Lemon, Paige, Zoldak, Feller, and Bearden on Saturday and Sunday, Boudreau had virtually no options left. He chose Don Black, who had pitched some strong games early in the season but had thrown only eighteen innings and started only twice since the All-Star break. The game on Monday, as it turned out, would be Black's last.

Three of the mythic figures of mid-century baseball—Joe DiMaggio, Dom DiMaggio, and Ted Williams—relax in the dugout at Fenway Park, moments before one of their critical contests. (Brearley Collection)

Bob Feller (*right*), who had pitched no-hitters in 1940 and 1946, and Don Black (*left*), who performed the feat in 1947, welcome future Hall of Famer Bob Lemon (*center*) into the club in late June 1948. (Cleveland State Library)

Satchel Paige greets another black American hero, heavyweight champion Joe Louis, before shutting out the White Sox at Comiskey Park on August 13, 1948. (Cleveland State Library)

The Red Sox lineup, one of the greatest long-sequence offenses in baseball history: (*left to right*) Dom DiMaggio, Johnny Pesky, Ted Williams, Vern Stephens, Bobby Doerr, Stan Spence, Billy Goodman, and Birdie Tebbets, in late August 1948. (UPI/Corbis-Bettmann)

Indians' catcher Jim Hegan responding to the unprecedented enthusiasm of young Cleveland fans outside Municipal Stadium. (Cleveland State Library)

Bill Veeck honors the "average fan" on Good Old Joe Earley Night at Cleveland's Municipal Stadium, September 1948. (Cleveland State Library)

Vern Stephens slides home behind Ted Williams to put Boston ahead of New York, 3-2, in the third inning of the final game of the season. (UPI/Corbis-Bettmann)

October 3, 1948. Boston fans line up outside Fenway Park to buy tickets for the next day's playoff game with the Indians. (Cleveland State Library)

A grim Indians' brain trust—general manager Hank Greenberg, owner Bill Veeck, manager Lou Boudreau, and coach Bill McKechnie—debate the Cleveland lineup before the game. (UPI/Corbis-Bettmann)

A confident Denny Galehouse warms up for the playoff game at Fenway. Behind him the American flag ominously signals a strong wind blowing out to left. (*Boston Herald*)

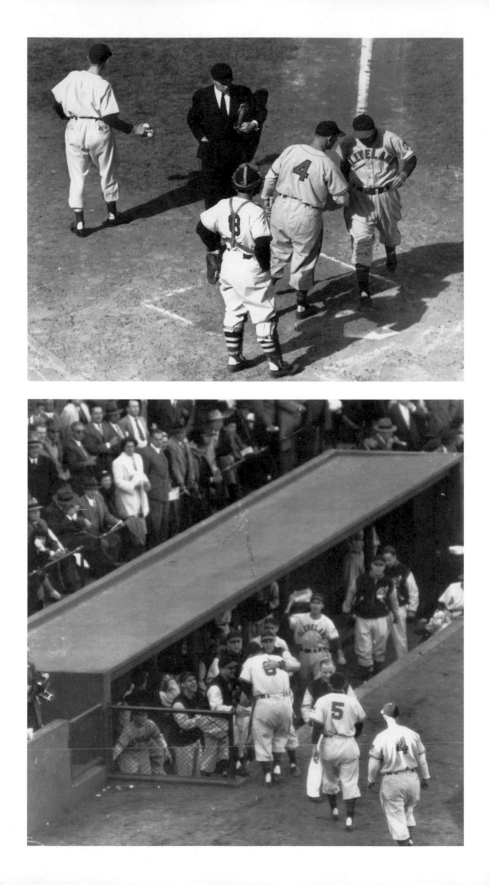

The jubilant Indians carry Gene Bearden off the field at the conclusion of his fourth complete game victory in the last ten days of the season. (Cleveland State Library)

(*Opposite, top*) Lou Boudreau receives congratulations from Joe Gordon after his first inning home run, as catcher Birdie Tebbets steps aside and home plate umpire Bill McGowan looks on. (UPI/Corbis-Bettmann)

(*Opposite, bottom*) Ken Keltner returns to the dugout in the top of the fourth inning after his three-run homer put Cleveland ahead, 4-1. (UPI/Corbis-Bettmann)

A gracious Joe McCarthy congratulates Lou Boudreau. (Sporting News/Archive Photos)

Winning pitcher Steve Gromek hugs Larry Doby, whose home run decided the fourth game of the World Series against the Boston Braves. The Indians went on to win the series, 4 games to 2. (Sporting News/Archive Photos)

STANDINGS
Monday Morning, September 13, 1948

Team	Won	Lost	Pct.	Games Behind
Boston	86	50	.632	—
New York	84	52	.618	2
Cleveland	84	53	.613	2½
Philadelphia	79	61	.564	9
Detroit	64	68	.485	20
St. Louis	54	80	.403	31
Washington	49	89	.355	38
Chicago	45	91	.331	41

The eastern clubs' last swing west featured ten games in nine days for the Red Sox and ten games in ten days for the Yankees—severe tests for the pitching staffs that had carried their teams to a combined 33–10 record during the last three weeks. Both teams had only a single game in Cleveland—the Yankees to open their trip, and the Red Sox to finish theirs. As the Yankees came into Cleveland, winners of three straight and twelve out of their last fifteen games, rumors were appearing in the press that Bucky Harris's two-year contract was not likely to be renewed. The excuse was Harris's lengthy disputes with George Weiss over the promotion of Porterfield and Bauer, but the real reason was that Harris had been hired by Larry MacPhail, and that Weiss wanted to replace anyone from the organization associated with MacPhail with his own man. Dan Topping, one of the two Yankee owners, denied the story, but the Yankees confirmed that no decision would be made on Harris's future until after the season.

The Yankees arrived early enough on Monday to watch the Indians take the field against the Browns for their makeup game. With the score 0–0 in the bottom of the first, pitcher Don Black came to the plate with two out. Black swung at Kennedy's second pitch and fouled it off. Like a man in a daze, he walked in a circle and stopped behind plate umpire Bill Summers. "My God, Bill, what happened?" he muttered.

"What's wrong, Don?" asked Summers.

"It started on that last pitch to Pellagrini," Black said. Then he collapsed on the ground unconscious.

Black was carried to the clubhouse and rushed to the hospital while the Indians tried to play the game. Bob Lemon finished his at bat and grounded out to end the inning, and Bob Muncrief, another forgotten hurler, came in to pitch. Muncrief rose to the occasion, holding the Browns scoreless for four innings, while Gordon gave the Indians a 2–0 lead with his 26th home run in the bottom of the fourth. But Zoldak's relief magic finally failed in the eighth and the Browns tied the game. Errors by Zoldak and Boudreau gave the Browns the lead run in the top of the ninth, and the Indians went out like lambs in the bottom of the inning to lose the game. In the clubhouse, they learned that Black had burst an aneurysm and suffered a cerebral hemorrhage. Doctors gave him only a fifty-fifty chance to live.

While Bucky Harris had Ed Lopat to try to beat the Indians for the fifth time on Tuesday, Boudreau's pitching crisis continued. After five games in three days, he had no option but Lemon, whose league-leading total of 265 innings included five on Wednesday and nine on Saturday. The two great teams finished their season series in style. Three singles in the first gave the Yankees a 1–0 lead, but Allie Clark tied it with a home run in the bottom of the inning. In the fourth DiMaggio's single and Brown's double made it 2–1 for New York.

The sixth began with singles by Dale Mitchell and Allie Clark, and Boudreau—batting third against a left-hander—raised a fly to Berra in right. Trying to catch Mitchell at home, Berra threw wildly to the plate, allowing Clark to reach second while Mitchell scored to tie the game. Then Joe Gordon drove his 27th homer into the left-field stands for a 4–2 lead, passing Keltner and tying Junior Stephens for second in the league. But Gus Niarhos opened the top of the seventh with a triple, and Charlie Keller pinch-hit for Lopat. It was the second time in two games that he had come up as a pinch hitter trailing by several runs—and for the second time in a row he homered, tying the game 4–4.

A shaken Lemon walked Stirnweiss. Boudreau decided that he had had enough, but he ignored Paige—who had yet to give up a run against the Yankees—and brought in Ed Klieman. Henrich promptly singled to send Stirnweiss to third, and Berra's fly scored Stirnweiss to take a 5–4 lead. Klieman solved the DiMaggio problem by hitting the Yankee Clipper in the hand and forcing him to leave the game. But Bobby Brown, breaking out of a slump with a vengeance, singled to left for his fourth hit, and Henrich scored to make the lead 6–4. Boudreau now called upon Christopher, who walked McQuinn to fill the bases and induced Rizzuto to ground to Keltner for a 5–2–3 twin killing to end the inning.

Disdaining Joe Page, who had apparently fallen into the doghouse again, Bucky Harris called on Porterfield after the seventh inning stretch, and the Virginian got the side out. One inning too late, Satchel Paige went in to pitch the eighth and retired Niarhos, Keller, and Stirnweiss in order. The two pitchers each retired the side once again to bring the Indians to bat in the bottom of the ninth. Ken Keltner opened the inning smartly with a single, and managed to prevent a double play when Thurman Tucker grounded to Rizzuto. Then Judnich singled to center to send Tucker to second and bring the winning run to the plate. Boudreau announced Doby to pinch-hit for Hegan, and Harris went to the bullpen for Joe Page to save the day. Boudreau, who never trusted Doby against a left-handed pitcher in a critical spot, countered with Bob Kennedy.

This move worked when Kennedy singled to right, but Tucker, playing conservatively, held at third and the bases were loaded with one out. A hit would tie the game, and Joe Tipton batted for Paige. Harris, perhaps remembering another ninth inning against the Browns two weeks earlier, removed Bobby Brown and inserted Bill Johnson at third base. Tipton flied to right, and Tucker beat Berra's throw to the plate to come within one run.

It was up to Dale Mitchell, hitting .335 and two for four on the day. He grounded to shortstop and Rizzuto tossed to Stirnweiss for the out. Two straight losses had dropped Cleveland five games behind the Red Sox in the loss column again. They were back to the same position they had occupied when their home stand had begun the previous Wednesday against the Tigers, with eight fewer games in which to make up the difference. The loss also dropped the Indians' record in one-run games back to 10–21, and gave the Yankees a 12–10 edge in the season series between the clubs. New York's fourth straight win moved them within a game of the lead.

With the Indians almost out of the race, Bill Veeck made an announcement to build interest for the Tribe's last night game of the season, exactly two weeks hence. September 28, when the Indians would play the White Sox, would be Joe Earley Night, with impressive but as yet unspecified festivities to honor the average fan. Win or lose, Veeck was going to end the season on a high note. "If it's a good laugh for everybody, it's a good thing," Mrs. Earley remarked, announcing that she and her husband were turning all the money they had received over to the Cancer Fund.

In Comiskey Park the Red Sox rebounded from Sunday's loss and maintained their two-game lead over New York with an easy 4–1 win over the White Sox behind Ellis Kinder, who won his fourth consecutive start. Ted Williams resumed his dominating role with a single, two doubles, and three runs batted in. His average rose to .371, giving him a comfortable lead over Boudreau, who had gone 0–4 against the Yankees that afternoon and slipped to .358. But the next day, Kramer failed for the second straight time and departed after the third inning trailing 4–1 against Al Gettel. Led by Williams, who went five for six on the day and drove in two runs, Boston closed the gap to 5–4 in the top of the seventh, but the White Sox scored ten runs in the bottom of the inning, as Earl Caldwell gave up his second grand slam in two appearances and the Red Sox made two awful misplays in the field. The final score was 17–10, and the Red Sox' lead over the Yankees fell to one. Now they were on to St. Louis for three games, followed by four in Detroit and one last game with the Indians in Cleveland.

STANDINGS
Thursday Morning, September 16, 1948

Team	Won	Lost	Pct.	Games Behind
Boston	87	51	.630	—
New York	85	52	.620	1½
Cleveland	84	55	.604	3½
Philadelphia	81	61	.567	8½
Detroit	67	68	.493	20
St. Louis	54	81	.400	31
Washington	49	91	.350	38
Chicago	46	92	.333	41

New York's series in Detroit began with a Thursday doubleheader. Bucky Harris had Raschi and Reynolds ready to go, but Frank Shea's arm was now too sore to lift above his shoulder. New York quickly lost its winning streak and its chance to move into the lead in the opener, as Fred Hutchinson gave up just one run—Joe DiMaggio's 36th homer—and outdueled Raschi, 2–1, in just one hour and thirty-five minutes. Things looked even grimmer in the nightcap, when the Tigers took a 3–0 lead over Reynolds in the first two innings behind Trout. Henrich tripled home a run in the third and the Yankees got two more in the fourth, but Reynolds, seeking his seventeenth victory, left the game after four innings trailing 4–3. The Yankees knocked Trout out in the seventh and took a 6–4 lead, and Joe Page pitched five shutout innings in relief to save a split of the doubleheader.

The next day, with the bases loaded in the first, Joe DiMaggio singled for two runs, raising his league-leading total to 139, and the Yankees eventually piled up thirteen tallies with the help of home runs by Henrich, Johnny Lindell, and Phil Rizzuto. Tommy Byrne, replacing the injured Frank Shea in the starting rotation, coasted to a 13–5 win. But on Saturday, Tiger ace Hal Newhouser drove in two runs himself and beat Lopat, 4–3, as he held the Yankees' right-handed power hitters—DiMaggio, Johnson, Lindell, and Bauer—to only one hit in fifteen at bats. The great lefthander's eighteenth win gave him a good chance for twenty.

Opening their three-game set in St. Louis on Thursday, the Red Sox ran into an equally inspired pitching performance. Browns right-hander Cliff

Fannin, who already owned three wins over the Yankees and two over the Indians, outdueled Mel Parnell and held the Red Sox to four hits in eight innings as the Browns built up a 3–0 lead. Ted Williams, one for two on the night, led off the ninth with a double and eventually scored, but Tebbetts lined out with the tying runs on base. One pitching collapse in Chicago and one hitting drought in St. Louis had been enough to cut Boston's lead to a single game. They had lost four of their last seven games, and as the Indians had discovered in mid-August, with three great teams in the pennant race, no lead could survive even a momentary lapse.

"The pressure," wrote *Boston Globe* columnist Harold Kaese after the season ended, "got too tough on the manager during the last western trip." After this loss, Joe McCarthy apparently "rode the White Horse" too far and too late into the night. When the team prepared to leave the Chase Hotel for the ballpark the next day, McCarthy was in no condition to go. Red Sox officials tried and failed to lock him in his hotel room, and a few of the 1,922 fans called, "You're drunk, McCardy!!!" when he staggered rather unsteadily out of the visiting team dugout.[5] But the play of the team was not affected, as Dobson stopped the Red Sox losing streak with his sixteenth victory, 9–3, with the help of a three-run double in the first by Sam Mele, to preserve at least a one-game lead. Doerr handled 10 chances in the field, setting a record of 396 consecutive chances without an error. And the next day the Red Sox finished their St. Louis series in style, surviving an early scare to emerge with a 13–5 victory against the Browns, as Earl Johnson got the win in relief of Galehouse. Doerr, who had returned to the lineup two days earlier, hit a three-run homer, and the team finished with 17 hits. Boston gained a half-game over the Yankees, who lost to Newhouser in Detroit, on the eve of their own Sunday doubleheader in the Motor City.

Having played nine games in seven days, the Indians had finally enjoyed a day off on Wednesday before entertaining the Senators. On Thursday evening, with Bearden pitching, Doby finally returned to the lineup and delivered a grand-slam home run in the bottom of the first, wiping out a 2–0 deficit and keying a 6–2 win, Bearden's fifteenth. The next afternoon, Bob Feller turned in his sixth consecutive good outing and fourth straight victory, fanning eleven Senators to take over the league strikeout lead from Lemon with 146. Jim Hegan drove in three runs on a single and his thirteenth home run, and Keltner hit his 27th homer, a solo shot, to give the Indians a 4–1 victory. And on Saturday, Zoldak pitched the Tribe to a

5. Curiously, while some members of the Red Sox—as well as one writer—have vivid memories of this incident, others appear to have forgotten it altogether. McCarthy enjoyed their almost unanimous respect, and they may have preferred not to remember this embarrassing day.

10–1 win. Boudreau broke out of an 0–15 slump with a single and a two-run homer, and Dale Mitchell's four hits raised his average to .335.

Helped by the Browns and Tigers, the Indians suddenly moved to within a game of the Yankees in second and three games of the Red Sox in first. They had rebounded from their latest low point, and complete games by Bearden, Feller, and Zoldak had rested the rest of the staff. Cool weather was taking the sting out of the hitters' bats around the Great Lakes—although not in St. Louis—and both the Red Sox and the Yankee pitching staffs were suffering from their exertions over the last six weeks. Cleveland, with deeper pitching and an offense that relied more upon the home run, was taking full advantage of the situation. In order to get the race back into their own hands, however, they had to draw within one game of the Red Sox before Boston returned to Cleveland for the last time for a single game on Wednesday.

As the team gave its fans a glimmer of hope, Bill Veeck announced that he had asked Tom Yawkey to shift that game to the evening, designate it as Don Black Night, and turn the entire home share of the gate receipts over to the stricken pitcher. Doctors now expected Black to recover, but his future as a pitcher was highly doubtful, and as Veeck put it, "I want the largest possible crowd." Yawkey offered to donate the Red Sox' share of the receipts as well, but Veeck declined, stating that he wanted the proceeds to be a Cleveland affair. The newspapers noted that Bob Feller would be available to pitch, although they could not yet know how critical the game would be for the pennant race.

> HANK GREENBERG: The only owner I ever knew who gave a damn about his players was Bill Veeck. Bill genuinely cared about them, and he always worried about them individually. It was almost like hero worship for Bill. The ballplayers were first in his book, and he would do anything to help their families, or ease the way if they got into trouble.[6]

On Sunday, September 15, Boudreau, his pitching crisis eased, sent two well-rested hurlers, Lemon and Gromek, to the mound against the Athletics. A crowd of 75,382 broke the all-time season attendance record of 2,265,512 set by the Yankees in 1947, and Cleveland had seven home dates left. Gordon staked Lemon to a 1–0 lead in the second with his 28th home run, but Lemon failed to hold a 3–1 lead, and the Athletics tied the game and knocked him out in the eighth—the third time in four outings that he had failed to win. Joe Gordon opened the bottom of the ninth with a single, and Keltner sacrificed. Doby needed only a base hit to win the game. He did better, clouting an opposite-field home run for a 5–3 victory, his second

6. Hank Greenberg, *The Story of My Life*, ed. Ira Berkow (New York, 1989), 223.

game-winning homer in four games. Cleveland completed the sweep in the second game, as Lou Boudreau's 15th and 16th home runs gave Gromek a brilliant, three-hit, 2–0 shutout victory. The Indians' win streak reached five games. They vaulted over the Yankees, regaining second place for the first time since August 28. Meanwhile, across Lake Erie, the Red Sox tried to hang on to their league in a long, nail-biting doubleheader with the Tigers before a packed house of 55,255 Detroiters who came to savor their team's part in the race.

Joe McCarthy had a well-rested Ellis Kinder ready for the opener, but Jack Kramer had to pitch the nightcap only three days after failing in Chicago. Kinder—winner of four straight games—pitched excellent ball for seven innings, and although Virgil Trucks was nearly as good, RBIs by Dom DiMaggio in the third and Stephens in the fourth allowed him to take a 2–1 lead into the bottom of the eighth. Then pitcher Fred Hutchinson—a good hitter—pinch-hit for Trucks and walked. With one out, Tiger manager Steve O'Neill sent up Dick Wakefield to pinch-hit, and Wakefield, always at his best at big moments, delivered a two-run homer for a 3–2 lead.

Dizzy Trout, relieving, retired Dom DiMaggio and Johnny Pesky to begin the ninth inning. One more out would end the game—but the batter was Ted Williams. Trout pitched to him, and the great hitter delivered his most dramatic blow of the campaign—a game-tying home run hit 420 feet to dead center field, his 24th of the season. Stephens also reached base, but Doerr was retired to end the inning. Having used Earl Johnson the day before, and having lost confidence in Earl Caldwell, McCarthy brought in Joe Dobson, Friday's victor, and Dobson retired the side in the ninth. The Red Sox seemed on the verge of a magnificent comeback when Wally Moses led off the tenth with a triple, but lefty Ted Gray walked Goodman and retired Tebbetts, pinch hitter Matt Batts, and Dom DiMaggio to end the inning with Moses stranded on third base. Like the Browns and the White Sox, the Tigers were giving nothing away before their own fans. The game had become a contest of pitching staffs.

Dave Ferriss now relieved and got the Tigers out in the tenth and the eleventh, while the Red Sox failed to score. The cool September breezes had stalled their great long-sequence offense. In the top of the twelfth Gray allowed two batters to reach base with one out, and went to a 3–0 count on Birdie Tebbetts. Stubby Overmire relieved him, and retired Tebbetts and pinch hitter Billy Hitchcock to end the inning. Now McCarthy yielded to necessity and brought in Earl Johnson. Two hits in the bottom of the twelfth brought pitcher Overmire to bat. Manager O'Neill let him hit, and Overmire hit a broken-bat single to right to score Campbell and win the game, 4–3—the first and only base hit that the pitcher delivered during the entire season.

Jack Kramer, shelled by the Yankees and the White Sox in his last two outings, now tried again for his seventeenth win, and this time the Red Sox got off to a quick start, scoring three runs in the first. But Kramer collapsed again, leaving after 3⅔ innings with the Tigers on top, 6–3. Once again the Red Sox came back. Stan Spence, restored to the lineup for the first time in the whole road trip, hit a two-run homer in the top of the fifth, and Pesky drove in another run to tie the game at six. But Dave Ferriss, relieving again, surrendered two more in the bottom of the seventh, as Wakefield homered for the second time of the day. Mother Nature and the league rules stopped the Red Sox after they failed to score in the top of the eighth. Five and a half hours after the first game began, the umpires halted the nightcap on account of darkness with the Tigers ahead, 8–6.

Playing seven games in six days, the Red Sox had scored 44 runs, allowed 42, and won just three while losing four. Their starting pitchers had delivered just three good outings—one of which, by Parnell, they wasted against the Browns—and their hitters had inevitably fallen off the pace they had set since the All Star game. Since mid-July, the Red Sox had repeatedly come up with the big hit, the big rally, and the late-inning victory. On this fateful Sunday, the cool weather and the laws of probability caught up to them, and they fell barely short. They still had a one-game lead in the loss column, but any chance of an easy victory in the pennant race was irretrievably gone.

STANDINGS
Monday Morning, September 20, 1948

Team	Won	Lost	Pct.	Games Behind
Boston	89	54	.622	—
Cleveland	89	55	.618	½
New York	88	55	.615	1
Philadelphia	83	63	.568	7½
Detroit	71	70	.504	17
St. Louis	56	85	.397	32
Washington	51	95	.349	39½
Chicago	49	96	.338	41

Clinging to the lead on Monday, Joe McCarthy had to choose between pitching Mel Parnell on three days' rest or turning to the very questionable Mickey Harris. Sticking with his usual strategy, he chose Harris, leaving

Parnell to face the Tigers on the following day and Joe Dobson to pitch Wednesday night against the Indians in Cleveland. Meanwhile the Red Sox added a new second baseman, Lou Stringer, whom they purchased from the Hollywood Stars of the Pacific Coast League. Doerr—forced back into service when Hitchcock injured a leg in St. Louis—had hurt himself again. Tom Yawkey, informed by Joe Cronin that the Sox' own farm system did not contain a single adequate middle infielder, was furious. Stringer, a lifetime .242 hitter with almost no power, had played for the Cubs in 1941–42 and 1946.

Harris barely came through, walking nine men but giving up just four hits, all singles, and two first-inning runs. The Red Sox rapped out twelve hits, and Stephens ended a twenty-seven-day home run drought with his 28th circuit clout in the top of the ninth, his first since beating the Indians back in the bottom of the ninth on August 24. Parnell apparently benefited from his fourth day of rest on Tuesday, and won his fifth start in six outings, 10–2. Dom DiMaggio went three for five, making him ten for seventeen on the series, Parnell hit a three-run single, and Stephens came up with a double, a triple, and two RBIs. He now had 128 on the season, but no chance at all for the league lead. Parnell raised his record to 14–7—10–2 since the All-Star break—and the Red Sox' 91st victory of the year kept them in first place. Having split their Detroit series, they boarded the train for Cleveland with a one-game lead over the streaking Indians.

By the time the Indians had taken the field Monday evening before another big crowd of 44,492, they knew that they needed another win just to stay in second. Bearden, facing Lou Brissie, had another shaky start, but double plays bailed him out of jams in the second, fourth, and sixth innings. The Indians, meanwhile, got a run in the first and two runs the fourth, and Gordon doubled home Boudreau in the fifth for a 4–0 lead. The Athletics scored three times against Bearden and Christopher in the seventh, but Joe Gordon—the hero of the series—promptly opened up a little distance in the bottom of the inning with his 29th home run. The Indians eventually won 6–3 as Christopher shut the A's out for the last two innings, and Bearden's record went to 16–6.

The Indians had now won six straight since losing to the Yankees the previous Tuesday, running their record on their current home stand to 12–2. While their hitters—led by Doby, Mitchell, Hegan, Gordon, and a rapidly reviving Keltner—had come to life, it was the depth of their pitching staff that was giving them the edge over the Red Sox and the Yankees. Since Labor Day, the Indians' pitchers had turned in seven complete-game victories and nine strong outings, compared to six complete games for the Red Sox and four for the Yanks. Their pitching and defense during their home stand had allowed just 2.7 runs per game, compared to 5.4 for the Red Sox and 5.7 for the Yankees. Best of all, the crisis in the schedule was over. With only nine games left in thirteen days, Boudreau could now rely almost exclusively upon Lemon (20 wins), Feller (16), and Bearden (16) for the rest of the way. In just one week they had moved from the edge of extinction to the verge of first place. After a day off, Feller would face the Red Sox on Wednesday, Don Black Night, with a chance to share the top spot.

Playing in St. Louis, the Yankees had tumbled into third, but remained right on the Indians' heels thanks to Joe DiMaggio. Desperate for pitching with Frank Shea injured, Bucky Harris called on Porterfield for the opener of Sunday's doubleheader and Raschi—with just two days' rest—for the nightcap. Porterfield had rested for a week, but it didn't matter. Leading 3–1, he gave up a two-run homer by Jerry Priddy in the bottom of the third and was removed in the next frame as the Browns scored three more runs. The incredible Henrich tied the game at 6–6 in the top of the sixth with his 24th homer, but in the bottom of the inning Al Zarilla delivered a two-run homer for an 8–6 lead. Browns manager Zack Taylor—taking every game very seriously—relieved with Cliff Fannin, who shut the Yankees out for the last three innings. Despite three hits by Henrich and two by a limping DiMaggio, the Yankees lost a chance to move into a tie for first as Boston dropped two in Detroit.

DiMaggio took charge in the second game. Coming up in the first inning with one on, he clubbed his 37th home run into the left-field seats for a 2–0 lead. Another two-run shot in the third made the lead 5–1, but he left the game in the fourth as his heel became too painful. Raschi, doing about as well as could be expected on two days' rest, let the Browns get back to 5–4 in the fifth, but yielded just one more run while the Yanks ran the score to 9–5.

The DiMaggio show resumed the next afternoon, with Reynolds pitching against Bill Kennedy. The Yankee Clipper's injury cost his team a run in the bottom of the third inning, when Priddy's routine fly was too much for his aching heel and fell for a triple, but he made up for it in the next inning with his 39th homer, cutting the Browns' lead to 4–2. The Yanks eventually tied the game at five in the sixth, and DiMaggio singled to help take the lead in the seventh and singled for two more runs off Ned Garver in the eighth for an 8–5 lead before once again leaving the game, with 30 RBIs for the month of September and 148 for the year. Joe Page struggled over the last three innings but managed to save an 8–7 victory and keep the Yankees within one game of the lead.

Only once before had Joe DiMaggio been involved in a close pennant race. In 1940, the Yankees, trying for their fifth straight world championship, had gotten an awful start, only to come roaring down the stretch to finish just two games back of the Tigers. Joe D had led the September charge, hitting .393 with 26 RBIs during the month. Now he was in a much tougher race, and he was rising to the occasion even more brilliantly. His pain was so obvious that writer John Debringer bluntly suggested that he should skip the two upcoming games in Chicago, take a train straight home, and rest for the three-game series coming up against the Red Sox. He did not take the advice, and on Wednesday New York finally came up with a relatively easy win, 7–2, behind Tommy Byrne, and moved into a tie for second in the loss column with the Indians. Then the Yankees repaired to their hotel to listen to the Red Sox take on the Indians in Cleveland in the biggest game of the season.

Facing Boston's Joe Dobson, Bob Feller—whose career had appeared to be threatened just a few weeks before—took the mound for one of the biggest games of his career. Since losing to the White Sox on August 22, the great right-hander had pitched four complete-game victories and a nine-inning, 3–3 tie. The fans of northern Ohio had turned out for Don Black in exactly the way that Veeck had hoped they would, and the crowd of 76,772 missed the Indians' month-old night attendance record by less than two thousand.[7] As the fans settled into their seats, Veeck stepped to a microphone near home plate and briefly thanked them for their support. He later announced that Black would receive about $40,000—at least $300,000 in 1998 dollars.[8] Feller, striding to the mound, received a tremendous ovation, and retired the Red Sox in order to start the game.

With one out in the bottom of the first, Thurman Tucker, playing center with Doby in right, drew a walk. Boudreau, batting third, ran the count to 3–2, and the fleet Tucker took off for second as Dobson delivered the payoff pitch. Shortstop Vern Stephens had the job of covering second, but Stephens had played against Boudreau for seven full seasons, and knew the Cleveland shortstop struck out about ten times a year. Holding his position, Stephens broke late for the bag after Boudreau swung and missed, dropped Tebbetts's throw, and couldn't make the tag on Tucker for what would have been the third out. Joe Gordon, up next, delivered a single to left, and Tucker, running with the crack of the bat, scored easily. Then Ken Keltner drove his 28th homer into the left-field stands for a 3–0 lead. The resurgent third baseman now had 107 RBIs, and his average was back to .289.

Feller responded with an overwhelming performance. Not until Doerr

7. The record, of course, had been set by the Indians against the White Sox on August 20, with Paige on the mound.
8. Black never pitched again. He died eleven years later, in 1959.

walked in the fifth inning did a Boston hitter reach base, and not until the sixth did the Red Sox get a hit, a double by Tebbetts. Dobson promptly singled the catcher home to make the score 3–1, but Mitchell threw Dobson out trying for second, and Feller got DiMaggio and Pesky to end the threat. In the seventh, four Indian singles ran the score to 5–1 and chased Dobson, and Feller survived a single run in the ninth to win, 5–2, and move into a first-place tie.

In the Boston locker room, Williams, generous as always, gave Feller credit for a tremendous curveball, and for forcing him to swing at fastballs that might have been off the plate—surely the ultimate tribute from the most discriminating hitter in the history of baseball. The game finished the season series between the two clubs at eleven wins each, and tied them with 90 wins and 55 losses, with the Yankees just one-half game behind.

The eastern clubs' trip west came to an end on the next afternoon, when the Yankees lost their third chance of the road trip to move into a tie for the lead. Behind Ed Lopat, 16–10, the Yankees scored just one run and lost 4–1, as lefty Frank Papish won his second game of the year before fewer than three thousand fans. The Yankees concluded their road trip with a record of 6–4. Just one game separated the Yankees from the other two contenders with eight games to play. Over the last two weeks, the weaker western clubs had put on an extraordinary display of professionalism. Despite the lack of any financial interest in the outcome, and despite some pathetic crowds in St. Louis and Chicago, the Tigers, Browns, and White Sox were playing a valiant role in the final weeks of the struggle. The Tigers had gone 4–4 in eight games against the Yankees and Red Sox; the Browns, who had suddenly begun knocking the cover off the ball, had given the Yankees all they could handle in their three-game set, and taken a game from the Red Sox as well; and even the White Sox had split four games against the Red Sox and Yankees. Their performances were a tribute to the integrity of baseball, as well as to its short-term unpredictability. With the eyes of the whole country on the American League, no one wanted to give anything away.

The Indians, now winners of seven straight games, were clearly back in the driver's seat. While they had six games left with the Tigers—consecutive weekend series in Detroit and Cleveland—and two home games with White Sox, the Red Sox and Yankees had five games on the next two weekends against each other. Bearden and Feller were pitching beautifully, and Lemon was the league's only twenty-game winner, while the Yankee staff, in particular, had worn itself out. Still, a photo finish was almost guaranteed. Veeck's off-season and in-season moves, Joe McCarthy's transformation of the Red Sox, Bucky Harris's lineup shifts, Williams's fantastic start, Junior Stephens's heroics, Boudreau's great year, Feller's comeback, Satchel Paige's brief, magnificent run of starts, and the unbelievable stretch drive of Joe DiMaggio—all this had done no more than earn their clubs a one-in-three chance of a flag. Interest in the race had reached unprecedented heights, and fans in all three cities could read not merely the box scores and lengthy accounts of the other contenders' games, but also the complete play-by-play supplied by wire services. Like tennis players in a fifth-set tiebreaker or marathoners with a mile to go, the teams had nothing left to do but play, hope, and let the final result take care of itself. Every player and manager now faced the most climactic nine days of his life.

They rose to the occasion.

11

Backing In

(SEPTEMBER 24–SEPTEMBER 30)

The climax of the season began in New York on Friday afternoon, September 24, as the Red Sox, still tied with Cleveland for first place, began a three-game series with the Yankees, who trailed by one game. Both teams—like the Indians—still had their regular lineups intact, although Bobby Doerr's leg still bothered him, Joe DiMaggio was limping badly on his right heel, and the Yankees were still missing the services of Frank Shea. To open the series Bucky Harris tapped Vic Raschi, now 19–7, who had not pitched since Sunday, to try once more for his first victory over the Red Sox. Harris also dropped Stirnweiss, who had failed to get his average over .260 for the last month, from the top spot in the batting order and replaced him with Phil Rizzuto, who was hitting only .258 himself. McCarthy chose Ellis Kinder, perhaps his most consistent hurler over the last month, with wins in four of his last five starts and a 9–4 triumph over New York in Fenway on September 9. The 33,609 New Yorkers who made their way to Yankee Stadium were not let down.

Raschi retired the Red Sox in the top of the first, and Rizzuto led off with a bunt down the first-base line and reached safely when Kinder failed to cover the bag. It was a fateful mistake. Doerr made a fine play on the grass to rob Henrich of a base hit and retire him, but Bobby Brown tripled to deep right-center to score Rizzuto, and Joe DiMaggio sent a fly ball to center to score Brown, his 149th RBI of the season. Kinder's miscue had given the Yankees a 2–0 lead. In the top of third, Tebbetts walked, Dom DiMaggio singled, and Raschi hit Pesky in the foot to bring Williams to the plate with one out and the bases loaded. On an 0–2 count, the Splendid

Splinter drove the ball deep to right field, where it glanced off a racing Yogi Berra's glove for a double that tied the game. Pesky scored the lead run when Stephens grounded to third.

All season long, both the Yankees and the Red Sox had hit each other's pitching so well that their games had become struggles between batters and fielders more than batters and pitchers. With one out in the bottom of the third, the left-handed Henrich crossed up the Boston defense with a drive to deep left-center, but Williams saved the day with a one-handed catch at full tilt facing halfway away from the plate. He could not, however, reach Bobby Brown's line drive to left center, which went through to the wall for Brown's second triple of the game. Joe DiMaggio, who had hit a sacrifice fly with one out and Brown on third in the first, now delivered a base hit to tie the game 3–3 with RBI number 150.

A wild Vic Raschi walked Stan Spence and Billy Goodman to open the fourth, but when Tebbetts bunted, Raschi made a fine play and threw Spence out at third. Playing to go ahead on the road, McCarthy sent Wally Moses up to hit for Kinder, and Moses lined sharply to Berra in right for the second out. But Dom DiMaggio seized the opportunity with a single to center for his 81st RBI, and the Red Sox took a 4–3 lead. With the game possibly on the line, Harris removed Raschi and brought in Joe Page to face the left-handers Pesky and Williams with two out and two on. Page induced Pesky to ground the ball to the right side. Stirnweiss snagged it, but this time it was the Yankee pitcher who failed to cover first base, and Pesky reached safely to load the bases with Williams coming to bat.

The tall, lean man at the plate, who finished the day's proceedings hitting .370, had averaged 125 runs batted in during his first six seasons in baseball. Despite this, some Boston writers liked to argue that he habitually fattened his average with no one on base and drove in runs when they were least needed. In later years, as the team declined, these whispers grew to a chorus, as the Boston scribes shamelessly blamed the Red Sox' failures upon their greatest player. None of this, however, had the slightest interest for Joe Page, who had to pitch not to the Williams created by the Boston writers, but to the Williams of flesh and blood. And Page did not hesitate. With the pennant on the line, he walked Williams on just five pitches to force in another run and give the Red Sox a 5–3 lead, and took his chances on *right-handed* Junior Stephens, who had 132 RBIs on the season. His strategy was rewarded when a shaken Stephens fouled out to Henrich to end the inning with the bases loaded, leaving the Yankees trailing by two runs.

Earl Johnson took over in the bottom of the fourth to try to hold the lead and pitched two scoreless innings. Page gave up singles to Spence and

Tebbetts in the top of the sixth, but Earl Johnson flied out with two out to end the inning. Johnson walked Henrich with one out in the bottom of the sixth. With Brown coming up, Harris would normally have pinch-hit Bill Johnson against the left-hander, but Brown had two triples in two at bats. Harris went with the hot hand, and the Golden Boy scored Henrich with a double to right to draw the Yankees within one. The Red Sox prudently walked Joe DiMaggio intentionally rather than give him a chance to drive in Brown for the third consecutive time, and now Harris sent Bill Johnson to bat for Berra.

Johnson's career as a Yankee regular—which had started in 1943 when he won the Rookie of the Year award—had ended one month earlier when Harris replaced him with Brown against right-handed pitching. Now, given a chance to make a difference, he cracked a three-run pinch-hit homer to give the Yankees a 7–5 lead. It was the third time such a home run had given the Yankees a lead in the last three weeks, with another veteran, Charlie Keller, having delivered the other two in Washington and in Cleveland. That was all for Earl Johnson, and Ferriss came in and got Lindell and Niarhos to end the inning.

The score was still 7–5 when Ferriss got Henrich and Brown to open the bottom of the seventh, but he walked DiMaggio and gave up a two-out triple to Hank Bauer—the Yankees' third three-bagger of the day. On the next play, Lindell's grounder to Pesky took a bad hop and scored another run. An angry Tebbetts ended the inning with a great snap throw to Goodman that picked Lindell off first, but the two-out rally gave the Yankees a 9–5 lead. Pesky, Williams, and Stephens loaded the bases with two out in the eighth, but Page got Bobby Doerr to fly to DiMaggio to end the inning.

The top of the ninth began with a single to right by Stan Spence, and Billy Goodman bounced the ball over the low left-field fence for a ground rule double. Tebbetts flied to Lindell, deep enough to score Spence and make the score 9–6, but pinch hitter Lou Stringer fanned for the second out. Dom DiMaggio drew a walk. Pesky came to the plate as the tying run, but Pesky had only three home runs on the season. The real threat, of course, was Williams, crouching in the on-deck circle hoping desperately for a chance to tie or win the game.

Page struck Pesky out to win the game, 9–6. The Yankees had tied the Red Sox and earned themselves a chance for a share of the lead.

In Detroit, Bob Lemon went for his twenty-first win and the Indians' eighth straight victory against Fred Hutchinson. Boudreau, trying to take advantage of Detroit's short right-field fence, restored Eddie Robinson—who had not started in sixteen games, since the Labor Day doubleheader—

to first base, and moved Walt Judnich to right and Doby to center. "Opinion on Lou Boudreau's ability as a manager may be—and in fact is—sharply divided," wrote Harry Jones in the *Plain Dealer*, "but you have to give the young man credit for having the courage of his convictions. Or is it the courage of his hunches."

The Tigers took a 1–0 lead in the bottom of the second inning on a single by Dick Wakefield, who was having a spectacular September against the pennant-contending clubs. Hutchinson kept the Indians completely under control until the fifth, when Doby drove a pitch 400 feet to dead center with two out and no one on, his 14th home run of the year. Then, in the next inning, Keltner delivered his 29th home run for a 2–1 lead. Boudreau immediately made a defensive change, inserting Thurman Tucker in center and moving Doby to right in place of Judnich. The carefree Wakefield promptly lined a ball exactly between Tucker and Doby that bounced into the stands for a ground rule double. He moved to third on a sacrifice and scored the tying run on a sacrifice fly.

Hutchinson started the Detroit seventh with a single, and Lipon sacrificed him to second. Boudreau now made another defensive shift, replacing left fielder Mitchell—currently hitting .337—with Bob Kennedy in the hope that Kennedy's arm might keep Hutchinson from scoring. But Lemon walked shortstop Neil Berry, and Vic Wertz crossed up the Indians' defense with a two-run double into the left-field corner that gave the Tigers a 4–2 lead. Boudreau relieved Lemon with Zoldak, who escaped two batters later when Wakefield lined a ball down the first-base line that Eddie Robinson turned into an unassisted double play. Boudreau had managed to take two of his best left-handed hitters—Mitchell and Judnich—out of the game, significantly weakening his batting order in a game the Indians had to win to stay ahead.

Larry Doby started the eighth with a single, but Boudreau—hitless on the day—grounded into a double play. The significance of his failure mushroomed a moment later, when Joe Gordon regained the team home run lead from Keltner with his 30th four-bagger—a record for Cleveland right-handed hitters. Keltner flied out to end the inning trailing 4–3, and Hutchinson got Tucker, Robinson, and pinch hitter Peck to hang on to the win in the bottom of the ninth. A worn-out Lemon had failed to hold a lead for the second time in three starts, and the Indians' winning streak was over.

With just nine days and seven games left in the season, the Indians, Red Sox, and Yankees were tied with 91 wins and 56 losses. And on that same Friday, a series of coin flips took place in the American League offices in

Chicago to assign the home field advantage for a playoff game—or games—to resolve a two-way or three-way tie. American League rules specified a one-game playoff to break a two-way tie, but the league had never had to implement this provision. The big winners in the coin flip were the Yankees, who won the right to face either the Red Sox or the Indians in New York should they finish in a two-way tie, and the right to face the winner of a single game between the Indians and the Red Sox in a game to decide the pennant should the race end in a triple tie. The preliminary game between the Indians and the Red Sox would take place in Boston, as would a playoff game to break a two-way tie between Cleveland and Boston. No playoff would take place in Municipal Stadium. Back in New York, the Yankees had something else to cheer about. After three unsuccessful attempts this month, and for the first time since their season opened back on April 20, the world champions had finally clawed their way into first place.

STANDINGS
Friday Evening, September 24, 1948

Team	Won	Lost	Pct.	Games Behind
Boston	91	56	.619	—
Cleveland	91	56	.619	—
New York	91	56	.619	—
Philadelphia	83	66	.557	9
Detroit	74	72	.507	16½
St. Louis	56	89	.386	34
Washington	53	95	.358	38½
Chicago	48	97	.331	42½

The Red Sox and the Yankees resumed their struggle on Saturday afternoon with Allie Reynolds and Jack Kramer each seeking his seventeenth victory. A crowd of 65,607 fans turned out, breaking the all-time Yankee attendance record set in the previous year. Tension told upon the players in the first inning again, as a walk, two Yankee errors, and a fielder's choice gave the Red Sox two runs without benefit of a hit. Kramer survived the first and second with the help of Doerr's great catch of Joe DiMaggio's pop fly near the right-field line, and Williams doubled to left with two out in the third to drive in Pesky for a 3–0 lead. Boston made it 5–0 in the fourth, and Harris pinch-hit for Reynolds in the bottom of the fifth and replaced him with Porterfield. The repeated failure of his starters, and his lack of confidence in his second-line pitching, had forced Harris virtually to abandon the distinction between starters and relievers.

Wally Moses hit an opposite-field home run in the top of the sixth to make the Boston lead 6–0. The Yanks scored twice, but great infield play by Stephens and Doerr and a shoestring catch by Dom DiMaggio snuffed out their rallies. Kramer finished the game with a 7–2 victory, one that owed at least as much to defense as to pitching. The Red Sox were sure of first place for one more day, while the Yankees slipped out of the lead again.

In Detroit, the Indians also had to win to retain a share of first place. After they took a 1–0 lead, Bearden survived the bottom of the first untouched when Mitchell made a tremendous running catch of Berry's liner and doubled up Johnny Lipon, who had walked, at first base. Keltner's 109th RBI, a single that drove in Boudreau, brought in another run in the third, and the Indians knocked Virgil Trucks out in the fifth. Bearden was almost untouchable, and the Indians coasted to a 9–3 victory to keep pace with the Red Sox, as Bearden won his fourth straight game and seventeenth overall.

Gene Bearden was nearing the climax of a season with few historical parallels. Bearden relied mainly on a knuckleball, at once the most devastating and the most unreliable of all pitching weapons. Because a knuckleball is thrown without spin, it breaks erratically in all directions. Because it is thrown with a minimum of pace, it immediately tends to throw off batters' timing. Because it requires little muscular effort, knuckleball pitchers can work longer and more often than any other hurlers of the lively-ball era. All this suggests that the knuckleball should be a more popular pitch than it has ever been, but alas, the peculiar pitch comes with its own curse: the curse of inconsistency. Few pitchers have ever been able to sustain a high level of knuckler effectiveness, especially in a starting role. The major exception, of course, was Phil Niekro, who from the late 1960s through the early 1980s used his knuckler to keep his ERA consistently below that of the league, and rode it into the Hall of Fame. Others, including Charlie Hough, Niekro's brother Joe, and Wilbur Wood, have had long careers and pitched remarkable numbers of innings, but with little better than average results overall. Jim Bouton—certainly baseball's most articulate knuckleballer—described the problem of inconsistency at length in 1970 in *Ball Four*. When the knuckler works, it is unhittable; when it does not, it produces a catastrophic mixture of walks and home runs.

It is not surprising, then, that on several occasions in history, unknown or apparently washed-up pitchers have knuckled their way to truly astonishing seasons, only to fall back very quickly to a much lower level of effectiveness. In 1940, at the age of thirty-nine, Fred Fitzsimmons used a knuckler to achieve a record of 16–2 and an ERA of 2.81 for the Dodgers. In the next year, his teammate Larry French knuckled his way to 15–4 with a 1.83 ERA. Hoyt Wilhelm entered the National League as a knuckleballing reliever in 1952 at the age of twenty-nine and posted a 15–3 record with a 2.43 ERA. Seven years later, with the Orioles, Wilhelm won his first nine starts and ran up a 15–11 record and a 2.19 ERA in his first full season as a starter. He quickly abandoned his starting role, however, remaining an effective reliever into his late forties. In 1992, Tim Wakefield won ten games against one loss for the Pirates in the second half of the season, including two wins against the Braves in the playoffs. Then in 1995, after two horrible years drove him back to the minors, Wakefield had another hot streak for the Red Sox before falling back to a lesser status in the second half of the season and in 1996.

Bearden was now in the same kind of zone. He had had three good outings in a row, and emerged as the Indians' most consistent pitcher. In the end, Bearden's career as a knuckleballing phenomenon was destined to be the shortest of all. But now he had a hot hand at the best possible time, and his gambling manager was determined to play it.

GENE BEARDEN: I had been practicing the knuckleball since I was a kid. It was always my big pitch, but my knuckler was a little different. It spun a little, it broke a little. I also threw sliders, sinkers, and changeups, but mostly knucklers. I suppose 70 to 80 percent of the pitches I threw were knucklers.

Bearden's latest win set the stage for a climactic finish to the series on Sunday, with Feller (17–14) set to pitch against Hal Newhouser (19–11), a two-time MVP in quest of his fourth twenty-game season in five years. Boudreau now announced his pitching plans for his remaining five games, tapping Lemon and Bearden to pitch against the White Sox back in Cleveland on Tuesday and Wednesday, and Feller, Lemon, and Bearden to wrap up the season against the Tigers on the last weekend. Despite the substantial second-half contributions of Zoldak, Gromek, and Satchel Paige, the Boy Manager was staking the pennant on his three aces.

The Sunday game at Detroit drew the largest Motor City crowd of the year, 57,888 fans. Allie Clark returned to the lineup in right for the first time in weeks and Robinson remained at first. The score was 0–0 with two out in the top of the third when Boudreau singled and Gordon smashed his 31st home run, giving him 118 runs batted in on the season. The Tribe stretched their lead to 3–0 in the fourth, when Doby singled, advanced to third on a ground ball and a wild pitch, and came home when Feller bunted safely down the third-base line. Feller gave up a run in the fourth, but the two great pitchers each faced the minimum six men in the fifth and sixth innings. Then, in the seventh, Hegan singled, Feller sacrificed, and Allie Clark drove Hegan home with a two-out single. The Indians, leading 4–1, scored no more runs, but Feller retired seventeen out of the last eighteen men who faced him to earn his eighteenth victory against fourteen losses.

The split of the first two games of the Red Sox–Yankees series had put enormous pressure on both teams to come away with Sunday's rubber game. Mel Parnell, trying for his fifteenth victory with four days of rest, tried to beat the Yankees for the first time against strong, wild Tommy Byrne. Byrne—like the young Bob Feller—had so much stuff, and so little control over it, that while he had good and bad outings, he never had a smooth or a dull one.

Byrne retired the Red Sox in the top of the first, but Parnell could not do the same. He walked Rizzuto, and Henrich—whose fantastic hitting had quieted down of late—set the enormous crowd alight with a line shot into the right-field seats, his 25th of the year. He had now scored an astonishing, league-leading 131 runs. Byrne held the Red Sox in check for the next two innings, and in the bottom of the third Rizzuto walked again with one out. Henrich singled to right, Lindell singled to left to score Rizzuto, and a limping Joe DiMaggio got his 152nd RBI of the season with a single to left, good for a 4–0 lead.

Byrne nearly lost the lead in the fourth, when he loaded the bases with none out and Wally Moses hit a drive down the left-field line that fell just foul before striking out. He eventually escaped with just one run scored. Denny Galehouse, who had not appeared in a game for eight days, took over for Boston and allowed single runs in the fourth and fifth, both of them with two out. One of them was Henrich's 100th RBI, an extraordinary achievement for a man who had batted second for most of the season and had just 41 RBIs at the All-Star break. The Red Sox threatened in the sixth and got a run in the eighth, but Byrne, who struck out seven and allowed just five hits, continued to dominate, shutting out Dom DiMaggio and Pesky and holding Williams to just one hit. The 6–2 victory tied the Yankees with the Red Sox, but only for second place.

Suddenly and dramatically, the whole complexion of the season had changed. Exactly one month earlier the Indians had fallen out of first place when Mel Parnell beat Gene Bearden 8–4 in the finale of their last three-game series in Boston, and eleven days later, on the evening of Labor Day, they had trailed by five games in the loss column. Now, with one week left, they had climbed back into uncontested possession of first. At the plate

Boudreau had slumped, but Keltner, Gordon, and above all Doby were back in stride. On the mound, Cleveland alone still appeared to have three consistently effective starting pitchers. Feller had now won six games in a row, making him the comeback story of the second half, and Bearden had four straight victories.

Buoyed by his success, Boudreau announced a characteristically bold decision after the game. On the previous day he had tapped Lemon to pitch on Tuesday, and perhaps to finish the season against the Tigers on Sunday. But Lemon had lost two of his last three decisions, and as Boudreau now told the reporters, he was utterly worn out. The Lemon of 1948 was a far cry from the chunky figure whom many fans will remember from baseball cards of the mid-1950s. A tall, lean athlete, he had weighed perhaps 185 when the season started. Now, after pitching a league-leading 286 innings, he was down to about 160 pounds.

Gambling, Boudreau now tapped Bearden and Feller to pitch against the White Sox in Cleveland on Tuesday and Wednesday—*each of them with just two days of rest.* Lemon would then open against the Tigers on Friday after a full week off, and Bearden and Feller could pitch the last two games of the season with three days' rest each. This arrangement would also give Feller a chance to reach twenty victories for the sixth consecutive season.[1]

The Indians' fate was completely in their own hands now, and the omens favored them. As Boudreau explained to the writers, he did not expect the Red Sox to lose any of their next three games with the Senators in Fenway, but they might easily drop one to the Yankees in Boston next weekend. Meanwhile, the Yankees could easily lose one of three to the Athletics in Philadelphia, dropping them two games back. If the Indians could take their two games with the White Sox, they would need just two out of three in the last series with the Tigers to wrap up the pennant. Bill McKechnie's months-old prediction was coming true. The Indians were backing into the pennant.

All three teams had the day off on Monday, but the Yankees—who surely faced the most difficult schedule of the three—got more bad news. Gus Niarhos, who had performed so well at bat and behind the plate since taking over the catching on August 13, had broken an index finger on Sunday and was lost for the rest of the campaign. Bucky Harris had no intention of putting Berra back behind the plate, and Charlie Silvera was hastily re-called from the minors to share catching duties with Sherman Lollar and Ralph Houk. With Joe DiMaggio still limping badly on his heel, Frank Shea out, and Bob Porterfield obviously exhausted, the Yankees, alone of

1. This does not count 1945, when Feller returned from the navy very late in the year.

the three contenders, would have to try to claw their way back into first place despite serious injuries.

Having left home two weeks' earlier with a 3½-game lead, the Red Sox now returned in second, having occupied at least a share of the top spot for exactly thirty days. A 6–7 road trip had left them with an uphill battle. Once again, much of their power had evaporated on the road. The team had only five home runs during the trip—one each for Williams, Doerr, and Stephens, and two for Stan Spence. Junior Stephens, worn out from playing shortstop for every inning of the season, had hit just .111 on the trip, dropping his average below .270. Like Bob Lemon, Reynolds, and Raschi, Dobson and Kramer were showing the strain of the long season, while Kinder and Parnell, McCarthy's second-half stalwarts, and Johnson and Galehouse, his key long relievers, had all failed during the series with the Yankees. But Williams had had a fine series in New York, and Dom DiMaggio and Johnny Pesky were finishing strongly.

The team, in any case, was back in Fenway, where it had won 31 out of 36 home games since the All-Star break. They awoke on Monday back in Boston with an extra incentive to catch the Indians. On the previous day, the Cinderella Boston Braves had defeated the New York Giants and clinched their first National League pennant in thirty-four years. The Red Sox could reward the fans who had bought well over three million tickets to Red Sox and Braves games during the 1948 season with a trolley series, the first in the history of the city. To do so, however, they could not afford to lose another game—at least until the Indians did.

A presidential election was also nearing its climax, and *Time* magazine had hit the newsstands on September 20 with California governor and Republican vice presidential candidate Earl Warren on the cover. The issue that would hit the stands on October 4 was scheduled to feature Dixiecrat candidate Strom Thurmond. But the issue that the nation awoke to read on Monday, September 27 showed Joe DiMaggio on the cover, and the story recapped the American League pennant race, complete with a graph that charted the progress of the three leaders over the entire season. The story described DiMaggio's early life and career, his relaxed training habits, and some of his recent heroics, but it made no mention of his heel. It concluded with an account of a recent telephone call between Joe D and his mother, who had reported that brother Dom had now scheduled his marriage to a Boston-area girl on October 7—or, if the Red Sox won the pennant, October 17. "Mama," Joe reportedly replied, "I'll see that Dom is free to get married on the seventh."[2]

2. *Time,* October 4, 1948, 72. (The October 4 issue hit the newsstands on September 27.)

STANDINGS
Monday, September 27, 1948

Team	Won	Lost	Pct.	Games Behind
Cleveland	93,	56	.624	—
Boston	92	57	.617	1
New York	92	57	.617	1
Philadelphia	83	66	.557	10
Detroit	74	74	.500	18½
St. Louis	57	90	.388	35
Washington	53	95	.358	39½
Chicago	49	98	.333	43

After the season's last full day of rest, a well-rested Joe Dobson took the mound for the Red Sox in Boston against the Senators on Tuesday. Washington sported a miserable 19–53 record since the All-Star break, and was struggling to avoid falling into the cellar for the first time since Clark Griffith had taken over the team more than thirty years before. The Red Sox had beaten them nine times in their last ten meetings, but the Senators' pitcher was Ray Scarborough, whose remarkable 13–8 record included two victories over the Sox. The last time Scarborough had pitched in Boston— on August 20—only Junior Stephens's dramatic ninth-inning home run had avoided defeat.

The score was 0–0 when Senator Mickey Vernon, finishing up a dreadful season, started the second off with a double to right. A walk and a single loaded the bases, and Dobson induced catcher Jake Early to ground the ball to Billy Goodman. The rookie first baseman made an uncharacteristic mistake, throwing home rather than going for a double play, and his wild peg scored Vernon and left the bases loaded. Scarborough, next up, singled to left for two runs and a 3–0 lead. After an out, Al Kozar sent a ground ball up the middle which Stephens reached but couldn't hold, scoring the fourth Washington run. Joe McCarthy, showing a little bit of panic himself, removed Dobson, who could easily have been out of the inning with considerably less damage, and replaced him with Mickey Harris. Harris got out of the inning, but the Sox trailed 4–0.

When Scarborough struck out Williams on a bad pitch to end the bottom of the third, the great hitter lost control of himself for the first time all season and hurled his bat up the third base line. The Red Sox got a run in the bottom of the fourth, but their rally died when McCarthy let Harris hit with two men on and two out, and the pitcher flied to center to end the inning. Williams made two good plays to open the top of the fifth, in which the Senators failed to score again, but fans in left field heckled him as he ran in at the end of the inning and he gestured to them in return—another 1948 first. Scarborough survived a solo homer by Doerr, his 26th, in the bottom of the sixth to lead 4–2. Williams grounded out to end the seventh with Dom DiMaggio on base. The crowd of 10,485 sat in stunned, unbelieving silence. After all the magnificent victories they had witnessed since the All-Star game, the pennant was slipping away before their eyes against the worst team in the American League. In the bottom of the ninth, down 4–2, McCarthy finally pinch-hit Stan Spence for Harris with two out. He walked, but Dom DiMaggio flied to center to end the game.

"Stay loose, stay loose," McCarthy said as he walked into the sepulchral locker room. "We're going to win this thing the last game of the season." Then he walked into his office, slammed the door, and presumably vented his real feelings in private. A few minutes later he emerged and went over to Ted Williams for a long talk. The two men, who were almost always the last to leave the locker room, had become increasingly close over the season.

The situation was desperate. Even if Boston swept their last four games against the Senators and Yankees, the Indians would have to lose twice against the White Sox and Tigers just to bring about a tie. That afternoon, in the late editions of the evening *Boston American,* beat writer Steve O'Leary and columnist Austen Lake openly gave up all hope.

In Philadelphia, the Yankees faced an Athletics team with nothing left to win or lose. Secure in fourth place, the team that had contended well into August was now a full ten games off the pace, but several of their hitters were finishing outstanding seasons. Barney McCosky had raised his average all the way to .325, fifth in the league among regulars behind Williams, Boudreau, Dale Mitchell, and Al Zarilla; Hank Majeski had hit .317 and driven in 117 runs; Elmer Valo had hit .309, with 69 runs in just 109 games; and shortstop Eddie Joost, with a mere .246 average, had scored 97 runs on just 122 base hits. To pitch Connie Mack tabbed Carl Scheib, now 13–8, while Raschi, 8–0 lifetime against Philadelphia, took another shot at his twentieth victory.

The Yankees' problems became glaringly apparent in the bottom of the very first inning, when Eddie Joost's fly to center fell over the head of a limping Joe DiMaggio and rolled to the wall for a triple. McCosky promptly scored him with a single, and Raschi eventually loaded the bases but escaped down just 1–0. The roof fell in on Raschi in the bottom of the third, when the A's made it 4–0 and Page relieved. They picked up another run in the fourth, while Scheib's mastery of the Yankees continued. Keller pinch-hit unsuccessfully for Page in the fifth, and Harris sent in Allie Reynolds, who had failed in his last three starts. Reynolds stopped the

Athletics the rest of the way, but Scheib took a 5–0 lead into the ninth. The Yankees, like the Red Sox, found themselves on the verge of extinction.

Lindell opened the ninth with a single to right, and Sherman Lollar walked. Harris sent up late-season call-up Joe Collins to hit for Stirnweiss, and Collins doubled down the left-field line for two runs. Bill Johnson, batting for Reynolds, flied out to Valo in right for the first out, and Joost threw out Rizzuto for the second. Henrich, 0–4 on the day, came up with a chance to bring the Yankees within one run, and sent a line drive into right-center. Valo, running hard, stretched his gloved hand across his body and made the catch on the dead run to end the game. The Yankee rally had fallen short. Like the Red Sox, they were now two games off the pace with just four games left to play. Their greatest star could hardly run, their pitching staff was exhausted, and, alone among the three contenders, they had to play the rest of their games against winning teams.

The Indians' game against the White Sox that evening in Cleveland was their last night game of the season. Weeks earlier, Veeck had designated it as "Good Old Joe Earley Night," and dedicated it to the average fan, without knowing whether the Indians would still be in the pennant race or not. Now the game might turn out to be a double celebration, as a Cleveland win could reduce the Tribe's magic number to three. With the Yankees and Red Sox both struggling—and scheduled for two games against each other on the weekend as well—the Indians' fans could almost taste their first pennant since 1920. In the clubhouse, Sam Zoldak sent telegrams to Ray Scarborough and Ferris Fain. "Love and kisses," they read.

Veeck began the evening by distributing twenty thousand packaged orchids, flown in from Hawaii in a special air-conditioned plane, to the first twenty thousand women to come through the turnstiles. (The total attendance was 60,405.) Then he set up shop at a microphone at home plate and began calling down lucky fans to receive gifts. The presents included three stepladders (all given to the same fan); four white rabbits; and a bony, swaybacked horse, described by Chuck Heaton of the *Plain Dealer* as a fugitive from a glue factory.

Last but not least came Good Old Joe Earley himself, the real author of this, Veeck's last big promotion of the year. Veeck began by announcing that the Cleveland ball club was presenting the war veteran with a house, done in early American architecture, and a truck carrying an outhouse drove in from left field. To go with the house, Veeck then announced a car, and a Model T, filled with young women hired for the occasion, followed. Then came a new convertible, and a truck packed with household appliances—"everything," as Veeck wrote more than ten years later, "we could talk the local merchants into contributing to the cause." Joe himself also received an impressive assortment of livestock, and a lifetime pass to any American League ballpark. A reporter noted the next day that the grounds crew eventually managed to get the animals off the field, but not before Gene Bearden had begun his warmup pitches "ankle-deep in week-old pigs."

The ball game that followed, of course, was anything but a joke. The White Sox, who had started the Indians on their big skid on August 21 and completed it on Labor Day, had beaten the Tribe in five of their last six meetings, and Bearden was pitching on two days' rest. This game, however, was never in doubt. After Bearden retired the White Sox in the first, Mitchell opened the bottom of the inning with his fourth home run of the year, and hits by Boudreau, Gordon, Keltner, and Doby scored three runs. The Tribe picked up another run in the second and batted around in the fifth, scoring six runs. Meanwhile Bearden was virtually untouchable, allowing just four hits and two walks. The biggest night of all belonged to Allie Clark, with three singles, a home run, three runs, and three RBIs. The 11–0 game was the first real blowout enjoyed by the Indians in more than a week. Bearden had his eighteenth victory.

STANDINGS
Wednesday Morning, September 29, 1948

Team	Won	Lost	Pct.	Games Behind
Cleveland	94	56	.627	—
Boston	92	58	.613	2
New York	92	58	.613	2
Philadelphia	83	66	.557	10
Detroit	74	75	.497	19½
St. Louis	58	90	.392	35
Washington	54	95	.362	39½
Chicago	49	99	.331	44

It was one thing for knuckleballer Gene Bearden to go on two days' rest; it was quite another for Bob Feller, perhaps the hardest thrower in baseball. Feller faced lefty Frank Papish, whose two victories on the season included his masterful performance against the Yankee just one week earlier. In the top of the second inning, a walk and three singles brought Papish to the plate with one out, two on, and two runs in. Another hit would probably take Feller out of the game, and Papish ripped the ball between Gordon and Robinson. The magnificent Gordon speared it, whirled, fired to Boudreau, and watched as the Cleveland manager completed a double play.

Feller, clearly off form, survived one hit in the third, two in the fourth, and a double in the fifth, while Papish stopped the Indians cold. The Tribe came to bat in the bottom of the sixth trailing 2–0, having made just four hits.

Boudreau, hitless on the day, walked to open the inning. Then Gordon took charge with his 32nd home run of the year, tying the game, and Keltner followed with his 30th to take the lead. An inning later, Gordon and Keltner repeated their instant replay act, this time contenting themselves with RBI doubles instead of home runs. Gordon finished the day with 121 RBIs, and Keltner 114—both of them career highs. Continuing to struggle, Feller gave up two more hits in the eighth and one in the ninth, but the White Sox did not score. The Indians won, 5–2, their sixteenth victory in their last nineteen games. "I didn't have a thing out there," Feller commented with characteristic bluntness, "but the boys sure helped me out." Unable to overpower the opposition, he had simply thrown the ball up to the plate and let the White Sox hit it.

"We're over the hill, boys, we're over the hill," old Bill McKechnie commented in the locker room. Boudreau now allowed himself the luxury of discussing the World Series. If the Indians clinched the pennant before Sunday, he told the writers, then Feller would forgo his chance for his twentieth win and start the World Series on Wednesday instead. If Feller was needed on Sunday and the Indians emerged with the flag, Lemon would probably open against the Braves in Boston. He said nothing about a playoff, which was looking more and more unlikely.

In Boston, the desperate Red Sox faced the Senators behind Ellis Kinder. A double by Dom DiMaggio and an RBI single by Stephens—his 133rd run batted in—gave Boston a 1–0 lead in the first, but the Senators tied the game in the top of the third. The Red Sox finally broke through in the bottom of the third when singles by Pesky, Williams, Spence, and Tebbetts combined with two Washington errors to give them three more runs and a 4–1 lead. The game now became a severe test of the nerves of Joe McCarthy and the mere 7,247 on hand. Kinder gave up a hit and a walk in the fourth, but Gil Coan popped to Pesky with runners on second and third to end the inning. He gave up two hits and a walk to load the bases with one out in the fifth, but induced Eddie Yost to ground to Pesky for a double play. Two more hits and a walk loaded the bases with two out in the sixth, but outfielder Sherry Robertson grounded out to end the inning. Bud Stewart doubled to start the seventh, but Kinder got the side out. He eventually ran his record to 10–7 with a remarkably unimpressive 5–1 victory that kept the Red Sox two games out.

In Philadelphia, Bucky Harris tapped Porterfield, another weary hurler who had not started for ten days, to face Dick Fowler, now 15–7. The A's took a 2–0 lead and held it through five. Twelve outs away from almost certain elimination, Henrich opened the sixth with a single. Brown flied to right, but Joe DiMaggio singled to center. Berra flied out for the second out, but Hank Bauer hit the left-field roof for three runs and a 3–2 lead. Porterfield held the Athletics in check through the sixth, seventh, and eighth, and in the top of the ninth Brown's sacrifice fly increased the lead to 4–2.

Carl Scheib, one of the league's best hitting pitchers, batted for Fowler to open the top of the ninth. He lifted a short pop fly to center, where Joe DiMaggio—perhaps distracted by pain—dropped the ball. Eddie Joost flied out, but Barney McCosky doubled to right field, sending pinch runner Mike Guerra to third base. With the tying runs in scoring position, Harris brought in Joe Page to face the left-handed-hitting Ferris Fain. Page walked Fain, and Harris brought in Allie Reynolds to face Majeski, who came to the plate with 119 runs batted in on the year. A base hit would tie the game, and an extra-base hit would win it and almost surely dispatch the Yankees from the pennant race. On deck was Elmer Valo, a .300 hitter himself. Majeski grounded to Stirnweiss, who flipped to Rizzuto, and the Scooter made the throw to first for a game-ending double play that kept the Yankees alive.

The remaining American League game that Wednesday also involved the pennant race. In Detroit, Hal Newhouser shut out the Browns, 4–0, for his twentieth victory of the year. Although Newhouser had pitched eight full innings in a losing cause on Sunday against the Indians, Tiger manager Steve O'Neill had sent him up against the Browns with just two days' rest rather than save him for the game scheduled for the next day. There could be only one reason. Only in this way could O'Neill give the great lefthander a shot at his twentieth win against the Browns, and also have him ready to pitch against the Indians on Sunday, the last day of the season, if the pennant race was still undecided. Having won four of eight games against the Red Sox and Yankees, O'Neill was going to give it his best shot against the Indians as well.

With the Indians off on Thursday, the agonizing pressure on the Red Sox and Yankees continued. Faced with the need to decide upon his pitching for the last three games, McCarthy had the ball placed in Mel Parnell's locker. Parnell would be pitching on just three days' rest, but he had lasted only three innings in Sunday's game, and it made more sense to let him seek his fifteenth win against the Senators, whom he had beaten three times, rather than against the Yankees, who had beaten him twice, and save Kramer and Dobson for the weekend.

Parnell put five men on base in the first two innings, but escaped without a run. The bottom of the Red Sox order came through with two out in the bottom of the second, as Goodman, Parnell, Dom DiMaggio, and Pesky singled for two runs. Parnell continued to hold the Senators, and the Red Sox had their first big inning of the series in the bottom of the fifth. Spence homered, Goodman, Tebbetts, Pesky, and Williams singled, and DiMaggio added a two-run double as the Sox knocked out Early Wynn and scored five runs. Like Kinder on the day before, however, Parnell struggled to hold the 7–0 lead. He surrendered a two-run homer to Bud Stewart in the sixth, and McCarthy yanked him in the seventh with one run in, two on, two out, and Stewart at the plate. Earl Johnson preserved the win. Parnell had his fifteenth win against eight losses, but he had given up seven hits and four walks in less than seven full innings. Indeed, since Parnell's fine complete-game win against the Tigers ten days before, only one Red Sox pitcher—Kramer—had turned in a really impressive performance, beating the Yankees 7–2 on the previous Saturday. In the last ten days Dobson had lost twice, while Kinder and Parnell each had one loss and one unimpressive win in two starts. The forgotten man of the staff was Galehouse, who had made just one brief relief appearance in the twelve days since his last start in St. Louis. Writing in the *Herald* after the game with the Senators, Arthur Sampson speculated that Galehouse and Mickey Harris—who had pitched strongly in Detroit on the previous Monday, and who, like Galehouse, owned a win over the Yankees—might start against the Yankees over the weekend.

Eddie Lopat, trying for his eighteenth win, faced Joe Coleman in Philadelphia. On a rainy day, with only 1,231 fans present, the Yankees finally seemed on their way to an easy win, as doubles by Berra and Brown helped run up a 6–0 lead in the first two innings. The game continued in a drizzle, and both sides began to hit. When Lopat got the side out in the bottom of the fifth, the Yankees led 9–3, but the umpires, mindful of the game's importance, refused to call it despite the rain. In the top of the sixth Joe DiMaggio was hit on the leg by a pitched ball and left the game.

With the Yanks still leading 9–3 in the bottom of the eighth, the A's suddenly rallied for three runs, and in the bottom of the ninth, they made a last, valiant bid to leave their stamp on the pennant race that had left them behind six weeks earlier. Joost grounded out to start the frame, but Rizzuto could not make a play on left fielder Don White's grounder, and Ferris Fain singled to right, sending White to third. With the dangerous Majeski representing the tying run at the plate, Bucky Harris removed Lopat and brought in Frank Shea, whose injury had kept him out of action for weeks. It was not a happy choice, as Shea promptly walked Majeski to fill the bases, and ran the count to 3–1 on Elmer Valo. Harris, dipping into his starting rotation for the third day in a row, replaced him with Raschi. Raschi completed the base on balls, forcing in a run and putting the winning run on first. The A's, who had tormented the Yankees in the earlier part of the season, had a magnificent chance to kill them off once and for all.

Raschi struck out Sam Chapman for the second out, and catcher Buddy Rosar sent a long fly to Berra in right. The Yankees, like the Red Sox, had their 94th victory of the year, with two games against the Red Sox left to play.

In Cleveland, Lou Boudreau gave his team the day off and took a train to Harvey, Illinois, to see his wife and family, who had returned home after Labor Day. Almost the only Indian to show up at the ballpark was Feller, who put in his usual two-hour off-day workout. The whole team would go to work again the next day, with a well-rested Bob Lemon taking on the Tigers. With a two-game loss column lead, a victory on Friday would clinch a tie for the title. In the front office, Bill Veeck and his staff worked on plans for distributing World Series tickets, while Veeck angrily denied, for perhaps the hundredth time, the rumors that he intended to sell the club.

Front-office stories were also brewing in the East. Arriving in Boston on Friday, Yankee manager Bucky Harris met his old friend and *Washington Post* columnist Shirley Povich, who asked Harris about the rumors that his contract would not be renewed. "No one has said anything to me, Shirley," replied Harris, "but where there's so much smoke, there's usually got to be some firing." Meanwhile, the Red Sox' millionaire owner, Tom Yawkey— who did not yet enjoy the saintly image he later acquired—had lost his temper over the team's loss of the lead over the last few weeks. He had been especially angered by hearing, after Bobby Doerr had pulled his hamstring on the eve of the last western trip, that the Red Sox' whole farm system did not include one suitable replacement, necessitating the purchase of veteran Lou Stringer. Now Yawkey fired George "Specs" Toporcer, the farm system director, and assistant general manager Phil Troy.[3] The news—intended to be kept a secret—leaked out on Friday and was confirmed by the club the next day.

Harris's fate, like that of his team, was out of his hands as he prepared for the last weekend of this amazing season. The schedule, combined with the Indians' more durable pitching staff and the resurgence of their right-

---

3. The two men were replaced by former Yankee pitcher Johnny Murphy, and by Dick O'Connell, who became the key figure in the Red Sox organization for most of the next thirty years.

handed power, had practically wrapped up the pennant for the Tribe. At bat, on the mound, and in the field, the Indians had turned in a truly extraordinary September. Since returning home after Labor Day, they had won seventeen out of twenty games, turning a four-game loss column deficit into a two-game lead. Fully fourteen of their seventeen wins had been complete-game victories, including four in a row by Feller and five in a row by Bearden. Over the same stretch, the Red Sox had just nine complete-game wins and the Yankees only five. The hitters, however, also deserved much of the credit. Joe Gordon had hit 8 home runs and driven in 19 runs during the Indians' last twenty games, while Keltner delivered 4 homers and 18 RBIs. Doby was doing his best hitting of the season, going 19 for 48 (.398) with three homers during this stretch. Boudreau was slumping, hitting only .270, but Mitchell had held steady at .333. The Red Sox, with Stephens and Doerr slumping, were depending almost entirely upon Ted Williams for power, while even the Yankees—despite the brilliance of Brown, Henrich, and DiMaggio—could not match the Indians for offensive production.

Boudreau now had Lemon ready to pitch on Friday with a full week of rest, followed by Bearden and Feller, each with their customary three days. The team had packed, enthusiastic houses to root them home over the weekend, and they had beaten the Tigers in five of their last six meetings. Their return from the dead was almost complete, and the pennant was surely theirs if they could just win two out of the last weekend's three games. The Indians—from Veeck all the way down to Johnny Berardino— could look forward to winning the race in front of yet another packed Municipal Stadium house on either Saturday or Sunday.

STANDINGS
Friday Morning, October 1, 1948

Team	Won	Lost	Pct.	Games Behind
Cleveland	95	56	.629	—
Boston	94	58	.618	1½
New York	94	58	.618	1½
Philadelphia	84	68	.553	11½
Detroit	76	75	.503	19
St. Louis	58	92	.387	36½
Washington	54	97	.358	41
Chicago	49	100	.329	45

12

A Long Weekend

(OCTOBER 1–OCTOBER 4)

The Cleveland Indians took the field in Municipal Stadium on Friday afternoon against Virgil Trucks and the Tigers to try to clinch a tie for the pennant. After Bob Lemon survived two hits in the top of the first, Dale Mitchell led off with a single—the fourth consecutive game that he had started with a hit—and eventually scored in the bottom of the inning. The lead held up until the top of the sixth, when Vic Wertz's triple over Doby's head keyed a two-run Tiger rally.

Trailing 2–1, Boudreau singled with one out in the Indian sixth. Gordon promptly grounded back to Trucks, but when Trucks threw to second to start a double play Berry dropped the ball and both men were safe. Keltner walked on four pitches to load the bases, and Walt Judnich, playing right field against a right-hander, worked Trucks for another walk and forced in Boudreau with the tying run. Eddie Robinson, next up, had gone just 4 for 29 since Boudreau had restored him to the lineup one week earlier in Detroit, and Boudreau gambled and sent a different left-handed hitter, Hal Peck, to hit for him. Peck struck out, and Hegan grounded out to end the inning with the game tied, 2–2. It was neither the first nor the last humiliation of the season for Robinson.

Judnich moved to first base and Bob Kennedy went out to right field to begin the seventh inning, and Detroit failed to score. With one out in the bottom of the seventh, Mitchell got his second single of the day, and reached second when Doby grounded out to Vico at first. Up came Boudreau, and the boy manager brought his team a giant step closer to the pennant with a long double to right that scored Mitchell with his 103rd run

219

batted in. Entering the eighth with a 3–2 lead, Lemon quickly got two outs, but Wertz came through again with a double down the right-field line, and Pat Mullin walked. Lemon had pitched more than 290 innings and the entire Cleveland bullpen had not thrown a ball in anger in a week, but Boudreau let Lemon pitch to Wakefield and was rewarded when the dangerous Tiger popped to Keltner for the third out. The Indians failed to score in the eighth.

Three outs away from clinching a tie for the pennant, Lemon went out to face the bottom of the Tiger order in the top of the ninth. The frame began well when third baseman Ed Mayo tapped a slow roller down the third-base line, and the catlike Lemon darted in for the ball, straightened up, and fired to first in quest of his league-leading 87th assist. He slipped, and the ball hit Mayo in the back for Lemon's fourth error of the season, allowing Mayo to reach second. Lemon then retired pinch hitter John Bero, but walked another pinch hitter, Johnny Groth. With Christopher and Zoldak warming up in the Cleveland bullpen, Boudreau let Lemon pitch to yet another pinch hitter, twenty-one-year-old catcher Joe Ginsberg, and Ginsberg walked to fill the bases. That was enough, and Russ Christopher came in to try to finish the game.

After a great first half, the chronically ill Christopher—who was destined to die of his heart problem only six years later—had frequently been too sick for Boudreau to use, but he had done well on rare occasions during September. Looking for a double play, Christopher kept the ball low to batter Johnny Lipon, but Lipon did not bite, and walked to force in a run and tie the game at three, taking Lemon's chance for his twenty-first win with him. The next batter, second baseman Neil Berry, grounded obediently to Keltner at third. Twice during September the Indians had pulled off a 5–2–3 double play in a critical situation, and now they would go into the bottom of the ninth with a chance to win against a much-depleted Tiger squad if they could do it again. Keltner charged the ball and threw to Hegan for one out, and Hegan turned and fired to Judnich at first to complete the double play. Umpire Bill McKinley called Berry out, only to reverse himself as the ball squirted out of Judnich's glove to leave the bases loaded.

Jimmy Outlaw, up next, singled for two runs and a 5–3 Tiger lead—the first hit of the inning. Zoldak replaced Christopher and retired Mullin to end the inning, but the Indians trailed by two runs. Five Tigers moved to new positions in the field for the bottom of the ninth, and young Art Houtteman—an awful 2–16 on the year—got Tucker, Mitchell, and Doby on three ground balls to end the game. The Indians stormed into their clubhouse, where they apparently indulged in a brief, pungent orgy of mutual recrimination.

For the third time in a row, the exhausted Lemon had failed to hold a lead. Another key to the defeat, of course, was the error by Judnich, who but for Boudreau's bizarre decision to pinch-hit for Robinson would not have been at first base at all. Boudreau later wrote in his autobiography that the players had "second guess[ed] each other a little" after this game, but he did not say if they second-guessed him.[1] A more crushing defeat could hardly be imagined under the circumstances, and with the benefit of the years, the Indians have dealt with it in the only possible way. Of all the players and other members of the organization interviewed for this book, not one of them has any specific memories of this game.

The Indians' lead was back down to one game over both the Yankees and the Red Sox. Suddenly, the schedule was no longer such an advantage. Since either Boston or New York must win on Saturday, the Indians could not increase their lead even with a victory, and could not possibly clinch the pennant until Sunday at the earliest. The pennant race was now irrevocably destined for its only appropriate end: it could not be decided before the 154th game of the 154-game season. Should the Indians lose to the Tigers on Saturday they would be tied for the lead, and need a victory on Sunday to be assured of place in a playoff. A three-way tie was again a possibility— and the Indians, who alone of the three contenders had lost all the coin tosses in Chicago a week earlier, would have to go to Boston or New York to face either or both of the other contenders. They could still win the race outright, but suddenly, in yet another traumatic emotional reversal, they found themselves in essentially the same position as the Red Sox and Yankees: they could not afford to lose another game.

A tense, excited crowd of 31,118 fans turned out on Saturday in Fenway Park to watch the Red Sox and the Yankees battle for a chance at the flag. The game—and the game to follow on the next day—capped the first close pennant race involving the two most distinguished franchises in the American League. The great Red Sox teams of the 1910s—winners of four world championships—had never had to face a strong Yankee team, and the Yankees' rise during the 1920s occurred after Red Sox owner Harry Frazee had destroyed his team by unloading a series of players—led by Babe Ruth—to the Yankees for cash. While the Red Sox had finished second in 1941 and 1942, they had not seriously challenged the Yanks, and Boston and New York had run away with pennants in 1946 and 1947, making this the first time that both teams had gone down to the wire. Indeed, of all the players on the two teams, only four—all Red Sox—had ever *won* a close pennant race: Birdie Tebbetts, the catcher for the 1940 Detroit Tigers; and

1. Boudreau with Fitzgerald, *Player-Manager,* 206.

Denny Galehouse, Jack Kramer, and Vern Stephens, stars of the 1944 St. Louis Browns. For the two teams, the two pitchers, and the two great stars—Joe DiMaggio and Ted Williams—this was the most important series they had ever played. The loser of today's game would need a miracle—two more losses by the Indians against the Tigers—to stay in the race. Harris and McCarthy chose their most effective hurlers of the previous weekend, Tommy Byrne and Jack Kramer, to open the series. Harris also put Bauer, whose home run had won the last game in Philadelphia, in left in place of Lindell, with Charlie Silvera behind the plate. With DiMaggio barely able to walk, Keller's back still bothering him, and Rizzuto nursing a sore arm, only four of the Yankees' regulars were fully fit and ready.

Kramer got Rizzuto to open the game, and Henrich singled to right. Bobby Brown, who had devastated the Sox the previous weekend in Yankee Stadium, sent the ball to deep center, but Dom DiMaggio ran it down. Joe DiMaggio—with 152 runs batted in on the season—stepped in. In his last at bat at Fenway, he had hit the grand-slam home run that had kept the Yankees in the race, but this time Kramer rose magnificently to the occasion and struck him out to end the frame. It was only the thirtieth whiff of the year for the Yankee Clipper, the most difficult of all the great power hitters in baseball history to fan.

In the bottom of the first, Byrne retired Dom DiMaggio but walked Pesky. Williams, like Joe DiMaggio, came to the plate in the first inning with a man on. Byrne was one of the hardest of pitchers for Williams to face because he combined excellent stuff with poor control. The Splendid Splinter concentrated above all on looking for a good pitch to hit, and he knew he could not expect very many from a thrower like Byrne. This time the first pitch fooled him, and he checked his swing and took a strike. A ball evened the count, and then Williams got a good look at a fastball and lifted it deep to right. It landed in the bullpen Tom Yawkey had built in 1940 to give his young star from San Diego a more inviting target, and Williams had his 25th homer and his 125th and 126th runs batted in. Containing his natural exuberance, he crossed the plate and accepted Pesky's congratulations with his head down and his eyes shut. Byrne walked two more batters, but eventually retired Billy Goodman to escape down just 2–0.

With the wind blowing in from left field, Kramer and Byrne got through the next three half-innings without incident. But Pesky walked again to open the bottom of the third, and Williams drove the ball deep to right-center again. It fell in for extra bases, but Joe DiMaggio, sprinting on his bad heel, made a sensational pickup to hold Williams to a double and stop Pesky at third base. Byrne struck Stephens out for the first out, but Bobby Doerr walked again to fill the bases, and Stan Spence singled sharply to right to score Pesky, with Williams holding at third. That was enough for Harris, and Joe Page came in to relieve Byrne. Goodman, next up, lifted a fly ball near the left-field line, and when Bauer made the catch less than three hundred feet away from home plate, Williams dashed for the plate and slid in safely for a 4–0 lead.[2]

Kramer got the Yankees out in the fourth to preserve the four-run lead, and DiMaggio and Pesky singled and doubled with one out in the bottom of the frame. To no one's surprise, Page gave Williams an intentional pass to face Stephens with the bases loaded, and Stephens flied deep enough to center to score the fifth Red Sox run. Kramer retired the side in the fifth, running his string of consecutive outs to twelve, and survived a hit by Henrich in the sixth. The Fenway Park scoreboard now told the Yankees that time was running out: the Indians had scored five runs in the bottom of the fourth inning in Cleveland to take a 5–0 lead behind Bearden. Allie Reynolds relieved again in the bottom of the sixth. With two out, Williams walked again and stole second—his fourth theft of the campaign—but failed to score.

The Yankees finally managed to score in the seventh when Joe DiMaggio drove the ball against the left-center-field wall for a double, limped to third as Berra grounded out, and came home on a sacrifice fly by Lindell. Entering the ninth with a 5–1 lead, Kramer retired Joe DiMaggio, gave up a single to Berra, and got Bauer for the second out. Making his last major league appearance, George McQuinn stepped up to hit for Ralph Houk with the season riding on his shoulders and grounded out to Goodman. Jack Kramer and Ted Williams had led Boston to a 5–1 victory, and more news was in from Cleveland. Bearden had beaten the Tigers. The Yankees were out of the race.

The New York Yankees of 1948 were superior to the team that won the world championship the next year, and only marginally inferior to the world champion 1947 edition. Both Tommy Henrich and, arguably, Joe DiMaggio, had turned in their greatest seasons, and they had enjoyed fine performances by Berra, Bobby Brown, Lindell, and—for most of the year— their starting pitchers. Their manager, Bucky Harris, had made a critical August adjustment that had allowed the team to catch fire and vaulted them into the pennant race. After fighting all season to reach the top, they had finally done so on the next-to-last Friday of the year, only to fall out of the race by losing three of their next six games.

Nothing could have been more appropriate than the Yankees' elimina-

2. Many fans will remember George Foster throwing out Denny Doyle on the same play in the ninth inning of the sixth game of the 1975 World Series.

tion at the hands of the Red Sox. Boston's win gave the Red Sox thirteen wins and eight losses in the season series with the Yankees, with one more game to play. The Red Sox' domination of the defending world champions had determined the character of the pennant race. While the Indians and the Red Sox had split their season series exactly and the Yankees had managed to beat the Indians twelve times while losing ten, the Red Sox had taken a five-game lead in their series with the Yanks. Had the Yankees played .500 ball against Boston, they would have won the pennant. The story of the 1948 season makes nonsense of all the theories that the Yankees "had" to beat the Red Sox, for financial or other reasons.

Having failed in 153 games ever to take undisputed possession of first place, New York had one more day left to play spoiler. Bucky Harris declined to name his pitcher for the next day. The obvious choice was Raschi, who could make yet a fourth try for his twentieth victory against the team he had never beaten, but Harris's silence suggested to most of the writers that he preferred the rookie Porterfield. The teams' two center fielders, the brothers DiMaggio, left the ballpark together on their way to dinner with their parents. Their family had congregated for the wedding of Dominic DiMaggio, scheduled to take place immediately after the season ended, but now liable to be postponed should the Red Sox find themselves in the World Series. Joe and Dom shared a cab on the way to the restaurant, and the elder brother spoke first about the next day.

Although he had been limping on his degenerated right heel for the better part of a month, no one, on either team, had the slightest doubt that Joe DiMaggio would play the next day's game. A different kind of man, or a player from another era, might easily have played with somewhat mixed feelings. Even in the intensely competitive world of professional baseball, some men, speaking to a friend or brother on the opposing team, might well have indicated that while they would certainly do their best to win, they would feel some pleasure if their friend or brother kept his pennant chances alive. Joe DiMaggio, however, was not such a man. The ultimate competitor, he hated to lose to anyone—especially, perhaps, to his brother— and in this campaign, everyone fought to the finish. "You put us out today," Joe told his younger, smaller brother on the evening of October 2, "but we're going to get even tomorrow. Enjoy yourself watching my fortieth home run going over that left-field wall." Dominic was giving nothing away, either in pride or in spirit. "Giuseppe," he replied, "you're all wet this time. This year it's our baby. The only DiMaggio home run tomorrow will be my number nine."

In Cleveland, the 56,238 fans who came to Municipal Stadium on a dark, cold, windy day to watch the Indians try to clinch a tie had gotten a pleasant surprise when the batteries were announced. Fred Hutchinson, a good pitcher having a wretched season, was the scheduled Tiger hurler, but manager Steve O'Neill announced that Hutchinson had the flu and a 102-degree fever, and replaced him with rookie right-hander Lou Kretlow. O'Neill called both Joe McCarthy and Bucky Harris before the game to apologize. Boudreau stuck with Bearden, pitching his third game in eight days, this time with three days' rest.

For three and one-half innings the two rookies pitched scoreless ball, helped by three rally-killing double plays. In the bottom of the fourth, Doby's double, Gordon's double, two Tiger errors, a walk, and Hegan's two-run single gave the Indians a 5–0 lead and chased Kretlow in favor of Trout. The Tribe went back to work in the bottom of the fifth as Mitchell singled, Doby doubled again, Trout balked, and Boudreau delivered a sacrifice fly for two runs. Robinson led off the next inning with his 16th home run, completing the Indians' scoring, while Doby—four for four on the day—raised his average to .302. Bearden gave up eight hits and walked three, but only one Tiger hit for extra bases, and the Indians turned three double plays. Bearden—7–3 at the All-Star break—had run his record to 19–6 with his sixth shutout, 8–0. He did not feel the least bit tired. The Indians stayed one game ahead of the Red Sox with one game to play.

The pennant race seemed to have boiled its way down to two possibilities. If the Indians won or the Red Sox lost on Sunday, Cleveland would be victorious, but if the Indians lost and the Red Sox won, the Tribe would have to go to Boston to play a one-game playoff on Monday. The odds would then turn back in favor of the Red Sox, but their chances of reaching that playoff seemed to be less than one in four. There was, however, a third possibility—one that had occurred to the fertile brain of Bill Veeck. The Indians would win the pennant outright no matter what happened in Boston if their last game with the Tigers did not take place at all. American League rules did not allow for games to be made up after the end of the season, and the Red Sox needed an Indians loss to force a tie. Bad weather might indeed make Sunday's game in Municipal Stadium impossible. The Tigers and Indians had played some of Saturday's game in a drizzle, and *New York Times* reporter Louis Effrat wrote that he had seen games postponed in comparable weather. Veeck, however, was thinking about calling the game even if the sun was shining.

Under the rules of baseball, the decision to start a regular-season game lay not with the umpires, but with the home team. Veeck had concluded that he had the power simply to declare the game unplayable on Sunday no matter what, and therefore assure the Indians the pennant. Whether he really entertained such plans, he felt sufficiently tempted by the possibility to inform the American League office in Chicago that it might be best for a representative of the league to make the decision to play, or not to play, the game. Will Harridge obliged, sending supervisor of umpires Tom Connolly. Veeck naturally released the whole story to the Cleveland press, which played it up in Sunday's papers.

In the press box in Municipal Stadium after Saturday's game, Gordon Cobbledick, the sports editor of the morning *Plain Dealer,* went to work on his Sunday column. A veteran in his trade, Cobbledick had been a key figure in the Indians' last big pennant race, in 1940. It was he who had broken the story of the players' delegation that had gone to team president Alva Bradley to ask him to fire their manager, Oscar Vitt, in midseason. His story turned that season into an orgy of recrimination, culminating in the loss of the pennant on the last Friday of the campaign. This time—win or lose—Cobbledick wanted no recriminations or second-guessing. On the eve either of a magnificent victory or a calamitous defeat, he tried to put the whole season in perspective.

> One of two things will be true about the Indians before sundown this evening: They will have won their first pennant since 1920 OR they will have finished in a tie with the Boston Red Sox.
>
> If they should be forced into a playoff and lose, it will be heartbreakingly easy to go back over the season's records and say, "Here's where they blew it. Here and here and here are ball games they should have won that they allowed to slip away from them."
>
> If they win it will be as easy to look back and say, "This and this and this are the games that did it. They had no license to win these, but they did."
>
> Since one game will have represented the difference in any case, there isn't a man on the ball club who can't be pointed out as the man who won the pennant, for there isn't a man but who contributed some bit above and beyond the call of duty that made one victory possible.
>
> Conversely, there isn't a man but who can be pointed to as the goat if they lose, for every man has been guilty at one time or another of a fielding slip or a careless pitch or a strikeout in the clutch that cost a ball game. And one ball game was enough.
>
> There was a tense overtime game in Washington in July when the Nats put the winning run on third with one out. Lou Boudreau called Bob Kennedy off the bench and sent him into right field on the long chance that his magnificent arm might be the instrument that would keep that run from scoring.
>
> The outfield and infield were both drawn in close when Al Kozar, the batter, hit a fly to right. It was well back over Kennedy's head, and Bob turned his back and ran with all his speed—not to the point where his judgment told him the ball would come down, but beyond. Then he stopped and turned and

dashed back in so that the momentum of his movement would be behind the throw.

He took that fly as he ran and he threw in the same instant the ball hit his glove. It was a perfect strike to Jim Hegan and the run that would have ended the game was headed off and the Indians went on to win in the 12th.

If a pennant flies from the Stadium flag pole, Kennedy, then, is the hero. One of them, anyhow.

It is as easy to remember the game in which Larry Doby lost a fly in the sun and was hit on the head by the ball, allowing the Philadelphia Athletics to score the tying and winning runs in the eighth. If the Indians lose the pennant, Doby is the goat.

But it is equally easy to remember a half-dozen games he won with his bat or his speed in the field and on the bases, so that if the Indians win you can call him one of the heroes without fear that any man can challenge you.

You can make Bob Feller the hero for his superb pitching in the grueling stretch, or you can make him the goat for his poor pitching in the middle stages of the season. . . .

Lou Boudreau and Joe Gordon and Ken Keltner have been brilliant, but even they have contributed to defeats. What are they—heroes or goats?

But win or lose, there's one thing you can't take away from them. They've given it the best they had, right down to the wire. And they've given us the most exciting baseball season in history.[3]

STANDINGS
Sunday Morning, October 3, 1948

Team	Won	Lost	Pct.	Games Behind
Cleveland	96	57	.627	—
Boston	95	58	.621	1
New York	94	59	.614	2
Philadelphia	84	69	.549	12
Detroit	77	76	.503	19
St. Louis	59	93	.388	36½
Washington	55	97	.362	40½
Chicago	50	101	.331	45

With their fate halfway out of their hands, the Red Sox ran out on the field to face the Yankees for the last time of the year before 31,304 prayerful fans on a clear autumn day. To oppose Dobson, shooting once again for his seventeenth win, Harris chose Porterfield, who had had a good outing in Philadelphia, and sent Raschi to the bullpen. The Indians and Tigers were also starting at 2:00 P.M. Eastern Time, and while most fans sat with one

---

3. *Cleveland Plain Dealer,* October 3, 1948.

eye on the scoreboard, some eagerly followed the game in Cleveland on bulky portable radios.

Phil Rizzuto flew out to open the game, and Henrich drew his 76th walk of the season. Brown popped out, but with two out, a determined Joe DiMaggio drove Dobson's pitch to deepest center field, where it landed out of his brother's reach at the base of the wall for a double and drove in Henrich for his 153rd run of the campaign. Porterfield walked Dom Di-Maggio and Williams in the bottom of the inning, but got Stephens and Doerr to escape unscathed.

Hank Bauer—again preferred to Lindell—walked to open the top of the second, and Charlie Silvera singled him to third. Stirnweiss broke out of a long slump with a single into short right, scoring Bauer and sending Silvera to second, and Porterfield sacrificed the runners along. McCarthy brought the infield in to try to hold the Yankee lead at two runs, and when Rizzuto grounded to Stephens, the league leader in assists rifled the ball home to get Silvera for a very big second out. Henrich grounded to Goodman to end the inning leading 2–0.

The bottom of the Red Sox order went down in the bottom of the second, and Dobson got Brown, DiMaggio, and Berra with the help of two fine plays by Junior Stephens in the top of the third. The scoreboard showed nothing but goose eggs in Cleveland as Dom DiMaggio opened the bottom of the third with a single and Pesky flied out. As Williams came to the plate, the Yankees again swung around into their version of the Boudreau shift. As he had done so many times all season, Williams crossed them up yet again with a double to left, and the fleet DiMaggio made it all the way around the bases for the Red Sox' first run.

Junior Stephens, next up, ripped the ball toward the hole. Rizzuto was set to take it, but Bobby Brown cut in front of him and muffed it, as Stephens reached first and Williams third. Then Doerr crossed up the Yankee defense with a fly to right center that Berra could not quite reach. Stephens, late starting, tore around the bases as Berra retrieved the ball and threw to Stirnweiss. The relay to Silvera was good, but Stephens made a fine hook slide around the tag to score behind Williams for a 3–2 lead. The Yankee left-handed batters, Berra and Brown, had been inserted in right and at third in August to hit. They had hit, but their fielding still left something to be desired.

It had been a long time coming, but the Red Sox were enjoying the second really big inning of their last home stand. As the crowd roared their approval, Stan Spence walked. As Yankee coach Charlie Dressen went to the mound to talk to Porterfield, loud shouts erupted around Fenway and fans behind the first-base dugout began trying to get the Red Sox' attention. When the conference was over, Goodman singled to right to score Doerr and send Spence to third, but an even louder cheer erupted when Bob Feller's number 19 disappeared from the scoreboard on the left-field wall and Zoldak's 26 replaced it. Meanwhile, Bucky Harris removed Porterfield and Vic Raschi came in with a chance to win his twentieth victory after all. Tebbetts grounded to Rizzuto, but the Yankees failed to turn the double play and Spence scored the fifth Red Sox run. Dobson struck out to end the inning with a 5—2 lead. Happily congratulating each other as they came off the field, the Red Sox players hardly heard some enthusiastic fans behind their dugout trying to get their attention. Portable radios among the crowd were telling an amazing story. Eight hundred miles away in Cleveland, another big inning was under way.

The weather in Cleveland was cool but sunny, and the crowd of 74,181 set an attendance record of 2,620,627 that lasted for more than thirty years. The city had declared Bill Veeck Day, and the owner accepted congratulations before the game from a committee including Mayor Thomas Burke and the city's newest celebrity, Joe Earley. Veeck donated the home share of the receipts—$55,000—to the Community Chest, the ancestor of the United Way. To match the value of that contribution, a present-day owner would have to contribute about half a million dollars.

Bob Feller took the mound with a chance to cap his second-half comeback with the greatest victory of his career. Since losing to the White Sox in the first game of a doubleheader on August 22, Feller had started nine times without a loss. His 5—2 win over the Red Sox on Don Black Night had given the Indians a tie for the lead, and his 4—1 win over the Tigers just one week before had gotten them back into sole possession of it. He had a 7—1 lifetime record in his matchups with Tiger ace Hal Newhouser, and one more victory would give him his sixth consecutive twenty-game season and his first shot at a World Series. Warming up, however, Feller knew that he would need some good fortune. His stuff was not there.

The situation on the other side of the diamond was almost as interesting. Having won his twentieth game on just two days' rest against the Browns on the previous Wednesday, Hal Newhouser was furious that he had to pitch. His teammate Fred Hutchinson had missed his turn the day before, and Newhouser, like so many players at this time of the season, wanted nothing more than to go home. Tiger manager Steve O'Neill, however, knew that he could not possibly depart from his rotation again. Having pitched the Tigers to a wartime pennant and world championship three years earlier, Newhouser would have to try to stop the Indians today.

With the crowd roaring, Feller put two men on in the top of the first, but escaped. Newhouser retired Mitchell, Clark, and Boudreau in order in the bottom of the frame. Keltner walked with one out in the bottom of the second, but a strike-'em-out, throw-'em-out double play with Doby at bat ended the rally. The top of the third began with Newhouser himself grounding to Robinson. Then Lipon walked, and Berry singled to right to move him to third. Rookie Vic Wertz doubled to left, scoring Lipon to break the ice and give the Tigers a 1–0 lead, and the huge crowd began to quiet down.

The dangerous Pat Mullin, who had beaten Feller earlier in the year with one of his 23 home runs, was next. Giving up the platoon advantage in favor of the double play, Feller walked him to face Dick Wakefield, the carefree one-time bonus baby who had already contributed so much to the September pennant race. Feller's pitch fooled Wakefield, but the Tiger outfielder got his bat on the ball and lifted a short pop fly to left field. With the defense swung around to the right, no one—not Keltner, not Boudreau, and not Mitchell—could possibly reach it. Runners dashed around the bases as Wakefield made it into second, and Berry and Wertz scored before the Indians could get the ball back into the infield. The enormous crowd sat silent and horrified.

BOB KENNEDY: You could have heard a pin drop on grass.

Bob Feller had faced fourteen batters and retired only six of them. He had given up five hits, walked three, struck out none, and trailed 3–0. Boudreau quickly brought in Zoldak to face left-handed second baseman Eddie Mayo. The great right-hander's bid for his twentieth victory was over; the Indians would have to win their last victory without him. It was Feller's second-earliest exit of the entire season.

Mayo promptly crossed up Boudreau's strategy with a double to right for another run. Zoldak walked Vico intentionally to load the bases, and Boudreau waved in Ed Klieman, one of his forgotten men, to try to get out of the inning. Catcher Bob Swift grounded into a 4–2–3 double play, but the Indians were down, 4–0. Up in the press box, the wire service reporters typed the news into their machines.

The job of scoreboard operator, in those distant, preelectronic days, was usually a pleasant, entertaining sinecure. The Boston incumbent, located inside the left-field wall, had two particular advantages: an excellent view of the playing field, and a daily opportunity to gossip with Ted Williams, who always wanted to know what the other big hitters in the American League were doing. But now, reading his wire-service ticker as the Red Sox third inning came to a close, the scoreboard operator knew that the biggest moment of his career was at hand. First, recording what his viewers already knew, he placed a 5 in the bottom of the Red Sox third. Then—after a pregnant pause—a 4 appeared in the Tigers' third. The roar that rocked Fenway was heard more than two miles away, across the Charles River in Harvard Yard. Suddenly, for the first time in almost a month, destiny was turning the Red Sox' way again.

Leading 5–2, Dobson threw another strong inning in the fourth, and Raschi survived the bottom of the inning when Stephens popped out after Williams had doubled to left for the second straight time. Rizzuto opened the Yankee fifth with a single, and Henrich flied to center for the first out. Bobby Brown then drove the ball off the wall in deepest center, but so quick was Dom DiMaggio that he managed to hold Rizzuto at third base. For the second time that day Joe DiMaggio came to bat with runners on. "I don't care what the rule is about putting the tying run on base," said a reporter in the press box, "they *have* to put him on."

McCarthy ordered Dobson to pitch to DiMaggio, and the Yankee Clipper, shooting for his 40th home run and a 5–5 tie, lifted the ball deep to left. Missing by a couple of feet, the ball struck the top of the wall and DiMaggio settled for a two-run double that brought New York within one. "The Yankees," Red Smith wrote in the press box, "have a guy named Joe DiMaggio. Sometimes a fellow gets a little tired of writing about DiMaggio; a fellow thinks, 'there must be some other ball player in the world worth mentioning.' But there isn't really, not worth mentioning in the same breath with Joe DiMaggio."[4]

With Denny Galehouse and Earl Johnson throwing in the Red Sox bullpen, McCarthy brought in the lefty Johnson to try to stem the tide, and Harris countered by pinch-hitting Lindell for Berra. Big John, who had practically disappeared from the Yankee lineup after a fine summer, hit the ball sharply toward third, and Pesky grabbed it, touched Joe DiMaggio for one out, and fired to first for an inning-ending double play that preserved the 5–4 lead. With Bauer moving to right field and Lindell to left, Raschi got the Red Sox out without incident in the bottom of the fifth. The Yankees threatened again in the top of the sixth but did not score.

Trailing 4–0 in the bottom of the third, the Indians had a flicker of hope when Eddie Robinson singled to right. But Hegan hit into a force play, and

4. *New York Herald Tribune*, October 4, 1948.

rookie call-up Al Rosen, hitting for Klieman, banged into a double play. Gromek, who had seen no service for two full weeks, took over for the top of the fourth, and promptly gave up a single and two doubles before retiring the side trailing 6–0. Totally in command, Newhouser went into the sixth having faced only one more than the minimum number of batters. The Indians had exactly one hit.

LARRY DOBY: Newhouser was unhittable.

Jim Hegan grounded out, and Boudreau chose Berardino to bat for Gromek. Johnny had not had a hit in 30 times at bat—since the sixth of August, almost sixty days before. He singled, raising his average to .190, and for a brief moment, Boudreau allowed himself to hope. The top of the order might rally, and Boudreau had taken Bearden up on his offer to relieve and sent him to the bullpen just in case the Indians caught fire. Dale Mitchell, up next, flied to Mullin in left, but Allie Clark roused the crowd with a single. It was up to Boudreau himself now, but the manager grounded out. The inning was over, the Indians still trailed, 6–0, and the scoreboard told more bad news. Boudreau, on his way out to shortstop, had a brief conversation with Joe Gordon. Then he turned toward the dugout and relayed a message for the Cleveland bullpen. Bearden sat down.

With the Red Sox' fate squarely in their own hands, Dom DiMaggio led off the bottom of the sixth. He kept his promise to his brother and sent his 9th home run over the left-field wall for his 127th run of the campaign and a 6–4 lead. Pesky beat out a perfect bunt. Williams—with two doubles and a walk on the day—tried to go to left again, but Bobby Brown snagged his pop-up, the first time the Yankees had retired Williams all weekend. But Williams did not have to do it all today, and Junior Stephens, batting with a man on base for the fourth time in the game, blasted the ball high and far over the left-center-field wall for his 29th home run and his 135th and 136th RBIs of the season. The Red Sox' lead was up to 8–4, and the crowd erupted in a frenzy. "It was the type of enthusiasm and delight your fan never can forget after having experienced it," Arthur Sampson wrote in the *Herald.* "History was being made, and it was great to sit and watch it unfold." Doerr followed with a single, and Harris removed Raschi and relieved with Allie Reynolds for the third consecutive game. Spence walked for the third time and Goodman singled to score Doerr, but the valiant Joe DiMaggio threw him out trying for a double, and Tebbetts grounded out to end the four-run inning.

Trailing 9–5, Henrich walked to open the seventh, and after Johnson struck out Brown, Joe DiMaggio singled for his third hit of the day. Johnny Lindell followed with another single to left-center, but Henrich held at third. With the bases loaded, a home run would tie the game. Leaving Galehouse in the bullpen, McCarthy brought in the sidearming right-hander Dave Ferriss to face Hank Bauer with one out. Bauer flied to Williams in left, and Henrich scored his 138th tally of the campaign to make the score 9–6. Charlie Keller now batted for Silvera in quest of his third big pinch-hit home run of the stretch drive, and Ferriss walked him to load the bases again. The crowd was on the edge of their seats as Bill Johnson, who had beaten the Sox with a pinch homer in New York nine days earlier, batted for Stirnweiss, but Ferriss—who had salvaged a disastrous season with some good relief appearances down the stretch—got him to ground to Pesky to end the threat.

Ferriss promptly astonished everyone by doubling to open the Red Sox seventh. Dom DiMaggio beat out another fine bunt, sending Ferriss to third, and after Pesky struck out, Williams lifted a sacrifice fly to Lindell for the Red Sox' tenth run. Stephens struck out, but the damage of the top of the inning had been repaired, and the lead was back up to 10–6. Both sides went quickly in the eighth, and as the Yankees came to bat for the last time, the loudspeaker announced that playoff tickets would go on sale immediately after the game. The scoreboard posted the final from Cleveland—Detroit 7, Cleveland 1—and the fans roared as the last act of the drama began. It was the greatest day in the history of the ballpark.

Bobby Brown fouled to Pesky for the first out. Joe DiMaggio, next up, singled to left for his fourth hit of the day. The hit gave him a .433 average with 7 homers and 30 RBIs since the second of September, and completed his season with a .320 average, a league-leading 39 homers—and 155 runs batted in. Bad heel and all, the Yankee Clipper had led an injury-racked team with an exhausted pitching staff down the stretch, keeping them in the race until the next-to-last day of the season. And today—with his team out of the race—he had turned in one of his most amazing performances.

Making his last move of the year, Bucky Harris removed DiMaggio for pinch runner Mike Souchock.

The 31,304 New England fans in attendance were overwhelmed with feelings they could experience only once in a lifetime. Arriving almost without hope, they had seen the Red Sox come from behind to mount two of their classic big-inning rallies and win the game they had to win. The scoreboard told them that fortune had smiled upon them hundreds of miles away on the shores of Lake Erie, bringing this tremendous season to a climax and turning the odds back in their favor yet again. Now, breathlessly awaiting the last out of the game, they were making ready to dash onto

Jersey Street and line up for tickets for the first playoff game in the history of the American League against the Indians the next afternoon. But now, as DiMaggio left first and began walking slowly toward the Yankee dugout, all this was forgotten.

The crowd rose to pay tribute to this magnificent athlete and unequaled competitor, whom destiny, on this day and in this year, had cast in the role of Hector. They honored him with an ovation the likes of which no one present had ever heard, longer and louder than any of the many hands for the Red Sox that day, and more memorable even than the reaction to Carlton Fisk's winning home run in the sixth game of the 1975 World Series, or the legendary Mudville ovation that rumbled through the valley and rattled in the dell. The cheering continued as he walked toward the dugout, and lasted well after he lifted his cap in a brief acknowledgment. On this day, as always, the greatness of the victor reflected the strength of the vanquished, and even the Red Sox found themselves overcome with emotion in what paradoxically was probably the greatest moment of the Yankee Clipper's career. In the Yankee dugout his teammates shook his hand one by one, and across the diamond Boston reserve catcher Matt Batts saw tears in men's eyes.

Johnny Lindell, as if on cue, grounded to Stephens, and the shortstop flipped the ball to Doerr and watched the great second baseman fire it to Billy Goodman for a double play to end the game. The crowd erupted again, and stampeded for the ticket window. Within an hour, all the tickets were gone.

New York, the nation's preminent city, would miss the climax of this great national drama. The final struggle would match an industrial giant, Cleveland, swollen with the huge demands of the Second World War, against the nation's intellectual capital, Boston, the center of a region already in industrial decline. Boston had waited thirty years for a pennant, and Cleveland twenty-eight. And the Red Sox, of course, would be fighting for the chance to give their city a trolley series, an honor previously enjoyed by New York, Chicago, and St. Louis.

"There's a game gang," Joe McCarthy exclaimed to the press in the locker room. "We were counted out as late as last Wednesday night. But those players never gave up." Dom DiMaggio shared the story of his conversation with his brother the evening before, including his prediction of his 9th home run. Junior Stephens noted that his 29th homer had been a long time in coming, "but it certainly came at the right time and in just the right spot."

Ted Williams had capped an amazing season. For the weekend he had three doubles and a home run in six at bats, three walks, four runs, and four runs batted in. His batting average, at .370, easily led Boudreau, who had dropped to .351, and guaranteed him his fourth batting title in his last five seasons. Largely because of his two July injuries, he had failed for the first time in his entire career to lead the league—or, for that matter, his team—in either runs scored or RBI, his 124 runs and 127 RBI trailing Dom DiMaggio and Vern Stephens, respectively, and he had only 25 home runs. But he had learned to beat the Boudreau shift, and in the field and on the bases he had had the greatest season of his life. After carrying the team almost single-handedly during the first two and one-half months of the season, he had turned in a magnificent performance in the last two games. Now he sat quietly in front of his locker for nearly half an hour before asking his neighbor, Wally Moses, who he thought might pitch for Cleveland the next day.

"I guess it will be Bob Lemon," said Moses, "and he's been tough for us all year."

"I don't give a damn if he's beaten us twenty games this year. We'll knock his brains out tomorrow!" Williams yelled.

The reporters, of course, crowded around McCarthy to ask who the Red Sox pitcher would be. Mel Parnell and Ellis Kinder, who had pitched Thursday and Wednesday, were regarded in Boston and around the country as the most likely candidates. "I had everybody working in the bullpen this afternoon," said McCarthy, "and I haven't the ghost of an idea who I'll start tomorrow. I'll try to dream up a starter tonight." Beyond that he would not go. Meanwhile, in private, Birdie Tebbetts cornered Denny Galehouse. "You may be pitching tomorrow," he said.[5]

Johnny Pesky was donning the unusual costume in which he had arrived at the game—his naval lieutenant's dress uniform, which he was wearing to a friend's wedding that evening. As he began to leave, several teammates demanded that he wear it the next day, too, for good luck. After some resistance, Pesky—yielding to the chronic superstition of athletes—gave in to please his mates, but he hardly cared one way or another. Williams had spoken the team's mind. Neither he nor any of the other Red Sox—except the pitchers themselves—was worried about the choice of a hurler for the next day. Counted out only five days earlier, they had done the impossible—and now they were the favorites again. They had a new four-game winning streak, their bats had come alive, and they would meet the Indians the next day *at home*, in Fenway, where their incredible 35 wins in 42 games since the All-Star break included five out of six against the Indians themselves. Twice in the second half of the season the Indians had come into Fenway

5. Interviews with Galehouse and Tebbetts.

Park in first place, and twice they had left it in second. For the Red Sox, the hard part was over. Having come back from the brink, they went home— happy, excited, and certain that they would win.

Things were different in Cleveland.

Virtually giving up after the collapse of the Indians' mini-rally in the bottom of the sixth, Boudreau allowed two rookies, Mike Garcia and Ernie Groth, to finish the game at the cost of one more run. Newhouser set the Indians down in order in the seventh and eighth, facing just twenty-seven batters over the first eight innings, before giving up two hits and a run in the ninth before Ken Keltner flied to left to end the game. The huge crowd had begun filing out in large numbers by the seventh inning. Bill Veeck himself paced back and forth in the press box during most of the contest, and eventually retreated into a stony, uncharacteristic silence.

Boudreau—0 for 3 on the day—had begun thinking about the next day's game as early as the seventh inning, when the scoreboard announced that the Red Sox lead was up to five runs again. And with the game still in progress, he had determined upon one last, daring gamble for the playoff in Boston. He would not risk Steve Gromek, or Sam Zoldak, or Satchel Paige in the biggest game of his managerial career. A few writers were speculating that he might come back with Feller, who after all had pitched less than three innings, but he apparently never considered that either. Lemon, with two full days of rest, was the consensus prediction among writers around the country, but Lemon, Boudreau knew, was utterly exhausted.

Instead, the Boy Manager was leaning toward the pitcher with the hottest hand—and the man who always seemed eager to pitch. As Boudreau went out on the field in the top of the seventh, he had told Gordon he was thinking about Gene Bearden for the next day—with just one day of rest. Gordon apparently concurred, and Boudreau sent the bat boy from the dugout to the bullpen to tell Bearden to sit down for the rest of the day. Now, with the game over, the Indian players met in the clubhouse. Boudreau some weeks earlier had begun banning the writers from the clubhouse after the game, and the team could talk the matter over in private.

Boudreau told the players he wanted to share his pitching plans with them and give them a chance to voice their opinion. "This game we're going to play tomorrow means as much to you men as individuals as it does to me," he said. Then he told them he had decided upon Bearden. "He's the best pitcher we have right now," he said, "better than Feller and better than Lemon and better than Gromek." In addition, he did not think that the Red Sox would be able to pull Bearden's knuckleball against the left-field wall.[6]

The choice was, to put it mildly, a gamble. Left-handers traditionally fared poorly in Fenway, and Bearden had lost his last start there five weeks before. He was not an overpowering pitcher, and he would be trying for his fourth complete game in just ten days. After a moment of silence, one player quickly asked Boudreau if they could look at the records of the various Cleveland pitchers at Fenway, hoping perhaps that they would bring the manager to his senses. Boudreau asked Marsh Samuel, the team public relations director who doubled as the club statistician, to bring them in.

MARSH SAMUEL: I had picked up a skin infection about a week before, so I was staying away from the players as much as I could. But I brought in those records. There was very little to choose from between those pitchers.

Indeed there was not. Bearden had started two games in Fenway Park. On the cold, foggy night of the eighth of June, he had shut out Mel Parnell, 2–0, winning behind Boudreau's foul home run. But on the twenth-sixth of August—in the game that dropped the Indians out of first place for the next four weeks—Parnell had beaten him soundly, 8–4, with the help of a big home run by Bobby Doerr. Bearden had also pitched against the Red Sox twice in Cleveland, shutting them out on May 22 and leaving in the second inning on July 30 in a game the Red Sox came from behind to win. After shutting Boston out twice, Bearden had failed in his last two outings against them.

Lemon had beaten the Red Sox three times—twice in Cleveland and once with a masterful four-hit, 9–0 shutout in Boston on August 25, the only game since the All-Star break that the Indians had won in Fenway Park. But he too had two losses against them, one each in Cleveland and Boston. Feller had beaten the Red Sox three times—once in Boston and twice in Cleveland—but he had lost once in each park and failed to finish a game in Cleveland as well, and he had always hated pitching in Fenway. The history of the season, in short, gave no clear guide to the decision. In the crisis, Boudreau was going with his gambler's instincts and choosing the man with the hottest hand.

Joe Gordon, the most experienced of all the Indians, spoke up. "Lou," he said, "we went along with your choice for 154 ball games and finished in a tie. There's not a man in this room who two weeks ago wouldn't have settled for a tie. I'm sure we can go along with you for another ball game."

6. Boudreau with Fitzgerald, *Player-Manager*, 210–11.

In any critical situation, athletes—and managers—tend to fall back upon their most characteristic strategies. Boudreau's choice was quite in keeping with his pitching plans over the last few weeks of the season. One could equally well imagine that Boudreau would put a new wrinkle into his lineup the next day—as indeed he did. The players agreed to keep the decision a secret to protect Bearden from reporters' questions, and Boudreau, who met with the press immediately afterward, said that any one of six pitchers was a possibility. Speculation continued to center on Lemon, with Parnell his expected opponent.

GENE BEARDEN: I felt fine. I wasn't surprised. I got along real well with Boudreau. He knew what he was doing. He made his own decisions, he told you the way it was going to be, and that was it.

Boudreau was pleased to have gotten the team's mind on the next day, and he told the writers that the Indians were simply going to Boston a day early, before the opening of the World Series against the Braves. Privately, however, the team was worried. Without even a chance to go home to their families, they had to dress and go directly to the station for a nine o'clock special train for Boston. No club ever felt very confident playing the Red Sox in Fenway, and although the Indians had won four of their first five games there during 1948, they had lost five out of their last six. Several of them—including Ken Keltner—doubted that Bearden would be likely to last very long. And despite Boudreau's brave front, he too had lost some of his confidence. As he left the park for the station, a *Plain Dealer* photographer snapped a picture of him in suit and overcoat. The Boy Manager's head was down, his shoulders hunched and his eyes on the ground: a picture of dejection.

In Boston, Joe McCarthy, alone in the hotel room he had occupied all season, was thinking about his pitcher for the next day as well. Earlier, he had met with his catcher, Birdie Tebbetts, to discuss the situation, as he had done routinely all season before every series. His choice, which also remained a secret until just before 1:30 on Monday the next day, has become the most controversial choice of a starting pitcher in the history of baseball. It was a choice that most managers—certainly including Lou Boudreau—would not have made, and one which generations of fans and writers have found it easy to criticize. McCarthy never explained it at any length, and the one man who claims to know how the manager reached his decision, Birdie Tebbetts, refuses to tell all he knows. Yet there is *not* necessarily any mystery about McCarthy's selection. Surprising though it may seem, it was very much in character, and reflects the pitching strategy he had used all season. To one who has followed the whole season it is not at all difficult to reconstruct the Boston manager's thinking.

Six Red Sox pitchers had started more than ten games each during 1948: Joe Dobson (32), Jack Kramer (29), Mel Parnell (27), Ellis Kinder (22), Mickey Harris (17), and Denny Galehouse (14). Although the left-handed Harris had contributed a few strong performances, he had been hit hard most of the season (his ERA was 5.29) and was not really a possibility. Nor did McCarthy apparently consider pitching Dobson, with no rest, or Kramer, with one day's worth—although at least one Red Sox player, Dom DiMaggio, had thought that Kramer might have been given the assignment. In their talk late Sunday, Birdie Tebbetts raised the name of Tex Hughson, the ace of the 1946 pennant-winning club who had spent part of the year in the minors recuperating from injury and the rest of it doing mop-up duty in the Red Sox bullpen, but McCarthy had declined to consider it. "It wouldn't be fair," he said, "after going all this way without him, to call on him for the last game."[7]

Parnell, Kinder, and Galehouse were the remaining candidates. McCarthy did not have a statistician to call upon to help him with his decision, but he did not need one. A few years later, when McCarthy's former player Red Rolfe was managing the Detroit Tigers, McCarthy went into Rolfe's office and discovered that all the walls were plastered with statistical charts. "He hasn't got much of a memory," said McCarthy, whose memory of players' tendencies had frequently astonished players like Tommy Henrich. This was his first year with the Red Sox, and he presumably knew, without looking, how these pitchers had done against the Indians and in various situations generally.

Of the three pitchers available, Mel Parnell (15–6) had by far the best record, with Kinder at 10–7 and Galehouse at 8–7. Postseason statistics eventually showed Parnell leading the team in ERA with a 3.14 mark (Kinder, as of October 3, had a 3.64 ERA, and Galehouse 3.86). That Parnell was left-handed would not apparently have weighed decisively with McCarthy, who had shown no inhibitions about using him in Fenway Park, even against the Indians. Parnell, moreover, had beaten the Indians three times: in Cleveland on June 15 (7–3), in Boston on July 24 when he shut them out 2–0, and in Boston again on August 26, when he gave up ten hits and four runs but beat Gene Bearden 8–4. He had also, of course, lost 2–0 on June 8 to Boudreau's foul home run, and he had been knocked out in the first inning of a game in Cleveland on July 31, the game that Galehouse had

7. Interview with Birdie Tebbetts.

finished so brilliantly. And Parnell, who had pitched against the Senators on Thursday, would have three days' rest. It was this that convinced Boudreau—who might easily have given up several years of his life to have had one of his three top men available with three days' rest—that Parnell would be McCarthy's choice.

Yet while we are not privy to McCarthy's thinking, we know that the three days' rest Parnell had enjoyed—and which was generally regarded by Boudreau and most other managers as ample—had not normally been viewed by McCarthy as sufficient for his pitchers, either during 1948 or for most of his managerial career. During the whole of the 1948 season, McCarthy had started pitchers on three days' rest on only nine occasions, and he had never started a pitcher on three days' rest twice in succession. Mel Parnell did have the best record on three days' rest, with three wins and one defeat, but this would have been his second consecutive outing with three days' rest, and his last two starts had not been encouraging. A week earlier, on Sunday, he had been knocked out by the Yankees, and on Thursday, he had pitched an undistinguished victory over the Senators, leaving the game in the eighth inning. Whether or not Parnell had a sore arm on October 4—a rumor which found its way into print a few weeks later, but which Parnell denies today—his performances over the last week of the season suggested that he might not be terribly effective.

Ellis Kinder might pitch with four days' rest instead of three, but he had not had a really good outing in almost three weeks. He had failed against the Yankees on the previous Friday and given up eleven hits against the lowly Senators on Wednesday while winning, 5–1. Kinder—a thirty-four-year-old veteran of eight years in the minors, who had shown up late for spring training and earned a reputation for heavy drinking—was one of the year's pleasant surprises, but he had not established himself in 1948 as a really exceptional pitcher. He had no wins and one defeat against the Indians that year.

The last possibility was Denny Galehouse.

Readers of this book already know full well that Galehouse was *not* the washed-up journeyman that he has often been portrayed as. Although he had not won a game since September 11, started one since September 18, or pitched in one since the previous Sunday, he had been an important member of the staff all year and a very valuable one in the second half. The ace of the Red Sox during the second half of 1947, he had started on Opening Day against the Athletics, losing a tight ball game to Lou Brissie. All year long he had mixed a few disastrous outings with some very strong performances both as a starter and as a long reliever. Since coming back from an injury to his left shoulder in late July, he had a 6–3 record, including three wins against the Athletics and one each against the Yankees and the Indians. Like Parnell, he had had good and bad outings against the Tribe. In his last outing against them, in Fenway on August 25, he had lasted only a few innings as Cleveland breezed to a 9–0 win. But on the evening of July 31, in Cleveland, he had relieved Mel Parnell in the very first inning and allowed just two hits and one run over the last 8⅔ innings of the ball game, handing Satchel Paige his first and only loss of the season in the bargain. His ERA of 3.86 was virtually identical to Kinder's, and actually superior to Jack Kramer's (4.35).

Every manager, moreover, is influenced by his entire history. It is possible, though not particularly likely, that McCarthy had thought of his first World Series game in 1929, when Connie Mack had stunned his heavy-hitting Chicago Cubs with his choice of a veteran right-hander, Howard Ehmke. More to the point, Galehouse had been known to McCarthy since 1936 as a good pitcher. In Cleveland that summer Galehouse had stopped the Yankees in relief in three consecutive games, prompting McCarthy to comment to Indian manager Steve O'Neill, "My boys can't seem to find him."[8] Galehouse's career statistics are not very impressive largely because he spent his entire career pitching in good hitters' parks—League Park in Cleveland, Sportsman's Park in St. Louis, and Fenway—but as of October 4, 1948, he had won 109 games and lost 117 in fourteen years in the majors. (Ellis Kinder eventually retired in 1957 with 102 career wins.) In 1944, the only other occasion in which he was involved in a pennant race, Galehouse had won a critical shutout victory to help sew up the flag for the Browns in the last week of the season—against Joe McCarthy's Yankees. And in the subsequent World Series against a strong Cardinal club, he had started and pitched two complete games, winning the first 2–1 and losing the second 2–0.

Galehouse, finally, was well rested. In the last two weeks he had pitched only once, for three innings in New York on the previous Sunday. He had warmed up in the bullpen for much of the game on the last day of the season, but McCarthy had brought in Dave Ferriss instead of him to finish the game. Given Ferriss's generally poor record during the season, it seems that McCarthy, like Boudreau, had at that point begun thinking about who would pitch the playoff for the Red Sox. And Birdie Tebbetts had told Galehouse that afternoon that he might indeed be the starter the next day.

McCarthy's decision to have the ball placed in Galehouse's locker on

8. Interview with Denny Galehouse.

October 4, then, was not as illogical as many have suggested. There is no reason to credit the story that sprang up later, that McCarthy asked Tebbetts to sound out all the Boston starters on Sunday afternoon, and that Galehouse alone seemed to want the assignment, or to believe that McCarthy changed his mind with a few minutes to go before the game.[9] And according to one retired Cleveland executive, at least one man on the Cleveland team was not surprised. That was Bill McKechnie, the most experienced baseball man in the whole pennant race, who after the Indians' defeat had speculated that Galehouse, who had turned in one of the most brilliant pitching performances the Indians had faced all season, might be McCarthy's choice.

The fans around the country who expected Lemon to face Parnell were in for a shock. Both McCarthy and Boudreau had made daring choices, and both of them had to live with the ever-present possibility that their strategy might not work.

As the Red Sox went to bed early, the Indians boarded the night train from Cleveland.

GENE BEARDEN: We had a little crap game going in the Pullman—me, Satchel Paige, Keltner, Allie Clark. It was just nickel and dime stuff—didn't last long. I went to bed around ten or ten-thirty. I slept.

The small army of writers that accompanied the Indians included a scribe from the *Boston Globe*, Cliff Keane, who had covered the Red Sox for most of the season before traveling to Cleveland to do the Indians' last game. Around midnight, Keane, who like everyone else was wondering who the Indian pitcher would be, made his way into the club car. There he noticed Bob Lemon and Ken Keltner—probably the most notorious party animal among the Indians—having a few drinks. Keane concluded that Lemon probably would not be pitching the next day. He also made a mental note to notice exactly what Keltner did against the Red Sox.[10]

BOB KENNEDY: Keltner told off a couple of the Cleveland writers during the evening.

KEN KELTNER: I probably went to bed around two-thirty. Bob Lemon's father was there, and I was explaining to him everything we planned to do against the Red Sox. I was staying loose.

9. Birdie Tebbetts still refuses to discuss his Sunday afternoon conversation with McCarthy in any detail, but he has confirmed, after reading this chapter, that it presents a fairly accurate picture of McCarthy's thinking.

10. Interview with Cliff Keane.

MARSH SAMUEL: If Keltner had been drinking water, I would have been worried.

Joe Gordon, who had become a kind of assistant manager to Lou Boudreau, found Bob Kennedy during the evening and told him that he might be starting the next day. He also offered him a sleeping pill, which Kennedy—who had never before taken one—accepted. In Boston and on the train through Pennsylvania, New York, and Massachusetts, the players tried to get some sleep.

Monday, October 4, dawned sunny but cool in Boston, and at eleven o'clock Bob Kennedy awoke sleepily to find himself in a Pullman berth in a Boston rail yard. Looking around, he found himself alone with Joe Gordon and Bob Feller. The three of them dressed quickly, ran out of the yards and took a cab to Fenway Park, stopping on the way to grab milk shakes with eggs in them at a drugstore. They were the last players to reach the park.

In the Cleveland locker room, Boudreau confirmed that Bearden would start, with both Feller and Lemon in the bullpen ready to relieve. Then he told catcher Jim Hegan to use a special sign for Bearden's knuckleball, which he figured to throw about 80 percent of the time. If a new pitcher came in, they would use their regular signs. Bearden arrogantly exclaimed that there would be no change in pitchers.

Meanwhile, Boudreau had been pondering his lineup. As the Indians went out on the field to work out, he went over to the visitors' box to talk to Bill Veeck and Hank Greenberg. There, Veeck and Greenberg learned for the first time that Bearden was pitching. They also learned something else.

The more important the ball game, the more determined was Lou Boudreau, manager, to find an edge. And it was hardly surprising, given that he had used at least thirty different lineups during the season, that he would come up with yet another new one for the last and biggest game of the year. The details, however, *were* surprising.

Boudreau assumed that Parnell would be pitching for the Indians, and he wanted to use the maximum number of right-handed hitters. All year long his platooning had been hampered by the lack of a right-handed first baseman. Today, Boudreau chose Bob Kennedy, who had hit .300 in less than 100 at bats and had hardly ever started a game, to play right field and bat seventh. He dropped Eddie Robinson from the lineup, and put Allie Clark—a better hitter than Kennedy, but a poorer outfielder—at first base. There was only one problem. Clark—who found a first baseman's glove in his locker when he came to Fenway that morning—was an outfielder and occasional third baseman who had never played first in his entire big-league career.

Veeck and Greenberg were rather astonished to hear Boudreau's plans, but Veeck—who had never warmed to Boudreau's managerial style, but had left the manager alone all year—told him to stick with his own judgment. Greenberg, a former first baseman himself, was flabbergasted. The decision stood.

> GENE BEARDEN: I heard the argument sitting in the dugout. Veeck wasn't happy because Clark had never played first base; Boudreau wanted him there for his bat. Boudreau got his way. He's a strong-willed person.

> ALLIE CLARK: I was a little scared. Playing first base—especially playing first base against Ted Williams—a lot of things could go wrong.

> BOB FELLER: I thought it was a great idea. Unless of course some one hit a ground ball at him.

Boudreau got the shock of his life when Galehouse, rather than Parnell, came out to warm up for the Red Sox. His lineup of six right-handed hitters had been designed to face the southpaw, and, suspecting a trick, he apparently dispatched a Cleveland executive to see if Parnell was warming up under the stands, ready to replace Galehouse and neutralize one or two left-handed Cleveland bats. (This was the gambit that Bucky Harris had used to beat John McGraw's Giants in the seventh game of the 1924 World Series.) Parnell was not warming up, and Boudreau concluded that McCarthy was serious. Noting that the wind was blowing out to left field, he stuck with his lineup.

> LARRY DOBY: We were very surprised that Parnell was not pitching. But we had Boudreau and Keltner and Gordon, and I can see why McCarthy decided on a right-hander.

The biggest game in American League history began at 1:30 with 33,957 fans on hand. The same Red Sox lineup that had played most of the second half of the year would face Mitchell, Clark, Boudreau, Gordon, Keltner, Doby, Kennedy, and Hegan. The plate umpire, in a specially assembled crew, was Bill McGowan.

Dale Mitchell, hitting .337 on the year, led off and flied to Williams in left field, and Allie Clark grounded to Pesky for out number two. Boudreau, next up, took two balls and fouled off a pitch. The next pitch was a curve, low and toward the outside part of the plate. Boudreau swung flatly and rather awkwardly, with little follow-through, and lifted the ball high toward left field.

> DENNY GALEHOUSE: As soon as he hit the ball, I looked toward left field. I saw Ted Williams start to come in towards it. Then the wind began to carry it, and he began to move back. Then he turned towards the wall. It just made it over the fence.

Boudreau had done what he wanted—he had lifted the ball into the twenty-mile-an-hour wind for his 17th home run of the year. Gordon now hit the ball solidly to short, and Stephens bobbled it, picked it up, and threw him out at first base. Cleveland led, 1–0, and the crowd roared as the Red Sox ran in from the field.

Dom DiMaggio, leading off, grounded to Boudreau, and Clark handled the throw at first for the out. Johnny Pesky promptly brought the crowd to its feet with a drive into right-center, and slid into second for a double.

JOHNNY PESKY: It was probably a fast ball down the middle. They didn't worry much about me hitting it out.

Up came Williams, fresh from two brilliant games against the Yankees.

GENE BEARDEN: I had pretty good luck with Williams, maybe because I pitched him a little differently. I thought everybody else tried to keep the ball away from him. I pitched him inside.

The extreme Boudreau shift had become a thing of the past thanks to Williams's year-long adjustments, and Boudreau was playing just to the left of second with Keltner in the hole. Williams grounded the ball up the middle, and Boudreau reached it and threw him out as Pesky sprinted into third.

GENE BEARDEN: Any time you got Williams out, it was a good play.

Once again it was up to Junior Stephens, who had broken out of his slump with three RBIs the day before. Stephens ripped the ball through the hole past Keltner for a single to tie the game, and the crowd erupted. Doerr, next up, had beaten Bearden with a three-run home run on his last trip to Fenway. This time he grounded to Keltner for the third out, ending the inning in a 1–1 tie.

Keltner, leading off the second, got the first really solid hit off Galehouse and rattled the left-field wall, but Williams, playing the carom well as usual, held him to a single. Larry Doby had gone 6 for 13 during the Indians' last visit, raising his average against Boston pitching to .388 on the year. This time he made another bid for a hit with a fly to right-center, but Dom DiMaggio ran it down for the out. Bob Kennedy flied to DiMaggio as well, and Jim Hegan struck out to end the top of the second.

Stan Spence led off the bottom of the second with his fifth consecutive walk, and Bearden managed to get two strikes on Billy Goodman. In 441 at bats, Goodman had struck out 43 times and grounded into 18 double plays. All year McCarthy had taken relatively few chances on the bases, with only 55 steal attempts compared to the Indians' 98, and the Red Sox had the highest stolen base percentage in the league. But now, McCarthy sent

Spence, apparently hoping to stay out of the double play against the ground-ball pitcher, Bearden.

GENE BEARDEN: I figured, if he's going to run, fine—Hegan will throw him out.

Goodman struck out, and Hegan's throw to second nailed Spence for the second out.

Tebbetts, up next, singled. Then Denny Galehouse, who, like most of the Red Sox, understood that many of Bearden's pitches broke out of the strike zone, took four pitches and found himself on first base. In the Cleveland bullpen, Feller and Lemon began warming up. Bearden was probably only one big hit away from leaving the game, and neither Feller nor Lemon had been especially effective for a week. Because the decision to send Stan Spence had gone awry, Dom DiMaggio now came up with two out and two on, rather than one out and the bases loaded. He grounded the ball to Keltner, who fumbled it, picked it up, and threw him out to end the inning. A potential big inning had slipped away, and the game was still tied 1–1.

Galehouse, returning the favor, walked Bearden on just five pitches to open the third, but Dale Mitchell grounded sharply to Stephens and the Red Sox turned a lightning-fast double play. Allie Clark grounded right back to the pitcher, who threw him out. He had allowed two hits in three innings.

DENNY GALEHOUSE: Bill McGowan said I had good stuff.

JOHNNY PESKY: We thought he had good stuff, too.

KEN KELTNER: He did have good stuff.

With the fans full of anticipation in the bottom of the third, Pesky grounded the ball toward first and Allie Clark made the play unassisted. Williams, up next, fouled the ball to the left side, where Boudreau called off Keltner and made the play for the out. With two down, Stephens drove Mitchell back to the left-field wall to take his line drive to end the inning. The score was still 1–1, but both teams seemed to be hitting the ball fairly well.

Boudreau led off the top of the fourth with a single to left, and Joe Gordon followed with another hit. For the first time, Cleveland had two men on base, and Ellis Kinder got up in the Boston bullpen.

KEN KELTNER: With two on and nobody out, I walked up looking for the bunt sign. It wasn't there.

Galehouse, pitching carefully, ran the count to 2–2.

DENNY GALEHOUSE: I saw Keltner leaning over the plate, as if he was looking for an outside pitch, and I decided to brush him back. But as I threw the pitch, he straightened up.

KEN KELTNER: The pitch was inside, but I managed to get around on it.

Keltner hit the ball squarely on a rising line toward left field, and it cleared both the wall and the screen and hit the light tower for a three-run homer. The man who had gotten the Indians off fast with a fantastic start and broken out of a slump down the September stretch had done it again. The crowd sat quietly as he circled the bases and accepted congratulations at home plate. It was the second consecutive game against the Red Sox in which he had delivered a big home run. In Fenway Park, the Indians' great right-handed power had come through.

KEN KELTNER: I still wasn't all that confident. There was a long way to go.

When Denny Galehouse was good, he was very good; when he was bad, he was horrid. Today he had been very good for three innings, and horrid for three batters. McCarthy decided to go no further, and Kinder came in to relieve.

Larry Doby nearly duplicated Keltner's feat with a drive to left-center that missed the screen by about a foot and bounced off the top of the wall for a double. With no one out, Boudreau ordered Kennedy to sacrifice, and his bunt moved Doby to third. The ploy worked when Hegan grounded to shortstop and Doby raced home for a 5–1 lead. Bearden flied to right to end the inning, but the Indians were in charge.

First baseman Eddie Robinson replaced Allie Clark—0–2 on the day— for the bottom of the fourth. "Clark," wrote Rud Rennie of the *New York Herald Tribune*, "played the position as one might expect it to be played by a man who had never played it before. He did not drop any balls, but he always looked as if he might."[11] Bearden struck out Bobby Doerr to start the inning, but Stan Spence walked for the sixth time in a row. This time McCarthy did not send the runner, and this time Goodman did hit into a double play, Gordon to Boudreau to Robinson, to end the inning.

Mitchell flied to Williams to open the Indian fifth, and Robinson, who found himself in the second spot in the order for the first time all year, popped to Stephens in short center. Boudreau, next up, lifted another long fly to left that found the screen for his 18th home run, making the lead 6–1. He had scored three of the Indians' six tallies. Gordon flied to center for the last out.

11. *New York Herald Tribune*, October 5. During the remaining five years of his career, Clark appeared at first base four more times.

The Red Sox still confidently expected to get to Bearden as they came up in the bottom of the fifth. Tebbetts, opening the inning, grounded to Boudreau. Kinder—hitting for himself—lined the ball to center, but Doby was there for the out. Dom DiMaggio ripped the ball toward third, but Keltner came up with it and made the play. Boston had four more chances to get back in the game.

Leading off the sixth, the great Keltner hit the wall again for a double, matching Boudreau with three consecutive hits on the day. Kinder got Doby to pop up to Stephens, and Bob Kennedy grounded to Pesky, with Keltner reaching third on the play. Kinder struck out Hegan, retiring the Indians without a run for the first time since the third.

The top of the order was up for the Red Sox again, but Pesky grounded to Gordon for the first out. Then Williams lifted a high, lazy pop to center, and the brilliant autumn New England sun—the same sun that blinded Lou Piniella exactly thirty years later in another playoff game—was too much for Joe Gordon, who dropped the ball. Bearden fanned Stephens for the second out, but Bobby Doerr came through with a drive that cleared the left-field wall for his 27th home run of the year—only his third since his leg injury in early September. Spence, who had walked six straight times in two critical games, struck out to end the inning, but the Indians' lead was cut to 6–3, with three innings to go.

GENE BEARDEN: Gordon came in laughing—"Well, I finally dropped one!" he said. That was the way Joe was.

Bearden himself opened the seventh with a single to center field, and Dale Mitchell, 0 for 3 on the day, followed with another single to center. Robinson sacrificed. To no one's surprise, the Red Sox gave Boudreau an intentional walk—the fourth consecutive time he had reached base. But with the bases loaded, Kinder got Gordon to pop up to Pesky, and performed a miracle by getting Keltner to fly to Williams for the third out. The fans rose for the seventh-inning stretch.

The Red Sox bench was continually shouting to their hitters to take more pitches. Billy Goodman opened the bottom of the seventh with a walk, but Tebbetts promptly bounced right back to Bearden for another double play. Down by three runs with two out, McCarthy let Kinder hit again, and he grounded to Boudreau at short to end the inning.

GENE BEARDEN: As you go along in a ball game, you've got tunnel vision. As far as I was concerned, there was nobody there but Jim Hegan and myself. All we knew was who was hitting and who was up next. I knew what the score was but I never looked at the scoreboard.

Doby led off with yet another double off the left-center-field wall, and Kennedy sacrificed again as Boudreau went for another insurance run. Hegan was walked intentionally, and Boudreau signaled for a squeeze. Tebbetts, behind the plate, anticipated it perfectly, called a pitchout, and rifled the ball to third to trap Doby for the second out, as Hegan alertly made it to second. But this fine piece of baseball in a desperate situation went for naught when Bearden lifted a long, high fly to left-center, and Williams made a long run, caught up to it, and dropped it for a two-base error and the Indians' seventh run. Mitchell popped out to Johnny Pesky to end the inning with Cleveland leading 7–3.

GENE BEARDEN: I called it a base hit!

Dom DiMaggio, leading off again, grounded to Keltner, his fourth ground ball out of the day. Pesky, with one of the Red Sox' four hits, struck out. Williams, up for the fourth time, reached base for the second time with a single to left field. Junior Stephens, with a chance to bring the Red Sox within two runs, grounded to Keltner, and Keltner forced Williams at second.

Eddie Robinson, leading off for the Indians, went the wrong way and grounded toward the hole, where Stephens made a fine stop but could not make a throw to first. Boudreau, three for three on the day, made it four for four with a single to left, sending Robinson to second. As the ball came back to the infield, the generous Boston fans gave Boudreau a hand—nothing like the ovation for Joe DiMaggio the day before, but nonetheless a respectful hand for the outstanding player of the game and the season.

Pitching to Gordon, Kinder let go a wild pitch, and both runners moved up. Gordon then received an intentional pass, loading the bases, and Kinder performed another miracle, getting Keltner to bang the ball to Stephens for a double play, with Robinson scoring. Doby struck out to end the inning with the Tribe leading, 8–3.

Bobby Doerr, owner of one of the Red Sox' five hits, managed only a grounder back to the box. Billy Hitchcock batted for Stan Spence and walked, and rookie Tom Wright ran for him. Billy Goodman—0 for 3 on the day—struck out. Birdie Tebbetts, with one hit, chopped the ball just to Bearden's right. The pitcher took two steps toward it, but saw Keltner coming quickly across the diamond and ducked away. The third baseman grabbed the ball and threw to first to end the frame.

Bearden was thinking about the last inning to come—a pinch hitter, followed by Dom DiMaggio and Johnny Pesky—as he turned toward the Cleveland bench.

He never made it to the dugout. Suddenly he saw Keltner and Hegan and Robinson converging around him, with Gordon close behind. As the rest of the team mobbed Bearden, Boudreau ran to a box behind third base and hugged and kissed his wife. The Indians struggled to get Bearden onto their shoulders, while horns began honking in Cleveland and millions of northern Ohio fans leapt up from beside their radios in pure joy. As the crowd headed quietly for the exits, Bearden was half-dragged and half-carried across the field to the dressing room entrance by the first base dugout. And following the Indians came Bill Veeck, who jumped over the railing and ran across the field looking like a kid who had just broken into the biggest candy store in the whole wide world—which, of course, was exactly what he was. Pitching his fourth game in ten days, Bearden had actually lost track of the inning and retired the last batter without knowing it. The game was over. The pennant race was over. The season was over. The Indians had won.

In the bedlam of the Indian locker room, Boudreau, the star of the biggest day of the amazing season, was naturally the center of attention. After he cleared the locker room briefly, Joe McCarthy, Red Sox general manager Joe Cronin, Tebbetts, and Doerr all came to offer congratulations, and McCarthy posed for pictures. Old Bill McKechnie, who had watched Boudreau through the season more closely than anyone, came over to him quietly and put his arm around him. "You did it, Lou," he said quietly. "You did it." As McKechnie walked around the room grinning and shaking hands with one and all, a writer remarked, "You look as happy as if this was a new experience for you." "It never gets old, son," said McKechnie, who had won his first pennant for Pittsburgh in 1925.[12]

Joe Gordon did the best job of putting things in perspective. "There's never been one like this before," he said. "We were never more than four and a half games out of first place and we never had a lead of more than four and a half games. What a battle, right down to the final day and now through this playoff. I'm as happy as I'll ever be in baseball. Sure, this is the biggest kick I've ever got."

Bearden, meanwhile, tried to preserve the lucky sweatshirt that he had worn during his last ten victories—four of them since the preceding Saturday. His accomplishments over the last week of the season are unmatched in the lively-ball era: four complete-game victories in his team's last eight games. Today's victory gave him twenty wins in his rookie season, and the league ERA title to boot. Joyful and relieved, Bearden explained to the

---

12. Boudreau with Fitzgerald, *Player-Manager,* 216.

writers how surprised he had been when his teammates had surrounded him. "I'll bet I was the most surprised person in the ballpark," he said. "I thought it was the eighth inning until the fellows carried me off the field on their shoulders."

"He pitched a great game," said catcher Jim Hegan, "but it wasn't his best of the season. He has a very effective knuckler—sometimes it breaks down and sometimes it breaks in."

In his column the next morning, Red Smith referred to Boudreau's long-standing problems with Veeck and the doubts about his leadership. The playoff, he said, was Boudreau's chance "to prove himself a manager. He started managing in the first inning," when he homered off Galehouse. "It made him the greatest manager in the world," Smith wrote. "Connie Mack couldn't have done it." After singling to start the big rally in the fourth, he homered again in the fifth to make it 6–1. "John McGraw couldn't have done it." In the ninth he singled and scored again. "The Manager had now made four hits in four times at bat, scored three times, driven in two runs and contributed to the scoring of another. He had handled six chances in the field without a flaw and taken part in two double plays. Not even Miller Huggins could have managed a club so well."

Boudreau wanted to talk more about Bearden than himself, and shrugged off questions about his two homers. "Off Galehouse," he finally said, "it was on a curve ball; the next one was a change of pace off Kinder." He told the story of the meeting twenty-four hours earlier at which he had announced his remarkable choice of pitchers, and then defended it. "I wasn't concerned about his pitching with only one day's rest," he said. "He's that type. You can't keep him off the mound. After pitching Saturday, he was in the bullpen yesterday."

All year long Boudreau had had to live with his reputation as a hunch player, with occasional gibes from the Cleveland writers, with Veeck's known distrust of his managerial ability, and, above all, with his own pre-season promise to step down should the Indians fail to win the pennant. Now, in the locker room, he permitted himself a brief, restrained moment of triumph. "That's what comes of being with your own team for 154 games," he said. "You know what the men can do."

Boudreau and Bearden were the biggest heroes of the day, but Keltner had struck the decisive blow in the fourth inning. He apparently had little to say to the writers. A veteran of many seasons with the Indians, he had seen the Cleveland press hit the players when they were down, and he apparently felt no need to help them now, on the greatest day of his life. And indeed, after several drinks at the subsequent victory party at the

Kenmore Hotel, he struck another blow for himself and his mates. Celebrating in style, Keltner decked the *Cleveland Plain Dealer* beat writer Harry Jones, who back in early July had quoted an unnamed veteran player's statements that the team preferred playing on the road.[13]

The Red Sox locker room was quiet—perhaps more stunned than disappointed. Once again, and for the last time, the team had gone from the heights of victory to the depths of despair, finishing unexpectedly at the bottom after the tremendous excitement of the previous day. The players found things to say, but the depth of their feelings would only become clear months and years afterward. For now, everything had happened too quickly to absorb.

"This isn't the first time. I've been licked before," Joe McCarthy told a small pool of writers in his office. "The Indians hit better than we did and that Bearden pitched a nice game. It's just one of those things. We played them even all season and now they come up with the odd game that wins the pennant. My congratulations to Boudreau and his players.

"I feel sorry for our boys that they couldn't win this one," he continued. "They've been the most courageous group I've ever managed. They fought an uphill fight and almost made it."

Bobby Doerr sat peeling the tape away from his injured hamstring. "Give credit where credit is due," he said. "Bearden was remarkable. He had all kinds of stuff. That he could come back with so much stuff after only one day was remarkable."

Ted Williams echoed Doerr's comments. "We really teed off on him the first time we faced him," he said, "but he has had something on us since then." (This was a rare lapse of memory for Williams: Bearden had shut the Red Sox out the first two times they faced him and failed the next two.) "He throws a slider, a curve and a knuckler. And he seems to get tougher to hit each time we face him."

Off the record, the bemused Williams had another comment about Bearden. "That guy will never have another year anything like that again," he said. He was right.

"You know that fly ball of Bearden's I dropped?" he asked, and the reporters nodded. "That's the first fly I've dropped all this year. I booted a couple of grounders, but I've held on to every fly until today. And maybe I wasn't mad to see that ball pop out of my glove." This time Williams's

13. See the various stories in the *Cleveland Plain Dealer*, October 5.

memory was accurate. Finishing at .369, he retained the batting title over Boudreau (.355), but no one wanted to talk much about that.

Dom DiMaggio, whose wedding now would take place on schedule, also paid tribute to Bearden and noted that the Red Sox, in any event, had not kicked the game away. Owner Tom Yawkey came in to speak to the players, and said he hoped to win by twenty games the next year. "I'm sorry I let you down," said Denny Galehouse. "All anyone can do is the best he can," Yawkey said, "and I know you always do that, Denny." Johnny Pesky angrily climbed back into his naval officer's uniform and swore off superstition for life.

"The clubhouse was practically empty," wrote Arthur Sampson of the *Herald,* "when Birdie Tebbetts, already dressed for an hour, said to a reporter, 'Wish me luck, now. I'm going to see if Ted will go on my exhibition tour.'" As he left the clubhouse himself, Sampson saw Tebbetts talking things over with Williams, who, "with the season over and everyone else on his way home, was still sitting on a stool completely attired in his baseball uniform." "Eventually," wrote Sampson, "it seemed likely that Ted and his manager Joe McCarthy, as is almost the daily routine, would have the dressing room and showers all to themselves."[14]

Williams had finally showered and dressed and was on his way out when he heard his manager's voice behind him.

"Well, we fooled 'em, didn't we?" the manager said.

Williams turned around. "What do you mean, Joe?"

"They said you and I couldn't get along. But we got along pretty good, didn't we?"

Williams smiled. "Yeah, we did, Joe."

And the great hitter and the great manager shared something that only they could fully understand.[15]

14. *Boston Herald,* October 5.
15. Williams with Underwood, *My Turn at Bat,* 164.

Epilogue

How the Best Team Won

FINAL STANDINGS

Team	Won	Lost	Pct.	Games Behind
Cleveland	97	58	.626	—
Boston	96	59	.619	1
New York	94	60	.610	2½
Philadelphia	84	70	.545	12½
Detroit	78	76	.506	18½
St. Louis	59	94	.386	37
Washington	56	97	.366	40
Chicago	51	101	.336	44½

Although a pennant race that ends in a one-game playoff has effectively come down to a flip of a coin, in this case, the outcome of the playoff bore out the evidence of the whole season. The Indians of 1948 far outperformed the Red Sox and the Yankees. Their accomplishments at bat, on the mound, and in the field indeed stamp them as one of the ten greatest ball clubs of all time.

Runs win ball games, and the true, raw measure of a team—to repeat once more—is the total of runs it scores and allows over the course of a season. As we have seen, Bill James's Pythagorean formula—$(Runs^2)/(Runs^2 + Opposition Runs^2)$—yields the expected winning percentage of a team based upon its overall performance. The following table shows the runs, runs allowed, Pythagorean or projected percentage, and actual percentage of the eight American League teams during 1948.

Team	Runs	Runs Allowed	Pyth. %	Actual %
Cleveland	840	568	.686	.626
Boston	907	720	.613	.619
New York	857	633	.647	.610
Philadelphia	729	735	.496	.545
Detroit	700	726	.482	.506
St. Louis	671	849	.384	.386
Washington	578	796	.345	.366
Chicago	559	814	.320	.336

The Indians' raw totals of runs scored and runs allowed should have given them the pennant quite handily. Their *projected* percentage of .686 was good enough to have won 106 games out of 154—a full ten games more than they actually won during the regular 1948 season. The Yankees, moreover, were projected to have won 100 games—six more than they actually managed—while the Red Sox won exactly one more game than their totals predicted. Had all gone according to form, the Indians would have won by a comfortable six games over the Yanks, with the Red Sox five games behind them.

How the Indians and Yankees managed to fall so far short of their projections requires more analysis. Before turning to the individual teams, however, a look at another table will provide a much better idea of their true strengths and weaknesses. The teams' raw totals of runs scored and runs allowed must be adjusted to reflect the effects of their parks. While Municipal Stadium and Yankee Stadium both favored defense, Fenway Park, of

Team	Runs	Runs Allowed	Adj. Runs	Adj. Allowed
Cleveland	840	568	892	603
Boston	907	720	852	676
New York	857	633	887	655
Philadelphia	729	735	730	736
Detroit	700	726	679	704
St. Louis	671	849	642	812
Washington	578	796	590	812
Chicago	559	814	580	844

course, favored offense. The following table shows the effects of corrections for ballpark effects.[1]

The superiority of the Indians emerges even more clearly when these adjustments are made: they both scored more runs than any other team in the league and gave up fewer. Since the league average of runs for the season was 730, their superiority totals 162 runs offensively and 127 defensively—a truly remarkable feat. We shall now see exactly how much the individual members of the team contributed to this extraordinary season—and why it was that one of the greatest teams in history had to fight all the way to a playoff to carry home the flag.

The 162 extra runs scored by the Indians' offense would in themselves have been enough to give the team a percentage of .599, or 92 wins, even if the Indians' pitching and defense had been perfectly average. Bill James's Runs Created formula, which measures the offensive contribution of each individual hitter, enables us to identify which Indians created how many of those 162 extra runs and won those eleven games for the Indians.

The Indians' lineup did not include a single below-average offensive ballplayer. Three of their regulars—first baseman Eddie Robinson, catcher Jim Hegan, and outfielder Thurman Tucker[2]—were almost exactly average offensive players. This does not mean that they made no contribution to the Indians' pennant, but rather that a team composed entirely of Robinsons, Tuckers, and Hegans, together with average pitching and defense, would have finished with a record of about 77–77. One other player—Johnny Berardino—actually cost the Indians a game over the course of the season. His failure, however, was counterbalanced by the tremendous hitting of Bob Lemon, who with a .286 average, 5 homers, and a .487 slugging average in 119 at bats contributed enough extra runs to give the Tribe one more win—over and above what he did on the mound.

The rest of the Indians' lineup performed at close to a Hall of Fame level. At second, Joe Gordon created 36 runs more than an average player, worth more than three extra wins. (To understand this analysis, one must keep in mind that the Indians—or any other American League team in 1948— needed slightly more than 10 additional runs for every win after their 77th, or every win over .500.) At third, Keltner's 47 extra runs created were worth four wins more. In the outfield, Doby and Mitchell contributed a total of

---

1. The adjustments are based on five-year averages of runs scored at home and away by each team and its opponents, 1946–50. The year 1946 has been left out for Cleveland's Municipal Stadium because of changes in the fences in 1947.

2. While Tucker was not a regular for most of the season, he had the third-highest total of at bats of the Indians' outfielders, behind Mitchell and Doby.

five more wins, with Doby slightly more effective despite his shorter time in the lineup. Allie Clark and Walt Judnich added one more win each. And at shortstop, Lou Boudreau's runs created—adjusted for the effects of Municipal Stadium—totaled an extraordinary 147, 81 more than an average player, and good for eight full wins for the Indians. All told the Indians' offense created enough runs to finish fifteen games over .500, with 92 wins. This total, however, would have left them in third place. The contribution of their pitching and defense was nearly as remarkable.

Pitchers' contributions can be measured more simply, since the actual number of innings they pitched and runs they allowed is already known. We can measure their value by comparing the number of runs they gave up—adjusted for the park they played in—to the number an average pitcher would have allowed in the same number of innings, and once again translating the difference into games won or lost, using the same figure of 10.8 runs per win. (In contrast to what baseball fans have been taught to believe, runs allowed, rather than won-lost record or ERA, is the true measure of a pitcher's effectiveness. Won-lost is overwhelmingly influenced by runs scored during the particular games a pitcher pitches, and errors—as Craig Wright recently showed—are largely a function of the pitcher himself, and particularly his tendency to allow ground balls.)[3] It will come as a surprise to many fans—raised on Connie Mack's famous dictum that pitching is 75 percent of the game—that outstanding pitching contributes considerably less to winning pennants than outstanding hitting. Lou Boudreau, as we have seen, won eight extra games for the Indians during 1948; no American League pitcher won more than four extra games for his club. We have seen that the Indians' hitters as a whole contributed more to their success than their pitching and defense, and this, too, is normal.

The Indians' pitchers nonetheless made a vital contribution. Both Lemon, who pitched a league-leading 294 innings, and Bearden, with 230, saved enough runs to have won four games each for their team. Feller over the season was only one game better than an average pitcher—considerably worse than that until August, clearly, and considerably better than that afterward. Gromek, Klieman, Paige, Christopher, and Zoldak were also good enough to provide one extra win each, for a total of five between them. (Overall effectiveness depends, of course, on total innings pitched, as well as the rate of runs allowed. Paige was just as effective as Lemon while he was on the mound, but pitched only one-fourth as many innings.) Meanwhile, Don Black, Al Gettel, and Bill Kennedy—the last two of

3. Wright and House, *The Diamond Appraised* 59–61.

whom were traded early in the year—all pitched poorly enough to lose one game apiece. Taken together, the Indians' staff saved 134 runs, enough to have finished thirteen games above .500.

How many of those runs were truly saved by the Indians' pitching, and how many by their defense, is something that available statistical tools do not enable us to say. While my hunch would credit the defense with between one-third and one-half, it is only a hunch. The Indians led the league in assists—partly because Lemon and Bearden threw so many ground balls—but also committed the second-fewest errors, one more than the Athletics, confirming the greatness of their infield. Overall, the Indians' pitching and defense were good enough to have won 90 games with an average offense.

Together, then, the offense and defense were good enough to have won about 106 games—the figure indicated by the Pythagorean percentage of .686, which is given by their raw totals of 840 runs scored and 568 runs allowed. Before trying to explain why their actual record fell so far short of that, we may note that this figure places them among the ten best ball clubs since 1901. Three of these teams came from the dead-ball era: the 1906 Cubs, whose 116 wins closely reflect their Pythagorean percentage of .773; the little-known Pirates of 1909, who actually won 110 games and who had a projected percentage of .710; and the 1912 Red Sox, whose .684 projection is almost exactly the same as that of the 1948 Indians, and who *did* win 105 games.

In the lively-ball era, two clubs—both Yankee teams—tower above the field. One, to no one's surprise, is the 1927 club, which won 110 games, but whose projected percentage of .726 was good enough to have won 112. (That team scored 975 runs and gave up 599.) Yet the raw figures of another Yankee team are even more impressive. The 1939 Yankees—a club built and managed by Joe McCarthy—scored 967 runs and allowed just 556, for a projected winning percentage of .752. This club—winners of 106 games—was unlucky not to have won 114. In short, it was the most dominant team in the history of the American League, or of modern baseball.

Behind these giants come the 1942 Cardinals, winners of 106 games, with a projected percentage of .710 to go with their actual .688, and the 1969 Baltimore Orioles, with 779 runs scored and only 517 allowed, a projected percentage of .694 (they actually won 109 out of 162 games, a .673 figure). Then, just .001 in front of the 1948 Indians, come their 1954 cousins, winners of an all-time record 111 games. The 1954 Tribe were almost as fortunate as their predecessors were unfortunate, winning five extra games. There can be little doubt that the 1948 team was, in fact, markedly superior. The American League deteriorated substantially between 1948 and 1954, and the 1954 Red Sox, in fourth place, finished with a 69–85 record, 42 games out. Rounding out the top ten teams of all time come the 1929 Athletics, with a projected percentage of .682.

Three relatively recent, very famous clubs actually fall well short of this group. The 1961 Yankees, who won 109 out of 162 games, were not as good as their record indicated. Their projected percentage was only .646, and they won about four more games than it projected. The 1986 Mets were astonishingly similar. They also had a projected percentage of .647, but won four more games than expected, giving them 108 wins and an actual percentage of .667. The 1995 Indians, who won 100 games and lost 44 in a shortened season, had a projected percentage of only .657, compared to their actual .694.

A few remarkable facts about this extraordinary group of ten teams should be noted. All of them won the pennant, and all but three of them won the World Series. They had a combined 31–20 record in games in the fall classic. The three teams that failed to win the series were the 1906 Cubs, who fell to the hitless wonder White Sox; the 1954 Indians, who dropped four straight to Willie Mays, Dusty Rhodes, and the rest of the New York Giants; and the 1969 Orioles, victims of the miracle Mets. And all but two of these ten teams won the pennant rather comfortably. The two exceptions were the 1942 Cardinals, who won by just two games over a great Dodger team that played slightly above its head while the Cardinals played slightly below theirs, and, of course, the 1948 Indians, who of the eight teams fell the furthest below their projected number of wins.

And why did the Indians, who played well enough to win 106 out of 154 games, win just 96 and find themselves in a playoff? The answer is at first glance quite simple: their abysmal 10–22 record in one-run games. Had they merely divided those games evenly, they would have coasted to the pennant with 102 victories, and had they won one-run games at the same rate that they won others, they would have won 109. Their problems in one-run games plagued them all season: they had a 2–7 record in them before the All-Star break, and an 8–15 mark thereafter. The reasons were somewhat different.

Luck, of course, played a big role throughout the season. The idea that good teams win close games is another misleading tenet of popular mythology, frequently embraced by writers and broadcasters who argue that "character" or "guts," rather than superior skill, wins pennants. Good teams almost always win a higher percentage of games decided by three runs or more than they do close games, which are games in which chance plays a bigger part. In the Indians' case, several of their one-run losses in the second half were low-scoring games in pitchers' parks where their right-handed power was ineffective: 2–1 in Washington on July 20, and 3–2 and 4–3 against the White Sox at home on August 21 and 22. Three others came in wild, high-scoring games against the Red Sox: 6–5 on July 24, 8–7 on July 30, and 9–8 on August 24, when Vern Stephens's two-out, two-run ninth-inning homer catapulted the Red Sox into first place. In such games, no blame should attach to either party. Another fluke loss occurred on July 28 in Cleveland against the Athletics, when an overanxious Larry Doby ran in front of Dale Mitchell, took a fly ball on the cap, and allowed the tying and winning runs to score. Another occurred against the Browns on Monday, September 13, in a makeup game, when Don Black suffered a hemorrhage in the bottom of the second inning and the team managed just three runs.

Four of the team's one-run losses, however, followed a similar pattern—a failure to hold a lead in the late innings, due either to mediocre relief pitching or to the weakening of a starting pitcher who stayed in too long. In several of these cases, moreover, Boudreau's frantic pitching changes played a role. And while it would be unbecoming and unfair to rehash these in detail now, any interested reader can once again check the accounts of the Indians' games of July 24, against the Red Sox; of August 28 against the Yanks; of September 14, again against the Yankees; and of September 24 and October 1, against the Tigers. The exhaustion of Bob Lemon was a key factor in the last three of these games. Second-guessing is a dangerous and almost inevitably unfair pastime: Boudreau saved some rather dramatic games with hunch plays as well, and his biggest gamble of the year—the choice of Bearden to pitch the playoff—was a smashing success. But a more consistent use of his bullpen might well have saved him some of those games, and saved the Tribe the need to make the extra trip to Boston for the playoff.

Boudreau eventually managed a total of fourteen years in the majors, and rarely was able to improve his teams. Overall his teams *underperformed* their expectations by 21 games, while Bucky Harris's teams outperformed theirs by 52 games, and Joe McCarthy's exceeded their expectations by 106 games.[4] But such criticism must not be allowed to obscure Boudreau's extraordinary season—one of the greatest of all time. In the field he was second in the league in putouts, behind Eddie Joost, and second in assists, behind Stephens, while leading the league in double plays with 119 and in fielding percentage. As we have seen, his hitting contributed an extra eight wins to his team. He walked 98 times and struck out just 9. He went four for four, with two home runs, two singles, and a walk, in the biggest game

4. These figures are from *Bill James Guide to Baseball Managers*, 149–52.

of his life, the playoff. And although his average of .355 trailed Williams by fourteen points, Boudreau in 1948 was without question a better hitter for average than the Splendid Splinter. In fact, allowing for the effects of their home parks, Boudreau in 1948 probably hit better than Williams had in 1941, when he hit .406.

Boudreau played 78 games in Municipal Stadium; Williams played 78 in Fenway Park. In his home games, Williams hit .370; on the road, he hit .368. Boudreau hit .310 at home, and .403 on the road. Williams never hit .400 on the road, peaking at .380 in 1941. Boudreau's offensive season was the greatest ever by any shortstop other than Honus Wagner of the dead-ball era. He was a unanimous MVP selection, and he deserved it. In a year of heroics, he was the greatest hero of all.

The Indians demonstrated their superiority fairly clearly in the World Series, in which they defeated the Boston Braves convincingly in six games, and might easily have won four straight. Playing in two good pitchers' parks, the Indians hit just .198, but got four home runs from Gordon, Doby, Dale Mitchell, and Hegan. Lemon, finding form again, won two games handily—the second, 4–1, and the sixth and last, 4–3, with relief help from Bearden, of all people, in the last inning. Bearden also pitched a shutout in the third game, and Steve Gromek won the fourth, 2–1, against Braves ace Johnny Sain—the first game Gromek had started since the nineteenth of September. Meanwhile, the Indians set two all-time World Series attendance marks in Cleveland, topping off at 86,288 in the fifth game. That figure is still the largest crowd ever to watch baseball in a baseball stadium.[5]

The hard-luck man of the series was Bob Feller. Opening in Boston, he threw perhaps his best game of the season, a two-hitter, against Johnny Sain. But in the eighth inning he walked Bill Salkeld, and pinch runner Phil Masi was sacrificed to second. As they had many times during the season, Feller and Boudreau tried to pick Masi off. A famous series of pictures seems to show that Masi was out, but the umpire, Bill Stewart, called him safe. Two batters later, Tommy Holmes singled home Masi with the only run of the game.

Four days later, in Cleveland, Feller tried to finish the series in front of the largest crowd in history. This time, alas, his stuff failed him. A three-run homer by Bob Elliott gave the Braves a 3–0 lead in the very first inning, but the Indians battled back, and Hegan's three-run homer gave Feller a 5–4 lead in the bottom of the fourth. It wasn't enough. The Braves tied the

---

5. The Los Angeles Dodgers, playing in the Coliseum, drew over 90,000 in each of their three 1959 World Series games.

game in the sixth and knocked Feller out with six runs in the seventh, winning 11–5. Feller never pitched in a World Series again.

The Indians of 1948 were not a dynasty. Keltner, Gordon, and Boudreau were all over thirty, and none of them ever had a great season again. Of the ten greatest teams in baseball history, they were one of only four not to have won a pennant in either the previous or the succeeding year. They were eight games off the pace in 1949, and Veeck had sold the club by the end of the year. Only Doby, Lemon, Mitchell, and Feller played on the next Indians' pennant winner, in 1954. For one year, however, they were one of the finest clubs of all time, and more than deserved to win the greatest of all pennant races.

Meanwhile, Bill Veeck, the one American League executive with real vision, got back into baseball as the owner of the Browns in 1951. As he explained years later in the most fascinating chapters of *Veeck—as in Wreck,* he knew that St. Louis could not support two major league teams, but he confidently expected to reduce the Cardinals—then owned by local businessman Fred Saigh—to the status of second banana and drive them out of town. He calculatedly signed several Cardinal legends as managers or coaches—including Harry Brecheen, Marty Marion, and, to his everlasting regret, the impossible Rogers Hornsby—plunged into a new round of promotional gimmicks, and doubled Browns attendance to over half a million in 1952. But during 1952, Fred Saigh was indicted for income tax evasion and sold the Cardinals to the Anheuser-Busch brewery. Veeck knew, at once, that the Cardinals, not the Browns, would remain in St. Louis.

Meanwhile, at annual meetings, Veeck was proposing suggestions that might have averted much of baseball's nationwide decline, and that would have solved the problem that *still* bedevils the majors today, nearly half a century later. First, he suggested reserving the right to sign new prospects to the independent minor leagues, which might have kept them operating far longer than they did. More important, he suggested that visiting teams receive a share of local television revenue—an idea that, properly implemented, could even now reduce the disparity between large and small markets to manageable proportions. Thanks to the Yankees and George Weiss—who controlled baseball's richest farm system, and who had no intention of sharing baseball's largest television contract—Veeck not only failed to win acceptance for his proposals, but acquired enemies determined to force him out of the league as soon as possible.

In early 1953, Veeck tried, and failed, to move the Browns to Milwaukee, the scene of his earliest triumphs, when his fellow American League owners blocked him and allowed the Boston Braves to secure what turned out to be one of the richest markets in the nation. A year later, in a freak combination of circumstances far too complex to describe here, they blocked his move to Baltimore, forced him to sell the Browns, and promptly allowed the new ownership to go ahead. He returned as White Sox owner in 1959, won one pennant, and had to quit two years later for reasons of health. Not until 1976 did he make it back, again with the White Sox. Within a year, the White Sox were in contention again.

Veeck in 1948 managed to more than compete with the Yankees, and played the critical role in bringing about the most exciting and profitable season in baseball history. He was the man that the league—and baseball—needed to stem its decline in the 1950s and 1960s. But for most of those two decades, he was zealously excluded by the owners, league presidents, and commissioners who presided over one of the most serious declines in fan interest in baseball history. Veeck was too happy a man to have suffered unduly. His three works of autobiography—*Veeck—as in Wreck*, *The Hustler's Handbook*, and *Fifty Tons a Day*—leave no doubt that Veeck enjoyed himself more than any of his fellow owners. It was the players and fans of the American League, alas, who were the poorer for his absence, and it is they who rejoiced early in 1990 when his well-deserved election to the Hall of Fame was announced.

The Red Sox performed quite differently. Alone of the three contenders, they won as many games as they deserved. In some ways, indeed, they did slightly better than their statistics would have predicted.

Fenway Park, as always, severely distorted the team's statistics. The team led the league in runs scored (907), but when the effects of Fenway Park are discounted, the Red Sox are found to have scored an adjusted total of 852 runs, compared to 887 for the Yankees and 892 for the Indians. (Both the Yankees and the Indians scored more runs on the road than the Red Sox.) Their pitching and defense, meanwhile, was still slightly inferior to the Yankees and 52 runs behind the Indians, but far superior to the rest of the league. All told their offense was 122 runs better than average, and their defense 54—figures that explain their 96 wins almost exactly. An interesting anomaly emerges, however, when we break down their offensive contribution.

Like the Indians, the Red Sox did not have a single below-average offensive player among their regulars, although Stan Spence and Birdie Tebbetts were almost exactly average and contributed no extra wins to the team offensively. And at first glance—despite the impressive statistics that Fenway Park allowed them to compile—their offensive performances, especially in the infield, were considerably less impressive than those of the

Indians. Despite his batting average of .310, Billy Goodman's adjusted 67 runs created contributed just one extra win to his team. Johnny Pesky and Junior Stephens also contributed only one extra win each, as Stephens's contribution was reduced by his late-season slump and a high total of double-play groundouts. (Stephens contributed much more in 1949 and 1950, when his totals were worth four and three extra wins.) Bobby Doerr, despite his injury, contributed three wins, the same as his great rival Joe Gordon. In the outfield, Dom DiMaggio's contribution was good for two wins, the same as Dale Mitchell.

One man's contribution, however, was not exaggerated by Fenway Park. Despite his injuries and two-week absence from the lineup, Ted Williams created a league-leading, park-adjusted 156 runs, nine more even than Lou Boudreau, and good for nine full wins over .500. As usual, Williams led the league both in on-base average (.494) and slugging (.615). He and he alone was responsible for more than half of the Red Sox' offensive edge.

The Red Sox offense for 1948, however, had strengths not immediately apparent to the naked eye. To repeat, the Runs Created formula, which I have used to measure the contribution of individual players, derives the number of runs created by each player from his hits, walks, outs, and total bases. The formula assumes that these are distributed fairly evenly, therefore resulting in a predictable number of runs. Repeated applications of the formula confirm that this is usually the case. It *was* the case for the 1948 Indians, for whom the Runs Created formula predicted 847 runs, compared to the 840 they actually scored. But for the Red Sox, the formula predicts only 847 runs—and the team scored 907, a full 60 runs more, or enough to win six full games.

What this means is that the Red Sox were that historical rarity, a clutch-hitting team. Over the course of the season, they bunched their hits and walks together well enough to produce an extra 60 runs, good for about six wins. Luck probably played a role here. The Red Sox did not repeat this feat in 1949, when they got more productive seasons from almost every regular on the team—including Williams and Stephens—but came away with only 897 runs. But in 1948, they did it. A much more thorough study—for which the play-by-play data are not readily available—would be required to determine exactly which Red Sox increased their team's run total by delivering hits with men on base. Two likely guesses are Junior Stephens, who created only 100 runs but drove in 137, and Dom DiMaggio, who drove in a remarkable 87 runs batting leadoff. Each of them may have contributed at least one extra offensive win through clutch hitting.

Defensively the Red Sox show a considerably different story from the

Indians. Their most valuable pitcher was Parnell, who saved enough runs to produce three extra wins, thereby ranking slightly below Lemon and Bearden. Dobson's pitching yielded two extra wins, and Kramer, Kinder, and Galehouse one each. Kramer's 18–5 record was a statistical fluke. As his 4.35 ERA also indicates, he enjoyed exceptional run support. On the debit side, Mickey Harris, Dave Ferriss, and Earl Caldwell all pitched badly enough to cost the team one game each, while Earl Johnson and Tex Hughson were average. All told, the pitching and defense was five games better than average.

Once again we must ask how many of those five games actually came from superior pitching, and how many from the Red Sox' outstanding defense. While we lack any really authoritative measure, I would not hesitate myself to assign at least three of them to Doerr, Stephens, Pesky, Dom DiMaggio, Williams, and catcher Birdie Tebbetts. Of the leading pitchers on the Red Sox staff, only Parnell actually proved himself an outstanding pitcher over the course of a long career.[6] The Red Sox' defense in 1948 probably contributed more to their 96 wins than their pitching staff.

It took a remarkable display of clutch hitting, then, for the Red Sox to win their 96 games and tie a superior Indian ball club. They were fortunate to beat out a superior Yankee team, and fortunate to find themselves playing at home on October 4 for the pennant against a team good enough to have won with ease. In the following year, with almost equal hitting and slightly superior pitching, they went into the last weekend of the year with 96 wins, needing just one more to win the pennant, but lost two close games and the pennant in Yankee Stadium to a Yankee team with almost identical figures. In 1950 they scored even more runs—1,027—but their pitching collapsed and they finished third, five games behind the Yankees. In none of these years, in short, were the Red Sox runs scored and runs allowed totals significantly better than their competition. "The irony of those 1948–49–50 teams," Ted Williams has written, "was that we were good enough to convince a lot of people we should have won pennants, but weren't good enough to actually win them."[7] Once again, he was absolutely right.

The playoff on October 5, 1948 was a coin flip, but happily enough, the outcome fairly reflected the strengths and weaknesses of the two teams. The Indians had more right-handed power, and more outstanding

6. Kinder, of course, had a truly remarkable season in 1949, and Kramer and Galehouse had had fine seasons for the Browns during the war. Hughson and Ferriss had been outstanding, but they had obviously declined in 1948.

7. Williams with Underwood, *My Turn at Bat*, 166.

pitchers. They delivered three right-handed home runs to one for the Red Sox, and came up with an excellent pitching performance. On that day—as in the entire season—they were the better team.

Like the Indians, the Yankees fell short of their projected winning percentage. Alone among the three contenders, the Yankee regulars included a player who actually cost them a game at the plate. That was Phil Rizzuto, who batted only .275 with very little power and an unimpressive on-base average, and whose figures cost the Yankees one game. Both McQuinn and Stirnweiss were average hitters who did nothing to raise the Yanks above .500. Steve Souchock, a .203 hitter in 118 at bats, was the Berardino of the Bronx, and also cost his team a full game.

The rest of the Yankees, however, more than made up for these deficiencies. At third, the platoon of Johnson and Brown contributed one game each. Behind the plate, Berra contributed two offensive games, and Niarhos one. In the outfield, the Yankees were in a class by themselves. Lindell and Keller—who shared left field for most of the season—hit well enough for three extra wins. In right field (and on first base), Henrich had a truly fantastic season, creating an adjusted 130 runs, good for five full wins. In overall offensive effectiveness Henrich trailed just three other players: Williams, Boudreau, and Joe DiMaggio, whose 138 adjusted runs created won six full games for the Yankees. And the Yankees, like the Red Sox, hit well in the clutch. Their actual runs scored total of 845 was 28 more than that predicted by the Runs Created formula, thus giving them the benefit of two or three extra games. Joe DiMaggio, it seems safe to say, deserves much of the credit. All told, they scored an adjusted 157 runs more than average— good enough for 14 wins over .500, or 91 wins.

The Yankee pitching was remarkably consistent, but not brilliant. Their five leading pitchers—Reynolds, Lopat, Raschi, Shea, and Byrne—each pitched well enough to contribute exactly one extra win to the team's record. The erratic Page and the tired rookie Porterfield together cost the team about one game. In the end, the Yankees, alone among the three teams, lacked even one really commanding hurler.

The Yankee defense in the field was almost surely the weakest of the three contenders. While Johnson's numbers suggest that he was a fine third baseman, Brown struggled in his place, and the figures of Stirnweiss at second and Rizzuto at short were far behind those of Doerr, Stephens, Gordon, and Boudreau.[8] In the outfield, Joe DiMaggio trailed his brother

8. This partially seems to reflect the tendencies of the Yankee pitching staff, which led the league in strikeouts, indicating a tendency to allow fly balls.

by almost 100 putouts despite registering the highest total of his career. Interestingly enough, Lopat, Raschi, and Reynolds all posted much better ERAs in subsequent years, as Lindell, Keller, Henrich, Brown, and Stirnweiss gradually gave way to Hank Bauer, Gene Woodling, Mickey Mantle, Jerry Coleman, Andy Carey, Gil McDougald, and Billy Martin.

The Yankees' deviation from their projected winning percentage—.037, or about six games—is considerably more common than the Indians' ten-game difference. They had a reasonably good 8–6 record in one-run games during the second half, compared to 11–10 in the first. Joe Page, who had been responsible for several key close losses in the first half, did better in the second. The biggest single reason for their defeat, as we have seen, was their 8–14 record against the Red Sox. Their biggest problem, relative to their championship year of 1947, was the loss of Spud Chandler, Bobo Newsom, and Bill Bevens, who had thrown 376 good innings in 1947. From a Pythagorean percentage of .661 in 1947, they had slipped to .647 in 1948. Their 94 wins would have been enough to win the 1947 pennant by eight games, but this time they earned them third place. The biggest difference between their 1947 and 1948 seasons was the competition they faced.

General manager George Weiss, however, did not see it that way. On the morning of October 4, before the playoff game, he announced that Bucky Harris's contract would not be renewed. That night, when Harris asked for his room at the Copley Plaza Hotel in preparation for the World Series, the clerk informed him that he was not on the Yankees' list. Harris spent the Series in the room of his old friend, *Washington Post* columnist Shirley Povich. A few months later, Weiss hired Casey Stengel. Stengel did not improve the Yankees' overall performance in 1949. Their projected percentage actually dropped from .647 to .629, but they won 97 games and edged out the Red Sox by one victory—the first of five consecutive world championships.[9] Meanwhile, Larry MacPhail—who had promised Harris the general manager's job when he convinced him to manage the Yankees in late 1946—made such a public stink over Harris's dismissal that the Yankees awarded him $25,000—at least $175,000 in 1998 dollars—in severance pay.

Two years later, Harris went back to Washington to manage the Senators for the third time. He got the team back up to .500 in 1952 and 1953, but left after 1954 and finished off his career with two .500-plus years with Detroit. Although Harris spent most of his career managing mediocre to poor ball clubs, his teams as a whole outperformed their expectations sig-

---

9. In fairness, it should be noted that the 1949 team was riddled with injuries.

nificantly, and Bill James's most accurate ranking lists him as the twelfth best manager of all time.[10] In 1975, two years before his death, he was elected to the Hall of Fame.

Thanks to their splurge of one-run victories in the first half of the season, the Athletics managed to remain seven games ahead of their Pythagorean projection. Essentially a .500 team, they finished with 84 wins and 70 losses. The Tigers, six games behind in the standings, were nearly as good. The Browns, Senators, and White Sox lost 94, 97, and 101 games.

A very large portion of the top talent in the league was concentrated among the three contenders. The five most valuable hitters in the league— Williams, Boudreau, Joe DiMaggio, Henrich, and Keltner—all played for Cleveland, Boston, or New York. Half of the six next best also played for the three contenders—Gordon, Doby, and Doerr, each worth three wins to their team. (The others were Pat Mullin of the Tigers and Jerry Priddy and Al Zarilla of the Browns, each worth three extra wins.) The outstanding pitchers in the league were Lemon, Bearden, Hal Newhouser, and Parnell. Meanwhile, in the nether regions of the league, the Senators had only one above-average hitter, Bud Stewart, while the White Sox' four leading starters were each two full games worse than average over the course of the season. It was not a year for parity; it was a year for fantastic excitement.

The Past and the Future

In retrospect, a highly significant event in baseball history took place at the winter meetings before the 1948 season opened, when the Pacific Coast League asked to be designated as a third major league. Permission was denied. Had it been granted either then or at any time during the next ten years, the structure of baseball would obviously be far different—and, quite possibly, far more exciting—than it is today. To have enlarged the majors by elevating the PCL would have solved several problems. The National League, to begin with, would not have deserted the strongest market in the country, New York City, and the league and the city would not have had to wait twelve years before a National League contender returned to the Big Apple. And while some sensible franchise shifts—the Browns to Baltimore, the Boston Braves to Milwaukee, and the Athletics to Kansas City—might have taken place, large-scale carpetbagging could have been long delayed, or even avoided altogether. Best of all, baseball could have adjusted to the shift in the country's population without destroying the intimacy and sym-

10. *Bill James Guide to Baseball Managers*, 149.

metry of the eight-team league. And divisional play, which drastically cheapens the 162-game season and sometimes keeps the league's best team out of the World Series, could have been avoided.

Instead, however, the existing teams and leagues decided to reserve all the benefits of expansion for themselves. The American and National leagues have used the tradition they built up during the first six decades of the century to monopolize major league baseball, and the players—preferring to exploit this monopoly themselves, rather than to increase playing opportunities as widely as possible—have collaborated with them. Not only have the American and National leagues controlled the pace of the growth of major league baseball, collecting huge entrance fees during every round of expansion, but they have also kept the supply of baseball *below* the demand in metropolitan areas like New York and Boston, which could easily support three and two teams, respectively, once again. As it was, the Dodgers' and Giants' move to the coast and the creation of the Angels destroyed the old PCL, and baseball initially went to ten-team leagues.

Ten-team leagues actually produced great baseball in the years 1961–68, and three ten-team leagues would fill the needs of the majors very well today. The American League had fine pennant races in 1961, 1962, 1964, and 1967, while the National League had a dogfight in every year from 1962 through 1966. Unfortunately for baseball, most of the drama took place in minor markets. The serious crisis in baseball attendance during the 1960s probably occurred for two reasons: a decline in offense, which always reduces fan interest, and the weak teams in Chicago, New York, Boston, and, after 1966, in Los Angeles. Stronger teams in these key cities could have avoided much of the slump in the game's popularity. Many cities, in addition, took too long to build new stadiums, and most of them built unattractive multipurpose parks when they did. Then, after the 1967 season, Charlie Finley's move of the Athletics to Oakland forced another round of expansion to placate Kansas City. The selection of Seattle, which could not support the 1969 Pilots, paved the way for yet another round of American League expansion eight years later, and the National League eventually followed suit in 1994.

In the late summer of 1993, the Atlanta Braves put on a tremendous stretch drive and came from behind to defeat a fine San Francisco Giants ball club for the National League West title. In 1994, the two leagues split into three divisions each, with four teams—including a wild-card team—to make the playoffs. Close races and even one-game playoffs remained possible, as the 1995 and 1996 seasons showed, but as long as this system persists, *never again* will the two best teams in a league have to battle one another for a pennant flag, since one of them will be guaranteed a wild card. Television contracts now drive the schedule, and baseball now prefers a guaranteed system of playoffs that it can sell for a long-term contract to the *possibility* of a much more dramatic struggle for the pennant that might last two weeks, a month, or, as in 1948, an entire season. The adoption of wild cards was the last of a series of changes dating back to the 1950s that have gradually eroded the significance of pennant races. Despite the phenomenal growth of baseball attendance in the 1980s and 1990s, owners still want to squeeze more September dollars out of the public by giving more and more teams a chance at postseason play.

Divisional play changed the character of baseball, and wild cards have changed it even more. Rivals battling for the pennant play considerably fewer games against each other. Fans, now faced with fourteen teams in each league, have a much harder time remaining familiar with their home team's competition. The intensity of combat is inevitably diluted. And a full season's fine effort can be wiped out in the playoffs—all the more so because of the advent in 1994 of wildcard teams.

"To everything there is a season"—and the new structure of baseball reflects the different age in which we now live. Rather than design leagues—or even divisions—that fight all year to produce a single winner, the leadership of baseball has substituted a system that allows more cities to have a chance, and thus—they hope—creates more profitable markets every year. The new system gives less scope for the kind of sustained heroism that so many teams demonstrated during the 1940s, but we no longer live in a heroic age. The divisive national climate of the 1990s has found expression in baseball—wracked by the worst labor troubles in its history and a complete failure in leadership—as well as in government and other areas of national life. Players and owners have subordinated everything to the pursuit of more dollars. It is entirely possible that yet another crisis—comparable in scope if not in its specifics to the Black Sox scandal—looms in the future, leading once again to the appointment of a real and effective commissioner, and to a new era in our national game.

Nationally, too, we may face another great crisis during the next twenty years, one whose exact nature we cannot yet foresee.[11] But that crisis in turn may—if we cope with it successfully—lead us into a new heroic age. In a new era, while the nation tries to redefine itself, a new generation of ballplayers, who should begin to reach the majors early in the next century, could revive the more purely competitive, less commercial spirit of the 1930s and 1940s. Meanwhile, the great players and seasons of the 1940s,

---

11. On this point see Strauss and Howe, *The Fourth Turning.*

like the broader American triumphs over the Depression and in the Second World War, live on as heroic archetypes which in the next few decades may inspire us in facing new tasks.

Baseball will always have a unique role in American life as an arena of heroic struggle, not merely because of the beauty of the game itself, but also because of the statistical tools that allow its skills to be measured and studied far more accurately than literally any other human activity. It is a never-ending panorama of strategy and tactics, of victory and defeat, which, like all human institutions, moves according to rhythms that we are only beginning to understand. Its hold on our imagination cannot be denied, and the documentary record it leaves behind is unparalleled. For nearly a century, the reporters and statisticians have carefully told the story of every year's drama on the field. And thus, the epic 1948 season—and others almost equally magnificent—still belongs to us all, and lives as a story of what has gone before, and what may come again.

INDEX